LOEB CLASSICAL LIBRARY

FOUNDED BY JAMES LOEB 1911

EDITED BY

JEFFREY HENDERSON

AUGUSTINE

CONFESSIONS

I

LCL 26

AUGUSTINE

CONFESSIONS

BOOKS 1–8

EDITED AND TRANSLATED BY

CAROLYN J.-B. HAMMOND

HARVARD UNIVERSITY PRESS
CAMBRIDGE, MASSACHUSETTS
LONDON, ENGLAND
2014

First published 2014

LOEB CLASSICAL LIBRARY® is a registered trademark of
the President and Fellows of Harvard College

Library of Congress Control Number 2013948584
CIP data available from the Library of Congress

ISBN 978-0-674-99685-4

*Composed in ZephGreek and ZephText by
Technologies 'N Typography, Merrimac, Massachusetts.
Printed on acid-free paper and bound by
The Maple-Vail Book Manufacturing Group*

CONTENTS

For Nicholas Purcell,
who gave me a chance
and taught me to think.

PREFACE

The original Loeb Classical Library edition of Augustine's
Confessions was published in 1912, when the series was
in its infancy. It contained the 1909 Teubner edition of the
Latin by Pius Knöll with a facing translation by William
Watts (ca. 1590–1649). Long after I had begun work on
this new translation, I discovered that not only had Watts
been a student at Gonville and Caius College in Cambridge, he had also spent ten years there as the chaplain,
where I am now dean. If two scholars make a tradition,
that gives Caius the best part of a four-hundred-year-old
tradition of translating *Confessions*. The work of adapting
Watts' translation to fit what was then the latest thinking
on the text of *Confessions* fell to William Henry Denham
Rouse (1863–1950). Rouse remarks in his 1912 preface
that for making his revision he used the 1838 translation
of E. B. Pusey, and the new commentary of J. Gibb and
W. Montgomery; I have made use of both works myself,
as their scholarship has stood the test of time. I referred
frequently to Verheijen's edition in making decisions
about individual variants and found it always helpful.
James O'Donnell's three-volume commentary with critical text is the scholarly foundation for this volume. Its
depth and lucidity called to my mind Cicero's ideals for
the perfect orator, which, in *Doctr. Chr.* 4.12.27, Augus-

tine records as being "to convince, to delight, to persuade" (*ut probet, ut delectet, ut flectat*; *Orat.* 21.69). O'Donnell did so at almost every turn.

Watts called the act of translating *Confessions* "the hardest task that ever I yet undertook": an evaluation with which I can heartily concur, as Rouse also did before me. There are so many translations already that a word explaining this one is unavoidable; of English versions readily available, the 1991 translation by Henry Chadwick helps by closely following the Latin and providing excellent notes; that of Maria Boulding OSB captures much of the rhetoric and lyricism of Augustine without sacrificing accuracy. As well as conveying the factual content of Augustine's prose, the aim of this translation is twofold: to give the reader with no Latin a sense of its sound and structure, and at the same time to give the reader with some Latin enough help to make out the syntactical structures and rhetorical casting of the original.

Sincere thanks are due to the Master and Fellows of Gonville and Caius College, Cambridge, for supporting me with sabbatical leave to complete this work, and for allocating me rooms above the Gate of Virtue to inspire my efforts. In a different way I owe an equal debt to Graham, Elizabeth, and Jonathan, who put up with the inevitable backwash of a mind busy with other things. My gratitude to the Loeb Classical Library must also find expression: even that it exists is a cause for celebration, and that I could contribute to it—following in the footsteps of D. R. Shackleton-Bailey (and indeed working in the same college room as he did)—is a source of pride to me. The Hebrew reading group I share in with Andrew Macintosh,

Morna Hooker, David Ford, and Simon Perry has been an invaluable source of intellectual energy when I hit biblical or theological *cruces*. To Richard Howells, who made it happen, I express last the thanks I owe first.

> *Ex alia in aliam linguam ad verbum expressa translatio, sensus operit et veluti laeto gramine sata strangulat. Dum enim casibus et figuris servit oratio, quod brevi poterat indicare sermone, longo ambitu circumacta vix explicat. Hoc igitur ego vitans ita beatum Antonium te petente transposui ut nihil desit ex sensu, cum aliquid desit ex verbis.*

> A word-for-word translation from one language to another conceals meanings like rampant weeds choking crops. While the words preserve the case-endings and the figures of speech, what could be expressed concisely is scarcely encapsulated even by long periphrases. So I have avoided this when translating the *Life of Antony* at your request, so as to give the full sense, even without a complete correspondence in the precise words.

> Evagrius, *Vita Sancti Antoni*
> Prologue to his translation of Athanasius

INTRODUCTION

1. GENRE

Marcus Aurelius (AD 121–180) insisted on first principles:

> A particular thing—what is it in itself, in the way it
> is arranged? What is its essence? From what mate-
> rial is it constructed? What is its function in the
> universe? How long does it endure? (*Med.* 8.11)

In engaging with these universal questions, the reader of
Confessions has a chance of making some sense of a text
that manages to be both opaque and translucent. Beginning with the nature of the text itself avoids the pitfall of
treating it as a straightforward autobiography with a disappointing exegetical section tacked on, and clarifies the
kind of questions that must have prompted Augustine to
write it in the first place. Though it is formulated as a
prayer, a conversation between Augustine himself and
God, there are occasional glimpses of another audience
beyond, the audience he must have been writing for if the
act of committing these thoughts to paper were not to have
been an expensive waste of time and papyrus. At *Conf.*
2.3.5 he admits as much when he asks, "Who am I telling
this? Certainly not you, my God! But I am narrating this
story in your presence to my kind, to the whole human

race, whatever the tiny fraction of it which happens to come across these writings of mine." So too at *Conf.* 6.9.14–15, for example, Augustine tells God about an accident that befell Alypius: but his real interlocutor must be (as well as God) the readers he expected, otherwise he is merely telling God what God knows already: "You, Lord, went to the help of his innocence, of which you were the sole witness."

This casting of *Conf.* in the form of a prayer shows that it can be categorized as essentially dramatic, because it is entirely a mimesis of speech rather than being mediated through third-person narrative. Augustine draws the reader into his emotions, constructing his self-disclosure by means of *peripeteia* (overthrow; a sudden change in circumstances), *anagnōrisis* (recognition), and *pathos* (suffering). For Aristotle, the key criteria of the worth of *Conf.* would have been how realistically it portrayed a principal character, how successfully it constructed a catharsis of the emotion evoked by the text, and how well it helped the hearer or reader to assimilate truth (*Poet.* 1452, 1454). As a first-person discourse, *Conf.* certainly belongs in Aristotle's category of the "most mimetic," perhaps most of all in terms of Augustine's skillful use of *anagnōrisis*. His moments of recognition of the divine message in the interactions of his ordinary life were, to him, proof enough that God was at work in and for him.

In addition to questions of genre and intended audience, there is the matter of focalization, which is common to all texts with an autobiographical core. Through whose eyes are we seeing what is set before us? The reader has to keep in mind two characters, both called "I"—the narrator outside the work, producing it for the audience or readership; and the character within the narrative, the protagonist who, unlike the narrator, acts without awareness of future outcomes and full contexts of his actions. This binary viewpoint sharpens the difficulty of keeping in mind the true chronology of the events narrated: not only the time when they happened (AD 354–386) but also the time when Augustine composed this account of them (probably AD 397) and the time when he looked back much later at what he had written and evaluated it (AD 426 or 427):

> The thirteen books of my confessions, and about my good and evil deeds, praise God who is just and good, and encourage the human understanding and feeling toward him. As far as they concern me, anyway, they did this for me when I was writing them, and they still do when people read them now. What other people think about them is up to them; but I know that they have brought pleasure, and continue to do so, to many of my brothers. From the first to the tenth book, they tell my story; in the last three, on the Holy Scriptures, they cover the text from "In the beginning God made heaven and earth" up to "the Sabbath rest."[1] As for the fourth book, when I was confessing the pitiable state of my mind at the death of my friend, and said that our soul had somehow become fused into one instead of two, "perhaps

---

[1] In A.'s time, Scripture was not yet divided into chapter and verse.

that was why I was afraid to die, in case he whom I had loved so much would therefore die completely," this seems to me more a frivolous piece of pleading than a serious confession, although my foolishness may have been tempered to some extent by the "perhaps" which I added. And what I said in the thirteenth book, "The firmament was made between the higher, spiritual waters, and the lower, physical ones" was said somewhat incautiously. For it is an extremely abstruse subject. This work begins with the words "Great are you, Lord." (*Retr.* 2.6)

Whether he sees himself as unique in his experiences or more emblematic of a universal experience for Christians is a matter for debate. If we are trying to work out what kind of text *Conf.* is, we find help in that later overview of it, which gives both a title, *Confessions,* and an incipit, "Great are you." Both point to an ongoing dialogue between creator and created. But we also find a programmatic element: Augustine exposes his awareness that *Conf.* as a whole is a text of enormous persuasive power—in other words, a work saturated with the substance of rhetoric, which is to say, persuasive speech.

For the opening of the text, in prayer form, Augustine draws on classical as well as scriptural conventions for addressing God directly. In other respects, however, it stands apart from classical predecessors: there is no prefatory dedication to a friend, teacher, or pupil; no elaboration of the defects of previous authors or of his own compositional principles, which would drag it more into the category of history or *bios* ($\beta \acute{\iota} o \varsigma$ [life]) writing; no insistence

on continuity with the efforts of earlier writers either. Nor
is there any claim to be treading on new ground in terms
of literary innovation. Instead, he follows a familiar prayer-
pattern by beginning with an elaborate invocation of the
deity, named as "Lord" (the regular scriptural substitute
for the true Hebrew name of God), praise of his attributes
(power, wisdom), the petitioner's statement of need, and
then the request for divine assistance. But Augustine goes
beyond the familiar literary form by entering into an extended investigation of those divine attributes and of ways
of accessing God. This immediately signals to his contemporary readership that they are encountering a form of
literature that is new.

Clusters of scriptural quotation flag the intensity of
Augustine's Christian fervor throughout *Conf.* So it may
prove impossible to categorize *Conf.* straightforwardly as
autobiography, prayer, memoir, or didactic; but what remains clear across the work as a whole is a reasoned pro-
gression from intense focus on the doings of one human
individual to a reorientation toward the activities of God
in creation, which, though implicit, clearly mirrors Augustine's view of how a Christian life should progress (Condon, *Limits of Rhetoric*, 46–63). This ultimate aim is a
working out of what was present from the first: that the
human search for God is initiated by, and desired by, God
himself (*Conf.* 1.1.1).

2. STRUCTURE AND COMPOSITION

Conf. consists of thirteen books. This odd number has
always caused puzzlement, but the fact that it is an odd

number, which does not correspond to any classical literary model, may partly be explained by Augustine's growing hostility to his formation in such literature and a desire to make the text stand apart from possible antecedents (Hagendahl, *A. and the Latin Classics,* 715–17). Books 1–9 cover Augustine's life, conversion, and the immediate aftermath, Book 10 explores the nature of memory, and Books 11–13 are an interpretation of the text of Genesis 1. There is a marked reprise at the beginning of 11 when he repeats the invocation from the start of the work. The care with which the whole has been put together confirms that this peculiar structure is intentional and (to the author at least) meaningful. Arguments that the last three books are an afterthought, similar to the later addition of a fourth book to the initial three books of Augustine's *Doctr. Chr.,* have not proved persuasive, nor has the idea of an initial seven-book scheme, to parallel the creation story of Genesis, that was later expanded (Pranger, *Time and Narrative,* 377–93).

If we follow the order in which Augustine reviewed his literary output in *Retr.,* then *Conf.* was composed after his consecration as bishop, probably in AD 395. As a work it defies categorization in terms of content; but it does include major explorations of alternative religious viewpoints (Neoplatonism, Manichaeism) as well as autobiographical material and the concluding theological exegesis. Part of the answer lies in the carefully chosen title: *confessio* means a declaration, either of belief, praise, or sin—and the text is a commixture of all three. In his preaching, Augustine made this explicit to his congregation:

If Christ who is set far apart from all sin, has said "I confess," then that word belongs not just to the sinner but also to the one who praises. So whether we praise God or condemn ourselves, that is called "confessing." (*S.* 67.1)

So nuanced is his deployment of the term that wherever *confessio* and cognates like *confiteor* (I confess) occur in this translation, they are always rendered by the English equivalent "confess/ion," even though the English term, in normal usage, has a more restricted, and more negative, semantic range. To substitute a variety of terms, such as "declaration of praise" or "affirmation of belief," would obscure for the reader this vital connective thread running through the text.

The same approach is taken with the recurring term *vanitas* and its cognate adjective *vanus* (e.g., *Conf.* 1.13.22, 1.18.28, 4.1.1, etc.), which encapsulate the pointlessness of Augustine's search for truth outside Christianity. In addition to its classical Latin meaning (emptiness, nothingness, falsehood, pretension), a scriptural sense of "futility" is present in his use of the term. This is drawn principally from the book Ecclesiastes (also known as Qoheleth), where the term rendered in the Latin Bibles as *vanitas* is the Hebrew *hebel* (vapor, breath, emptiness, delusion), and from Psalms and Job, where (as well as *hebel*) the Hebrew term *shav'* (deceit, worthlessness) closely parallels the classical Latin semantic range of *vanitas*. No single English word can express this range of nuance better than "vanity" itself.

3. AUGUSTINE'S BACKGROUND
AND EARLY LIFE

Augustine tells us the names of the towns where he grew up—Thagaste—and was educated—Madauri—but adds no detail beyond what is strictly necessary to forwarding the narrative. Only archaeology and cross-referencing yield further detail about these formative locations. He tells us little more than this of Carthage too, though it was a principal city of the western empire. This corroborates the view that *Conf.* is not an autobiography. Only what is directly relevant to the main theme is included, and at least for the author that main theme is not himself; this principle likewise governs what he tells his audience about his friends and family. His references to his father, Patricius, show no great affection, though this need not entail that there was none. His relationship to his mother, Monnica, was remarkable for its intensity and, at the end, spiritual fervor; but to a modern reader it may seem tinged with an unhealthy degree of manipulative pressure on her part.

As for his friends, Augustine introduces quite a few, though the text is studiously opaque concerning personal details (cf. Konstan, *Friendship,* 151, 161–62). Nebridius stands out among them, as a close friend from childhood and as a correspondent. Writing to a fellow bishop (*Ep.* 98.8), Augustine said of him: "I remember my friend Nebridius; he was the most scrupulous and keen examiner of difficult matters concerning true doctrine—but he hated a short answer on a weighty question" (Gavigan, *Nebridius,* 47–58). Alypius plays a different role, as the *fidus Achates,* in the garden where Augustine finally capitulates to his Christian calling (*Conf.* 8.8.19, 12.28–29); and they remained close in later life, when Alypius was bishop of Thagaste.

In a different way Romanianus too stands out, for Augustine dedicates two extant works to him, *C. Acad.* (AD 386) and *Vera Rel.*, to encourage him to convert from Manichaeism to Christianity, which he did in AD 396. It is possible that he is the addressee of *Ep.* 259 (Gabillon, *Romanianus*, 58–70); if so, he becomes a more problematic character, in that although his life as a Christian was not one of exemplary morality, his financial support made him too important for Augustine to ignore. Ambrose is another character both named and honored in *Conf.*, but with a shadow of ambiguity woven into the text: Augustine depicts himself as approaching a number of distinguished teachers and seeking their approval, including Faustus and then Ambrose. In the case of the latter, the depiction in *Conf.* (e.g., 5.12.23, 6.1.1–3.4) is positive but perhaps reflects a later revision of Augustine's reaction to his cool reception by the bishop of Milan. It is certainly apparent that Ambrose was careful not to let him have the close contact he was seeking and allowed him only the same public access as other students, perhaps because he was tainted by his connections to Manichaean heresy.

Only sixteen of the people who were close to Augustine are named in *Conf.*: Adeodatus, Alypius, Ambrose, Elpidius, Evodius, Faustus, Firminus, Monnica, Nebridius, Patricius, Ponticianus, Romanianus, Simplicianus, Symmachus, Verecundus, and Vindicianus. The one thing they have in common is that they forwarded (unwittingly in the cases of Faustus, Symmachus, and Patricius) the progress of Augustine's conversion to Christianity. He does not include the names of those who did not further it, not even the friend to whom he was so devoted, and whose death he describes in *Conf.* 4.4.7–4.5.10, nor his long-term partner, the mother of his son Adeodatus, whom he abandoned under pressure from Monnica.

Augustine's parents, Monnica and Patricius, invested a great deal in his education, which followed a familiar pattern. His knowledge of Greek was limited (*Conf.* 1.14.23; Bonner, *Augustine of Hippo*, 394–95); in an answer to the Donatist bishop Petilianus (*C. Litt. Pet.* 2.38.91) he writes, "I have acquired only a slight knowledge of Greek, hardly any at all; but I have enough confidence to assert that I know *holon* does not mean 'one' but 'the whole,' and *kath' holon* means 'according to the whole'; from which the Catholic Church takes its name." However, he was entirely at home with the corpus of Latin literature, which became the subject of his first studies.

According to that standard pattern, the initial level of teaching began with a *primus magister*, or primary teacher for reading and writing, then a secondary teacher, or *grammaticus*, for language and literature, and finally a *rhetoricus* for eloquence and oratory (Kaster, *Guardians of Language*, 21–28). The full syllabus of the liberal arts was variously recorded as consisting of geometry, music, literature and poetry, natural science, ethics, and political affairs (Cic. *De or.* 3.127); they were called "liberal" because they were the heritage of a free man (*liber*). According to Cicero (*Tusc.* 2.27; cf. *Rep.* 1.28, "only true men are cultured in the arts appropriate to humanity," *politi propriis humanitatis artibus*). Another list, in *Retr.* 1.6, gives the seven liberal disciplines (or "arts") as grammar, music, dialectic (logic), rhetoric, geometry, arithmetic, and philosophy.

Augustine describes his efforts at composing classical Latin poetry, which is written according to strict conventions of rhythm, meter, and genre (and with no conception of free verse). At *Conf.* 3.7.14 he uses the composition of a poem, with rules of genre governing the choice of word placement, as an analogy for the way in which certain rules abide through time while others are mutable according to circumstance, in order to make sense of the different social conventions governing the Old Testament patriarchs.

Augustine gives the impression that he is searingly explicit in describing his early adulthood as a time of (from a Christian point of view) sexual immorality and questionable conduct. But he turns out to be extremely reticent about the actual nature of that conduct. It may have included homosexual experiences (*Conf.* 2.1.1–2.2.4) as well as the antisocial behavior he describes in *Conf.* 3.3.6; but he is deliberately imprecise in his narrative. Even so, the impression of reflective openness is enough to make *Conf.* the first work of classical literature to construct for its readership a self-portrait of a human individual that is psychologically, emotionally, and intellectually rounded. When the reader encounters Augustine isolating the paradox (*Conf.* 3.2.3) of wanting bad things to happen to people so that he can enjoy the feeling of pitying them, it is difficult not to be impressed by his insight and self-analysis. In a similar way, he questions the nature of enjoyment: "So why did I get pleasure from something that I would not have done at all if left to myself? Is it perhaps because no one finds it easy to laugh when they are alone?" (*Conf.*

2.9.17: cf. Provine, *Laughter*, 215). Likewise he gives a dispassionate analysis of curiosity, which he consistently treats as a negative characteristic (e.g., *Conf.* 3.3.5).

4. THEORIES OF MEANING

At the root of almost all the theories about the world and the right way for human beings to live that were current in Augustine's time was a conviction that there was a force or essence (variously defined) governing all that existed and giving to life a purpose and meaning. This sense of a metaphysical connection between the actions of human individuals and groups, and the eternity of this force understood as some kind of divinity, is articulated by the fifth-century historian Socrates of Constantinople:

> [I want] to make it clear to you that whenever state affairs were in turmoil, by a kind of sympathy [συμπάθεια, or "coordination of experience"] the churches' affairs were in turmoil also . . . As a result, I cannot believe that this succession of events happens by chance—rather it originates in our trespasses (πλημμελήματα). (*Hist. Eccl.* 5 proem)

As a counter to this uncertainty, Augustine was attracted to what promised to interpret his sense experience and his intellectual and spiritual experiences to him in a connected way. He dabbled in astrology until Vindicianus talked him out of it (*Conf.* 4.3.5) by arguing that the stars and planets had no capacity for predicting the future. In the garden where his conversion happened, he picked up a text of Saint Paul and used it to indicate what his next step should be (*Conf.* 8.13.20). This action mirrored the "pagan" use of *sortes Virgilianae* as well as what was later termed bibliomancy or stichomancy: finding a text at random to give guidance for the future. The predictions, foreshadowings, and types that Christians detected in their Old Testament and regarded as fulfilled in the New came to be a principal appeal of Christianity for Augustine, once he conquered his squeamishness about the poor quality of biblical Latin. His development of a theology of divine providence in *De civ. D.* points to the continuity of this priority in his exegetical and theological thinking.

Though he was initiated as a catechumen at birth (*Conf.* 1.11.17), Augustine did not become a Christian. Delaying the full initiation rite of baptism was not unusual in this period, for postbaptismal sin was a serious matter, with (as yet) no adequate theology to explain how God could accommodate forgiveness of such sin. But it was also because as a young man he found the Christian holy writings to be crude in comparison to the high literature in which he had been educated. Instead, he turned to a group, or sect, known as Manichaeans, for the enlightenment he craved. Manichaeism was a popular and powerful religious movement that originated with a third-century Persian teacher, Mani ("Manichaeus" in Latin). Manichaeism imaged the universe in terms of an eternal battle between Good and Evil, Light and Darkness. It emphasized ascetic practices, with a hierarchical separation of the lesser rank ("Hearers") from the inner circle ("Elect": cf. A. *Ep.* 236.2 to Bishop Deuterius). It also had the attraction of seven volumes of the writings of Mani, or Manichaeus, providing Augustine with the kind of sacred text that he clearly found a potential attraction, as his later devotion to Christian Scriptures suggests. Manichaeans did not accept that Old Testament prophets could foretell the future; but Augustine was later to argue elsewhere that the behavior as well as the prophecies of Old Testament characters were a foreshadowing of Christ: "Whatever Scripture says about Abraham is both a historical fact and a prophecy" (S. 2.6; cf. Tert. [ca. AD 170–ca. 225], *De Res. Carn.* 28).

Everything that Augustine tells the reader in *Conf.* about the famous Manichaean teacher Faustus, from whom at one time he was eager to learn, is written from the perspective of someone who has abandoned one faith and embraced another (cf. *Conf.* 5.3.3, 6.11.18); it is inherently hostile. He opens *Conf.* 4.1.1, for example, with a long sentence of extraordinary rhetorical virtuosity mocking Manichaeism. The sentence includes antithesis, irony, bathos, and an outlandish metaphor of the bulbous water vessel (here meaning a paunch or belly) as a workshop or laboratory belching out divinities. At the heart of Augustine's criticism is the failure of Manichaeism to deal rigorously with the question of the existence of evil, and that question becomes the focus of his rejection of the old faith and his embracing of the new. The challenge of Manichaeism to Christianity was based on questions (*Conf.* 3.7.12) about the origin of evil (dealt with in *Conf.* 7.12.18), anthropomorphism in the representation of God (*Conf.* 7.1.1–7.2.3), and the questionable behavior of Bible characters accounted righteous (*Conf.* 5.14.24 and 6.4.6).

In *C. Faust.* 20.2, Faustus is represented as saying, "Paul called Christ the power of God and the Wisdom of God; we believe his power abides in the sun, his wisdom in the moon." At *Conf.* 3.6.11 Manichaeism is shown as teaching five caverns in the realm of darkness, containing the elements of darkness, smoke, wind, fire, and water. There is enough congruence with Christian doctrine and praxis to confuse the unwary seeker: just the kind of heretical pollution of the faith that Irenaeus of Lyons (*Haer.* preface) identified in the second century AD as a primary threat to the purity of true Christianity. Augustine too recognized the danger and must have known that he was uniquely qualified to refute the pretensions of this *ersatz* Christianity.

Once Augustine had abandoned Manichaeism after nine years of adherence, he considered the New Academic school of skeptical philosophers who followed the second-century BC teacher Carneades (*Conf.* 6.11.18). But not for long. Even before this (*Conf.* 4.16.28), he had read, and been impressed by, Aristotle's *Categories* (in a Latin translation; cf. Lössl and Watt, *Bible and Aristotle,* 111–20), a work that encouraged him in using philosophical terminology of substance and predicates. He was yet to encounter Plotinus' reasoning that such categories do not apply in the metaphysical realm because "we are investigating things that are existent, not the one that is beyond existence" (τὰ ὄντα ζητοῦμεν, οὐ τὸ ἐπέκεινα, *Enn.* 6.2.3). Stoicism was too materialist a philosophy, though attractive for its ethical rigorism, and Epicureanism not only appeared to be too hedonistic but also taught that the soul disperses into nothingness after death, which he could not accept (*Conf.* 6.16.26).

"Neoplatonism" is a modern term used to identify philosophers of the third century AD and later who followed in the tradition of Plato and the Academy but whose teach-

ing differed substantially from that of Plato himself. It is
a moot point whether Plotinus (AD 204/5–270) is better
termed a Platonist or a Neoplatonist: at any rate, he was
an Alexandrian philosopher whose teachings affected Augustine both indirectly and directly. Augustine probably
read both the master and his pupil Porphyry (ca. AD
234–301), so the "books of the Neoplatonist" (*Conf.*
7.9.13) cannot be identified securely. From Plotinus Augustine absorbs the principle or Intellect, which combines
with Plotinus' "Word" (Logos [λόγος]: similar to, but not
identical with, the Christian "Word" [Jn 1:1]), to bring
about motion, change, and separation from the One (τὸ
ἕν). This provides a cause for the shift from an aboriginal
perfect One to a world of separation and change: "In reality Intellect (ὁ νοῦς) holds together in itself and is not
disintegrated by reason of its closeness to the One, though
it somehow dared to stand apart from the One" (*Enn.*
6.9.5).

Two themes that run throughout *Conf.* and other works
but that are not self-evidently Christian in origin are the
dyad unity/multiplicity and its correlative alienation/in-
dwelling. Both show Augustine's debt to Neoplatonism in
general and Plotinus in particular; even his famous opening observation to God that "you have made us for yourself, and our hearts are restless until they rest in you" is a
reflection of an understanding of God and the soul in
which the soul, fragmented and alienated from its true
home, longs to return to the place where it belongs. Augustine repeatedly expresses this in terms of God abiding
in him, but of him being outside of, alienated from, himself. Plotinus argues (cf. *Conf.* 2.1.1) that a unity divided

INTRODUCTION

into very small parts loses its identity: "The soul, even if it is a unity and lacks distinct parts, is manifold; it contains many capacities within itself—reasoning, yearning, apprehension—all these coinhere in a unity as if chained together. So the soul supplies unity, and is itself a unity" (*Enn.* 6.9.1).[2] The theme of alienation from God is finally resolved at *Conf.* 13.35.50–38.53. Augustine owes to Plotinus (or found in him a confirmation of his own insight) the idea that the self is a proper subject of philosophical inquiry, for example, *Enn.* 1.6.9–11; the focus on "withdrawing into oneself," and "seeing oneself," provides the foundation upon which the subject matter of *Conf.* itself is constructed.

At the time he wrote *Conf.*, Augustine had been a Christian for years. But in presenting his journey toward that faith from an external perspective, he allows the reader a glimpse of Christianity from the outside: as not only a set of beliefs with some philosophical foundations but also a corpus of holy writings and a long and continuous tradition of teaching and learning, like other philosophical schools. On top of this was the Christian way of gathering for worship by reading and singing sacred words, which was so distinctively different from the "pagan" religious observance based on votive offerings and blood sacrifice. It is important to bear in mind that readers

---

[2] πάντα τὰ ὄντα τῷ ἑνί ἐστιν ὄντα, "beings are beings in virtue of their unity"; ἔπειτα δὲ πολλὴ ἡ ψυχὴ καὶ ἡ μία κἂν εἰ μὴ ἐκ μερῶν· πλεῖσται γὰρ δυνάμεις ἐν αὐτῇ, λογίζεσθαι, ὀρέγεσθαι, ἀντιλαμβάνεσθαι, ἃ τῷ ἑνὶ ὥσπερ δεσμῷ συνέχεται. ἐπάγει μὲν δὴ ψυχὴ τὸ ἓν ἓν οὖσα.

who base their impression of Augustine on his writings encounter a man mainly occupied with doctrine, i.e., correct theological teaching. They will see relatively little of his pastoral preoccupations as bishop of Hippo (but cf. van der Meer, *Augustine the Bishop*, 388–402), or of what came to be the ritual and spiritual focus of his life, as of all orthodox (or "catholic") Christians: the celebration of the sacrament of the Eucharist. Yet this was fundamental to how he lived and prayed (cf. *Conf.* 9.11.27).

At the time when Augustine was writing, the Christian doctrine of the Trinity, that God is both One and Three (one substance and three persons), was emerging out of a long-accepted baptismal formula ("In the name of the Father and of the Son and of the Holy Spirit," Mt 28:19) and a great deal of theological, and sometimes social and political, disputation. So long as the focus remained on the unity, rather than the trinity, of God, Christian understanding of God's nature had much in common with the "pagan" philosophical schools. It was the place of the Word that made Christianity both distinctive and problematic. The "Word" (which in Greek—λόγος—can mean "word" and "speech" and "reason") was a term of Stoic philosophy that denoted how divinity pervaded the universe and made it meaningful and comprehensible. The term may have been adapted by the author of the fourth gospel from Philo of Alexandria (ca. 20 BC–AD 50) as a way of explaining the divine identity of the man Jesus, showing how he can be, as well as human, the "Christus," or anointed, chosen, Son of God (cf. Phil 2:6–7, with *Conf.* 7.18.24; *De civ. D.* 21.15). The *logos*-christologies of the early Christian apologists witness to the appeal of this idea as a way of harmonizing the new Christian faith with older philosophical teachings. In the fourth and fifth centuries, such harmonization was beginning to happen in the sphere of cultic practice as well as theological debate: Augustine relates how Monnica followed her African Christian tradition of venerating the dead at their tombs (in a way strongly reminiscent of ancient Greek hero-cult) but was forbidden to continue the practice in Milan, for Ambrose regarded it as improper (*Conf.* 6.1.1–6.2.2).

The term used in Latin theology for the making of the Word into a human being, usually Englished as "incarnation," is *incarnatio*, or "fleshification." In Greek it is *enanthropesis*, or "humanification." Both terms strive, however inadequately, to give expression to the idea of making a universal force or principle—the Word, or *Logos*—into an individual human person, Jesus the Christ. Nevertheless, Augustine is always insistent on the full humanity of this Word incarnate, which is so fundamental to his sense of having been "saved" in *Conf.*:

So these heretics said that our Lord Jesus Christ did not have a human soul . . . But what do they say? That this, the actual Word of God, was in that human being in place of a mind . . . The catholic faith has spat them out . . . It has been confirmed in the catholic faith that the one whom the Wisdom of God took had, in respect of the wholeness of his nature, nothing less than other people. For other people can be called participants in the Word of God, having the Word of God, but none of them can be called the Word of God, which he has been called when it was said, "The Word was made flesh" (*verbum caro factum est*). (*En. Ps.* 29, 2.2)

5. LANGUAGE AND RHETORIC

Augustine's higher education was primarily an education in rhetoric (the art and techniques of persuasive speaking) built on a primary foundation of the study of literature. His writing finds its own distinctive style, echoing but not imitating his great classical predecessors Cicero, Sallust, and Livy, as well as borrowing from the poets, mainly but not exclusively Virgil. Discourse, as he was taught to handle it, was then primarily an oral phenomenon, not a written one; most literary documents are composed in accordance with the principles and habits of spoken rhetoric (Schaeffer, "Orality and Literacy," 1133–40). *Conf.* itself is imagined as a speech, an address to God, who gives only occasional glimpses of himself (e.g., *Conf.* 7.17.23). At the same time as *Conf.* was taking shape, A. was composing *Doctr. Chr.,* to teach preachers how to use rhetoric properly and (seemingly in passing) to consider fundamental questions of language and semiotics as well (Murphy, "Debate about a Christian Rhetoric," 205–18; Fortin, "Problem of Christian Rhetoric," 219–33).

As a teacher of rhetoric himself, Augustine had mastered the use of techniques that could sway an audience or readership on the macrocosmic level (structure, arrangement, style) and the microcosmic. In the case of the latter, devices called "figures of rhetoric" are easy to find throughout *Conf.*: irony, bathos, paronomasia, antithesis, anaphora, polysyndeton, and the like. Metaphor is used to careful effect, for example, at *Conf.* 2.3.6, where he uses a vivid metaphor to express his reaching sexual maturity: "Thorny growths of sexual immorality sprouted up higher than my head, and there was no hand to uproot them." His despondent friends are described as "dragging their hearts in the dust" (*Conf.* 8.6.15); when he writes, more than once, of the "glue trap that is death," he expects the reader to have seen birds trapped in this way, frantically and hopelessly struggling to escape (*Conf.* 6.5.8). More idiosyncratic but equally vivid is his prayer at the start of Book 5: "Receive the sacrifice of my confessions from the hand of my tongue." Oxymoron is also used for more than decoration; it often points the contrast between what a thing appears or a person wishes to appear and the thing or person's inner reality, hence the "cheated cheats and speechless speakers" (*Conf.* 7.2.3) and "fruitful barrenness of the desert" (*Conf.* 8.6.15). Such figures would have added to his reader's enjoyment of the text; though in the case of rhetorical questions, it might be argued that they are sometimes overabundant (*Conf.* 1.1.1–5.6). These figures can also work in a more expansive way. The apparently trivial incident of the theft of pears (*Conf.* 2.4.9–10.18) is an extended synecdoche: it stands for more than itself, acting, in fact, as a proof to the text of Romans 7.19–24 and a parallel for Adam and Eve taking forbidden fruit in the garden of Eden (cf. OD *Commentary*, 2:205).

Augustine's attitude to his own mastery of rhetoric is ambivalent. He is acutely aware of its power both to inspire and inculcate the good and to manipulate and mislead hearers. It is evident from his extant writings that he knows how to vary his style to suit different audiences; in *Doctr. Chr.* he explores the tricky question of how preachers can learn to take up such expertise for their Christian message, thus appropriating and, as it were, Christianizing, this equivocal phenomenon.

6. AUGUSTINE'S BIBLE

The Bible as Augustine encountered it was a collection of holy writings, *scripturae*. Once he became a Christian, his attitude to this heterogeneous assemblage of texts changed from contempt to devotion: "I decided to fix my mind on the Holy Scriptures, to see what kind of thing they really were. What do I find? Something not disclosed to the proud nor made plain to children, but requiring humility in the approach, yet becoming sublime and cloaked in mystery as one goes deeper" (*Conf.* 3.5.9). His reverence did not, however, extend as far as treating the text as magically powerful in its own right, though some heretical sects did practice rearranging syllables and lines to produce new teachings and works (cf. Iren. *Haer.* 1.8.1, 14–15; 6.37; and Falt.; with Bowman and Woolf, *Literacy and Power,* 126). One of Augustine's first criticisms of Manichaeans in *Conf.* is their mistreatment of the Scriptures (3.6.10).

Augustine's "Old Testament" consisted of a Latin version of a Greek text, the Septuagint (conventionally abbreviated LXX); his "New Testament" was the same collection of writings as in a modern Bible, with minor differences in the arrangement. There was a wide variety of Latin versions available in his time, but no single text was authoritative. These older texts are known collectively as *vetus Latina* or "old Latin" (conventionally abbreviated VL); the "authorized" version produced by Jerome at the turn of the fourth century (known as the Vulgate, conventionally abbreviated Vg) was based for the most part on Hebrew, but also on Greek versions of the Old Testament. Augustine was cautious about it, to say the least; as bishop first, rather than scholar, he considered the pastoral damage that changing long-venerated words might provoke (Robinson, "Ascetic Western Translatology," 3–8, 14–25). But he did not persuade Jerome to translate only from LXX and not from the Hebrew (*Ep.* 71.4, ca. AD 404; with Jerome's acidic reply, *Ep.* 112.20–22, ca. AD 404). In time, Vg came to supersede VL almost completely.

So Augustine's attitude to Jerome's project was ambivalent. He was no polyglot himself and preferred a secure agreed text to a scrupulously accurate one, as their earlier correspondence on the subject showed (A. *Ep.* 38 to Jerome, ca. AD 394). But Augustine was a master of words, able to absorb and deploy elements of biblical style and idiom as part of his rhetorical armory, especially in the elevated sections of *Conf.* Just as the clusters of Scripture signal a heightened spiritual mood, so does repetition of "and" at the start of sentences, which is a distinctive feature of narrative Hebrew prose adopted in LXX and absorbed by VL. On occasion, a reader consulting the marginal Scripture references in this translation will find that the modern biblical text does not match Augustine's words (e.g., *Conf.* 4.8.13); this is usually because he was working with a version of the text later superseded. In particular, the numeration of Psalms in VL and Vg does not always match that of a modern English Bible; the marginal references here follow the latter for the reader's convenience. "Cf." before a marginal Scripture reference indicates a significant difference between Augustine's Old Latin Bible and a modern critical text.

So to return to Marcus Aurelius, and to his fundamental question, "A particular thing: what is it in itself, in the way it is arranged? What is its essence? From what material is it constructed? What is its function in the universe? How long does it endure?" It is possible to answer that the arrangement of *Conf.* is a reflection of the journey of a human person away from self and toward God; that their essence is understanding of the identity of God, both as he is in himself and as he is revealed in creation; and that the material from which they are constructed is Augustine's life experiences, lived and reflected on in a blending of classical and Christian learning and dialectic fused together by the self-aware narrator. Their function is to speak to Augustine's fellow Christians, as he remarks that they did, even within his own lifetime (*Retr.* 2.6). As for how long this text will endure, sixteen centuries have passed; people are still reading it and finding themselves in it. Few texts that are not themselves accounted sacred can have been either so influential or so enduring.

7. THIS TRANSLATION

Augustine's Latin, being both more concise and more elaborate than English, as well as inflected (i.e., modulating the verb itself to indicate mood, number, tense, and person, rather than using pronouns and auxiliary verbs, as in English), has its own special difficulties for the translator. This version aims at a lucid, natural English style, from which it is possible for a reader with some knowledge of Latin to make some sense of the original, and which tracks the syntactic movement wherever possible (cf., e.g., *Conf.*

2.3.5, with Raffel, *Translating Prose*, 71–77; Crystal, *Translation Theory*, 322–29). The problem of translating "confess" and "vain" has been noted already; *animus* and *anima* are consistently rendered as "mind" and "soul," respectively. Where the word "pagan" is used, it is enclosed in quotation marks to indicate that this is a pejorative term used by Christians, not a self-descriptor for Greek and Roman religious praxis. The terms *ecce* ("Look!" or "Behold!") and *vide* ("See!") cause a little awkwardness in that they sound archaic when Englished, and yet they cannot be left untranslated, because they are fundamental to how emphatically Augustine draws the reader's attention to key points in his argument; they also remind the reader repeatedly that *Conf.* is a dialogue with God and the reader, not a soliloquy.

8. HISTORY AND CONSTITUTION OF THE TEXT

By the time the first extant manuscript of *Conf.* was being written, Augustine had been transformed from a recently deceased African bishop, teaching his flock and intervening in the worldwide theological disputes of his day, into a European saint: his body had been translated back to Italy (his bones now rest in the church of San Pietro in Ciel d'Oro in Pavia: Saak, *Creating Augustine*, 58–63). There is a vast number of manuscripts of *Conf.*, testifying to an ongoing fascination with Augustine's description of his coming to Christian faith, perhaps fueled by the disputatious monastic orders laying claim to historical priority in following Augustine's rule (cf. A. *Ep.* 211 = Loeb Classical Library 239, Augustine, *Select Letters,* 49). Despite wide differences in the quality and accuracy of the manuscripts, the text itself is relatively unproblematic. Only one of the many manuscripts is earlier than AD 800: a sixth-century Italian codex S (Sessorianus 55) now in the Biblioteca Nazionale in Rome (cf. Gorman, "Early Manuscript Tradition," 114–45); though early, it is full of errors. Other principal manuscripts (full descriptions in Ver., lxvi–lxxi) include:

A   Stuttgart, Württembergische Landesbibliothek, HB.vii 15. (ninth century, France)

C   Paris Bibliothèque Nationale, lat. 1913 (ninth century, France); tends to Vg assimilation (cf. OD 1:lxvi)

D   Paris Bibliothèque Nationale, lat. 1913A (ninth century, France). C and D are almost identical, but each has different parts of the complete text missing.

E   Paris Bibliothèque Nationale, lat. 12191 (ninth and tenth century, France)

G   Paris Bibliothèque Nationale, lat. 12193 (ninth and tenth century, France). E, from Tours, and G, from the Loire region, are closely related.

H   Paris Bibliothèque Nationale, lat. 12224 (ninth century, France)

O   Paris Bibliothèque Nationale, lat. 1911. (ninth century, France; "perhaps the best single MS" [OD 1:lvii]). With corrections by two later hands.

P   Paris Bibliothèque Nationale, lat. 1912 (ninth century, Germany)

V   Vatican City, Bibliteca Apostolica Vaticana, Vat lat. 5756 (ninth century, north Italy). A, H, and V are closely related.

A number of critical editions are widely available. The introduction, text, and commentary of OD are all freely accessible online. OD provides a concise survey of manuscripts and editions (*Comm.* 1:lvi–lxxi) but integrates detailed comments on individual points of textual disagreement or difficulty into the commentary ad loc. Ver. gives a more detailed presentation of the transmission history and editing of *Conf.*, but the trend of his revisions is, as OD remarks, "to move further away from S and closer to the Maurist *textus receptus*" (*Comm.* 1:lx). Verheijen's critical apparatus is essentially the same as that of Skut. Ver. also makes use of an early sixth-century anthology (*excerpta*) of Augustine made by Eugippius (ca. 455–ca. 535), which preserves some ancient readings.[3]

The translation in this book follows the text printed by OD, with its revised punctuation, except for a few minor variants; the Maurist subdivisions of books are given in parentheses.

Among the editions of *Conf.*, the following may be especially noted:

Editio princeps: J. Mantelin (Strasburg, 1465–1470).

J. Amerbach (Basle, 1506). Based on P; revised by Erasmus, 1528.

C. Plantin (Louvain, 1576–1577).

A. Arnauld (Paris, 1649). Based on twelve MSS, including C G H); Arnauld was the first editor to use sigla to denote the MSS he used.

Benedictine or "Maurist" edition [Maur.] (Paris, 1679–1700). Made extensive use of Arnauld, and added

---

[3] Migne, *PL* 62.0561D; ed. P. Knöll, *CSEL* (Vienna, 1885).

three MSS, two still extant: D E. A major scholarly enterprise in its time.

L. E. Rondet (Paris, 1776). First to use the ninth-century MS O.

Oxford Bibliotheca Patrum edition (E. B. Pusey, 1838). With English translation: based on Maur. with a number of other MSS.

Patrologia Latina edition vol. 32 (J.-P. Migne, 1841–1849). Based on Maur. with a number of other MSS.

P. Knöll. Vol. 33, *Corpus Scriptorum Ecclesiasticorum Latinorum* (Vienna: Teubner, 1898). First to use (and indeed base his edition on) S.

J. Gibb, W. Montgomery [GM] (Cambridge, 1908; revised 1927). Followed Knöll closely: with "excellentes annotations" (Verheijen, viii).

P. de Labriolle (Paris: Budé, 1925). With French translation.

A.-C. Vega (Madrid: El Escorial, 1930). First to use *excerpta* of Eugippius.

M. Skutella [Skut.] (Stuttgart, 1934, rev.1981). Bibliotheca Teubneriana: moved away from Knöll's reliance on S.

M. Pellegrino [Pell.] (Paris, 1960). With commentary.

L. Verheijen [Ver.]. Vol. 27, Corpus Christianorum Series Latina (Turnhout: Brepols, 1981; revised 1990).

J. J. O'Donnell [OD]. (New York: Clarendon Press, 1992). 3 vols. (vol. 1, Introduction and Commentary; vol. 2, Commentary on Books 1–7; vol. 3, Commentary on Books 8–13). OD has comprehensively reviewed the punctuation of *Conf.*

ABBREVIATIONS

A.	Augustine	
Ad.	*Adelphoe*	*The Brothers*
Adn. Iob	*Adnotationes in Iob*	*Comments on Job*
Aen.	*Aeneis*	*Aeneid*
Amic.	*De Amicitia*	*On Friendship*
Apol.	*Apologia*	*Apology (Defense)*
Arist.	Aristotle	
B. Coniug.	*De Bono Coniugio*	*On the Good of Marriage*
Beata V.	*De Beata Vita*	*On the Blessed Life*
C. Acad.	*Contra Academicos*	*Against the Academics*
C. Adim.	*Contra Adimantum*	*Against Adimantus*
Carm.	*Carmina*	*Odes*
Cat.	*Catilina*	*Catiline*
Cath. Hist. Rev.	*Catholic Historical Review*	
Catull.	Catullus	
Cent. Virg.	*Centones Virgiliani*	*Virgilian Compilations*

ABBREVIATIONS

C. Faust.	*Contra Faustum Manichaeum*	*Against Faustus the Manichaean*
Cic.	Cicero	
C. Litt. Pet	*Contra Litteras Petiliani*	*Against the Letters of Petilianus*
Corrept.	*De Correptione et Gratia*	*On Admonition and Grace*
C. Symm	*Contra Symmachum*	*Against Symmachus*
Cura Mort.	*De cura pro mortuis gerenda*	*On the Care of the Dead*
De civ. D.	*De Civitate Dei*	*City of God*
De Res. Carn.	*De Resurrectione Carnis*	*On the Resurrection of the Body*
Dial.	*Dialogi*	*Dialogues*
Doctr. Chr.	*De Doctrina Christiana*	*On Christian Teaching*
DRN	*De Rerum Natura*	*On the Nature of Things*
Ecl.	*Ecloga*	*Eclogues*
Enn.	*Enneades*	*Enneads*
En. Ps.	*Enarrationes in Psalmos*	*Expositions of the Psalms*
Ench.	*Enchiridion*	*Handbook*
Ep.	*Epistulae*	*Letters*
Epod.	*Epodes*	*Epodes*
Eun.	*Eunuchus*	*The Eunuch*
Eur.	Euripides	

xlii

ABBREVIATIONS

Falt.	Faltonia Betitia Proba, *Cento Vergilianus de laudibus Christi*	
Fast.	*Fasti*	*Fasti (Rome's Calendar)*
Fin.	*De Finibus*	*On Ends*
G.	*Georgica*	*Georgics*
Gell.	Aulus Gellius	
GM	*J. Gibb and W. Montgomery edition (Cambridge, 1908)*	
Gn.c.Man.	*De Genesi contra manichaeos*	*On Genesis, against the Manichees*
Gn. Litt.	*De Genesi ad Litteram*	*The Literal Meaning of Genesis*
Gn.litt. Imp.	*De Genesi ad Litteram Inperfectus Liber*	*Unfinished Literal Commentary on Genesis*
GR	*Greece & Rome*	
Haer.	*Adversus Haereses*	*Against Heresies*
Hist. Eccl.	*Historia Ecclesiastica*	*Church History*
Hom.	Homer	
Hor.	Horace	

xliii

ABBREVIATIONS

HThR	Harvard Theological Review	
IA	Iphigenia Aulidensis	Iphigenia at Aulis
Il.	Ilias	Iliad
In Cat.	In Catilinam Orationes	Speeches against Catiline
Inst.	Institutio Oratoria	The Orator's Education
Io. Ep. Tr.	Tractatus in Iohannis epistulam ad Parthos	Tractates on the Epistle of John to the Parthians
Io. Ev. Tr.	Tractatus in Evangelium Iohannis	Tractates on the Gospel of John
Iren.	Irenaeus of Lyons	
Iug.	Iugurtha	Jugurtha
JBL	Journal of Biblical Literature	
JHI	Journal of the History of Ideas	
JHSex	Journal of the History of Sexuality	
JR	Journal of Religion	
JRS	Journal of Roman Studies	

JThS	*Journal of Theological Studies*	
Juv.	Juvenal	
Lib. Arb.	*De Libero Arbitrio*	*On Free Will*
Lucr.	Lucretius	
Maur.	Benedictine or "Maurist" edition (Paris, 1679–1700)	
M. Aur.	Marcus Aurelius	
Med.	*Meditationes*	*Meditations*
Met.	*Metamorphoses*	*Metamorphoses (Transformations)*
Mus.	*De musica*	*On Music*
NA	*Noctes Atticae*	*Attic Nights*
Nat. D.	*De Natura Deorum*	*On the Nature of the Gods*
OD	J. J. O'Donnell edition (Oxford, 1992)	
Op. Mon.	*De opere monachorum*	*On the Work of Monks*
Orat.	*Orator*	*The Public Speaker*
Ord.	*De Ordine*	*On Order*
Ov.	Ovid	
PBSR	*Papers of the British School at Rome*	

Pell.	M. Pellegrino edition (Paris, 1960)	
Persev.	*De Dono Perseverantiae*	*On the Gift of Perseverance*
Pl.	Plato	
Phaedr.	*Phaedrus*	*Phaedrus*
Poet.	*Poetica*	*Poetics*
P&P	*Past & Present*	
Prudent.	Prudentius	
Qu.Ev.	*Quaestiones Evangeliorum*	*Questions on the Gospels*
Quint.	Quintilian	
REAug	*Revue des Études Augustiniennes*	
Rem.Am.	*Remedia Amoris*	*Remedies for Love*
Rep.	*De Republica* (Cic.)	*On the Republic*
Resp.	*Resp.* (Pl.)	*Republic*
Retr.	*Retractationes*	*Reviews*
Rhet.	*Rhetorica*	*Rhetoric*
S.	*Sermones*	*Sermons*
Sall.	Sallust	
Sat.	*Saturae*	*Satires*
S. Dom. M.	*De Sermone Domini in Monte*	*On the Lord's Sermon on the Mount*
Sen.	Seneca	

Skut.	M. Skutella edition (Stuttgart, 1934; rev. 1981)	
SO	*Symbolae Osloenses*	
SPh	*Studies in Philology*	
TAPhA	*Transactions and Proceedings of the American Philological Association*	
Ter.	Terence	
Tert.	Tertullian	
Thuc.	Thucydides	
Trin.	*De Trinitate*	*On the Trinity*
Tusc.	*Tusculanae Disputationes*	*Tusculan Disputations*
Util. Cred.	*De Utilitate Credendi*	*On the Point of Believing*
VChr	*Vigiliae Christianae*	
Ver.	L. Verheijen edition (Turnhout, 1981)	
Vera Rel.	*De vera religione*	*On True religion*
Virg.	Virgil	
VL	*vetus Latina*	old Latin

REFERENCES

EDITIONS

Gibb, J., and W. Montgomery. *The Confessions of Augustine.* Cambridge: Cambridge University Press, 1908. With commentary.

Verheijen, L. *Sancti Augustini Confessionum libri XIII.* Corpus Christianorum Series Latina 27. Turnhout, 1981. With critical apparatus. Available online.

O'Donnell, J. J. *Augustine: Confessions.* Introduction, text, and commentary. 3 vols. Oxford: Oxford University Press, 1992. Available online.

TRANSLATIONS

Boulding, M. *The Confessions: Saint Augustine.* Hyde Park, NY: New City Press, 1997.

Chadwick, H. *Saint Augustine: Confessions.* Oxford: Oxford University Press 1991.

Pine-Coffin, R. S. *Saint Augustine: Confessions.* New York: Penguin Books, 1961.

REFERENCES

COMMENTARIES

Campbell, J. M., and M. R. P. McGuire. *The Confessions of Saint Augustine: Books 1–9 (selections)*. New York: Prentice-Hall, 1931.

Clark, G. *Augustine: Confessions Books I–IV*. Cambridge: Cambridge University Press, 1995.

BOOKS

Arts, M. R. "The Syntax of the Confessions of Saint Augustine." PhD diss., Washington, DC: Catholic University of America, 1927.

Bartelink, G. J. M., ed. and trans. *Vie d'Antoine. Athanase d'Alexandrie. Introduction, texte critique, traduction, notes et index*. Sources Chrétiennes 400. Paris: Editions du Cerf, 1994.

Bickersteth, E. *The Testimony of the Reformers*. London, 1836.

Bidez, J. *L'empereur Julien. Oeuvres complètes*. Vol. 1.1. Paris: Les Belles Lettres, 1932.

Bonner, G. *St. Augustine of Hippo: Life and Controversies*. Canterbury Press Norwich, 1963 (revised 1986).

Bowman, A., and G. Woolf. *Literacy and Power in the Ancient World*. Cambridge: Cambridge University Press, 1994.

Brown, P. R. L. *Augustine of Hippo: A Biography*. 2nd ed. London: University of California Press, 2000.

Charlesworth, J. H., ed. *The Old Testament Pseudepigrapha*. Vol. 2, *Expansions of the "Old Testament" and Legends, Wisdom and Philosophical Literature, Prayers, Psalms and Odes, Fragments of Lost Judeo-Hellenistic*

l

Works. Garden City, NY: Doubleday, 1985. Reproduced in Michael G. Reddish, ed., *Apocalyptic Literature: A Reader* (Nashville: Abingdon, 1990).

Enos, R. L., and R. Thompson, eds. *The Rhetoric of Saint Augustine of Hippo: de doctrina Christiana and the Search for a Distinctly Christian Rhetoric*. Waco: Baylor University Press, 2008.

Hagendahl, H. *Augustine and the Latin Classics*. 2 vols. Stockholm: Almquist et Wiksell, 1967.

Hegedus, T. *Early Christianity and Ancient Astrology*. New York: Peter Lang Publishing, 2007.

Hunt, H. *Clothed in the Body: Asceticism, the Body and the Spiritual in the Late Antique Era*. Farnham, UK: Ashgate, 2012

Knauer, G. N. "Psalmenzitate in Augustins Konfessionen." PhD diss., Hamburg, 1955; reprinted in *Three Studies*. New York: Garland, 1987.

Konstan, D. *Friendship in the Classical World*. Cambridge: Cambridge University Press, 1997.

Lössl, J., and J. W. Watt. *Interpreting the Bible and Aristotle in Late Antiquity: The Alexandrian Commentary Tradition between Rome and Baghdad*. Farnham, UK: Ashgate, 2001.

Meer, F. van der. *Augustine the Bishop: The Life and Work of a Father of the Church*. Translated by B. Battershaw and G. R. Lamb. Sheed & Ward: London, 1961.

Provine, R. "'Laughter, Tickling, and the Evolution of Speech and Self." *Current Directions in Psychological Science* 13 (2004): 215.

Raffel, B. *The Art of Translating Prose*. University Park: Pennsylvania State University Press, 1994.

Saak, E. *Creating Augustine: Interpreting Augustine and

REFERENCES

Augustinianism in the Later Middle Ages. Oxford: Oxford University Press, 2012.

ARTICLES

Condon, Matthew G. "The Unnamed and the Defaced: The Limits of Rhetoric in Augustine's 'Confessiones.'" *Journal of the American Academy of Religion* 69 (2001).

Crystal, D. "Some Current Trends in Translation Theory." *The Bible Translator* 27 (1976): 322–29.

Diggle, J. "Theophrastus: Characters." *Cambridge Classical Texts and Commentaries* 43 (2004).

Fortin, E. L. "Problem of Christian Rhetoric." In Enos and Thompson, *The Rhetoric of Saint Augustine of Hippo.*

Gabillon, A. "Romanianus Alias Cornelius." *REAug* 24 (1978).

Gavigan, J. J. "S. Augustine's Friend Nebridius." *Cath. Hist. Rev.* 32 (1946).

Gillard, F. D. "More Silent Reading in Antiquity: Non Omne Verbum Sonabat." *JBL* 112 (1993).

Gorman, M. M. "The Early Manuscript Tradition of St. Augustine's *Confessiones.*" *JThS* 34 (1983).

———. "Aurelius Augustinus: The Testimony of the Oldest Manuscripts of Saint Augustine's works." *JThS* (1984): 35.

Levick, B. "Morals, Politics, and the Fall of the Roman Republic." *GR* 29 (1982).

Löfsted, B. "Notizen zu den Bekenntnissen des Augustin." *SO* 56 (1981).

Murphy, "Debate about a Christian Rhetoric." In Enos

and Thompson, *The Rhetoric of Saint Augustine of Hippo*.

Plumpe, J. C. "Ecclesia Mater." *TAPhA* 70 (1939).

Pranger, M. B. "Time and Narrative in Augustine's 'Confessions.'" *JR* 81 (2001).

Quasten, J. "Vetus Superstitio et Nova Religio: The Problem of Refrigerium in the Ancient Church of North Africa." *HThR* 33 (1940).

Rist, J. "Augustine on Free Will and Predestination." *JThS* 20 (1969).

Robinson, D. "The Ascetic Foundations of Western Translatology: Jerome and Augustine." *Translation and Literature* 1 (1992): 3–25.

Williams, R. "Language, Reality and Desire in Augustine's *de doctrina Christiana*." *Journal of Literature & Theology* 3 (1989).

GENERAL BIBLIOGRAPHY

Brennan, J. *"A Study of the Clausulae in the Sermons of Saint Augustine."* PhD diss., Washington, DC: Catholic University of America, 1947.

Brown, P. R. L. *The Making of Late Antiquity.* Cambridge, MA: Harvard University Press, 1978.

———. *The Body and Society: Men, Women, and Sexual Renunciation in Early Christianity.* New York: Columbia University Press, 1988.

———. Power *and Persuasion in Late Antiquity: Towards a Christian Empire.* Madison: University of Wisconsin Press, 1992.

Burnaby, J. *Amor dei: The Religion of Saint Augustine.* London, 1938. Reissued by Canterbury Press Norwich, 1991.

Burton, P. *Language in the Confessions of Augustine.* Oxford: Oxford University Press, 2007.

Clark, E. A., and D. F. Hatch, trans. *The Golden Bough, The Oaken Cross: The Virgilian Cento of Faltonia Betitia Proba.* Chico, CA: Scholars Press, 1981.

Clark, G. *Augustine: The Confessions.* Cambridge: Cambridge University Press, 1993.

Courcelle, P. *Recherches sur les Confessions de Saint-Augustin.* 2nd ed. Paris: Editions É. de Boccard, 1968.

Courcelle, P. *Les Confessions de saint Augustin dans la tradition littéraire*. Paris: Études Augustiniennes, 1963.

Dobell, B. *Augustine's Intellectual Conversion: The Journey from Platonism to Christianity*. Cambridge: Cambridge University Press, 2009.

Fitzgerald, A. D. *Augustine through the Ages: An Encyclopedia*. Grand Rapids, MI, 1999.

Harmless, W. *Desert Christians: An Introduction to the Literature of Early Monasticism*. Oxford: Oxford University Press, 2004.

Hrdlicka, C. L. *"A Study of the Late Latin Vocabulary and the Prepositions and Demonstrative Pronouns in the Confessions of St. Augustine."* PhD diss., Washington, DC: Catholic University of America, 1931.

Kaster, R. A. *Guardians of Language: The Grammarian and Society in Late Antiquity*. Berkeley: University of California Press, 1988.

Lancel, S. *Saint Augustine*. Librairie Arthème Fayard, 1999. Translated by Antonia Nevill. London: SCM Press, 2002.

Markus, R. A. *The End of Ancient Christianity*. Cambridge: Cambridge University Press, 1990.

McMahon, R. *Augustine's Prayerful Ascent: An Essay on the Literary Form of the Confessions*. Athens, GA: Georgia University Press 1989.

O'Meara, D. J. *Plotinus: An Introduction to the Enneads* Oxford: Oxford University Press, 1993.

O'Meara, J. *The Young Augustine:* London: Longmans, 1954.

Reynolds, G. *"The Clausulae in the De Civitate Dei of St. A."* PhD diss., Washington, DC: Catholic University of America, 1924.

Rist, J. *Augustine.* Cambridge: Cambridge University Press, 1994.

Robinson, D. *Western Translation Theory: From Herodotus to Nietzsche.* Manchester, UK: St. Jerome Publishing, 2002².

Sandnes, K. O. *The Gospel "According to Homer and Virgil": Cento and Canon.* Supplements to Novum Testamentum 138. Leiden: Brill, 2011.

Stock, B. *Augustine's Inner Dialogue: The Philosophical Soliloquy in Late Antiquity.* Cambridge: Cambridge University Press, 2010.

Stump, E, and N. Kretzman. *The Cambridge Companion to Augustine.* Cambridge: Cambridge University Press, 2001.

Verheijen, M. J. *Eloquentia pedisequa; observations sur le style des Confessions de saint Augustin.* Nijmegen: Dekker & van de Vegt, 1949.

ARTICLES

Bonner, G. "Christ, God and Man in the Thought of S. Augustine." In *God's Decree and Man's Destiny: Studies on the Thought of Augustine of Hippo.* London: Variorum Reprints, 1987.

Brown, P. R. L. "The Diffusion of Manichaeism in the Roman Empire." *JRS* 59 (1969).

Camargo, M. "Non solum sibi sed aliis etiam: Neoplatonism and Rhetoric in Saint Augustine's *De doctrina Christiana.*" *Rhetorica: A Journal of the History of Rhetoric* 16 (1998).

Ferrari, L. C. "The Pear Theft in Augustine's 'Confessions.'" *REAug* 16 (1970).

Markus, R. A. "Saint Augustine on Signs." *Phronesis* 2 (1957), 60–83.

Mathewes, C. T. "The Liberation of Questioning in Augustine's 'Confessions.'" *Journal of the American Academy of Religion* 70 (2002).

Mazzeo, J. A. "St. Augustine's Rhetoric of Silence." *JHI* 23 (1962).

McCarthy, M. "Augustine's Mixed Feelings: Virgil's Aeneid and the Psalms of David in the *Confessions.*" *HThR* 102 (2009).

O'Connell, R. J. "The Enneads and St. Augustine's Image of Happiness." *VChr* 17 (1963).

———. "Ennead VI, 4 and 5 in the Works of St. Augustine." *REAug* 9 (1963).

Rothfield, L. "Autobiography and Perspective in the Confessions of St. Augustine." *Comparative Literature* 33 (1981).

Schaeffer, J. D. "The Dialectic of Orality and Literacy: The Case of Book 4 of Augustine's 'De doctrina christiana.'" *Proceedings of the Modern Language Association* 111 (1996).

Shaw, B. D. "The Family in Late Antiquity: The Experience of Augustine." *P&P* 115 (1987).

Soble, A. G. "Correcting Some Misconceptions about St. Augustine's Sex Life." *JHSex* 11 (2002).

Suchoki, M. "The Symbolic Structure of Augustine's 'Confessions.'" *Journal of the American Academy of Religion* 50 (1982).

Taylor, J. H. "St. Augustine and the 'Hortensius' of Cicero." *SPh* 60 (1963).

Tell, D. "Augustine and the 'Chair of Lies': Rhetoric in

The Confessions." Rhetorica: A Journal of the History of Rhetoric 28 (2010).

Wallace-Hadrill, A. "The Social Structure of the Roman House." *PBSR* 56 (1988).

Walsh, P. G., "The Rights and Wrongs of Curiosity (Plutarch to Augustine)." *GR* 35 (1988).

LIFE OF AUGUSTINE

THE WIDER CHURCH AND
THE EMPIRE

TIMELINE

386	Reads Neoplatonist books; converts to orthodox Christianity (July/August); stays in Cassiciacum; writes first Christian works; baptized by Ambrose Easter Day, April 24, 387
387	Monnica dies at Ostia; anti-Manichaean writings
388–90	Returns to Africa and Thagaste; Adeodatus and Nebridius die
391–95	Priested at Hippo Regius 391; in 395 consecrated as co-bishop to Valerius; begins *En. Ps.*
397	Develops skills in preaching and controversy; participates in local church councils; begins *Conf.*
400–403	Negotiates with Donatists; writes *Trin.*
407	*Io. Ep. Tr.* 7.8: "Love, and do what you want" (*dilige et quod vis fac*)
411	Involved in Catholic-Donatist conference (*collatio*) at Carthage
412	*De civ. D.* begun; works on theology of grace and original sin; begins his challenge to Pelagianism
416	Attends council at Milevis, where Pelagius is condemned
418	Council of Carthage upholds A. on original sin and infant baptism

TIMELINE

TIMELINE

TIMELINE

THE CONFESSIONS OF
AURELIUS AUGUSTINE

LIBER I

1. Magnus es, domine, et laudabilis valde. magna virtus
tua et sapientiae tuae non est numerus. et laudare te vult
homo, aliqua portio creaturae tuae, et homo circumferens
mortalitatem suam, circumferens testimonium peccati sui
et testimonium quia superbis resistis; et tamen laudare te
vult homo, aliqua portio creaturae tuae. tu excitas ut laudare te delectet, quia fecisti nos ad te et inquietum est cor
nostrum donec requiescat in te.

Da mihi, domine, scire et intellegere utrum sit prius
invocare te an laudare te, et scire te prius sit an invocare
te. sed quis te invocat nesciens te? aliud enim pro alio
potest invocare nesciens. an potius invocaris ut sciaris?
quomodo autem invocabunt, in quem non crediderunt?

The praenomen, "Aurelius," is never mentioned by A. or his col-
locutors; but A. very rarely mentions his cognomen, "Augustinus," either, and never in *Conf.*

[1] A. refers to *Conf.* in *Retr.* 2.6.1, *Persev.* 20.53, etc., both by
its familiar title and by its incipit, *magnus es domine* (the placing
of the first word is emphatic; cf. the first word of *De civ. D.*, *glo-
riosissimam*, and the last of *Conf.*, *aperietur* [Mt 7:7]).

[2] "And" at the start of a narrative sentence evokes biblical
idiom.   [3] The theme of alienation from God introduced
here concludes at *Conf.* 13.35.50–38.53; it is rooted in Plotinus,
cf. Introduction, pp. xxvii–xxix.

BOOK I

1. (1) Great are you, O Lord,[1] and surpassingly worthy of praise. Great is your goodness, and your wisdom is incalculable. And[2] humanity, which is but a part of your creation, wants to praise you; even though humanity bears everywhere its own mortality, and bears everywhere the evidence of its own sin and the evidence that you resist the proud. And even so humanity, which is but a part of your creation, longs to praise you. You inspire us to take delight in praising you, for you have made us for yourself, and our hearts are restless until they rest in you.[3]

O Lord, let me know and understand which comes first—is it invoking you in prayer or praising you? And again, which comes first—knowing you or invoking you in prayer? Yet how can anyone invoke you without knowing you?[4] In ignorance they may invoke something else, mistaking it for you.[5] Perhaps then you should be invoked instead, so that you can be known? Yet how will they invoke one in whom they have not believed? Or how will

Ps 145:3

Ps 147:5

2 Cor 4:10

Jas 4:6

---

[4] A. uses sequences of rhetorical questions when working through intellectual problems.

[5] A key theme: experiments with fruitless alternatives to the Christian God.

3

aut quomodo credent sine praedicante? et laudabunt dominum qui requirunt eum: quaerentes enim inveniunt eum et invenientes laudabunt eum. quaeram te, domine, invocans te et invocem te credens in te: praedicatus enim es nobis. invocat te, domine, fides mea, quam dedisti mihi, quam inspirasti mihi per humanitatem filii tui, per ministerium praedicatoris tui.

2. (2) Et quomodo invocabo deum meum, deum et dominum meum, quoniam utique in me ipsum eum vocabo, cum invocabo eum? et quis locus est in me quo veniat in me deus meus, quo deus veniat in me, deus qui fecit caelum et terram? itane, domine deus meus? est quicquam in me quod capiat te? an vero caelum et terra, quae fecisti et in quibus me fecisti, capiunt te? an quia sine te non esset quidquid est, fit ut quidquid est capiat te? quoniam itaque et ego sum, quid peto ut venias in me, qui non essem nisi esses in me? non enim ego iam inferi,[1] et tamen etiam ibi es, nam etsi descendero in infernum, ades. non ergo essem, deus meus, non omnino essem, nisi esses in me. an potius non essem nisi essem in te, ex quo omnia, per quem omnia, in quo omnia? etiam sic, domine, etiam sic. quo te invoco, cum in te sim? aut unde venias in me? quo enim recedam extra caelum et terram, ut inde in me veniat deus meus, qui dixit, "caelum et terram ego impleo"?

---

[1] (Reading *inferi* as locative) inferi *S codd. Knöll Skut.*: in infernis *Maur*: in ⟨profundis⟩ inferi *Ver*

---

[6] Perhaps an allusion to Ambrose; cf. *Conf.* 5.13.23, etc.

they believe without a preacher?[26] Those who seek the Rom 10:14 Lord will praise him: those who search, find him; and Mt 7:7 when they have found him they will praise him. So let me seek you, Lord, while I invoke you in prayer; and let me invoke you while I believe in you. You have been preached to me. That faith of mine, Lord, which you have given to me, which you breathed into me by the incarnation of your Son, invokes you in prayer through the ministry of your preacher.

2. (2) And how shall I invoke my God, my God and my Lord, in prayer? Certainly, when I do invoke him in prayer, Jn 20:28 I shall be summoning him into my very being. What place is there in me where my God may enter in, where that same God who made heaven and earth may enter into me? Gn 1:1 Is it so, O Lord my God? Is there any part of me capable of encompassing you? Or is it the case that heaven and earth, which you made, and in which you made me, encompass you? Is it the case that because whatever exists would not exist but for you, whatever exists must contain you? Therefore since I too exist, why do I ask you to enter into me, when I would not exist but for your presence in me? After all, I am no longer in Hell; and yet there too Ps 86:13 you are present: for even if I go down into Hell, you are there. So I would not exist, my God, I would not exist at Ps 139:8 all, unless you existed in me. Or rather, I would not exist unless I existed in you, by whom everything is, and through whom everything is, and in whom everything is. So it is, Rom 11:36 Lord, so it is. How am I to invoke you in prayer when I exist within you? Where would you come *from,* into me? Where would I have to withdraw *to,* beyond heaven and earth, to reach a place from which my God could enter into me?—for he declares, "I fill heaven and earth." Jer 23:24

3. (3) Capiunt ergone te caelum et terra, quoniam tu imples ea? an imples et restat, quoniam non te capiunt? et quo refundis quidquid impleto caelo et terra restat ex te? an non opus habes ut quoquam continearis, qui contines omnia, quoniam quae imples continendo imples? non enim vasa quae te plena sunt stabilem te faciunt, quia etsi frangantur non effunderis. et cum effunderis super nos, non tu iaces sed erigis nos, nec tu dissiparis sed conligis nos. sed quae imples omnia, te toto imples omnia. an quia non possunt te totum capere omnia, partem tui capiunt et eandem partem simul omnia capiunt? an singulas singula et maiores maiora, minores minora capiunt? ergo est aliqua pars tua maior, aliqua minor? an ubique totus es et res nulla te totum capit?

4. (4) Quid es[2] ergo, deus meus? quid, rogo, nisi dominus deus? quis enim dominus praeter dominum? aut quis deus praeter deum nostrum? summe, optime, potentissime, omnipotentissime, misericordissime et iustissime, secretissime et praesentissime, pulcherrime et fortissime, stabilis et incomprehensibilis, immutabilis mutans omnia, numquam novus numquam vetus, innovans omnia et in vetustatem perducens superbos et nesciunt. semper agens semper quietus, conligens et non egens, portans et implens

---

[2] es *codd. Maur. Ver.*: est S *Knöll Skut. GM*

---

[7] Cf. Plotinus *Enn.* 5.5.9: "That source (ἀρχή), which has nothing prior to it, does not subsist in anything other than itself . . . in itself it encompasses all other things . . . and it possesses but is not possessed."   [8] "Most merciful" is A.'s distinctive superlative for God: three examples in *Conf.* (6.5.7, 8.13; 9.2.4), more than fifty in extant writings, rare otherwise.

3. (3) So: because you fill them, does it follow that
heaven and earth contain you?[7] Or do you fill them, and
yet something remains because they cannot contain you?
Where do you pour out whatever of yourself is left over,
once heaven and earth are filled? Or have you no need to
be contained *by* anything, since you contain all things, and
since whatever you do fill, you fill it by containing it? For
it is not vessels full of you which render you immutable,
since even if they are broken you do not spill out of them.
When you are poured out upon us, you do not merely   Jl 2:28
settle on the ground; instead you lift us up. And you are   Ps 146:8
not dispersed; instead you bind us together. As for all
those things which you fill, you fill all of them with all of
yourself. Or is it the case that because all things cannot
contain all of yourself, they contain a part of you, and all
of them contain the same part at the same time? Or do
individual things contain individual parts of you?—the
greater things greater parts, and the smaller things smaller
parts? In sum: is one part of you greater, another lesser?
Or are you altogether everywhere, so nothing contains you
completely?

4. (4) So what is my God? What, I want to know, is God
if not the Lord? Who is lord except *the* Lord? And who
is God except *our* God? Highest, best, most powerful,   Ps 18:31
most omnipotent, most merciful[8] and most just, most hidden and most evident, most beautiful and most sovereign,
steadfast and inconceivable, unchanging yet changing all
things; never new, never old, renewing all things and   Ws 7:27
bringing the proud into decrepitude without their knowl-
edge.[9] Always active, always at rest; uniting and needing   cf. Jb 9:5^VL

---

[9] See Introduction, p. xxxv.

et protegens, creans et nutriens et perficiens, quaerens cum nihil desit tibi. amas nec aestuas, zelas et securus es, paenitet te et non doles, irasceris et tranquillus es, opera mutas nec mutas consilium, recipis quod invenis et numquam amisisti. numquam inops et gaudes lucris, numquam avarus et usuras exigis, supererogatur tibi ut debeas: et quis habet quicquam non tuum? reddis debita nulli debens, donas debita nihil perdens. et quid diximus, deus meus, vita mea, dulcedo mea sancta, aut quid dicit aliquis cum de te dicit? et vae tacentibus de te, quoniam loquaces muti sunt.

5. (5) Quis mihi dabit adquiescere in te? quis dabit mihi ut venias in cor meum et inebries illud, ut obliviscar mala mea et unum bonum meum amplectar, te? quid mihi es? miserere ut loquar. quid tibi sum ipse, ut amari te iubeas a me et, nisi faciam, irascaris mihi et mineris ingentes miserias? parvane ipsa est si non amem te? ei mihi! dic mihi per miserationes tuas, domine deus meus, quid sis mihi. dic animae meae, "salus tua ego sum": sic dic ut audiam. ecce aures cordis mei ante te, domine. aperi eas et dic animae meae, "salus tua ego sum." curram post vocem hanc et apprehendam te. noli abscondere a me faciem tuam: moriar, ne moriar, ut eam videam.

---

10 A. notes elsewhere that "All things can be said of God, and yet nothing about God can be said worthily," *Io. Ev. Tr* 13.5.

11 *misereor, misericordia* and cognates refer to compassion for suffering apart from the element of guilt.

12 The Latin word *salus* encompasses literal safety, health, and rescue, as well as spiritualized salvation.

13 Intricate phrasing, also evoking Ex 33:20 and Dt 31:17 to produce the conceit.

nothing, bringing and filling and protecting, creating and nurturing and bringing to perfection, seeking even though you lack nothing. You love, yet do not burn with passion; you are zealous in your love and yet peaceable; you repent without regretting; you are angry yet serene; you change Gn 6:6–7 your works yet do not change your purpose; you accept what you find and have never lost. You are never poor and you take pleasure in gain; you are never greedy yet you exact interest; you receive more in payment than you ask Mt 25:14–30 for so as to put you under an obligation—yet who owns Lk 10:35 anything that is not, in reality, yours? You pay off debts, though you owe nothing to anyone; you remit debts, yet suffer no loss. After all this, what have we said, my God, my life, my holy sweetness? What is anyone to say when they speak of you? Woe betide those who stay silent about you, because even the loquacious become like those who cannot speak a word.[10]

5. (5) Who will allow me to find rest in you? Who will allow me to let you enter my heart and intoxicate it so that Ps 65:10 I forget my troubles and embrace my one and only good, namely yourself? What are you to me? Have mercy[11] so that I may speak. What am I myself to you, that you insist on my loving you—and, unless I do so, you are angry with me and threaten me with great unhappiness? Is my unhappiness insignificant if I do not love you? Pity me! Tell me, O Lord my God, by your mercies, what you are to me. Say to my soul, "I am your salvation":[12] speak in such a way Ps 35:3 that I may hear. Look—the ears of my heart are before you, Lord. Open them and say to my soul, "I am your salvation." I shall run after this voice and embrace you. Do not hide your face from me: let me die—in order not to Pss 27:9, 143:7 die—so that I may see it.[13]

(6) Angusta est domus animae meae quo venias ad eam: dilatetur abs te. ruinosa est: refice eam. habet quae offendant oculos tuos: fateor et scio. sed quis mundabit eam? aut cui alteri praeter te clamabo, "ab occultis meis munda me, domine, et ab alienis parce servo tuo?" credo, propter quod et loquor, domine: tu scis. nonne tibi pro-locutus sum adversum me delicta mea, deus meus, et tu dimisisti impietatem cordis mei? non iudicio contendo tecum, qui veritas es, et ego nolo fallere me ipsum, ne mentiatur iniquitas mea sibi. non ergo iudicio contendo tecum, quia, si iniquitates observaveris, domine, domine, quis sustinebit?

6. (7) Sed tamen sine me loqui apud misericordiam tuam, me terram et cinerem sine tamen loqui. quoniam ecce misericordia tua est, non homo, inrisor meus, cui loquor. et tu fortasse inrides me, sed conversus miserebe-ris mei. quid enim est quod volo dicere, domine, nisi quia nescio unde venerim huc, in istam dico vitam mortalem an mortem vitalem? nescio. et susceperunt me consola-tiones miserationum tuarum, sicut audivi a parentibus carnis meae, ex quo et in qua me formasti in tempore: non enim ego memini. exceperunt ergo me consolationes lactis

---

14 Cf. *En. Ps.* 18.14 (= Ps 19:13), "He who keeps himself pure from sin of his own (*mundus a suis*) is not ensnared by the sins of others."   15 A. is sharply aware of the mystery of human origins. He writes to Jerome, "Certainly God makes individual souls for every child that is born" (*Ep.* 166.4.8).

16 A double oxymoron—perhaps "deathly life" or "lively death."

17 The "flesh" is (Rom 8:13, Gal 5:17, etc.) the earthly part of human substance (Greek *sarx* [σάρξ], Hebrew *basar*) with its

(6) The house of my soul is too narrow for you to enter it: it needs you to widen it. It is in ruins: rebuild it. It contains things that will displease your eyes: I admit it, I know it. But who will cleanse it? Who else can I cry to, if not to you?—"cleanse me from my secret faults, O Lord, and keep your servant safe from the sins of others."[14] I Ps 19:13
believe, and therefore I also speak, Lord: you know. Surely Ps 116:10
I have denounced my sins to you against myself, O my God, and surely you have forgiven my heart's lack of reverence? I am not contending in a court of law against Ps 32:5
you who are Truth; and I have no desire to deceive myself, Jer 2:29
lest my sin bear false witness against itself. So I do not contend with you in a court of law, because if you were to examine my sins closely—Lord, Lord, who shall endure that? Ps 130:3

6. (7) Still let me speak in the presence of your mercy. I am earth and ashes—but let me speak. After all, it is your Gn 18:27
mercy, rather than some person or other mocking me, to which I am addressing my words. Perhaps even you are laughing at me: but if so, turn again and have mercy upon Ps 2:4
me. What is it that I wish to say, Lord? Only that I have Mi 7:19
no idea where I came from, so as to be here;[15] and came to this life which is mortal—or is it perhaps life-giving death?[16] I do not know. The consolation of your mercies has embraced me, just as I heard from my parents according to the flesh[17] from which, and in which, you shaped me in time. I—of course—do not remember this. The comforts of human milk sustained me; but neither my mother

embodied desires, at war with the divine or spiritual element. A. means that, being human, he is both composed of flesh (physical) and ensnared by "the flesh" (metaphysical).

11

humani, nec mater mea vel nutrices meae sibi ubera im-
plebant, sed tu mihi per eas dabas alimentum infantiae
secundum institutionem tuam et divitias usque ad fundum
rerum dispositas. tu etiam mihi dabas nolle amplius quam
dabas, et nutrientibus me dare mihi velle quod eis dabas:
dare enim mihi per ordinatum affectum volebant quo
abundabant ex te. nam bonum erat eis bonum meum ex
eis, quod ex eis non sed per eas erat. ex te quippe bona
omnia, deus, et ex deo meo salus mihi universa. quod
animadverti postmodum, clamante te mihi per haec ipsa
quae tribuis intus et foris. nam tunc sugere noram et adquiescere delectationibus, flere autem offensiones carnis
meae, nihil amplius.

(8) Post et ridere coepi, dormiens primo, deinde vigi-
lans. hoc enim de me mihi indicatum est et credidi, quoniam sic videmus alios infantes: nam ista mea non memini.
et ecce paulatim sentiebam ubi essem, et voluntates meas
volebam ostendere eis per quos implerentur, et non poteram, quia illae intus erant, foris autem illi, nec ullo suo
sensu valebant introire in animam meam. itaque iactabam
membra et voces, signa similia voluntatibus meis. pauca
quae poteram, qualia poteram:[3] non enim erant vere[4]

---

[3] signa similia voluntatibus meis, pauca quae poteram, qualia
poteram *OD*   [4] vere *similia OD coniecit*: veresimilia *S codd.
Skut. Ver.*: verisimilia (veri similia *GM) edd.*

---

[18] A. thinks the instinct to feed a baby is God given, and that
breast milk appears as if by divine decree.
[19] A rhetorical figure called syllepsis or zeugma: A. uses the
verb literally ("fling, throw") and metaphorically ("utter, boast").

nor those who nursed me filled their own breasts with milk. You were the one who used to give me nourishment through them in my babyhood, according to your own plan for creation, and the bountiful riches you have put in place right in the foundation of reality. You even inspired me to want nothing more than what you provided, and you inspired my wet nurses to give me what you gave to them.[18] They always wanted to give me what they had from you in abundance, as if prompted by a proper and instinctive affection. The good that came to me from them was also good for them, for it did not really come from them but through them. All good things come from you, O God, even my whole salvation. I only realized this later on, when you called to me by means of these very gifts which you bestow both inwardly and outwardly. Back then I knew how to suck, and to accept pleasures, while crying at any physical discomfort. That was all.

2 Sm 23:5; cf. 1 Chr 29:11

(8) Later I also started to smile, at first in my sleep, but then also while I was awake. I was told this fact about myself much later on, and I believed it, because we see the same thing in other babies. I do not remember all this with respect to myself. And look—gradually I became aware of where I was, and wanted to make my desires known to those who would fulfill them. I was not able to do this myself, because my desires were internal, whereas those adults were external to me, and none of their senses gave them the capacity to enter into my soul. So I began to wriggle my limbs and show off my crying,[19] as signs to represent my wishes: meager as they were, these were the sort of signs I could do. They did not really resemble what

13

similia. et cum mihi non obtemperabatur, vel non intellecto vel ne obesset, indignabar non subditis maioribus et liberis non servientibus, et me de illis flendo vindicabam. tales esse infantes didici quos discere potui, et me talem fuisse magis mihi ipsi indicaverunt nescientes quam scientes nutritores mei.

(9) Et ecce infantia mea olim mortua est et ego vivo. tu autem, domine, qui et semper vivis et nihil moritur in te, quoniam ante primordia saeculorum, et ante omne quod vel ante dici potest, tu es, et deus es dominusque omnium quae creasti, et apud te rerum omnium instabilium stant causae, et rerum omnium mutabilium immutabiles manent origines, et omnium inrationalium et temporalium sempiternae vivunt rationes, dic mihi supplici tuo, deus, et misericors misero tuo dic mihi, utrum alicui iam aetati meae mortuae successerit infantia mea. an illa est quam egi intra viscera matris meae? nam et de illa mihi nonnihil indicatum est et praegnantes ipse vidi feminas. quid ante hanc etiam, dulcedo mea, deus meus? fuine alicubi aut aliquis? nam quis mihi dicat ista, non habeo; nec pater nec mater potuerunt, nec aliorum experimentum nec memo-

---

20 On A.'s theory of signs, and words as signs, cf. *Doctr. Chr.* 1–3; Markus, "Saint Augustine on Signs," 60–83.

21 Cf. M. Aur. *Med.* 9.21, "Dismiss the stages of life such as childhood, adolescence, manhood, and old age: all of them are change (μεταβολή), are death."

22 A. later rejects the Pythagorean theory of *metempsychosis*, or the transmigration of souls: *De civ. D.* 10.30, 11.23 (cf. *Ep.* 166.27 to Jerome).

23 Indeed he had. He looked on while his own son grew in the womb.

they represented.[20] When my demands were not fulfilled (either because they misunderstood me or to avoid harming me) I became furious with my elders who disobeyed me, and with those who were independent and who did not bow to my will: I got my revenge on them by crying. I have learned that infants are like this from the ones I was able to observe; and although they did not know me, they have shown me more clearly what kind of a creature I was than did my nurses (who knew me well).

(9) Now look—my infancy is long ago, dead: and I am alive.[21] But you, Lord, live for ever, and nothing in you dies: for before the beginning of time, and before everything which can be described as "before," you yourself exist, and you are God and Lord of everything which you have made. In you the causes of all fluctuating things stand fast; and the origins of all mutable things remain immutable, and the reasons for all irrational and temporal things live forever. Tell me, O God, I beg you; in your mercy, tell me, pitiable creature that I am, did my infancy come after some other period of my existence, which is now extinct?[22] Or was that "other period" the time I spent within my mother's womb? For something of that subject has been made apparent to me, and I have also observed pregnant women.[23] What was there before that, my sweetness, my God? Did I exist somewhere? Was I someone at all? I have no one to explain this to me; my father and mother could not, nor could other people's experience, nor my own

ria mea. an inrides me ista quaerentem teque de hoc quod
novi laudari a me iubes et confiteri me tibi?

(10) Confiteor tibi, domine caeli et terrae, laudem dicens tibi de primordiis et infantia mea, quae non memini.
et dedisti ea homini ex aliis de se conicere et auctoritatibus
etiam muliercularum multa de se credere. eram enim et
vivebam etiam tunc, et signa quibus sensa mea nota aliis
facerem iam in fine infantiae quaerebam. unde hoc tale
animal nisi abs te, domine? an quisquam se faciendi erit
artifex? aut ulla vena trahitur aliunde qua esse et vivere
currat in nos, praeterquam quod tu facis nos, domine, cui
esse et vivere non aliud atque aliud, quia summe esse ac
summe vivere idipsum est? summus enim es et non mutaris, neque peragitur in te hodiernus dies, et tamen in te
peragitur, quia in te sunt et ista omnia: non enim haberent
vias transeundi, nisi contineres eas. et quoniam anni tui
non deficiunt, anni tui hodiernus dies.

Et quam multi iam dies nostri et patrum nostrorum per
hodiernum tuum transierunt et ex illo acceperunt modos
et utcumque extiterunt, et transibunt adhuc alii et acci-
pient et utcumque existent. tu autem idem ipse es et omnia crastina atque ultra omniaque hesterna et retro hodie
facies, hodie fecisti. quid ad me, si quis non intellegat?

---

[24] The verb "confess" is used for the first time, here with the
meaning "give praise to" uppermost, rather than "admit wrongdoing." Cf. Introduction, p. xix.

[25] The scriptural context refers to the spiritual perception of
infants.

[26] Because God does not have an eternal existence and a mortal life (within the created order).

memory. Or do you smile at me for asking these questions—and decree that I must praise you for what I do know about you, and confess my faith in you?[24]

(10) I make my confession to you, [25] Lord of heaven and earth, and I sing your praises for my origins and infancy, which I do not remember. You have allowed this mortal man to deduce facts about himself from the examples of others, and also to understand a great deal about himself from evidence given by mere women. For even then I existed and was alive; and as my infancy came to an end I began to investigate the signs by which I made my feelings known to others. Where could such a living creature come from, Lord, if not from you? Or can anyone be the artist of their own creation? Does some channel of heredity feed from elsewhere to where it pours existence and life into us, independently of what you make us, Lord? For to you existence and life are not two different things:[26] to exist as the most high, and be alive as the most high, are one and the same. For you are the most high and you do not change. In you the present time does not come to an end, and yet in you it does come to an end, because all things are in you: they would have no ways of changing unless you were maintaining them. Since your years do not fail, those years are the same as a "today."

How many days of ours and of our fathers have now traversed your eternal today, and have taken from it the measure and manner of their existence? And yet others will pass through in future: they will receive likewise the manner of their existence. And still you yourself remain the same: everything tomorrow and beyond, everything yesterday and before, all of it you will make, and you have made, your "today." Do I care if anyone cannot understand

Mt 11:25

Mal 3:6

Rom 11:35

Ps 102:27

17

gaudeat et ipse dicens, "quid est hoc?" gaudeat etiam sic, et amet non inveniendo invenire potius quam inveniendo non invenire te.

7. (11) Exaudi, deus. vae peccatis hominum! et homo dicit haec, et misereris eius, quoniam tu fecisti eum et peccatum non fecisti in eo. quis me commemorat peccatum infantiae meae, quoniam nemo mundus a peccato coram te, nec infans cuius est unius diei vita super terram? quis me commemorat? an quilibet tantillus nunc parvulus, in quo video quod non memini de me? quid ergo tunc peccabam? an quia uberibus inhiabam plorans? nam si nunc faciam, non quidem uberibus sed escae congruenti annis meis ita inhians, deridebor atque reprehendar iustissime. tunc ergo reprehendenda faciebam, sed quia reprehendentem intellegere non poteram, nec mos reprehendi[5] me nec ratio sinebat: nam extirpamus et eicimus ista crescentes.

Nec vidi quemquam scientem, cum aliquid purgat, bona proicere. an pro tempore etiam illa bona erant, flendo petere etiam quod noxie daretur, indignari acriter non subiectis hominibus liberis et maioribus hisque, a quibus genitus est, multisque praeterea prudentioribus non ad nutum voluntatis obtemperantibus feriendo nocere niti

---

[5] reprehendi *codd. edd.*: reprehendendi S

---

[27] A paradoxical conceit.   [28] A crucial passage: A. wrestles with the problem of sin. He sees in babies greed and jealousy but tries to understand how these can be wrong in adults and to what extent a baby can be culpable for such behaviors. He has not yet called it "original sin" (see *Conf.* 5.9.16).

[29] A. means the wordless movements and expressions by which an infant communicates need.

this? Let them rejoice and say, "What is this?" Let them be glad, even, and love discovering you by failing to discover you, rather than failing to discover you through attempting to discover you.[27]

7. (11)[28] Hear me, O God! Alas for the sins of humanity! And the man who says this is counted among them, and you have mercy on him, for you made him, yet you have not made the sin which is in him. Who can remind me of the sin of my infancy? After all in your sight no one is clean from sin, not even an infant whose life on this earth lasts but a single day. Who can remind me? Or take any little child you like, however small: is what I see in them what I do not remember about myself? So what were my sins back then? Was it the way my mouth was greedily open for the breast? For if I did that now, and started opening my mouth wide (not for breasts but for food appropriate to my age) I would be laughed at and very properly rebuked. So back then I was doing things which deserved to be rebuked, but because I could not understand anyone rebuking me, neither custom nor reason admitted of my being rebuked. But when we grow up we root out these practices and reject them.

I never saw anyone who knowingly threw away what was good when flushing out something bad. Was it really at that age a good thing to use crying as a way to obtain things that might do harm if given? And to be fiercely indignant that free persons, adults, those who had begotten me, did not comply with my demands? And to struggle to strike and do as much harm as possible to many other sensible people besides them who refused to give in to my gestures of will[29] simply because they would not obey

Ps 55:1

Jb 25:4

1 Cor 13:11

CONFESSIONS

quantum potest, quia non oboeditur imperiis quibus per-
niciose oboediretur? ita inbecillitas membrorum infanti-
lium innocens est, non animus infantium. vidi ego et expertus sum zelantem parvulum: nondum loquebatur et
intuebatur pallidus amaro aspectu conlactaneum suum.
quis hoc ignorat? expiare se dicunt ista matres atque nutrices nescio quibus remediis. nisi vero et ista innocentia
est, in fonte lactis ubertim manante atque abundante opis
egentissimum et illo adhuc uno alimento vitam ducentem
consortem non pati. sed blande tolerantur haec, non quia
nulla vel parva, sed quia aetatis accessu peritura sunt.
quod licet probes, cum ferri aequo animo eadem ipsa non
possunt quando in aliquo annosiore deprehenduntur.

(12) Tu itaque, domine deus meus, qui dedisti vitam
infanti et corpus, quod ita, ut videmus, instruxisti sensibus, compegisti membris, figura decorasti proque eius
universitate atque incolumitate omnes conatus animantis
insinuasti, iubes me laudare te in istis et confiteri tibi et
psallere nomini tuo, altissime, quia deus es omnipotens et
bonus, etiamsi sola ista fecisses, quae nemo alius potest
facere nisi tu, une, a quo est omnis modus, formosissime,
qui formas omnia et lege tua ordinas omnia.

Hanc ergo aetatem, domine, quam me vixisse non

---

30 English struggles to convey the range of meaning from "not
doing harm" to "moral purity" present in the Latin *innocentia*.

31 A rare lapse from the addressing God into a generalizing
second person.　　　32 Cf. Cic. *Fin.* 2.11.33, "Nature does not
prompt an infant to seek pleasure, but only to love itself, so as to
want to remain whole and safe. Every living creature . . . loves
both itself and all its parts."

33 A double *figura etymologica*: the contrast of "one" (*unus*:
here rendered "unique") with "all" (*omnis*), and "most beautiful"
(*formosissime*) with the verb "form" (*formas*).

my demands, even though carrying them out would be harmful? So the weakness of infant limbs compasses innocence,[30] but with the minds of infants it is not so. I have observed and experienced a little one expressing jealousy. Though he was not yet capable of speech, he glared, pale with envy, at his sibling at the breast. Surely everyone knows this! Mothers and wet nurses claim to avert this behavior by their own particular charms. Surely one cannot call it "innocence" when a baby prevents his sibling—who is completely dependent for care, and stays alive only because of that one source of sustenance—from having a share in the plentiful, abundant flow of milk. But these things are tolerated kindly: not because they are of little or no importance but because they will die away as the child grows older. You can agree[31] that this is permissible, although people find such behavior is completely unacceptable, from a fair-minded point of view, when it is encountered in someone older.

(12) So you, O Lord my God, give both life and a physical body to babies. As we have seen, you have endowed them with senses, you have shaped their limbs, you have graced their form; and for the preservation of the whole human race you have inculcated all the instincts of a living creature.[32] Therefore you direct me to extol you for these things, and to confess you, and sing praises to your name, O most highest, because you are God, almighty and good. Ps 92:1 Even if you had done nothing but that, no one else but you could do even so much: you are unique, and every kind of being comes from you; you are most beautiful, you who form everything and dispose it according to your law.[33]

So, Lord, as for that period when I do not remember being alive, and which I know about from other people,

memini, de qua aliis credidi et quam me egisse ex aliis
infantibus conieci, quamquam ista multum fida coniectura
sit, piget me adnumerare huic vitae meae quam vivo in hoc
saeculo. quantum enim attinet ad oblivionis meae tenebras, par illi est quam vixi in matris utero. quod si et in
iniquitate conceptus sum et in peccatis mater mea me in
utero aluit, ubi, oro te, deus meus, ubi, domine, ego, servus tuus, ubi aut quando innocens fui? sed ecce omitto
illud tempus: et quid mihi iam cum eo est, cuius nulla
vestigia recolo?

8. (13) Nonne ab infantia huc pergens veni in pueritiam? vel potius ipsa in me venit et successit infantiae? nec
discessit illa: quo enim abiit? et tamen iam non erat. non
enim eram infans qui non farer, sed iam puer loquens
eram. et memini hoc, et unde loqui didiceram post ad-
verti. non enim docebant me maiores homines, praebentes
mihi verba certo aliquo ordine doctrinae sicut paulo post
litteras, sed ego ipse mente quam dedisti mihi, deus meus,
cum gemitibus et vocibus variis et variis membrorum
motibus edere vellem sensa cordis mei, ut voluntati pare-
retur, nec valerem quae volebam omnia nec quibus volebam omnibus, prensabam[6] memoria. cum ipsi appellabant

---

[6] prensabam *codd. pauc. Ver. Pell.*: pensabam S *codd. mult.
Knöll Skut.*: praesonabam E G *Maur.*

---

[34] The English "world" includes both temporal (as here, *saeculo*) and spatial (Latin *mundus*).

[35] See Introduction, pp. xx–xxi, xxv.

[36] Another *figura etymologica*, on *infans/farer* ("one who cannot speak"/"one who can speak").

[37] Text, punctuation, and sense are all disputed here. By

and the manner of which I have surmised from observing
other infants (even though it is a fairly safe supposition), I
am not keen to count that as part of the life that I am living
in this world.[34] How much does it matter to the shadows
of my unconsciousness? It is on a par with my existence in   Ps 88:10
my mother's womb. But if I was also conceived in wickedness, and in sin my mother nourished me in the womb,   Ps 51:7
where, I pray, O my God, where and when, O Lord, was
I, your servant, innocent of sin? But look, I am going to
say no more of that period. Why should it matter to me,
when I cannot remember even a trace of it?[35]

8. (13) Was it really I who went onward from infancy
and progressed to boyhood? Or was it rather that boyhood
entered into me and took the place of my infancy? Infancy
did not leave me—for where did it go *to*? Yet it was no
longer there. I was not an infant incapable of speech,[36] but
now I was already a boy, able to talk. This I do remember;
and later on I realized from what sources I had learned
the art of speech. It was not that older people were teaching me, giving me words in a logical framework of instruction, such as happened soon after with the alphabet.
Rather, I intended to give expression to the feelings of my
heart by all kinds of groaning, and crying, and moving
my limbs in different ways, to make people obey my will.
When I was incapable of achieving all that I wanted, and
by all the means I wanted, in my mind (which you gave to
me, o my God) I would instead snatch at it with my memory.[37] When people called something by name, and, in

"snatch at it with my memory," A. seems to strive to express his
eagerness to seize upon the power of words as a means of assert-
ing his will.

rem aliquam et cum secundum eam vocem corpus ad aliquid movebant, videbam et tenebam hoc ab eis vocari rem
illam quod sonabant cum eam vellent ostendere. hoc autem eos velle ex motu corporis aperiebatur tamquam verbis naturalibus omnium gentium, quae fiunt vultu et nutu
oculorum ceterorumque membrorum actu et sonitu vocis
indicante affectionem animi in petendis, habendis, rei-
ciendis fugiendisve rebus. ita verba in variis sententiis
locis suis posita et crebro audita quarum rerum signa
essent paulatim conligebam measque iam voluntates edo-
mito in eis signis ore per haec enuntiabam. sic cum his
inter quos eram voluntatum enuntiandarum signa com-
municavi, et vitae humanae procellosam societatem altius
ingressus sum, pendens ex parentum auctoritate nutuque
maiorum hominum.

9. (14) Deus, deus meus, quas ibi miserias expertus
sum et ludificationes, quandoquidem recte mihi vivere
puero id proponebatur, obtemperare monentibus, ut in
hoc saeculo florerem et excellerem linguosis artibus ad
honorem hominum et falsas divitias famulantibus. inde in
scholam datus sum ut discerem litteras, in quibus quid
utilitatis esset ignorabam miser. et tamen, si segnis in dis-
cendo essem, vapulabam. laudabatur enim hoc a maioribus, et multi ante nos vitam istam agentes praestruxerant
aerumnosas vias, per quas transire cogebamur multipli-

---

38 Possible echo of Ter. *Ad.* 867: *quam ibi miseriam vidi.*

39 A. dismisses the rhetorical training of his youth, from which
he made a living before his conversion. Cf. Juvenal, who refers to
"Africa the breeding ground of petty pleaders" (*nutricula cau-
sidicorum/Africa*), *Sat.* 7.147–48.

response to that word they turned their bodies toward it,
I observed it. I noted that they were calling the thing a
particular name, the sound they made when they wanted
to draw attention to it. What they meant was evident from
their physical movements, which constitute an instinctual
language in all peoples. It was conveyed through facial
expressions and eye movements and other bodily gestures;
and by the tone of voice, which conveys the mind's inclination to seek and possess things, or to reject or avoid them.
So I gradually pieced together the sense of words placed
in their proper position in different sentences, and after
hearing them frequently, established what they were signs
of. Then I schooled my mouth to produce these signs and
by using words I disclosed my wishes. In this way, I com-
municated the signs of those wishes which I needed to
express with the people around me. Thus I descended
deeper into the stormy society that is human life, though
still dependent on the authority of my parents and the
favor of my elders.

9. (14) O God, my God, what miseries and mockeries
I experienced there,[38] seeing that this was the plan set out
before me, while I was still a boy, for how to live my life
well: to obey those who instructed me so that I would
thrive in this world, and excel in the arts of persuasive
speech, which pander to the vainglory of humanity and to
false wealth.[39] So then I was dispatched to school to learn
to read and write. As to the point of mastering this, I remained wretchedly ignorant. But if ever I was slow to
learn, I was beaten. My elders approved of this method,
and many who lived before our time had constructed the
ways of sorrows through which we were compelled to pass
with the increased toil and suffering that is the lot of Ad-

cato labore et dolore filiis Adam. invenimus autem, domine, homines rogantes te et didicimus ab eis, sentientes
te, ut poteramus, esse magnum aliquem qui posses etiam
non apparens sensibus nostris exaudire nos et subvenire
nobis. nam puer coepi rogare te, auxilium et refugium
meum, et in tuam invocationem rumpebam nodos linguae
meae et rogabam te parvus non parvo affectu, ne in schola
vapularem. et cum me non exaudiebas, quod non erat ad
insipientiam mihi, ridebantur a maioribus hominibus usque ab ipsis parentibus, qui mihi accidere mali nihil volebant, plagae meae, magnum tunc et grave malum meum.

(15) Estne quisquam, domine, tam magnus animus,
praegrandi affectu tibi cohaerens, estne, inquam, quisquam (facit enim hoc quaedam etiam stoliditas: est ergo),
qui tibi pie cohaerendo ita sit affectus granditer, ut eculeos
et ungulas atque huiuscemodi varia tormenta (pro quibus
effugiendis tibi per universas terras cum timore magno
supplicatur) ita parvi aestimet, diligens[7] eos qui haec acer-
bissime formidant, quemadmodum parentes nostri ride-
bant tormenta quibus pueri a magistris affligebamur? non
enim aut minus ea metuebamus aut minus te de his
evadendis deprecabamur, et peccabamus tamen minus

---

[7] diligens *omn. al. codd.*: deridens *M*[2] *Maur.*

---

40 For this metaphor, cf. Gell. (whom A. admires as "a man of
the most polished eloquence"—*uir elegantissimi eloquii*—*De civ.
D.* 9.4); *NA* 5.9.2.

41 The allusion is obscure: elsewhere he construes Ps 22:2 as
meaning that refusing to give an answer is intended to teach
wisdom (*En. Ps.* 53.5).

42 A complex sentence, reflecting A.'s struggle to make sense

am's offspring. Still, Lord, we did come across people who prayed to you, and from them we learned (insofar as we were able) to be aware of you as some great being who—even without being apparent to our senses—could hear us and help us. For I was still a boy when I began to pray to you, my help and refuge, and I undid the knot of my tongue[40] in order to invoke you; and when I was a small child, I begged you with utter sincerity not to let me be beaten at school. Then, when you did not grant my request, which was to prevent my foolishness,[41] my elders and even my own parents (who had no desire to see any harm befall me) laughed at the marks of my beatings. But to me they were a grim and weighty evil.

(15) Is there any mind so great, O Lord, so attached to you by intense devotion; is there anyone, I want to know, who by reason of their deep attachment to you (for it is a fact that a thick-skinned type of character is capable of this too) is so intensely devoted that they can reckon racks and instruments of torture and all the manifold devices for inflicting pain a matter of indifference (when people in every land pray to you in terror for deliverance from them)? And who can still love those[42] who are desperately afraid of those horrors, just like our parents when they used to laugh at the torments that our teachers would inflict on us? We were just as afraid of our punishments, and we prayed just as vehemently to escape them. And still we

of how a loving parent can find the infliction of pain on a loved one a trivial matter (as well he might) and how human parental behavior might map onto the actions of God the Father. Ability to endure torture, like everything for A., must spring from a pure source.

scribendo aut legendo aut cogitando de litteris quam exi-
gebatur a nobis. non enim deerat, domine, memoria vel
ingenium, quae nos habere voluisti pro illa aetate satis, sed
delectabat ludere et vindicabatur in nos ab eis qui talia
utique agebant.

Sed maiorum nugae negotia vocantur, puerorum autem talia cum sint, puniuntur a maioribus, et nemo mise-
ratur pueros vel illos vel utrosque. nisi vero approbat quisquam bonus rerum arbiter vapulasse me, quia ludebam
pila puer et eo ludo impediebar quominus celeriter discerem litteras, quibus maior deformius luderem. aut aliud
faciebat idem ipse a quo vapulabam, qui si in aliqua quaes-
tiuncula a condoctore suo victus esset, magis bile atque
invidia torqueretur quam ego, cum in certamine pilae a
conlusore meo superabar?

10. (16) Et tamen peccabam, domine deus, ordinator
et creator rerum omnium naturalium, peccatorum autem
tantum ordinator, domine deus meus, peccabam faciendo
contra praecepta parentum et magistrorum illorum. poteram enim postea bene uti litteris, quas volebant ut discerem quocumque animo illi mei. non enim meliora eligens
inoboediens eram, sed amore ludendi, amans in certami-
nibus superbas victorias et scalpi aures meas falsis fabellis,
quo prurirent ardentius, eadem curiositate magis magisque per oculos emicante in spectacula, ludos maiorum—
quos tamen qui edunt, ea dignitate praediti excellunt, ut

---

[43] I.e., not the cause or originator.
[44] Cf. *Conf.* 4.8.13 (the false teaching of the Manichaeans).
[45] Cf. *Conf.* 3.2.2: *curiositas* carries a morally negative tinge in A.

went on sinning, by doing less writing, or reading, or reasoning, in our lessons than was required of us. Not that we lacked such memory or ability as you wanted us to possess, commensurate with our age—but we enjoyed playing, and put up with punishment by those who used to inflict it.

The affairs of adults, however trivial, are called "business"; while boys' affairs (however important they may be) are punished by their elders, and no one pities the boys or the adults, or both groups for that matter. Surely no sensible judge of affairs applauds my being beaten because I liked to play ball as a boy and my playing slowed my progress in learning to read and write! Because of this, when I grew up my playing might take a more crooked form. When the man who used to beat me was bested by his fellow teacher in some petty dispute, and so writhed in indignation and jealousy, was he doing anything different from me, when in my ball game I was outdone by my opponent?

10. (16) So I did sin, Lord God. And though you are both disposer and creator of all natural phenomena, of sins you are the disposer only.[43] O Lord, my God, I used to sin by acting against the instructions of my parents and of those teachers. After all, I was later able to handle the written word with some skill, which was what those adults wanted me to learn, whatever their attitude may have been. I was not disobedient because of choosing some better course, but from a desire to play. I loved the pride of victory in contests, and to have my ears tickled with false fables (which made them itch all the more),[44] and the same curiosity blazed more and more in my eyes for the public shows, the ancestral games.[45] Those who put on such shows gain prestige thereby, and are so distin-

2 Tm 4:3–4

29

hoc paene omnes optent parvulis suis, quos tamen caedi libenter patiuntur, si spectaculis talibus impediantur ab studio quo eos ad talia edenda cupiunt pervenire. vide ista, domine, misericorditer, et libera nos iam invocantes te, libera etiam eos qui nondum te invocant, ut invocent te et liberes eos.

11. (17) Audieram enim ego adhuc puer de vita aeterna promissa nobis per humilitatem domini dei nostri descendentis ad superbiam nostram, et signabar iam signo crucis eius, et condiebar eius sale iam inde ab utero matris meae, quae multum speravit in te. vidisti, domine, cum adhuc puer essem et quodam die pressu stomachi repente aestuarem paene moriturus, vidisti, deus meus, quoniam custos meus iam eras, quo motu animi et qua fide baptismum Christi tui, dei et domini mei, flagitavi a pietate matris meae et matris omnium nostrum, ecclesiae tuae. et conturbata mater carnis meae, quoniam et sempiternam salutem meam carius parturiebat corde casto in fide tua, iam curaret festinabunda ut sacramentis salutaribus initiarer et abluerer, te, domine Iesu, confitens in remissionem peccatorum, nisi statim recreatus essem. dilata est itaque mundatio mea, quasi necesse esset ut adhuc sordidarer si

---

46 Cf. *Conf.* 1.1.1 on the mystery of how people come to pray by invoking God (i.e., calling God by name).

47 On the Christian doctrine of incarnation, cf. Introduction pp. xxx–xxxii.   48 The sign of the cross and the giving of salt are marks of the catechumenate, an initiate status, and necessary preliminary to baptism. The imperfect tense of "signed" and "seasoned" hints that the signs were repeated.

49 See Introduction, p. xxv.

50 Lit., "according to the flesh"; cf. above, n. 17.

guished that almost everyone desires their own little ones
to achieve a like status. Yet they still happily let the children be beaten if such shows get in the way of studying—
even though studying is the route by which they long for
their offspring to achieve the status of provider of such
shows! In your mercy, Lord, observe all this; and set us
free as we invoke you in prayer;[46] and set free also those
who do not yet invoke you, so that they can invoke you in
prayer and you can set them free.

11. (17) Even when I was just a boy I had heard how
we are promised eternal life through the lowliness of our
Lord God descending to the level of our human pride;[47]
and I was signed with the sign of his cross, and seasoned
with his salt from the moment I left my mother's womb.[48]
My mother trusted in you completely. You saw, Lord,
when I was still a boy and developed a sudden fever one
day, and stomach pain, and was almost at death's door; you
saw, my God (for you were my protector), with what anxi-   Gn 28:15
ety and what faith I pleaded for baptism into your Christ,
my Lord and my God, and pleaded that it was the duty of   Jn 20:28
my mother and of your Church, which is the mother of us
all.[49] My earthly[50] mother was in great distress. By the   Gal 4:26
purity of her heart's faith in you, she was giving birth—at
an even higher cost[51]—to my eternal salvation. Now she
was in a hurry to ensure that I was initiated into the life-
giving sacraments, and was baptized, declaring belief in
you, Lord Jesus, for the forgiveness of my sins—but then
I suddenly recovered. So my baptismal cleansing was postponed, because it was inevitable that I would go on being

[51] Compared with the risks of physical childbirth.

viverem, quia videlicet post lavacrum illud maior et peri-
culosior in sordibus delictorum reatus foret. ita iam credebam et illa et omnis domus, nisi pater solus, qui tamen
non evicit in me ius maternae pietatis, quominus in Christum crederem, sicut ille nondum crediderat. nam illa sa-
tagebat ut tu mihi pater esses, deus meus, potius quam ille,
et in hoc adiuvabas eam, ut superaret virum, cui melior
serviebat, quia et in hoc tibi utique id iubenti serviebat.

(18) Rogo te, deus meus: vellem scire, si tu etiam velles, quo consilio dilatus sum ne tunc baptizarer, utrum
bono meo mihi quasi laxata sint lora peccandi. an non
laxata sunt?[8] unde ergo etiam nunc de aliis atque aliis so-
nat undique in auribus nostris: "sine illum, faciat: nondum
enim baptizatus est"? et tamen in salute corporis non dicimus: "sine vulneretur amplius: nondum enim sanatus est."
quanto ergo melius et cito sanarer et id ageretur mecum
meorum meaque diligentia, ut recepta salus animae meae
tuta esset tutela tua, qui dedisses eam. melius vero. sed
quot et quanti fluctus impendere temptationum post
pueritiam videbantur, noverat eos iam illa mater et terram
per eos, unde postea formarer, quam ipsam iam effigiem
committere volebat.

---

[8] (non laxata) sunt *codd. Maur. Ver.*: sint S *Knöll Skut.*

---

[52] *Figura etymologica*: A. plays with the repeated sound: *tu
. . . tu . . . tu.*

[53] A. shifts from a marine metaphor of shipwreck to the biblical idea of humankind made of earth yet in the divine image.
Monnica "saved up" his baptism, aware that he was not yet ready
to give up sinful ways. To her, postbaptismal sin posed the more
serious threat to her son's salvation.

defiled by sin if I survived—and it is certain that after that baptismal washing the guilt attached to the stain of sins would be more serious and dangerous than before. So I believed, as did my mother and all the household except for my father. But he did not overrule the power of my mother's devotion in me to prevent me from believing in Christ, although he himself was not yet a believer. My mother was active in ensuring that you were a father to me, O my God, rather than he. And you supported her in overcoming her husband—she was usually obedient to him, even though she was his moral superior—for in doing so it was really you that she was serving, and this was your command to her.

(18) My God, I ask you—I should like to know, if only you wanted me to—for what reason my baptism at that time was postponed, whether it was for my own good that I had the reins of sin loosened upon my neck, so to speak. Or were they not loosened after all? After all, why is it that even now, the words resound in our ears concerning someone or other, "Leave him be, let him do it—he's not yet been baptized!"? When it comes to physical health we do not say: "Let him be wounded some more: after all he has not yet been cured!" How much more quickly and completely would I then have been healed! Then my own love and that of my family would have brought it about that the salvation of my soul was secured, and through the protection of you who bestowed it, it would have been safe indeed.[52] Yes, that would have been the better course. But however many and great those floods of temptations were which seemed to threaten me after my childhood, that mother of mine knew of them already. And her wish was to consign to those floods that earth from which I was afterward formed, rather than the actual image itself.[53]

Ps 34:3

Gn 1:27, 2:7, 3:19

33

CONFESSIONS

12. (19) In ipsa tamen pueritia, de qua mihi minus
quam de adulescentia metuebatur, non amabam litteras et
me in eas urgeri oderam, et urgebar tamen et bene mihi
fiebat. nec faciebam ego bene (non enim discerem nisi
cogerer; nemo autem invitus bene facit, etiamsi bonum est
quod facit), nec qui me urgebant bene faciebant, sed bene
mihi fiebat abs te, deus meus. illi enim non intuebantur
quo referrem quod me discere cogebant, praeterquam ad
satiandas insatiabiles cupiditates copiosae inopiae et igno-
miniosae gloriae. tu vero, cui numerati sunt capilli nostri,
errore omnium qui mihi instabant ut discerem utebaris ad
utilitatem meam, meo autem, qui discere nolebam, utebaris ad poenam meam, qua plecti non eram indignus, tantillus puer et tantus peccator. ita de non[9] bene facientibus
tu bene faciebas mihi et de peccante me ipso iuste retri-
buebas mihi. iussisti enim et sic est, ut poena sua sibi sit
omnis inordinatus animus.

13. (20) Quid autem erat causae cur graecas litteras
oderam, quibus puerulus imbuebar? ne nunc quidem mihi
satis exploratum est. adamaveram enim latinas, non quas
primi magistri sed quas docent qui grammatici vocantur.

---

[9] de non *Maur. Pell. codd. pauc. min.*: non de S *codd. mult.*
Skut. Ver.

---

[54] An allusion to Socrates' dictum "no intelligent (*sophos*) person believes that anyone willingly does wrong (ἐξαμαρτάνειν)":
Pl. *Protagoras* 345d–e.

[55] Double oxymoronic *figura etymologica*: he was taught to
pursue worldly wealth, which was not real wealth at all (cf. Phil
3:8), and renown which bestowed no true honor.

[56] A rare example of A. using the indicative in an indirect

34

12. (19) During my boyhood, there was less cause for anxiety on my behalf than during my adolescence. But I had no love for reading and writing and I detested being pestered to do so. Yet still I was pestered, and it was for my own good. Even so I usually did it badly (for I would not learn unless forced to do so; but no one can do good against their will, even if the thing they do is good in itself).[54] Nor were those who kept pestering me doing any good. But you did me good, O my God. For they never paid any attention to the use I made of what they forced me to learn, except for the purpose of satisfying insatiable desires for prosperous poverty and ignoble glory.[55] Certainly you have counted all the hairs of my head; and you put to good use the error of all who stood over me to make me learn for my own benefit. As for my own error (i.e. being unwilling to learn), you used it to punish me: and it was punishment I deserved—so small a boy, yet so great a sinner! So it transpired that you turned the actions of those men, who were doing me no good, to my advantage; and even at the moment when I was sinning you always exacted a fair retribution from me. For this was your decree—and indeed it is so—that every disordered mind becomes its own punishment.

13. (20) Why was it that I loathed learning Greek, though I was immersed in it even as a little boy?[56] Even now I am not completely confident about it. Instead I was completely in love with Latin—not the basics which my primary teachers covered but the literature which the teachers known as grammarians taught me. At the ele-

question. On the disputed question of A.'s competence in Greek, see Introduction, pp. xxii, xxxv.

nam illas primas, ubi legere et scribere et numerare disci-
tur, non minus onerosas poenalesque habebam quam omnes graecas. unde tamen et hoc nisi de peccato et vanitate
vitae, qua caro eram et spiritus ambulans et non rever-
tens? nam utique meliores, quia certiores, erant primae
illae litterae quibus fiebat in me et factum est et habeo
illud ut et legam, si quid scriptum invenio, et scribam ipse,
si quid volo, quam illae quibus tenere cogebar Aeneae
nescio cuius errores, oblitus errorum meorum, et plorare
Didonem mortuam, quia se occidit ab amore, cum interea
me ipsum in his a te morientem, deus, vita mea, siccis
oculis ferrem miserrimus.

(21) Quid enim miserius misero non miserante se ipsum et flente Didonis mortem, quae fiebat amando Ae-
nean, non flente autem mortem suam, quae fiebat non
amando te, deus, lumen cordis mei et panis oris intus
animae meae et virtus maritans mentem meam et sinum
cogitationis meae? non te amabam, et fornicabar abs te, et
fornicanti sonabat undique: "euge! euge!" amicitia enim

---

57 Antimetathesis: *errorum* is used in two different senses
(one physical, the other moral).

58 A. enjoyed Virg. *Aen.,* but it was a guilty pleasure akin to
Jerome's shameful passion for Cicero (cf. Jerome *Ep.* 22).

59 English struggles to capture the *figura etymologica* here
(triple anaphora of *miser-*).

60 This phrase, unparalleled in earlier literature, reemerges
much later in, e.g., King Edward's Catechism (1552), "Faithful is
the mouth of the soul by which we receive this evidently sacred
food" (Bickersteth, *Testimony,* 100), and by S. John of the Cross,
Dark Night of the Soul 23.12.

mentary level, learning to read and write, and do arithmetic, I found this language just as tiresome and onerous as
all the Greek was. Where did this aversion come from, if
not the sin and vanity of mortal life, in which I was flesh
and spirit, traveling and not returning? Certainly the ba- Ps 78:39
sic language skills were better, because they were more
definite. They gave me the capacity and then the ability
that I still possess, of reading any piece of writing I come
across, and of writing for myself if I want to compose
something. They were better, that is, than the literature
in which I was made to master the wanderings of some
fellow called Aeneas (meanwhile neglecting my own wanderings),[57] and to weep for Dido's dying, just because she
killed herself for love.[58] And all the time—pitiable though
I was—in such matters I endured my own dying away from
you, O God, my life; and I shed not a single tear.

(21) What, after all, is more pitiful than a pitiable person who does not look with pity on their own pitifulness[59]
—and who weeps for the death of Dido, which came about
through her love for Aeneas; yet does not weep for their
own death, which was coming about because they had no
love for you, O God, who are the light of my heart and
bread of the mouth of my soul[60] deep within, and courage
wedded to my mind, and the bosom of my thoughts? I
did not love you, and by separating from you I pros- Ps 73:27
tituted myself; and as I prostituted myself the cry resounded from every side: "Well done, well done!"[61] For Ps 40:15

[61] A Greek exclamation of congratulation, preserved in A.'s
Latin; it translates a Hebrew word *hea'h*, which can convey gloat-
ing as well as joy.

mundi huius fornicatio est abs te et "euge! euge!" dicitur ut pudeat, si non ita homo sit. et haec non flebam, et flebam Didonem extinctam ferroque extrema secutam, sequens ipse extrema condita tua relicto te et terra iens in terram. et si prohiberer ea legere, dolerem, quia non legerem quod dolerem. tali dementia honestiores et uberiores litterae putantur quam illae quibus legere et scribere didici.

(22) Sed nunc in anima mea clamet deus meus, et veritas tua dicat mihi, "non est ita, non est ita." melior est prorsus doctrina illa prior. nam ecce paratior sum oblivisci errores Aeneae atque omnia eius modi quam scribere et legere. at enim vela pendent liminibus grammaticarum scholarum, sed non illa magis honorem secreti quam tegimentum erroris significant. non clament adversus me quos iam non timeo, dum confiteor tibi quae vult anima mea, deus meus, et adquiesco in reprehensione malarum viarum mearum, ut diligam bonas vias tuas, non clament adversus me venditores grammaticae vel emptores, quia, si proponam eis interrogans, utrum verum sit quod Ae-

---

62 The Latin can mean fornication, prostitution, or, in a Christian context, idolatry (e.g., Nm 14:33, Dt 31:16); A. is thinking of all these. 63 A.'s Bible probably said, "The love of this world is unlovely to God" (*amicitia huius mundi inimica est Dei*); if so, he redirects the phrase into a condemnation of the infidelity which is idolatry (cf. Hos 4:12).

64 Cf. Virg. *Aen.* 6.457. As A. cites it, it is a complete hexameter line, heavily spondaic and so underlining the sense of gloom. His sufferings parallel Dido's.

65 Vg has "dust returning to dust" (*pulvis* not *terra*); but Ambrose, *de sacramentis* 2.6.17 confirms the variant, *Terra es, et in terram ibis* (cf. Gn 3:19).

the love of this world is a physical infidelity[62] to you,[63] and the "Well done, well done!" is said in such a way as to make people ashamed, if that is not really the kind of people they are. I did not weep over this at all, but I did weep for Dido, "who died and secured her own destruction by a sword."[64] I pursued the meanest things in all of your creation, but abandoned you. I was earth returning to earth.[65] If I had been prevented from reading such works, I would have suffered, because I was not reading what would actually cause me to suffer! It is sheer madness to regard such literature as more respectable and fruitful than the texts by which I learned to read and write.

(22) But now let my God cry aloud in my soul! Let your truth say to me, "Not so, not so"! For that primary teaching is certainly more valuable. Just think—I would rather forget the wanderings of Aeneas and all that stuff than the skill of writing and reading. But wait: there are curtains hanging across the doorways where literature is taught;[66] yet they are symbols of a cloaking of error, as much as of a reverence owed to the mystery within. Do not let those whom I fear cry out against me any longer, O my God, while I confess to you what my soul desires: and I consent to the curbing of my wicked ways, so that I come to love your righteous ways. Do not let those who sell or buy the teaching of literature cry out against me because, if I put a question to them (whether what the poet says is true,

Jas 4:4

Ps 119:101; cf. Jer 18:11
Jer 7:3, 26:13

---

66 Such curtains were to prevent those who had not paid a fee from benefiting from the education. For A. the curtain also represents a segregation of clarity from obscurity and secrecy from knowledge.

nean aliquando Carthaginem venisse poeta dicit, indoctiores nescire se respondebunt, doctiores autem etiam negabunt verum esse. at si quaeram quibus litteris scribatur Aeneae nomen, omnes mihi qui haec didicerunt verum respondent secundum id pactum et placitum quo inter se homines ista signa firmarunt. item si quaeram quid horum maiore vitae huius incommodo quisque obliviscatur, legere et scribere an poetica illa figmenta, quis non videat quid responsurus sit, qui non est penitus oblitus sui?

Peccabam ergo puer cum illa inania istis utilioribus amore praeponebam, vel potius ista oderam, illa amabam. iam vero unum et unum duo, duo et duo quattuor, odiosa cantio mihi erat, et dulcissimum spectaculum vanitatis, equus ligneus plenus armatis et Troiae incendium atque ipsius umbra Creusae.

14. (23) Cur ergo graecam etiam grammaticam oderam talia cantantem? nam et Homerus peritus texere tales fabellas et dulcissime vanus est, mihi tamen amarus erat puero. credo etiam graecis pueris Vergilius ita sit, cum eum sic discere coguntur ut ego illum. videlicet difficultas, difficultas omnino ediscendae linguae peregrinae, quasi felle aspergebat omnes suavitates graecas fabulosarum narrationum. nulla enim verba illa noveram, et saevis terroribus ac poenis ut nossem instabatur mihi vehementer. nam et latina aliquando infans utique nulla noveram, et

---

67 Cf. n. 20.

68 On *vain* and *vanity*, see Introduction, p. xix.

69 An outline of the plot of Virg. *Aen.* 2.

70 A.'s knowledge of Homer is scanty: see *De civ. D* 3.2.

that Aeneas at one time came to Carthage) the less well-educated will reply that they do not know, while those who are better educated will go so far as to say that it is untrue. But if I were to ask how to spell the name "Aeneas," all those who have learned their letters will certainly reply according to that agreement and concordance by which people have defined those signs[67] among themselves. Likewise, if I were to ask each of them what would cause the greater disruption to his life were he to forget it—either how to read and write, or those poetic fictions: surely anyone who has not completely lost his senses would see clearly what the reply must be?

Thus I was sinning as a boy when I gave priority to that useless trivia over these more practical skills, or rather when I hated the latter, while adoring the former. Already indeed I found it a loathsome sing-song: "one plus one is two; two plus two is four"; while most delectable of all was that vain parade[68]—the wooden horse full of soldiers, and the burning of Troy, and the shade of Creusa herself.[69]

14. (23) Why then did I detest Greek literature when it told similar stories? For Homer too was skilled at weaving myths, and was just as delightfully vain; but when I was a boy I found him little to my taste. I suspect that Greek boys have the same reaction to Virgil, since they are made to learn him in the same way I learned Homer.[70] Evidently there is difficulty, real difficulty, in learning a foreign language at all, as if it sprinkled all the sweet flavor of the Greek mythical stories with a foul taste. I knew none of the vocabulary, and I was severely intimidated by harsh threats of punishment to make me learn. There was a time, after all, when I was a baby, when I knew absolutely no Latin either, but I still learned to speak it—without all the

41

tamen advertendo didici sine ullo metu atque cruciatu, inter etiam blandimenta nutricum et ioca adridentium et laetitias adludentium. didici vero illa sine poenali onere urgentium, cum me urgeret cor meum ad parienda concepta sua, †et qua†[10] non esset, nisi aliqua verba didicissem non a docentibus sed a loquentibus, in quorum et ego auribus parturiebam quidquid sentiebam. hinc satis elucet maiorem habere vim ad discenda ista liberam curiositatem quam meticulosam necessitatem. sed illius fluxum haec restringit legibus tuis, deus, legibus tuis a magistrorum ferulis usque ad temptationes martyrum, valentibus legibus tuis miscere salubres amaritudines revocantes nos ad te a iucunditate pestifera qua recessimus a te.

15. (24) Exaudi, domine, deprecationem meam, ne deficiat anima mea sub disciplina tua neque deficiam in confitendo tibi miserationes tuas, quibus eruisti me ab omnibus viis meis pessimis, ut dulcescas mihi super omnes seductiones quas sequebar, et amem te validissime, et amplexer manum tuam totis praecordiis meis, et eruas me ab omni temptatione usque in finem. ecce enim tu, domine, rex meus et deus meus, tibi serviat quidquid utile puer didici, tibi serviat quod loquor et scribo et lego et numero, quoniam cum vana discerem tu disciplinam dabas mihi, et in eis vanis peccata delectationum mearum dimisisti mihi. didici enim in eis multa verba utilia, sed et

---

[10] †et qua† *Skut.*: et qua S *codd. Vega Pell. Ver.*: et quia M^2 O V: quae *Maur.*: id quod *Knöll GM.*

---

[71] Cf. n. 46, above.   [72] The version here quoted differs from the Hebrew followed by Vg and English versions.

fear and torture—by paying attention, surrounded by my
nurses' encouragement and the amusement of those who
smiled at me, and the pleasure of those who played with
me. In a word, I learned without any pressure from looming punishment. I learned when my heart encouraged me
to generate its own ideas. It could not have done so had I
not learned some words, not from teachers but from people speaking to me. In turn, whatever I became aware of
at the time, I was trying to produce it for them to hear. So
it is perfectly clear that untrammeled curiosity is a more
effective aid to learning than any pressure born from
fear.[71] By your laws, O God, this kind of pressure restricts
the free flow of curiosity. Your laws extend their scope
from the rods of school teachers right up to the trials of
the martyrs. Your laws have power to impart a wholesome
severity that recalls us to you and away from the harmful
attractions that once caused us to fall away from you.

15. (24) Hear my prayer, Lord; do not let my soul fail   Ps 61:1
under your discipline, nor let me fail in confessing to
you your mercies, by which you rescued me from all my
wicked ways. Be sweeter to me than all the distractions
which I used to pursue. Let me love you with all my heart.
Let me grasp your hand with the core of my being. Rescue
me from all temptation forever and ever.[72] For you, O   Ps 18:29[VL]
Lord, are my king and my God. At your service is whatever   Ps 5:2
skill I learned as a boy: at your service is everything I say
and write and read and count. For when I was learning
those vain things, you were disciplining me, and you for-
gave me the sinful pleasure I took in such vanities. And
amid it all I did learn a lot of useful words, but then the

43

in rebus non vanis disci possunt, et ea via tuta est in qua pueri ambularent.

16. (25) Sed vae tibi, flumen moris humani! quis resistet tibi? quamdiu non siccaberis? quousque volves Evae filios in mare magnum et formidulosum, quod vix transeunt qui lignum conscenderint? nonne ego in te legi et tonantem Iovem et adulterantem? et utique non posset haec duo, sed actum est ut haberet auctoritatem ad imitandum verum adulterium lenocinante falso tonitru. quis autem paenulatorum magistrorum audit aure sobria ex eodem pulvere hominem clamantem et dicentem: "fingebat haec Homerus et humana ad deos transferebat: divina mallem ad nos"? sed verius dicitur quod fingebat haec quidem ille, sed hominibus flagitiosis divina tribuendo, ne flagitia flagitia putarentur et ut, quisquis ea fecisset, non homines perditos sed caelestes deos videretur imitatus.

(26) Et tamen, o flumen tartareum, iactantur in te filii hominum cum mercedibus, ut haec discant, et magna res agitur cum hoc agitur publice in foro, in conspectu legum supra mercedem salaria decernentium, et saxa tua percutis et sonas dicens: "hinc verba discuntur, hinc adquiritur

---

⁷³ A. apostrophizes the classical culture he has abandoned as a river full of filth, evoking human immorality and ungodliness; perhaps with Rome and the polluted Tiber in mind. ⁷⁴ An oblique reference to the saving power of the cross, and perhaps to Ws 14:7. ⁷⁵ Against the wicked; hence the implied inconsistency with his adulteries. ⁷⁶ *Paenulati* wear the cloak (*paenula*) as a mark of oratorical expertise. The dust is that of the floor where lawyers stand, not the earth from which humankind was created (as in n. 65, above). ⁷⁷ A. is quoting a text from Cicero (*Tusc.* 1.26.65); cf. *Deciv. D.* 4.26. ⁷⁸ "Children of men" (*filii hominum*, cf. 1.18.29, etc.) is biblical idiom.

same words can also be learned in a context which is not vain, and this is the safe way boys ought to walk in.

16. (25) To hell with you, you surging torrent of human custom![73] Who can withstand you? How long before you run dry? How much longer will you go on tumbling the children of Eve into this great and terrible sea, which those who have climbed aboard the wood[74] scarcely manage to cross? Is it not the case that I have read in you about Jupiter's thundering[75] and his adulteries? Certainly he could not do both at once, but the result was to give real adultery encouragement to follow that example, complete with fake thunder to pander to it. Who among the magistrates expert in oratory is ready to tolerate listening to a human being crying out from the same dust[76] and declaring: "Homer imagined these things and he transferred human characteristics to the gods: if only he had applied divine characteristics to us human beings instead!"[77] It would be more accurate to say that Homer certainly did imagine these things once: but that by attributing a divine character to sinful human beings, the result was that sin was no longer considered to be sin; and that anyone who had committed sin would be considered to have imitated the gods of heaven, not damned humanity.

(26) Yet for all this, O infernal torrent, the children of men[78] are cast into you along with their fees for learning such stuff. It is a matter of importance when such teaching takes place in the forum[79] at public expense, in front of the legal inscriptions defining salaries to be paid in addition to pupils' fees. So you clash your rocks together and you roar, "This is why you have to learn words, this is why

[79] *forum* refers to the main financial, commercial, and judicial center in a Roman city.

45

eloquentia, rebus persuadendis sententiisque explicandis
maxime necessaria." ita vero non cognosceremus verba
haec, "imbrem aureum" et "gremium" et "fucum" et "tem-
pla caeli" et alia verba quae in eo loco scripta sunt, nisi
Terentius induceret nequam adulescentem proponentem
sibi Iovem ad exemplum stupri, dum spectat tabulam
quandam pictam in pariete ubi inerat pictura haec, Iovem
quo pacto Danae misisse aiunt in gremium quondam imbrem aureum, fucum factum mulieri? et vide quemadmodum se concitat ad libidinem quasi caelesti magisterio:

> at quem deum! inquit, qui templa caeli summo sonitu
> concutit.
> ego homuncio id non facerem? ego vero illud feci ac
> libens.

non omnino per hanc turpitudinem verba ista commodius
discuntur, sed per haec verba turpitudo ista confidentius
perpetratur. non accuso verba quasi vasa electa atque pre-
tiosa, sed vinum erroris quod in eis nobis propinabatur ab
ebriis doctoribus, et nisi biberemus caedebamur, nec ap-
pellare ad aliquem iudicem sobrium licebat. et tamen ego,
deus meus, in cuius conspectu iam secura est recordatio
mea, libenter haec didici, et eis delectabar miser, et ob hoc
bonae spei puer appellabar.

---

80 The comic dramatist P. Terentius Afer (d. 159 BC) was a
standard school author in A.'s time; cf. nn. 46, 93.

81 Quotations from Ter. *Eun.* 583–91. It is an old argument:
see *De civ. D.* 18.13.   82 *libido* as a form of pleasure is for
A. always morally negative.   83 A. uses a diminutive of *homo*
to emphasize frailty and insignificance; cf. *Conf.* 9.3.6.

84 A vivid metaphor: classical literature is intoxicating, and
words are the containers for this potent liquor.

you have to achieve eloquence, which is absolutely indispensible for talking people into a course of action and explaining reasoning." Would we really have been incapable of recognizing phrases like "golden rain-shower" and "bosom" and "disguise" and "temples of heaven" and other phrases that are written in that text, had not Terence[80] brought on stage a worthless young man to argue that Jupiter is setting him an example of immoral behavior, when he looks at "a particular scene painted on the wall, which included this image: the tale of how Jupiter in this way once sent a kind of golden shower to Danae's bosom . . ."[81] and so deceived the woman? Note how he encourages himself to sensual pleasure[82] as if he had a heavenly teacher:

> But what a god! "he says," who strikes heaven's
>   temples with a mighty noise.
> I am only a weak and feeble human being[83]—why
>   shouldn't I do as he does? In fact I've done it
>   already—and enjoyed it!

It is definitely not the case that such words as these are more conveniently learned through this kind of immorality. Rather, using such words gives greater self-assurance to carry immorality off. I am not blaming the words themselves, for they are select and precious vessels. Nonetheless, drunken teachers prepared the wine of error in them for us to drink, and if we did not drink it they used to beat us.[84] There was no right of appeal to some sober judge. Even so, O my God, I learned it all gladly—now I am in your sight it is safe to remember this. Pitiful though I was, I took pleasure in it, and as a result I was called "a promising boy."

Jer 25:34

1 Kgs 17:1

47

17. (27) Sine me, deus meus, dicere aliquid et de ingenio meo, munere tuo, in quibus a me deliramentis attere-
batur. proponebatur enim mihi negotium, animae meae
satis inquietum praemio laudis et dedecoris vel plagarum
metu, ut dicerem verba Iunonis irascentis et dolentis quod
non posset Italia Teucrorum avertere regem, quae numquam Iunonem dixisse audieram. sed figmentorum poeti-
corum vestigia errantes sequi cogebamur, et tale aliquid
dicere solutis verbis quale poeta dixisset versibus. et ille
dicebat laudabilius in quo pro dignitate adumbratae personae irae ac doloris similior affectus eminebat, verbis
sententias congruenter vestientibus. ut quid mihi illud, o
vera vita, deus meus, quod mihi recitanti adclamabatur
prae multis coaetaneis et conlectoribus meis? nonne ecce
illa omnia fumus et ventus? itane aliud non erat ubi exer-
ceretur ingenium et lingua mea? laudes tuae, domine,
laudes tuae per scripturas tuas suspenderent palmitem
cordis mei, et non raperetur per inania nugarum turpis
praeda volatilibus. non enim uno modo sacrificatur trans-
gressoribus angelis.

---

85 Cf. *Conf.* 1.6.7; A. uses prayer for divine help to mark off
the sections of the book.

86 Virg. *Aen.* 1.37–49; cf. 1.8–11; the words were never heard,
because Juno did not exist to say them.

87 The same task was set for the whole class.

88 Cf. A. *Io. Ev. Tr.* 10.6, "Surely everything is smoke and
wind? Surely everything changes and hastens?"

89 Cf. Jn 15:4; perhaps A. is using the same image as Catull.
Carm. 62.49–55.

90 An oblique allusion to Virg. *G.* 2.60; cf. Ps 8:8 (the birds of
the air evoke pride because they abide in the realm of the angels
who fell through pride).

17. (27) O my God, let me say something[85] about my intellectual ability, which was your gift to me, and the way I squandered it on such absurdities. A task was assigned to me, which quite roused my soul with thoughts of a reward of praise (and perhaps with a fear of disgrace and beatings too). It was to perform the speech of Juno when she was angry and hurt because she could not divert the Trojan king from Italy, words that I had never heard Juno utter.[86] Instead we were obliged to go astray by following the footsteps of poetical inventions, and to declaim in prose something similar to what the poet had written in verse.[87] The one who was displaying a more realistic impression of anger and hurt in defending the honor of the character being delineated (using appropriate words to clothe the ideas) was the one whose speech won the most praise. For what does it matter to me, O my true Life, my God, that they acclaimed my performance as superior to those of my contemporaries and fellow students? Look, surely all that stuff is just smoke and wind?[88] Was there no other subject matter on which to hone my intellect and speaking skills? Your praises, Lord, your praises throughout your Scriptures would have supported the vine shoot of my heart,[89] and then it would not have been carried away by the vacuity of trifling matters as prey for the birds of the air.[90] There is more than one way of sacrificing to the rebel angels.[91]

---

91 The word "rebel" translates *transgressor*, a Christian term (equivalent to biblical Greek παραβάτης) for a sinner. A. thinks of the pagan gods pervading classical literature (who expect blood sacrifice) as demonic and identifies them with the rebel angels (Rv 12:9); cf. *De civ. D.* 9.19.

18. (28) Quid autem mirum, quod in vanitates ita fere-
bar et a te, deus meus, ibam foras, quando mihi imitandi
proponebantur homines qui aliqua facta sua non mala, si
cum barbarismo aut soloecismo enuntiarent, reprehensi
confundebantur, si autem libidines suas integris et rite
consequentibus verbis copiose ornateque narrarent, laudati gloriabantur? vides haec, domine, et taces, longanimis
et multum misericors et verax. numquid semper tacebis?
et nunc eruis de hoc immanissimo profundo quarerentem
te animam et sitientem delectationes tuas, et cuius cor
dicit tibi, "quaesivi vultum tuum:" vultum tuum, domine,
requiram: nam longe a vultu tuo in affectu tenebroso. non
enim pedibus aut a spatiis locorum itur abs te aut reditur
ad te, aut vero filius ille tuus minor equos vel currus vel
naves quaesivit, aut avolavit pinna visibili, aut moto po-
plite iter egit, ut in longinqua regione vivens prodige dis-
siparet quod dederas proficiscenti, dulcis pater quia dederas, et egeno redeunti dulcior: in affectu ergo libidinoso,
id enim est tenebroso, atque id est longe a vultu tuo.

(29) Vide, domine deus, et patienter, ut vides, vide

---

92 Cf. A., *Doctr. Chr.* 2.13.19.

93 Repetition of *longe* highlights the distance between his soul
and God (and recalls the alienation of *Conf.* 1.1.1). "Face of God"
is equivalent to "presence of God," e.g., *En. Ps.* 104.3; he asks,
"What does 'face of the Lord' mean, if not the presence of God?"

94 Cf. the parable of the prodigal son, Lk 15:11–32. For his
interpretation, cf., e.g., *Qu.Ev.* 2.33.

95 An allusion to a favorite passage of Plotinus for A.: *Enn.*
1.6.8: "This is our native land (πατρίς), where we came from, and
there is our father . . . We must let go of everything and not
go looking, but, as if closing our eyes, change one kind of sight

18. (28) It is hardly surprising, my God, that I was carried away into vain pursuits, and strayed far away from you. Men were set up as examples for me to imitate who would have been mortified if, when they were recounting some acts of theirs (acts not wrong in themselves), they had been criticized for mispronunciation or making a grammatical error.[92] But if they gave full and elaborate descriptions of their immoral behavior in rounded and well-constructed phraseology, they boasted of the praise they won for it! You see this, Lord, and remain silent. You are long-suffering, full of mercy and truth. But surely you will not always be silent? And now you pluck the soul that seeks you and thirsts for your pleasures out of this bottomless abyss, and its heart says to you: "I have sought your face"; your face, Lord, I shall seek. For I was far from your face,[93] and in the shadows of earthly passion. Not that physical movement or distancing can achieve a separation from you, or a return to you. Nor did that younger son of yours[94] get hold of chariots or ships, or fly off on visible wings or go as fast as his legs would carry him, just so as to waste what you had given to him, as he set out, through self-indulgent living in a faraway country. You were a kindly father because of what you had given to him, and you were even kinder to him when he returned penniless.[95] No. It is earthly pleasure, which is to say the darksome gloom of being far removed from your face, which creates separation from you.

(29) Look, Lord God, and when you do look, look with

for another, and restore the sight which all of us have, but few of us use."

Ps 86:15

Ps 82:2

Ps 27:8

51

quomodo diligenter observent filii hominum pacta litterarum et syllabarum accepta a prioribus locutoribus, et a te
accepta aeterna pacta perpetuae salutis neglegant, ut qui
illa sonorum vetera placita teneat aut doceat, si contra
disciplinam grammaticam sine adspiratione primae sylla-
bae hominem dixerit, magis displiceat hominibus quam si
contra tua praecepta hominem oderit, cum sit homo. quasi
vero quemlibet inimicum hominem perniciosius sentiat
quam ipsum odium quo in eum inritatur, aut vastet quisquam persequendo alium gravius quam cor suum vastat
inimicando. et certe non est interior litterarum scientia
quam scripta conscientia, id se alteri facere quod nolit
pati. quam tu secretus es, habitans in excelsis in silentio,
deus solus magnus, lege infatigabili spargens poenales
caecitates supra inlicitas cupiditates, cum homo eloquentiae famam quaeritans ante hominem iudicem circum-
stante hominum multitudine inimicum suum odio immanissimo insectans vigilantissime cavet, ne per linguae
errorem dicat, "inter hominibus,"[11] et ne per mentis fu-
rorem hominem auferat ex hominibus, non cavet.

11 (inter) hominibus *codd. Maur. Knöll Ver.*: homines S

---

96 Literally, "sons of humankind," a scriptural phrase.
97 Pronunciation or omission of an initial *h* as a subject of
social criticism goes back at least to Catullus (ca. 84–ca. 54 BC),
poem 84.   98 A. repeatedly associates silence with God; cf.
Conf. 1.18.28, 8.12.28.   99 The error in Latin is to use the
wrong case after the preposition.
100 Cf. Brown, *Augustine*, 238. A. was hostile on principle to
capital punishment.

patience at how scrupulously mortals[96] observe conventions of spelling and syllable division that they learned from those speakers who have gone before them; and yet they neglect the enduring terms of their everlasting salvation that they received from you. So if anyone who holds to the old conventions of pronunciation, or teaches them, contravenes the rules of grammar by saying the word "human" without pronouncing the initial aspirate,[97] folk find that more deserving of rebuke than if that person breaks your laws by hating another human being—despite themselves being human also! As if the feeling that someone is their enemy could do them more damage than the actual hatred which makes them infuriated with that person! Or as if one person would do more damage to someone else by persecuting them than to their own heart by the very fact of its hostility! The knowledge of letters is definitely not imprinted as deeply as the graven sense that it is wrong   Rom 2:15 to inflict on another what one does not wish to endure oneself. How enigmatic you are, God! You alone are great, and you dwell on high in the silence.[98] With your inex-   Is 33:5 haustible law you sprinkle blindness as punishment upon our unlawful passions. Say a man earnestly desires a reputation for skill in speaking: before a judge, who is also a human being, and with a crowd of men around him, he launches an attack, full of vitriolic hatred, upon his enemy. He takes the most scrupulous care not to make a slip of the tongue by saying "among they people"[99]—but he takes no trouble at all to prevent his furious temper causing another human being to be cast out of the land of the living.[100]

19. (30) Horum ego puer morum in limine iacebam
miser, et huius harenae palaestra erat illa, ubi magis timebam barbarismum facere quam cavebam, si facerem, non
facientibus invidere. dico haec et confiteor tibi, deus
meus, in quibus laudabar ab eis quibus placere tunc mihi
erat honeste vivere. non enim videbam voraginem turpitudinis in quam proiectus eram ab oculis tuis. nam in illis
iam quid me foedius fuit, ubi etiam talibus displicebam
fallendo innumerabilibus mendaciis et paedagogum et
magistros et parentes amore ludendi, studio spectandi
nugatoria et imitandi ludicra inquietudine? furta etiam
faciebam de cellario parentum et de mensa, vel gula impe-
ritante vel ut haberem quod darem pueris ludum suum
mihi quo pariter utique delectabantur tamen vendentibus.
in quo etiam ludo fraudulentas victorias ipse vana excellentiae cupiditate victus saepe aucupabar. quid autem tam
nolebam pati atque atrociter, si deprehenderem, arguebam, quam id quod aliis faciebam? et, si deprehensus ar-
guerer, saevire magis quam cedere libebat.

Istane est innocentia puerilis? non est, domine, non
est. oro te, deus meus: nam haec ipsa sunt quae a paeda-
gogis et magistris, a nucibus et pilulis et passeribus, ad
praefectos et reges, aurum, praedia, mancipia, haec ipsa

---

101 A. means that he was in danger of capitulating to conformity with such practices.

102 *Palaestra* can mean both wrestling ground and rhetorical
school.

19. (30) In my boyhood I lay prostrate and pitiable at the threshold of these conventions,[101] and the school of rhetoric[102] was the arena where I began to fear grammatical solecisms—rather than trying, once I had committed them, not to envy those who had made no mistake. I admit all this, O my God, and I confess to you, that this was the kind of thing I tried to be praised for, by those whose good opinion then seemed to me the mark of a successful life. I did not recognize the maelstrom of filth into which I was thrown headlong, away from your sight. What could be more foul than myself in their view? For at that time I was even disappointing the slave who took me to school, and my teachers, and my parents, by deceiving them with countless lies of that sort: because I loved to play games, and I enjoyed watching frivolous entertainments, and I longed to emulate sporting performances. I used to steal from my parents' storeroom, and from the table, either because I was constantly greedy or to obtain something to trade with the other boys, who charged me to join in their playing, which they enjoyed just as much as I did. In these games I was overmastered by my vain desire to excel, so I used to strive to win, even by cheating. But the thing I was so determined not to put up with, and which I denounced so harshly if I detected it, was the exact thing which I myself was constantly committing against others! If I was caught and denounced, I chose to become furious rather than to admit the truth.

So much for the innocence of youth. There is no such thing, Lord, truly there is no such thing! My God I entreat you—human failings are the same from the childhood time of slaves and teachers, trivia and ball games and birds as in the adult transition to magistrates and mon-

Ps 31:22

55

omnino succedentibus maioribus aetatibus transeunt,
sicuti ferulis maiora supplicia succedunt. humilitatis ergo
signum in statura pueritiae, rex noster, probasti, cum aisti,
"talium est regnum caelorum."

20. (31) Sed tamen, domine, tibi excellentissimo atque
optimo conditori et rectori universitatis, deo nostro gratias, etiamsi me puerum tantum esse voluisses. eram enim
etiam tunc, vivebam atque sentiebam meamque incolumi-
tatem, vestigium secretissimae unitatis ex qua eram, curae
habebam, custodiebam interiore sensu integritatem sen-
suum meorum inque ipsis parvis parvarumque rerum
cogitationibus veritate delectabar. falli nolebam, memoria
vigebam, locutione instruebar, amicitia mulcebar, fugiebam dolorem, abiectionem, ignorantiam. quid in tali ani-
mante non mirabile atque laudabile? at ista omnia dei mei
dona sunt. non mihi ego dedi haec, et bona sunt, et haec
omnia ego. bonus ergo est qui fecit me, et ipse est bonum
meum, et illi exulto bonis omnibus quibus etiam puer
eram. hoc enim peccabam, quod non in ipso sed in crea-
turis eius me atque ceteris[12] voluptates, sublimitates, veri-
tates quaerebam, atque ita inruebam in dolores, con-

---

[12] ceteris *codd. Maur. Skut. Ver.*: ceteras S *Knöll.*

---

[103] A. means that Jesus defined the "humility" of children as
physical, not ethical or spiritual; not a convincing historical exegesis. On the "symbol" (*signum*), cf. A.'s distinction between symbol
and referent, on which his understanding of sacraments depends
(Cf. *Doctr. Chr.* 1–3, with Williams, "Language, Reality, and Desire," 138).

archs, gold and estates and property: they are exactly the same—and likewise more severe punishments take the place of the schoolmaster's cane. So, my King, you meant that the image of humility consists in the physical stature of children, when you said, "Of such is the kingdom of heaven."[103]

20. (31) Thanks be to you, Lord our God, supreme and greatest, founder and ruler of the universe—even if your will had decreed that I not live beyond childhood. For I was an existing being even then, I was alive and self-aware, and able to safeguard my own wholeness, which was a vestige of that mystical unity of yours from which my existence derived. By an inner consciousness I kept watch over the purity of my senses and I delighted in truth, even in my trivial reflections on trivial matters. I disliked being deceived, I had an excellent memory, I was well taught as a speaker, I was mellowed by friendship;[104] I avoided pain, despondency, ignorance. Surely a living creature such as I is altogether wonderful and praiseworthy? But all these qualities are gifts from my God. I did not give them to myself, and they are good, and I am the sum of all their parts. Therefore the one who made me is good, and he himself is my good, and I rejoice in him for all the good things of which I consisted even in childhood. This was my sin: I sought pleasures, exaltations, truths[105] not in God himself but in his creations, which is to say, in myself and other things. As a result I tumbled headlong into distress,

[104] This final chapter is full of deliberately placed rhetorical triplets: patterns of three matter to A.

[105] The plurals suggest division and hence inferiority to God, who is One.

fusiones, errores. gratias tibi, dulcedo mea et honor meus
et fiducia mea, deus meus, gratias tibi de donis tuis: sed tu
mihi ea serva. ita enim servabis me, et augebuntur et per-
ficientur quae dedisti mihi, et ero ipse tecum, quia et ut
sim tu dedisti mihi.

disorder, delusion. I give thanks to you, my sweetness, my reverence and my confidence: my God. I give thanks to you for your gifts. Keep them safe for me, though. For then you will be keeping me safe, and all that you have given to me will grow and be perfected, and I myself will be with you, because even the fact that I exist was a gift from you to me.[106]

[106] The last word of *Conf.* 1 is "me."

LIBER II

1. (1) Recordari volo transactas foeditates meas et carnales corruptiones animae meae, non quod eas amem, sed ut amem te, deus meus. amore amoris tui facio istuc,[1] recolens vias meas nequissimas in amaritudine recogitationis meae, ut tu dulcescas mihi, dulcedo non fallax, dulcedo felix et secura, et conligens me a dispersione, in qua frustatim discissus sum dum ab uno te aversus in multa evanui. exarsi enim aliquando satiari inferis in adulescentia, et silvescere ausus sum variis et umbrosis amoribus, et contabuit species mea, et computrui coram oculis tuis placens mihi et placere cupiens oculis hominum.

2. (2) Et quid erat quod me delectabat, nisi amare et amari? sed non tenebatur modus ab animo usque ad animum quatenus est luminosus limes amicitiae, sed exhalabantur nebulae de limosa concupiscentia carnis et scatebra pubertatis, et obnubilabant atque obfuscabant cor

---

[1] istuc S Ver. Knöll Pell. : istud codd. Maur. Skut.

---

[1] I.e., "fleshly" or "carnal"; see Conf. 1.6.7, n. 17.
[2] Cf. Plotinus on singularity and number: Introduction, p. xxviii.   [3] Paronomasia on limes ("confine," "limit") and limosus ("slimy," "filthy").
[4] Either eruptions of acne or other kinds of discharge.

BOOK II

1. (1) I wish to put on record the disgusting deeds in which I engaged, and the corrupting effect of sensual experience[1] on my soul, not because I love them, but so that I may love you, my God. I do this because of my love for your love, to the end that—as I recall my wicked, wicked ways in the bitterness of recollection—you may grow even sweeter to me. For you are a sweetness which does not deceive, a sweetness which brings happiness and peace, pulling me back together from the disintegration in which I was being shattered and torn apart, when I turned away from you who are unity and dispersed into the multiplicity that is oblivion.[2] For there was a time during my adolescence when I burned to have my fill of hell. I ran wild and reckless in all manner of shady liaisons, and my outward appearance deteriorated, and I degenerated before your eyes as I went on pleasing myself and desiring to appear pleasing in human sight.

2. (2) What was it that used to delight me, if not loving and being loved? But there was no boundary maintained between one mind and another, and reaching only as far as the clear confines of friendship. Instead the slime[3] of fleshly desire and the spurts[4] of adolescence belched out their fumes, and these clouded and obscured my heart, so

1 Jn 2:16

61

CONFESSIONS

meum, ut non discerneretur serenitas dilectionis a caligine libidinis. utrumque in confuso aestuabat et rapiebat
inbecillam aetatem per abrupta cupiditatum atque mersa-
bat gurgite flagitiorum. invaluerat super me ira tua, et
nesciebam. obsurdueram stridore catenae mortalitatis
meae, poena superbiae animae meae, et ibam longius a te
et sinebas, et iactabar et effundebar et diffluebam et ebul-
liebam per fornicationes meas, et tacebas. o tardum gaudium meum! tacebas tunc, et ego ibam porro longe a te in
plura et plura sterilia semina dolorum superba deiectione
et inquieta lassitudine.

(3) Quis mihi modularetur aerumnam meam et novis-
simarum rerum fugaces pulchritudines in usum verteret
earumque suavitatibus metas praefigeret, ut usque ad
coniugale litus exaestuarent fluctus aetatis meae? si tran-
quillitas in eis non poterat esse fine procreandorum liberorum contenta (sicut praescribit lex tua, domine, qui
formas etiam propaginem mortis nostrae, potens impo-
nere lenem manum ad temperamentum spinarum a para-
diso tuo seclusarum; non enim longe est a nobis omnipotentia tua, etiam cum longe sumus a te)—aut certe sonitum
nubium tuarum vigilantius adverterem: "tribulationem
autem carnis habebunt huius modi; ego autem vobis
parco"; et "bonum est homini mulierem non tangere"; et
"qui sine uxore est, cogitat ea quae sunt dei, quomodo
placeat deo; qui autem matrimonio iunctus est, cogitat ea
quae sunt mundi, quomodo placeat uxori." has ergo voces

⁵ Cf. *Conf.* 10.27.38, 13.29.44.   ⁶ Anticipating the lyri-
cal prayer at *Conf.* 10.28.   ⁷ Oxymoron.
⁸ Double oxymoron.   ⁹ The "or" marks an anacoluthon
caused by the (unusual) long parenthesis.
¹⁰ Cf. *Conf.* 1.6.7, n. 17.

that it was impossible to distinguish the purity of love from the darkness of lust. Both of them together seethed in me, dragging my immaturity over the heights of bodily desire, and plunging me down into a whirlpool of sin. Your anger grew strong against me, but I was unaware of it. I had been deafened[5] by the loud grinding of the chain of my mortality, the punishment for the pride of my soul, and I went even further away from you, and you let me. I was shaken about and poured away and spilled out and burned up by my sexual immorality; and you said nothing. How long you took, my Joy![6] You were silent then, and I wandered far, so far, from you, toward more and more sterile seeds,[7] whose only fruit was grief, in my proud despondency and restless lethargy.[8]

(3) Who would bring order to my predicament? Who would turn the fleeting attractions of these most recent experiences to a proper purpose and fix limits to their luscious taste, to make the foaming waves of my youth surge toward the safe haven of marriage? If I were unable to find contentment in such experiences by being confined to the procreation of children (this is what your law prescribes, Lord, for you also cultivate the offshoots of our mortality, and in your power you set your gentle hand to keeping in check the thorns which you excluded from your paradise—for your omnipotence is not far from us, even when we are far from you)—or[9] I would surely have taken more notice of the sound from your clouds, "Such as are married will experience the troubles of the flesh:[10] but I am sparing you," and, "It is good for a man to not to touch a woman"; and, "He who has no wife thinks upon the things of God, how to please God; he who is joined in matrimony thinks upon worldly things, how to please his wife." I should have paid more careful attention to these voices,

Gn 1:28

1 Cor 7:28
1 Cor 7:1
1 Cor 7:32–33

exaudirem vigilantior, et abscisus propter regnum caelorum felicior expectarem amplexus tuos.

(4) Sed efferbui miser, sequens impetum fluxus mei
relicto te, et excessi omnia legitima tua nec evasi flagella
tua. quis enim hoc mortalium? nam tu semper aderas
misericorditer saeviens, et amarissimis aspergens offensionibus omnes inlicitas iucunditates meas, ut ita quaererem sine offensione iucundari, et ubi hoc possem, non
invenirem quicquam praeter te, domine, praeter te, qui
fingis dolorem in praecepto et percutis ut sanes et occidis
nos ne moriamur abs te. ubi eram? et quam longe exulabam a deliciis domus tuae anno illo sexto decimo aetatis
carnis meae, cum accepit in me sceptrum (et totas manus
ei dedi) vesania libidinis, licentiosae per dedecus huma-
num, inlicitae autem per leges tuas? non fuit cura meorum
ruentem excipere me matrimonio, sed cura fuit tantum ut
discerem sermonem facere quam optimum et persuadere
dictione.

3. (5) Et anno quidem illo intermissa erant studia mea,
dum mihi reducto a Madauris, in qua vicina urbe iam
coeperam litteraturae atque oratoriae percipiendae gratia
peregrinari, longinquioris apud Carthaginem peregrina-
tionis sumptus praeparabantur animositate magis quam
opibus patris, municipis Thagastensis admodum tenuis.

---

11 Echoing a famous expression in Cic. *In Cat.* 2.1, "He has
departed, withdrawn, escaped, burst out" (*abiit, excessit, evasit,
erupit*).   12 The first precise indicator of A.'s age.

13 Or "Madaura." A. tells us nothing of this small inland town
in North Africa, just further south of Hippo Regius than Thagaste: see Introduction, p. xx.   14 Cf. *Conf.* 4.4.7, 7.12;
6.7.11. The town of Thagaste was his birthplace.

and if I had become a eunuch for the sake of the kingdom
of the heavens I would now be anticipating your embraces   Mt 19:12
with more pleasure.

(4) I was in a pitiful state of turmoil, abandoning
you to follow the impulse of my own moral weakness.
I transgressed all your true ordinances, but I did not escape your scourges.[11] What mortal ever can? After all,
you were always there, merciful even in your severity,
sprinkling all my forbidden pleasures with the bitterest
of disappointments, so that I would seek a kind of pleasure that is free from disappointment, and when I did
so I would find none other but yourself, Lord, yourself
alone. You shape pain into precepts, and you strike us to   Ps 94:20
heal us, and you put us to death so that we do not die apart   Hos 6:2
from you. Where was I? And how far was I in exile from   Dt 32:39
the pleasures of your house in that sixteenth year of my   Mi 2:9
mortal age,[12] when the madness of lust seized dominion
over me (and I surrendered myself to it completely)? Such
passion was permissible by human standards, disgraceful
as they are: but it is forbidden by your laws. Not that my
family was concerned to rescue me from ruin by marrying
me off—their only concern was for me to master oratory
and rhetoric as thoroughly as possible.

3. (5) In that year, there was a break in my studies. I
was brought back from Madauri,[13] the nearby town where
I had now begun to lodge in order to study literature and
oratory. My father, with more temerity than wealth, was
saving up to pay for me to stay at Carthage in the longer
term, for even though he was a citizen and councilor at
Thagaste,[14] he was a man of modest means. Who am I

cui narro haec? neque enim tibi, deus meus, sed apud te
narro haec generi meo, generi humano, quantulacumque
ex particula incidere potest in istas meas litteras. et ut quid
hoc? ut videlicet ego et quisquis haec legit cogitemus de
quam[2] profundo clamandum sit ad te. et quid propius
auribus tuis, si cor confitens et vita ex fide est?

Quis enim non extollebat laudibus tunc hominem, patrem meum, quod ultra vires rei familiaris suae impende-
ret filio quidquid etiam longe peregrinanti studiorum
causa opus esset? multorum enim civium longe opulentio-
rum nullum tale negotium pro liberis erat, cum interea
non satageret idem pater qualis crescerem tibi aut quam
castus essem, dummodo essem disertus, vel desertus potius a cultura tua, deus, qui es unus verus et bonus dominus agri tui, cordis mei.

(6) Sed ubi sexto illo et decimo anno, interposito otio
ex necessitate domestica, feriatus ab omni schola cum
parentibus esse coepi, excesserunt caput meum vepres
libidinum, et nulla erat eradicans manus. quin immo ubi
me ille pater in balneis vidit pubescentem et inquieta indutum adulescentia, quasi iam ex hoc in nepotes gestiret,
gaudens matri indicavit, gaudens vinulentia in qua te iste
mundus oblitus est creatorem suum et creaturam tuam
pro te amavit, de vino invisibili perversae atque inclinatae

---

[2] quam S *edd.*: quo *codd.*

---

[15] A glimpse of A.'s awareness (usually cloaked) of his readers.

telling this?[15] Certainly not you, my God! But I am narrating this story in your presence to my kind, to the whole human race, whatever tiny fraction of it happens to come across these writings of mine. And why is this? Obviously so that I, and whoever reads this, may ponder the depths from which we must cry out to you. What is closer to your ears than a heart that makes its confession to you and a life that is faithful? Ps 130:1

Rom 10:9

Who was there, back then, who did not praise that man, my father, because he was spending on his son whatever he must, even beyond his means, so that his son could travel far away in order to pursue his studies? Many citizens, far richer than he, took less trouble than this for their children: although in the meantime this same father was not at all troubled about what kind of person I grew up to become before you, or whether I was chaste. So long as I was well-spoken, so what if I was estranged from worshipping you, O God?—though you are the one true Master over your field, which is my heart. 1 Cor 3:9

(6) In my sixteenth year I found myself obliged to be at leisure, for funds at home were low, and I had a break from all this education and started living with my parents. Thorny growths of sexual immorality sprouted up higher than my head, and there was no hand to uproot them. Rather, when we were at the baths my father saw that I was becoming a man and clothed with the turbulence of adolescence; he was delighted by this, at the prospect of grandchildren. In his pleasure he told my mother. It was a pleasure fueled by wine, which is the way this world has forgotten you, its creator, and loved—instead of you—creation; and all because of the invisible wine of its own will, which is perverse and inclined toward everything base.

67

in ima[3] voluntatis suae. sed matris in pectore iam inchoaveras templum tuum et exordium sanctae habitationis tuae, nam ille adhuc catechumenus et hoc recens erat. itaque illa exilivit[4] pia trepidatione ac tremore et, quamvis mihi nondum fideli, timuit tamen vias distortas in quibus ambulant qui ponunt ad te tergum et non faciem.

(7) Ei mihi! et audeo dicere tacuisse te, deus meus, cum irem abs te longius? itane tu tacebas tunc mihi? et cuius erant nisi tua verba illa per matrem meam, fidelem tuam, quae cantasti in aures meas? nec inde quicquam descendit in cor, ut facerem illud. volebat enim illa, et secreto memini ut monuerit cum sollicitudine ingenti, ne fornicarer maximeque ne adulterarem cuiusquam uxorem. qui mihi monitus muliebres videbantur, quibus obtemperare erubescerem. illi autem tui erant et nesciebam, et te tacere putabam atque illam loqui per quam mihi tu non tacebas, et in illa contemnebaris a me, a me,[5] filio eius, filio ancillae tuae, servo tuo.

Sed nesciebam et praeceps ibam tanta caecitate ut inter coaetaneos meos puderet me minoris dedecoris, quoniam audiebam eos iactantes flagitia sua et tanto gloriantes magis, quanto magis turpes essent, et libebat facere non

---

3 inclinatae in ima *D G edd.*: inclinata in ima *C*: inlicitae in anima *S*   4 exilivit *codd. Maur. Ver.*: exsiluit *S Knöll Skut.*
5 a me, a me *S Knöll Skut. Pell. Ver.*: a me *codd. Maur.*

---

16 Cf. *Conf.* 1.11.17, n. 48.   17 *fidelis* in A. always means a full member of the Christian community.
18 On the Christian view of *fornicatio*, cf. 1 Cor 5:1. Adultery was a more serious offense, a ground for divorce, because it cast doubt on the legitimacy of offspring.

But you had already laid the foundations of your temple in my mother's breast, and the beginning of your holy habitation, for my father was still just a catechumen,[16] and even that was only recent. So she was excited with holy fear and trembling, and although I was not yet a believer,[17] still she was afraid for me, because of the twisted ways in which they walk who turn their back to you and not their face.

    Eccl 24:14

    2 Cor 7:15

    Jer 2:27

(7) Pity me! How do I even dare to say that you were silent, my God, when I was the one withdrawing from you? Were you really so silent toward me then? Whose words were they if not yours that you chanted into my ears through my mother, who was your faithful servant! From that age on, nothing penetrated my heart deeply enough to spur me to act upon it. My mother's wish (and I recall how in great distress she warned me privately about it) was that I should not commit fornication or, still worse, adultery with a woman who was married.[18] This seemed to me to be mere women's nagging; it would be embarrassing to pay heed to it. But they were warnings from you, and I had no idea of it. I went on believing that you were saying nothing. I thought she was the one speaking, though all the time it was you speaking to me through her. So in rejecting her I was rejecting you—I who was her son, I who was the son of your handmaid, and your servant.

    Ps 116:16

    Ps 116:16

But I knew none of this. I rushed headlong so blindly that among friends of my own age I blushed over the slightest loss of prestige, for I would hear them boasting of their own scandalous deeds. The more discreditable the deeds, the more they bragged about them. So I began to take pleasure in such behavior not just because of the lust

solum libidine facti verum etiam laudis. quid dignum est vituperatione nisi vitium? ego, ne vituperarer, vitiosior fiebam, et ubi non suberat quo admisso aequarer perditis, fingebam me fecisse quod non feceram, ne viderer abiectior quo eram innocentior, et ne vilior haberer quo eram castior.

(8) Ecce cum quibus comitibus iter agebam platearum Babyloniae, et volutabar in caeno eius tamquam in cinnamis et unguentis pretiosis. et in umbilico eius quo tenacius haererem, calcabat me inimicus invisibilis et seducebat me, quia ego seductilis eram. non enim et illa quae iam de medio Babylonis fugerat, sed ibat in ceteris eius tardior, mater carnis meae, sicut monuit me pudicitiam, ita curavit quod de me a viro suo audierat, iamque pestilentiosum et in posterum periculosum sentiebat cohercere termino coniugalis affectus, si resecari ad vivum non poterat. non curavit hoc, quia metus erat ne impediretur spes mea compede uxoria, non spes illa quam in te futuri saeculi habebat mater, sed spes litterarum, quas ut nossem nimis volebat parens uterque, ille quia de te prope nihil cogitabat, de me autem inania, illa autem quia non solum nullo detrimento sed etiam nonnullo adiumento ad te adipiscendum futura existimabat usitata illa studia doctrinae. ita enim conicio, recolens ut possum mores parentum meo-

---

19 The city of Babylon in Mesopotamia is a biblical symbol for corruption and immorality (Rv 14:8, etc.); in *De civ. D.* it stands as the earthly polity (*civitas terrena*) in opposition to Jerusalem, the heavenly polity (*civitas dei*).

20 The "scented spice" is cinnamon; but A. is thinking of its scent rather than any culinary purpose.   21 His "mother according to the spirit" is the Church (Gal 4:26–27).

of the deed itself but also because of the kudos it won me. What is more deserving of disapproval than depravity? I faked the depravity to avoid the disapproval of my peers. If no actual wrongdoing took place that I could boast of to equal my peers in their abandon, I pretended to have done something wrong, though really I had not. I did not want my innocence to resemble weakness nor did I want to be scorned because of my sexual inexperience.

8. Look what kind of companions I had as I journeyed over the wide roads of Babylon[19] and wallowed in the city's filth as if it were scented spice[20] and expensive perfumes! The more my unseen enemy trampled me and seduced me, the more determinedly I clung to its center. How easy I was to tempt! For my mother according to the flesh[21] had already fled the center of Babylon (but was still lingering on that city's outskirts): though she urged me to be chaste, still she placed no such importance on what her husband had told her about me. Now she began to realize that it was already unhealthy and potentially a future danger too; something to restrain within the bounds of a marital relationship if it could not be pruned back to the quick. The reason why she did not take it more seriously was her fear of damaging my expectations by shackling me to a wife: not, in other words, that hope for the world to come which my mother maintained, but the hope of an academic career, which (as I knew) both my parents were all too eager for. In my father's case, this was because he gave virtually no thought to you and instead thought of my gaining such hollow achievements. My mother, though, thought that such customary academic study would not only be no hindrance but might even be some help in my striving to reach you. At least so I guess, when I recall my parents'

Sg 4:14

Ps 56:2

71

rum. relaxabantur etiam mihi ad ludendum habenae ultra
temperamentum severitatis in dissolutionem affectionum
variarum, et in omnibus erat caligo intercludens mihi,
deus meus, serenitatem veritatis tuae, et prodiebat tamquam ex adipe iniquitas mea.

4. (9) Furtum certe punit lex tua, domine, et lex scripta
in cordibus hominum, quam ne ipsa quidem delet iniquitas. quis enim fur aequo animo furem patitur? nec copio-
sus adactum inopia. et ego furtum facere volui et feci,
nulla compulsus egestate nisi penuria et fastidio iustitiae
et sagina iniquitatis. nam id furatus sum quod mihi abun-
dabat et multo melius, nec ea re volebam frui quam furto
appetebam, sed ipso furto et peccato.

Arbor erat pirus in vicinia nostrae vineae pomis onusta
nec forma nec sapore inlecebrosis. ad hanc excutiendam
atque asportandam nequissimi adulescentuli perreximus
nocte intempesta (quousque ludum de pestilentiae more
in areis produxeramus) et abstulimus inde onera ingentia,
non ad nostras epulas sed vel proicienda porcis, etiamsi
aliquid inde comedimus, dum tamen fieret a nobis quod
eo liberet quo non liceret.

Ecce cor meum, deus, ecce cor meum, quod miseratus
es in imo abyssi. dicat tibi nunc, ecce cor meum, quid ibi
quaerebat, ut essem gratis malus et malitiae meae causa
nulla esset nisi malitia. foeda erat, et amavi eam. amavi

---

22 See *Ord.* 2.8.5.

23 *quousque*: the word forever evoked Cicero's reproach to
Catiline, *In Cat.* 1; the parallel of A. with Catiline the arch-rebel
and conspirator develops in *Conf.* 2.5.11.

behavior as best I can. They gave me a loose rein, rather than an attitude of strict discipline, to indulge my volatility with whatever pleasures took my fancy—in all of which, my God, a mist was cutting me off from the brightness of your truth, while my wickedness was overflowing in its abundance.

Ps 73:7

4. (9) Your law, Lord, surely punishes theft; and that law is so written in human hearts that not even wrongdoing can efface it.[22] For what thief willingly puts up with a thief, even if one has all he needs while the other is driven by need? I wanted to commit theft, so I did. I was not driven by any kind of lack other than the absence of righteousness and a distaste for it: and the fact that I was bloated with sin. For I stole what I had already in plenty, and of far better quality. I had no desire to enjoy what I had aimed to steal; rather, what I enjoyed was the theft and sin themselves.

Ex 20:15
Rom 2:15

There was a pear tree near to our vineyard, laden with fruit which had no attractive appearance or flavor. So we set out in the dead of night—a gang of good-for-nothing youths—to shake it down and carry off its fruit; up till then[23] we had prolonged our sport in the usual vexatious fashion in the streets. We carried off great loads, not for ourselves to eat but for throwing to pigs—though we did eat some of them, on condition that what we were doing was something we enjoyed because it was forbidden.

Look, O God, and see my heart, see my heart! For you had mercy on it even in the depths of the pit. Let my heart tell you now to look upon it: what was it searching for there? And how was it that I became a wrongdoer for nothing, and the cause of my wrongdoing was none other than wrongdoing itself? It was loathsome and I loved it. I

perire, amavi defectum meum, non illud ad quod deficie-
bam, sed defectum meum ipsum amavi, turpis anima et
dissiliens a firmamento tuo in exterminium, non dedecore
aliquid, sed dedecus appetens.

5. (10) Etenim species est pulchris corporibus et auro
et argento et omnibus, et in contactu carnis congruentia
valet plurimum, ceterisque sensibus est sua cuique ad-
commodata modificatio corporum. habet etiam honor
temporalis et imperitandi atque superandi potentia suum
decus, unde etiam vindictae aviditas oritur, et tamen in
cuncta haec adipiscenda non est egrediendum abs te,
domine, neque deviandum a lege tua. et vita quam[6] hic
vivimus habet inlecebram suam propter quendam modum
decoris sui et convenientiam cum his omnibus infimis pulchris. amicitia quoque hominum caro nodo dulcis est
propter unitatem de multis animis. propter universa haec
atque huius modi peccatum admittitur, dum immoderata
in ista inclinatione, cum extrema bona sint, meliora et
summa deseruntur, tu, domine deus noster, et veritas tua,
et lex tua. habent enim et haec ima delectationes, sed non
sicut deus meus, qui fecit omnia, quia in ipso delectatur
iustus, et ipse est deliciae rectorum corde.

(11) Cum itaque de facinore quaeritur qua causa fac-

---

[6] quam S *edd.*: qua *codd.*

---

[24] If touch is the sense proper to sexual wrongdoing, it suggests that the theft of the pears is emblematic of such sins for A.
[25] Cf. *Conf.* 1.31 on different levels of good.

was in love with death, I was in love with my own failing—not the thing in which I was failing, but the actual failure itself was what I loved. My soul was foul and, becoming alienated from your firm foundation, it was disintegrating into oblivion. It did not use disgraceful means to achieve what it wanted; what it wanted was the disgrace itself.

5. (10) Certainly beautiful objects have an attraction about them, whether made of gold or silver or the like. Also, the sense of what feels right in the physical act of touching has a powerful influence upon us, while the other senses are all proportionately adapted to particular material objects.[24] Worldly honor and the power to rule and command have their own dignity, and from this the taste for vengeance arises. Yet there should be no escaping from you, Lord, and no turning away from your law, so as to obtain all these things. The life we live here on earth has its own particular attraction, because it possesses its own proper measure of honor and is in balance with all these things that are beautiful on a lower level. Human friendship is also sweetened by a precious bond on account of the unity it forges out of many souls. Yet it is in pursuit of all these things and the like that sin gains an entrance, while an ungoverned inclination for those things, even though they are only the lowest level of goods,[25] means that better and higher ends are abandoned—which is to say you, Lord our God, and your truth and your law. For even these lowly things bring with them pleasures, but not like my God, who has made everything; because the righteous shall rejoice in the Lord, and he himself is the delight of those who are true of heart.   Ps 64:10

(11) So when the cause of a crime is investigated, the

75

tum sit, credi non solet, nisi cum appetitus adipiscendi alicuius illorum bonorum quae infima diximus esse potuisse apparuerit aut metus amittendi. pulchra sunt enim et decora, quamquam prae bonis superioribus et beatificis abiecta et iacentia. homicidium fecit. cur fecit? adamavit eius coniugem aut praedium, aut voluit depraedari unde viveret, aut timuit ab illo tale aliquid amittere, aut laesus ulcisci se exarsit. num homicidium sine causa faceret ipso homicidio delectatus? quis crediderit? nam et de quo dictum est, vaecordi et nimis crudeli homine, quod gratuito potius malus atque crudelis erat, praedicta est tamen causa: "ne per otium," inquit, "torpesceret manus aut animus." quaere[7] id quoque: "cur ita?" ut scilicet illa exercitatione scelerum capta urbe honores, imperia, divitias adsequeretur et careret metu legum et difficultate rerum propter "inopiam rei familiaris et conscientiam scelerum." nec ipse igitur Catilina amavit facinora sua, sed utique aliud cuius causa illa faciebat.

6. (12) Quid ego miser in te amavi, o furtum meum, o facinus illud meum nocturnum sexti decimi anni aetatis meae? non enim pulchrum eras, cum furtum esses. aut vero aliquid es, ut loquar ad te? pulchra erant poma illa

---

7 quaere *codd. Ver.*: quare *S Maur. Knöll Skut.*

---

26 Quoting C. Sallustius Crispus (86–35 BC) *Cat.* 16.3. For L. Sergius Catilina's character, cf. Sall. *Cat.* 5; Cic. *In Cat. Orat.* 1–4. The conspiracy of the rebel patrician politician was foiled by Cicero as consul in 63 BC. For A. he exemplifies wickedness by universal rather than specifically Christian criteria.

27 The act of theft is briefly apostrophized. The question of evil's existence returns in *Conf.* 7.

usual reaction is disbelief, except when the desire to obtain any of those goods belonging to someone else that we have labeled "inferior"—or the fear of losing one—seems likely to be realized. After all they are beautiful and attractive, although they are still lowly and humble in comparison with the higher goods, which bestow blessings on us. Say a man has killed someone. Why has he done so? He was in love with another man's wife or property; or he wanted to ransack his property for something to live on; or he was afraid of losing a considerable part of his own wealth to that other man; or, after being injured, he burned to avenge himself. Surely he would not commit murder without a reason, just for the pleasure of the act of killing itself? Who would believe that? Even Catiline, a man who was said to be both insane and excessively cruel ("excessively" because he was evil and cruel for cruelty's sake) had his reasons for acting thus revealed: "So that neither hand nor heart would grow slack through idleness."[26] Now ask this too: "Why so?" Surely so that by criminal activity he could take over the city and appropriate honors, military command, riches—and shake off all fear of legal consequences and affairs encumbered by "straitened family circumstances and his awareness of the crime he had committed"! So not even Catiline himself loved his own criminal deeds; surely he was committing them for some ulterior motive.

6. (12) I was pathetic! What was it that I loved about you, my theft, my deed of darkness done in the sixteenth year of my age? For you were not beautiful, because you were an act of theft. Then again, should I be addressing you as if you were an actual thing?[27] The fruit we stole was

77

quae furati sumus, quoniam creatura tua erat, pulcherrime omnium, creator omnium, deus bone, deus summum bonum et bonum verum meum. pulchra erant illa poma, sed non ipsa concupivit anima mea miserabilis. erat mihi enim meliorum copia, illa autem decerpsi tantum ut furarer. nam decerpta proieci, epulatus inde solam iniquitatem qua laetabar fruens. nam et si quid illorum pomorum intravit in os meum, condimentum ibi facinus erat.

Et nunc, domine deus meus, quaero quid me in furto delectaverit, et ecce species nulla est: non dico sicut in aequitate atque prudentia, sed neque sicut in mente hominis atque memoria et sensibus et vegetante vita, neque sicut speciosa sunt sidera et decora locis suis et terra et mare plena fetibus, qui succedunt nascendo decedentibus—non saltem ut est quaedam defectiva species et umbratica vitiis fallentibus.

(13) Nam et superbia celsitudinem imitatur, cum tu sis unus super omnia deus excelsus. et ambitio quid nisi honores quaerit et gloriam, cum tu sis prae cunctis honorandus unus et gloriosus in aeternum? et saevitia potestatum timeri vult: quis autem timendus nisi unus deus, cuius potestati eripi aut subtrahi quid potest, quando aut ubi aut quo vel a quo potest? et blanditiae lascivientium amari volunt: sed neque blandius est aliquid tua caritate nec amatur quicquam salubrius quam illa prae cunctis formosa et luminosa veritas tua. et curiositas affectare vi-

---

28 The idea is that sin is a contest with God for supremacy.

beautiful because it was your creation, O most beautiful of all, creator of all, good God, God the supreme good, and my true good. Yes, the fruit was beautiful, but my pitiable soul did not desire the actual fruit. I had plenty of better fruit—I plucked these only for the sake of thieving. For I threw away what I had stolen. All that I feasted on from my theft was my own wickedness, and I was delighted to enjoy it. Even if one morsel of fruit passed my lips, it was sin that sweetened it.

Now, O Lord my God, I want to work out what it was about the theft that gave me pleasure. Look—it does not have a fine appearance. I do not mean in the same way as justice and wisdom, or indeed like human intelligence and memory, nor physical senses and organic growth; neither is it beautiful in appearance and shining like the stars in their courses, and the earth and the sea teeming with new life being born and replacing what falls into decay. My act of theft is not even like those deceiving vices that have a specious, shady illusion of beauty.

(13) This is how pride imitates sublimity. Yet you alone are God, supreme over all things.[28] As for ambition, what does it strive for if not honors and glory—although it is you who ought to be honored above all else, and you possess glory that lasts for ever. Moreover, the cruelty of the powerful is eager to be feared, whereas in truth no one should be feared but God alone—for how can any part of his power be snatched away or removed? And when? Where? Where to? By whom? The attractions of those who are immoral long to be found desirable; but nothing is more truly attractive than your love, and nothing that we find desirable can be more wholesome than your truth, which is fair and full of light beyond all else. Curiosity

detur studium scientiae, cum tu omnia summe noveris. ignorantia quoque ipsa atque stultitia simplicitatis et innocentiae nomine tegitur, quia te simplicius quicquam non reperitur. quid te autem innocentius, quandoquidem opera sua malis inimica sunt? et ignavia quasi quietem appetit: quae vero quies certa praeter dominum? luxuria satietatem atque abundantiam se cupit vocari: tu es autem plenitudo et indeficiens copia incorruptibilis suavitatis. effusio liberalitatis obtendit umbram: sed bonorum omnium largitor affluentissimus tu es. avaritia multa possidere vult: et tu possides omnia. invidentia de excellentia litigat: quid te excellentius? ira vindictam quaerit: te iustius quis vindicat? timor insolita et repentina exhorrescit rebus quae amantur adversantia, dum praecavet securitati: tibi enim quid insolitum? quid repentinum? aut quis a te separat quod diligis? aut ubi nisi apud te firma securitas? tristitia rebus amissis contabescit quibus se oblectabat cupiditas, quia ita sibi nollet, sicut tibi auferri nihil potest.

(14) Ita fornicatur anima, cum avertitur abs te et quaerit extra te ea quae pura et liquida non invenit, nisi cum redit ad te. perverse te imitantur omnes qui longe se a te faciunt et extollunt se adversum te. sed etiam sic te imi-

---

29 For A. "curiosity" is a negative characteristic.

30 A. is thinking of the Latin word *innocens* as encompassing freedom from guilt. Cf. *Conf.* 1.7.11, n. 30.   31 A reference to the ubiquitous pecuniary lubrication of Roman politics.   32 Cf. *Trin.* 11.5.8: "Even in their own sinning, souls are pursuing a certain likeness to God, with an arrogant and, so to speak, distorted freedom. So not even our first parents could be persuaded to sin, but for their being told, 'You will be like gods'" (Gn 3:5).

seems to affect a love of knowledge,[29] yet you are the one who knows everything absolutely. Also, actual ignorance and folly are disguised by labeling them "simplicity" and "innocence" because nothing can be found to be more pure than you. And what is more free from harm[30] than you, given that it is their own works that are injurious to those who are evil? Of course idleness seems to seek the peaceful life, but what sure peace can there be except the Lord? Luxury longs to be known as abundance and plenty, but you are the fullness and unfailing bounty of incorruptible sweetness. Lavish spending cloaks the dark side of generosity,[31] whereas you are the most beneficent giver of all gifts. Greed longs for many possessions, whereas you possess everything. Envy disputes over supremacy, but what is more supreme than you? Anger seeks revenge, but who is a more just vindicator than you? Terror takes fright Rom 12:19 at unexpected and sudden events that pose a threat to treasured possessions, and so takes thought for their safety in advance, but what is there that comes as a surprise to you, an unexpected surprise at that? And who can separate from you anything that you love? Where can true safety be found except in you? Grief consumes away when something is lost that the desire for possessing once used to delight in: this is because it never wishes to be deprived of anything—just as you can never be deprived of anything.

(14) So my soul behaves promiscuously when it turns Ps 73:27 away from you and looks away from you for what is untainted and pure, but cannot find it except by returning to you. In a perverse way they are imitating you, those who put themselves at a distance from you and who glorify themselves in contrast to you;[32] though even by the act of

81

tando indicant creatorem te esse omnis naturae, et ideo non esse quo a te omni modo recedatur.

Quid ergo in illo furto ego dilexi, et in quo dominum meum vel vitiose atque perverse imitatus sum? an libuit facere contra legem saltem fallacia, quia potentatu non poteram ut mancam libertatem captivus imitarer, faciendo impune quod non liceret tenebrosa omnipotentiae similitudine? ecce est ille servus fugiens dominum suum et consecutus umbram. o putredo, o monstrum vitae et mortis profunditas! potuitne libere quod non licebat, non ob aliud nisi quia non licebat?

7. (15) Quid retribuam domino quod recolit haec memoria mea et anima mea non metuit inde? diligam te, domine, et gratias agam et confitear nomini tuo, quoniam tanta dimisisti mihi mala et nefaria opera mea. gratiae tuae deputo et misericordiae tuae quod peccata mea tanquam glaciem solvisti. gratiae tuae deputo et quaecumque non feci mala. quid enim non facere potui, qui etiam gratuitum facinus amavi? et omnia mihi dimissa esse fateor, et quae mea sponte feci mala et quae te duce non feci.

Quis est hominum qui suam cogitans infirmitatem audet viribus suis tribuere castitatem atque innocentiam suam, ut minus amet te, quasi minus ei necessaria fuerit

---

33 "Grace" develops a technical sense in Christian theology; but its main usage in classical Latin is for the everyday giving and receiving of "favor." "For its own sake" (*gratuitum*) can also mean "free of charge."

imitation they disclose that you are the creator of all nature—and so there is nowhere for them to go where you can be avoided.

So what was it about the theft that gave me pleasure, and in which I imitated my Lord, albeit in a wicked and perverse way? Was it pleasing to contravene your law at least surreptitiously because I was not able to do so in an authoritative way? Was it that I myself was like a captive, imitating a maimed kind of freedom by doing what was forbidden without being punished, in a shadowy semblance of your omnipotence? Just look at me—that slave fleeing from his own master, and pursuing a fantasy! What rotten filth! What a deformity of life, what an abyss of death! Was it possible to take pleasure in something just because it was forbidden, and for no other reason than that it was forbidden? Jb 7:2

7. (15) How shall I make restitution to the Lord for the fact that my memory recalls these things and yet my soul is not afraid because of them? I will love you, Lord, and give thanks, and confess praises to your name because you have forgiven me my sins and all my wrongdoing. I count it a mark of your grace and your mercy that you have melted my sins like ice. I also count as a mark of your grace all the evils I did not do. What was I not capable of?—I who even loved wrongdoing for its own sake![33] I admit it, all these things were forgiven me, both the sins that I committed of my own volition and those that, under your guidance, I avoided committing. Ps 116:12
Ps 18:2
Ps 54:6

Sir 3:19

Among all humanity who can reflect on their own weakness and yet dare to attribute their chastity and avoidance of wrongdoing to their own efforts? As if they owed you less love, as if they had less need of your mercy,

misericordia tua, qua donas peccata conversis ad te? qui
enim vocatus a te secutus est vocem tuam et vitavit ea quae
me de me ipso recordantem et fatentem legit, non me
derideat ab eo medico aegrum sanari a quo sibi praestitum
est ut non aegrotaret, vel potius ut minus aegrotaret, et
ideo te tantundem, immo vero amplius diligat, quia per
quem me videt tantis peccatorum meorum languoribus
exui, per eum se videt tantis peccatorum languoribus non
implicari.

8. (16) Quem fructum habui miser aliquando in his
quae nunc recolens erubesco, maxime in illo furto in quo
ipsum furtum amavi, nihil aliud, cum et ipsum esset nihil
et eo ipso ego miserior? et tamen solus id non fecissem
(sic recordor animum tunc meum), solus omnino id non
fecissem. ergo amavi ibi etiam consortium eorum cum
quibus id feci. non ergo nihil aliud quam furtum amavi?
immo vero nihil aliud, quia et illud nihil est. quid est re
vera? (quis est qui doceat me, nisi qui inluminat cor meum
et discernit umbras eius?) quid est quod mihi venit in
mentem quaerere et discutere et considerare? quia si tunc
amarem poma illa quae furatus sum et eis frui cuperem,
possem etiam solus; si satis esset committere illam iniquitatem qua pervenirem ad voluptatem meam, nec confricatione consciorum animorum accenderem pruritum cupiditatis meae. sed quoniam in illis pomis voluptas mihi
non erat, ea erat in ipso facinore quam faciebat consortium simul peccantium.

---

[34] I.e., because the evil in which it consists has no existence
of its own. Cf. *Conf.* 3.7.12.

by which you forgive the sins of those who turn to you? As for anyone who was called by you, and followed your voice, and avoided what they read me recollecting and confessing about myself, let them not laugh at me in my sickness for being healed by the very doctor who ensured that they themselves were not sick, or rather were less sick. In fact, let them love you as much, or even more, because they discern that I have been freed from the great frailties of my sins by that same being through whom they discern that they themselves have escaped the toils of similar frailties of sin.

8. (16) What fruit did I obtain back then, wretch that I was, amid those actions which I now blush to remember?—particularly that theft in which I enjoyed nothing else but the actual thieving, both because it too was a nothing[34] and because it made me even more wretched! For had I been alone I would not have done it (I remember thinking so at the time), yes, I would definitely not have done it alone. So what I loved about it was participating with others in doing what I did. Did I not love anything, then, apart from the theft? Surely I loved nothing else, because that participation was not something real. What was it, in actual fact? Who is it who can teach me, except the one who illuminates my heart and penetrates its shadows? What is this thing that has come into my mind to seek out, and investigate, and weigh up? Because if then I loved those fruits that I had stolen and was longing to enjoy them, I could have done it alone. If it was enough to commit that sin by which I achieved my pleasure, I would not have had to kindle the itch of my greedy desire through the stimulus of complicit consciences. Because my pleasure was not in the pears, it was in the actual crime that a fellowship of sinners committed together.

Rom 6:21

9. (17) Quid erat ille affectus animi? certe enim plane turpis erat nimis, et vae mihi erat qui habebam illum. sed tamen quid erat? delicta quis intellegit? risus erat quasi titillato corde, quod fallebamus eos qui haec a nobis fieri non putabant et vehementer nolebant. cur ergo eo me delectabat quo id non faciebam solus? an quia etiam nemo facile solus ridet? nemo quidem facile, sed tamen etiam solos et singulos homines, cum alius nemo praesens, vincit risus aliquando, si aliquid nimie ridiculum vel sensibus occurit vel animo. at ego illud solus non facerem, non facerem omnino solus.

Ecce est coram te, deus meus, viva recordatio animae meae. solus non facerem furtum illud, in quo me non libebat id quod furabar sed quia furabar: quod me solum facere prorsus non liberet, nec facerem. o nimis inimica amicitia, seductio mentis investigabilis, ex ludo et ioco nocendi aviditas et alieni damni appetitus nulla lucri mei, nulla ulciscendi libidine! sed cum dicitur, "eamus, faciamus," et pudet non esse impudentem.

10. (18) Quis exaperit istam tortuosissimam et implicatissimam nodositatem? foeda est; nolo in eam intendere, nolo eam videre. te volo, iustitia et innocentia pulchra et decora, honestis luminibus et insatiabili satietate. quies est

---

35 Cf. *Conf.* 1.7.12, n. 35.

9. (17) What were my thoughts and feelings? Certainly they were self-evidently shameful, and augured ill for me as I maintained them. But still, what actually were they? Who understands their faults? It was for a laugh, to give us a bit of a thrill, at the thought of cheating people who had no idea we were capable of such behavior and who would strongly disapprove. So why did I get pleasure from something that I would not have done at all if left to myself? Is it perhaps because no one finds it easy to laugh when alone? It is a fact that no one finds it easy, but even so laughter sometimes overcomes people when no one else is present, and they are solitary and alone, if something overwhelmingly silly impacts upon their senses or thoughts. Yet on my own I would never have done it, no, I definitely would not have done it on my own.

O my God, see the living memory of my soul in your presence! I would not have committed that theft on my own, a theft in which it was not the stolen items that pleased me but the very act of thieving. It definitely would not have pleased me to do it alone, nor would I have done it. What an extremely alien alliance it was—an unsearchable distraction of the mind! Out of a game and a lark came an eagerness to do harm, a taste for inflicting losses on others without myself gaining anything, or enjoying settling a score. Once someone says, "Come on, let's do it," it is shameful to be anything but shameless.

10. (18) Who is going to untie that tangled, twisted mass of knots? How vile it is—I have no desire to turn my attention to it, I have no desire even to look upon it. I desire you—O Righteousness and Integrity, both lovely and becoming to the gaze that is true, with an appetite that can never cloy.[35] With you there is deep peace and life

Jb 10:15

Ps 19:12

87

apud te valde et vita imperturbabilis. qui intrat in te, intrat in gaudium domini sui et non timebit et habebit se optime in optimo. defluxi abs te ego et erravi, deus meus, nimis devius ab stabilitate tua in adulescentia, et factus sum mihi regio egestatis.

which cannot be disturbed. Those who enter into you enter into the joy of their Lord and will not be afraid, and   Mt 25:21
will abide perfectly in the One who is perfect. I deviated
from you, I have wandered from the path, my God; in my
teens I was too inconstant in your steadfastness, and I
made myself into a barren land.   Lk 15:13–14

LIBER III

1. (1) Veni Carthaginem, et circumstrepebat me undique sartago flagitiosorum amorum. nondum amabam, et amare[1] amabam, et secretiore indigentia oderam me minus indigentem. quaerebam quid amarem, amans amare, et oderam securitatem et viam sine muscipulis, quoniam fames mihi erat intus ab interiore cibo, te ipso, deus meus, et ea fame non esuriebam, sed eram sine desiderio alimentorum incorruptibilium, non quia plenus eis eram, sed quo inanior, fastidiosior.[2]

Et ideo non bene valebat anima mea et ulcerosa proiciebat se foras, miserabiliter scalpi avida contactu sensibilium. sed si non haberent animam, non utique amarentur. amare et amari dulce mihi erat, magis si et amantis corpore fruerer. venam igitur amicitiae coinquinabam sordibus concupiscentiae candoremque eius obnubilabam

[1] amare *S Knöll Skut. Ver.*: amari *codd.*
[2] fastidiosior *S codd. Knöll Skut. Pell. Ver.*: eo fastidiosior C^2 O^2 *Maur.*

---

[1] A disputed phrase, taken here to mean that A.'s desire for human love is superficial, while he is aware of a deeper desire (for God), and dislikes the fact that his desire does not match up to what God deserves.

BOOK III

1. (1) I came to Carthage and all around me a melting pot of illicit passions was seething. I was not yet in love, but I was in love with the idea of love; and because of the neediness I felt deep down I hated the thought of not being needy enough.[1] I was looking for something to love, loving to love, and I hated the safety of a course free from pitfalls. Ws 14:11 Within myself I was hungry from the lack of inner food: you yourself, my God; but that hunger did not make me want to feast—rather, I had no desire at all for the incorruptible food. This was not because I was already full of such food: instead the more empty I was, the more I disdained it.

So my soul was in a poor state of health, and covered in sores it lay prostrate out of doors, in a pitiable state, Lk 16:20; itching to be scratched through the sensual touch of phys- cf. Jb 2:7–8 ical things. Yet had those things not possessed a soul, they would definitely not be lovable.[2] I enjoyed loving and being loved, and even more so if I got to enjoy the body of my lover. So I used to defile the stream of friendship with the filth of sensual desire, and to overshadow its bright-

---

[2] His longing for reciprocity of love with other souls is a misdirection of his desire for the God who is Love.

CONFESSIONS

de tartaro libidinis, et tamen foedus atque inhonestus, ele-
gans et urbanus esse gestiebam abundanti vanitate. rui
etiam in amorem, quo cupiebam capi. deus meus, misericordia mea, quanto felle mihi suavitatem illam et quam
bonus aspersisti, quia et amatus sum, et perveni occulte
ad vinculum fruendi, et conligabar laetus aerumnosis
nexibus, ut caederer virgis ferreis ardentibus zeli et suspi-
cionum et timorum et irarum atque rixarum.

2. (2) Rapiebant me spectacula theatrica, plena imagi-
nibus miseriarum mearum et fomitibus ignis mei. quid est
quod ibi homo vult dolere cum spectat luctuosa et tragica,
quae tamen pati ipse nollet? et tamen pati vult ex eis dolorem spectator et dolor ipse est voluptas eius. quid est nisi
mirabilis[3] insania? nam eo magis eis movetur quisque, quo
minus a talibus affectibus sanus est, quamquam, cum ipse
patitur, miseria, cum aliis compatitur, misericordia dici
solet. sed qualis tandem misericordia in rebus fictis et
scenicis? non enim ad subveniendum provocatur auditor
sed tantum ad dolendum invitatur, et actori[4] earum ima-
ginum amplius favet cum amplius dolet. et si calamitates
illae hominum, vel antiquae vel falsae, sic agantur ut qui
spectat non doleat, abscedit inde fastidiens et reprehen-

---

3 mirabilis *S codd. Skut. Ver.*: miserabilis *G Maur. Knöll Pel.*
4 actori *O Maur. Pell. Ver.*: auctori *S codd.* Knöll Skut.

---

3 See Introduction, p. xxiii.
4 For Plato emotion was weakness (*Resp.* 10.606–7); for Aristotle watching tragedy effected a purgation (καθάρσις) of emotions (pity and fear: *Poet.*1449b).
5 A. is thinking both of theater and of other forms of representation (such as epic narratives).

ness with my fiendish lust.³ Disgraceful and dishonorable as I was, my overweening vanity made me long to appear refined and civilized. So I rushed into love, wanting love to take me prisoner. My God, my mercy, how good you were, sprinkling that sweet gratification of mine with so much bitterness! For I was loved; and I secretly attained a bond of pleasure; and I was happy to be constrained by burdensome bonds—with the result that I was being beaten with glowing iron rods of jealousy, mistrust, anxieties, rages and quarrelling.

Ps 144:2

Ps 2:9
Gal 5:20

2. (2) I was carried away by the stage shows, which were full of representations of my own unhappy experiences and added fuel to my flames. Why is it that in the theater people are willing to suffer distress when watching sad and tragic events that they nonetheless have no desire to endure themselves? Yet they are willing to suffer distress from watching such events, and the pain itself is their pleasure. What is this but a remarkable madness?⁴ For the more each person is upset by these kinds of emotion, the less they can stay unaffected by them. All the same, when someone endures something on their own it is described as "pitiable," whereas when it is endured together with others it is usually called "compassion." But what is the real meaning of compassion in imaginary events and stage plays?⁵ The audience is not being summoned to assist, but merely invited to feel distress; and the deeper their distress, the more they appreciate the performer of those representations. If, on the other hand, the usual human disasters, either historical or fictitious, are performed in a way that does not cause the spectator to feel distress, that spectator walks out in critical disgust—whereas if they do

dens; si autem doleat, manet intentus et gaudens lacrimat.[5]

(3) Ergo amantur et dolores. certe omnis homo gaudere vult. an cum miserum esse neminem libeat, libet tamen esse misericordem, quod quia non sine dolore est, hac una causa amantur dolores? et hoc de illa vena amicitiae est. sed quo vadit? quo fluit? ut quid decurrit in torrentem picis bullientis, aestus immanes taetrarum libidinum, in quos ipsa mutatur et vertitur per nutum proprium de caelesti serenitate detorta atque deiecta? repudietur ergo misericordia? nequaquam. ergo amentur dolores aliquando, sed cave immunditiam, anima mea, sub tutore deo meo, deo patrum nostrorum et laudabili et superexaltato in omnia saecula, cave immunditiam.

Neque enim nunc non misereor, sed tunc in theatris congaudebam amantibus cum sese fruebantur per flagitia, quamvis haec imaginarie gererent in ludo spectaculi. cum autem sese amittebant, quasi misericors contristabar, et utrumque delectabat tamen.

Nunc vero magis misereor gaudentem in flagitio quam velut dura perpessum detrimento perniciosae voluptatis et amissione miserae felicitatis. haec certe verior misericor-

---

[5] lacrimat. ergo *codd. Ver.*: lacrimae ergo S *codd. Knöll Skut. Vega*: lacrimatur. ergo *Maur.*

feel distress, they stay in their place, completely absorbed, and revel in their own weeping.

(3) Even feelings of distress, then, can be desirable. To be sure, everyone wants to feel enjoyment. Or is it more that, although no one likes to be pitiful, still there is pleasure in being full of pity? And because this state of showing pity incorporates aspects of distress, is it for this reason alone that distress can be desirable? This capacity for pity too is from that source, namely friendship. But what is friendship's course? In what direction does it flow? Why does its current plunge into the maelstrom of boiling pitch, that monstrous fever of hellish desires into which Is 34:9 friendship itself is mutated and transformed—distorted from heavenly serenity and abandoned, and this with its own acquiescence! Is showing pity to be rejected? By no means! So sometimes what is distressing should be embraced: but, O my soul, beware of impurity, for you are under the protection of my God, the God of our fathers, worthy of all praise and exalted for ever, beware of im- Dn 3:52^{LXX} purity!

Even now I still have the capacity to feel pity, but back then, at the theaters, I used to be united with the lovers in their pleasures, when they were reveling in sinful behavior though they were playacting the misdeeds on the stage for entertainment. When the protagonists got themselves lost, it made me feel sad as if I was full of real pity. Yet both contrasting cases caused me to experience delight!

Now, though, I feel more pity for someone who enjoys sinning than someone who has apparently suffered greatly through being deprived of some ruinous pleasure or letting go of some piece of good luck which was doing them

dia, sed non in ea delectat dolor. nam etsi approbatur officio caritatis qui dolet miserum, mallet tamen utique non
esse quod doleret qui germanitus misericors est. si enim
est malivola benivolentia, quod fieri non potest, potest et
ille qui veraciter sinceriterque misereretur cupere esse miseros, ut misereatur. nonnullus itaque dolor approbandus,
nullus amandus est. hoc enim tu, domine deus, qui animas
amas, longe alteque purius quam nos et incorruptibilius
misereris, quod nullo dolore sauciaris. et ad haec quis idoneus?

(4) At ego tunc miser dolere amabam, et quaerebam ut
esset quod dolerem, quando mihi in aerumna aliena et
falsa et saltatoria ea magis placebat actio histrionis meque
alliciebat vehementius qua mihi lacrimae excutiebantur.
quid autem mirum, cum infelix pecus aberrans a grege tuo
et impatiens custodiae tuae turpi scabie foedarer? et inde
erant dolorum amores, non quibus altius penetrarer (non
enim amabam talia perpeti qualia spectare), sed quibus
auditis et fictis tamquam in superficie raderer. quos tamen
quasi ungues scalpentium fervidus tumor et tabes et
sanies horrida consequebatur. talis vita mea numquid vita
erat, deus meus?

3. (5) Et circumvolabat super me fidelis a longe misericordia tua. in quantas iniquitates distabui et sacrilegam

---

6 *Infelix pecus*: combining Virgil's luckless sheep (*Ecl.* 3.3)
with the lost sheep of the gospel (Lk 15:4–8); hence, the defile-
ment of sin is described in terms of disease—"scab" or "mange."

no good. To be sure, this is a truer kind of pity, but not one in which grief finds any delight. For even though a person who is distressed at someone in a pitiful state is to be commended for the charity they show, it would be far preferable if that person who shows sincere pity had nothing to be distressed by in the first place. For if there were such a thing as malign goodwill, which is impossible, it is possible that a person who does feel genuine pity might actually want others to be pitiable, so as to have the experience of pitying them. Some distress, therefore, is acceptable, but none is desirable. For you, Lord, are a lover of souls, and you show pity far more deeply and purely and incorruptibly, because no distress can wound you. And who is equal to this?   2 Cor 2:16

(4) But in those days I was a pitiable creature, in love with feeling distress, and I would seek out occasions for being distressed: whenever the pretended troubles of other people on stage were involved, the more an actor's performance reduced me to tears, the more pleasure it gave me, the more completely it captivated me. Is it surprising that when I was an unfortunate sheep, finding your guardianship irksome and so wandering from your flock, I became defiled with disgusting disease?[6] This was the source of my love of distresses, not the kind to pierce me to my core, for I had no desire to suffer such things as I used to watch, but the kind of fictions that, when I heard them, would merely graze my surface. The consequence of those loves was an inflamed swelling and decay and repulsive pus, as when fingernails scratch a sore. That was my life then—but was it really life at all, O my God?

3. (5) Your constant mercy was encircling me, but at a distance. I was melting away into iniquity, and pursuing

curiositatem[6] secutus sum, ut deserentem te deduceret
me ad ima infida et circumventoria obsequia daemoniorum, quibus immolabam facta mea mala! et in omnibus
flagellabas me. ausus sum etiam in celebritate sollemnita-
tum tuarum, intra parietes ecclesiae tuae, concupiscere et
agere negotium procurandi fructus mortis. unde me ver-
berasti gravibus poenis, sed nihil ad culpam meam, o
tu praegrandis misericordia mea, deus meus, refugium
meum a terribilibus nocentibus, in quibus vagatus sum
praefidenti collo ad longe recedendum a te, amans vias
meas et non tuas, amans fugitivam libertatem.

(6) Habebant et illa studia quae honesta vocabantur
ductum suum intuentem fora litigiosa, ut excellerem in
eis, hoc laudabilior, quo fraudulentior. tanta est caecitas
hominum de caecitate etiam gloriantium. et maior etiam
eram in schola rhetoris, et gaudebam superbe et tumebam
typho, quamquam longe sedatior, domine, tu scis, et re-
motus omnino ab eversionibus quas faciebant eversores
(hoc enim nomen scaevum et diabolicum velut insigne
urbanitatis est), inter quos vivebam pudore impudenti,
quia talis non eram. et cum eis eram et amicitiis eorum
delectabar aliquando, a quorum semper factis abhorre-
bam, hoc est ab eversionibus quibus proterve insectaban-

---

[6] sacrilegam curiositatem O^1 *Maur. Ver. Pell.*: sacrilega curiositate: *S codd. Knöll Skut. OD*

---

[7] I.e., while attending church as a catechumen, as he had from
childhood, he was intent on seduction.

[8] A. quotes Ov. *Fast.* 4.188 and *Rem. am.* 670.

[9] One who teaches rhetoric and oratory; see Introduction,
p. xxii, on A.'s education.

profane curiosity: as a result, even as I was abandoning you, it dragged me down to the depths of impiety and to the sham service of the demonic forces to which I offered my sinful deeds as a sacrifice! In all this you were the one scourging me. At the celebration of your sacred mysteries, and within the walls of your church, I was so insolent that, when I felt passionate desire, I cut a deal to secure the fruit of death.[7] For this you chastised me with severe punishments, but they were scarcely in proportion to my blameworthiness, O my God, my limitless mercy, my refuge from the dreadful crimes which I deviated into—stiffnecked—as I retreated from you, preferring my own ways and not yours, preferring my freedom like a runaway slave.

Rom 7:5

Pss 59:17, 144:2

(6) The end to which my studies (which were deemed "respectable") were directed was "disputatious trials."[8] I was supposed to master these subjects—and the better I was at deceiving, the more praiseworthy I was. How great is the blindness of those who even boast about their being blind! I was top of the class in the rhetor's[9] schoolroom. I reveled in my arrogance, I was puffed up with pride, although, Lord, as you know, I was much more restrained than the Destroyers who were always causing destruction[10] (their name is sinister, devilish, but still a badge of sophistication), and firmly distanced from them. I lived among them, but with a kind of brazen embarrassment, for I was not one of them. I spent time with them and occasionally enjoyed friendships with them, but I used to shudder at what they got up to, namely the havoc that in

---

[10] Probably a group with a common sense of identity and a regular modus operandi, like a modern-day "gang."

tur ignotorum verecundiam, quam proturbarent gratis inludendo atque inde pascendo malivolas laetitias suas. nihil est illo actu similius actibus daemoniorum. quid itaque verius quam eversores vocarentur, eversi plane prius ipsi atque perversi, deridentibus eos et seducentibus fallacibus occulte spiritibus in eo ipso quod alios inridere amant et fallere.

4. (7) Inter hos ego inbecilla tunc aetate discebam libros eloquentiae, in qua eminere cupiebam fine damnabili et ventoso per gaudia vanitatis humanae. et usitato iam discendi ordine perveneram in librum cuiusdam Ciceronis, cuius linguam fere omnes mirantur, pectus non ita. sed liber ille ipsius exhortationem continet ad philosophiam et vocatur "Hortensius." ille vero liber mutavit affectum meum, et ad te ipsum, domine, mutavit preces meas, et vota ac desideria mea fecit alia. viluit mihi repente omnis vana spes, et immortalitatem sapientiae concupiscebam aestu cordis incredibili, et surgere coeperam ut ad te redirem. non enim ad acuendam linguam, quod videbar emere maternis mercedibus, cum agerem annum aetatis undevicensimum iam defuncto patre ante biennium, non ergo ad acuendam linguam referebam illum librum, neque mihi locutio[7] sed quod loquebatur persuaserat.

---

[7] locutio *Löfstedt*: locutionem *codd. edd.*

---

[11] A. was nineteen.

[12] Ironic. His readers would have been familiar with M. Tullius Cicero (106–43 BC).

[13] Or "love of wisdom"; that meaning of the Greek term is always in A.'s mind; cf. *Conf.* 3.4.8.

their insolence they used to inflict upon the modesty of strangers. They would attack without provocation, jeering and then gratifying their malevolent pleasures. There is no behavior more akin to demonic activity than this. So "Destroyers" is the perfect name for them. Certainly they are themselves destroyed and corrupted first, when the spirits of darkness and deceit mock and seduce them by that very behavior with which they love to mock and deceive others.

4. (7) In such company, and at that vulnerable age,[11] I was mastering works of rhetoric. I was desperate to excel on account of the pleasures of human vanity—what a conceited, damnable course of action! In the ordinary course of my studies I had arrived at a work by a certain person called Cicero,[12] whose use of language is almost universally admired even if his character is not. One of his works contains a call to philosophy:[13] it is called the *Hortensius*.[14] That same work effected a change in my feelings, and also changed my prayers to you, Lord. It altered the substance of my supplications and desires. All of a sudden every one of my vain hopes became worthless to me, and with an extraordinary passion of the heart I began to long for immortal wisdom, and I started to arise so as to return to you. Lk 15:18 Not to sharpen my style of delivery (which was what my mother's payments were ostensibly for, now that I had reached the age of nineteen and my father had died two years back[15]), no, not to sharpen my style was I applying myself to this work: and it was not the style of speaking but the content of what was said, that I found persuasive.

[14] A lost work of Cicero extolling the superiority of philosophy over oratory, cf. *Trin.* 14.19.26. Hortensius was an orator and contemporary of Cicero.   [15] Cf. *Conf.* 9.9.19.

(8) Quomodo ardebam, deus meus, quomodo ardebam revolare a terrenis ad te, et nesciebam quid ageres mecum! apud te est enim sapientia. amor autem sapientiae nomen graecum habet philosophiam, quo me accendebant illae litterae. sunt qui seducant per philosophiam magno et blando et honesto nomine colorantes et fucantes errores suos, et prope omnes qui ex illis et supra temporibus tales erant notantur in eo libro et demonstrantur, et manifestatur ibi salutifera illa admonitio spiritus tui per servum tuum bonum et pium: "videte, ne quis vos decipiat per philosophiam et inanem seductionem secundum traditionem hominum, secundum elementa huius mundi et non secundum Christum, quia in ipso inhabitat omnis plenitudo divinitatis corporaliter."

Et ego illo tempore, scis tu, lumen cordis mei, quoniam nondum mihi haec apostolica nota erant, hoc tamen solo delectabar in illa exhortatione, quod non illam aut illam sectam, sed ipsam quaecumque esset sapientiam ut diligerem et quarererem et adsequerer et tenerem atque amplexarer fortiter, excitabar sermone illo et accendebar et ardebam, et hoc solum me in tanta flagrantia refrangebat, quod nomen Christi non erat ibi, quoniam hoc nomen secundum misericordiam tuam, domine, hoc nomen salvatoris mei, filii tui, in ipso adhuc lacte matris tenerum cor meum pie biberat et alte retinebat, et quidquid sine hoc nomine fuisset, quamvis litteratum et expolitum et veridicum, non me totum rapiebat.

5. (9) Itaque institui animum intendere in scripturas sanctas et videre quales essent. et ecce video rem non

---

16 The apostle Paul, in Colossians 2.8–9.

(8) How I burned, my God! How I burned to fly back from earthly things to you, and yet I was unaware of what you were doing with me! For wisdom abides with you. But the love of wisdom, which in Greek is called "philosophy," was the means by which those books enkindled me. There are people who use that impressive, attractive, respectable word to camouflage and obscure their faults, and who lead people astray with their "philosophy." Almost all those who behaved in that way, up to and including Cicero's day, are recorded in the work and exposed: this makes plain the truth of that wholesome challenge of your Spirit, spoken through your good and faithful servant:[16] "See that no one deceives you by philosophy and vain deceit according to human teaching, according to the fundamental principles of this world, and not according to Christ, for in him all the fullness of godhead dwelt in bodily form."

You know, light of my heart, that in those days these writings of the apostle were as yet unknown to me, but this alone was what delighted me in his recommendation: to love and seek and pursue and hold and embrace with all my strength not one sect or another, but wisdom itself, wherever it was to be found. I was roused by his words, kindled and ablaze, and the one thing that checked me in my great passion was the fact that the name of Christ was not there—for in accordance with your mercy, Lord, in early childhood my heart had devoutly imbibed that name of my Savior, your Son, along with my mother's milk, and kept it deep within; and anything which lacked this name, however cultured and polished and truthful, could never take me over completely.

5. (9) So I decided to fix my mind on the Holy Scriptures, to see what kind of thing they really were. What do

compertam[8] superbis neque nudatam pueris, sed incessu humilem, successu excelsam et velatam mysteriis. et non eram ego talis ut intrare in eam possem aut inclinare cervicem ad eius gressus. non enim sicut modo loquor, ita sensi, cum attendi ad illam scripturam, sed visa est mihi indigna quam tullianae dignitati compararem. tumor enim meus refugiebat modum eius et acies mea non penetrabat interiora eius. verum autem illa erat quae cresceret cum parvulis, sed ego dedignabar esse parvulus et turgidus fastu mihi grandis videbar.

6. (10) Itaque incidi in homines superbe delirantes, carnales nimis et loquaces, in quorum ore laquei diaboli et viscum confectum commixtione syllabarum nominis tui et domini Iesu Christi et paracleti consolatoris nostri spiritus sancti. haec nomina non recedebant de ore eorum, sed tenus sono et strepitu linguae; ceterum cor inane veri. et dicebant, "veritas et veritas," et multum eam dicebant mihi, et nusquam erat in eis, sed falsa loquebantur, non de te tantum, qui vere veritas es, sed etiam de istis elementis huius mundi,[9] creatura tua, de quibus etiam vera dicentes philosophos transgredi debui prae amore tuo, mi pater summe bone, pulchritudo pulchrorum omnium.

---

[8] compertam *codd. Maur. Knöll Skut. Ver.*: confectam *codd. al.*   [9] huius mundi *codd. Maur. Ver. Pell.*: mundi *S Knöll Skut.*

---

[17] An echo of a favorite text, Prv 3:34[VL]. See Introduction, p. xxxiv, on A.'s Bible.   [18] Two images combined: a neck bent to the weight of a yoke (for servitude) and an arduous climb (for the weightiness of the task).   [19] Manichaeans. A. does not use that term until *Conf.* 3.10.18: see Introduction, p. xxv.
[20] Cf. Iren. *Haer.* 1.14–15, 6.37.

I find? Something not disclosed to the proud nor made
plain to children, but requiring humility in the approach
yet becoming sublime and cloaked in mystery as one goes
deeper.[17] I was not fit to enter into it, or to bend my neck
to making that ascent.[18] Back then, when I scrutinized
Holy Scripture, I did not feel the way I now do when I
speak of it. Instead it seemed to me unworthy of comparison with the merit of Cicero's writings. My pompos-
ity was repelled by its restraint, while my powers of perception could not penetrate its depths. It was something
which could keep pace in its growth with little children;
but I would not deign to become a little child—I saw
myself as full of importance, I was bloated with disdain.

Ps 8:8;
Lk 18:17

6. (10) And so I fell among men who were crazy in their
pride, excessively unspiritual and garrulous.[19] In their
mouths were demonic snares and birdlime concocted by
mixing together the syllables of your name and that of the
Lord Jesus Christ and of the Holy Spirit, the Advocate,
our Comforter.[20] Those names were on their lips perpetu-
ally, but as nothing more than sound and vocal noises. At
their heart there was not a particle of truth. And they were
constantly declaring, "truth!" and "truth!" They often used
to declare it to me, but it was nowhere among them. Instead they spoke lies, not only about you, who are truly
Truth, but also about the elements of this world (that is,
your creation); whereas I should have bypassed even those
philosophers who do speak truly about those things, and
preferred your love, my Father, my highest Good, Beauty
of all beauties.

Lk 10:30

1 Tm 3:7,
6:9; 2 Tm
2:26

O veritas, veritas, quam intime etiam tum medullae
animi mei suspirabant tibi, cum te illi sonarent mihi
frequenter et multipliciter voce sola et libris multis et
ingentibus! et illa erant fercula in quibus mihi esurienti te
inferebatur pro te sol et luna, pulchra opera tua, sed tamen
opera tua, non tu, nec ipsa prima. priora enim spiritalia
opera tua quam ista corporea, quamvis lucida et caelestia.

At ego nec priora illa, sed te ipsam, te veritas,[10] in qua
non est commutatio nec momenti obumbratio, esuriebam
et sitiebam. et apponebantur adhuc mihi in illis ferculis
phantasmata splendida, quibus iam melius erat amare istum solem saltem istis oculis verum quam illa falsa animo
decepto per oculos. et tamen, quia te putabam, manduca-
bam, non avide quidem, quia nec sapiebas in ore meo
sicuti es (neque enim tu eras illa figmenta inania) nec
nutriebar eis, sed exhauriebar magis. cibus in somnis si-
millimus est cibis vigilantium, quo tamen dormientes non
aluntur; dormiunt enim. at illa nec similia erant ullo modo
tibi, sicut nunc mihi locuta es, quia illa erant corporalia
phantasmata, falsa corpora, quibus certiora sunt vera corpora ista quae videmus visu carneo, sive caelestia sive ter-
restria, cum pecudibus et volatilibus. videmus haec, et
certiora sunt quam cum imaginamur ea. et rursus certius

---

10 te veritas *codd. Maur. Ver.*: veritas S *Knöll Skut.*

---

21 In Manichaeism sun and moon were worshipped as divine;
cf. A. *C. Faust.* 20.2.   22 See *Conf.* 12.7–10; *Gn. litt. imp.*
(AD 393/4; cf. *Retr.* 1.18) 3.7.

23 A. uses the Latin *phantasma* to mean what is imaginary; and
phantasia to mean what ones recalls visually by means of genuine
memory. Cf. *Vera Rel.* 10.18 on phantasms.

O Truth, Truth! How deeply, even then, the marrow of my soul was really sighing with longing for you, while their individual speakers and their many weighty books proclaimed you to me so often, and in so many ways. And as I hungered for you, those were the platters on which they served up to me (instead of you yourself) the sun and moon, which are beautiful works of yours, but "works" is all they are. They are not you yourself, they are not even your primary works,[21] for your spiritual works come before those physical ones, however luminous and heavenly they may be.[22]

But I was hungering and thirsting not for those primary Mt 5:6
works but for you yourself, you who are Truth, in whom is no variation nor shadow of turning. Still they kept plac- Jas 1:17
ing before me platters laden with gorgeous phantasms:[23] though it would have been better to love this sun, which is at least real to our eyes, than those fantastic visions by which our eyes deceive the mind. Because I thought that these were you, I fed on them. To be sure I did not do so eagerly, because in my mouth you did not taste as you really are, even though you were not one of those empty illusions. So I was not nourished by them, but instead was utterly drained. Food in dreams is very like food when we are awake, yet those who sleep are not nourished by eating it, precisely because they are asleep! Those things were not at all like you, O Truth, as you now speak to me—they were imaginary objects, not real physical objects at all. As for the real physical things (whether heavenly or earthly) which we see with our human sight, along with the cattle and birds of the air, those imaginary things made them more definite. We actually do see those things, so they are more definite than when we are imagining them. And

107

imaginamur ea quam ex eis suspicamur alia grandiora et infinita, quae omnino nulla sunt. qualibus ego tunc pascebar inanibus, et non pascebar.

At tu, amor meus, in quem deficio ut fortis sim, nec ista corpora es quae videmus quamquam in caelo, nec ea quae non videmus ibi, quia tu ista condidisti nec in summis tuis conditionibus habes. quanto ergo longe es a phantasmatis illis meis, phantasmatis corporum quae omnino non sunt! quibus certiores sunt phantasiae corporum eorum quae sunt, et eis certiora corpora, quae tamen non es. sed nec anima es, quae vita est corporum (ideo melior vita corporum certiorque quam corpora), sed tu vita es animarum, vita vitarum, vivens te ipsa, et non mutaris, vita animae meae.

(11) Ubi ergo mihi tunc eras et quam longe? et longe peregrinabar abs te, exclusus et a siliquis porcorum quos de siliquis pascebam. quanto enim meliores grammaticorum et poetarum fabellae quam illa decipula! nam versus et carmen et Medea volans utiliores certe quam quinque elementa varie fucata propter quinque antra tenebrarum, quae omnino nulla sunt et occidunt credentem. nam versum et carmen etiam ad vera pulmenta transfero; volantem

---

24 A reference to the invisible angelic sphere.

25 The terms "imaginary" and "imagined" reflect A.'s distinction between *phantasma* and *phantasia*, respectively.

26 Pagan literature (represented by the husks) is preferable to Manichaean heresy, because A. knew the former was only myth and story.

27 I.e., in a dragon chariot: cf. Ov. *Met.* 7.219–36.

28 Cf. Introduction, pp. xxvi–xxvii.

again, we imagine them more surely than we form concep-
tions, on the basis of real things, of other things both colossal and infinite that definitely do not exist. So at that time
I was feeding upon such vacuous things—except that I was
not being fed.

But to you, my Love, I am weak in order to be strong.
You are not one of those bodies that we observe, even if
they are in heaven, nor are you one of those things that we
do not see there,[24] for you created them and do not consider them among your greatest creations. How far removed you are from those imaginary creations of mine,
those imaginary creations that do not even exist! The
imagined[25] forms of things that do in fact exist are more
definite than nonexistent things; and the actual things
themselves are more real than both—but still none of
these things is you. Then again neither are you a soul, for
that is the life in any body, and as the life of bodies, it is
better and more definite than the bodies themselves—
rather you are the life of every soul, the life of lives, yourself a living thing, and what is more, Life of my soul, you
do not change.

(11) Where were you then for me, and how far were
you from me? I was wandering far from you, and was even
denied the pigs' husks, the husks on which I used to feed
them. How much better are the myths of teachers and
poets than those traps![26] The verses and poems and the
"flight of Medea"[27] are of more use than five elements,
complicated in different ways by means of five caves of
shadows, which definitely do not exist and bring death to
anyone who believes in it all.[28] For I can turn even verses

Ps 119:81;
cf. 2 Cor
12:10

Ps 102:27

Lk 15:16

autem Medeam etsi cantabam, non adserebam, etsi cantari audiebam, non credebam. illa autem credidi—vae, vae! quibus gradibus deductus in profunda inferi, quippe laborans et aestuans inopia veri, cum te, deus meus (tibi enim confiteor, qui me miseratus es et nondum confitentem), cum te non secundum intellectum mentis, quo me praestare voluisti beluis, sed secundum sensum carnis quaererem. tu autem eras interior intimo meo et superior summo meo.

Offendi illam mulierem audacem, inopem prudentiae, aenigma Salomonis, sedentem super sellam in foribus et dicentem, "panes occultos libenter edite, et aquam dulcem furtivam bibite." quae me seduxit, quia invenit foris habitantem in oculo carnis meae et talia ruminantem apud me qualia per illum vorassem.

7. (12) Nesciebam enim aliud vere quod est, et quasi acutule movebar ut suffragarer stultis deceptoribus, cum a me quaererent unde malum, et utrum forma corporea deus finiretur et haberet capillos et ungues, et utrum iusti existimandi essent qui haberent uxores multas simul et occiderent homines et sacrificarent de animalibus. quibus rerum ignarus perturbabar, et recedens a veritate ire in

---

29 He means either that he could earning a living from teaching literature or that even these classical sources contain grains of truth, whereas Manichaeism is altogether false.

30 Literally, "the sense of the flesh"; cf. above, *Conf.* 1.6.7, n. 17.

31 Prv 9:13–17^{VL} underpins this, contrasting wisdom and folly.

32 "Outside" for A. often (including here) means "outside the soul/self"; cf. also "within."

33 See Introduction, p. xxvi.

and poetry into true food.[29] Even if I sang of Medea's flight I was not thereby defending it as fact; even if I listened to it being performed I was not believing that it actually happened. But I did believe those teachings—God help me, by what steps was I being dragged down to the depths of Hell! Certainly I was struggling and feverish through my want of truth. For I was seeking you, my God—I confess this to you because you had mercy upon me even before I put my trust in you; I was seeking you not by following my mind's understanding—that capacity by which you willed me to be superior to dumb animals—but according to my capacity for physical sensation.[30] Yet you were deeper within me than the most secret part of me, and greater than the best of me.

I ran up against that shameless woman, totally lacking in wisdom, that riddle of Solomon, sitting upon her chair in the marketplaces and declaring: "Eat willingly of the bread of secrecy! Drink of the sweet water that was stolen!"[31] She seduced me because she found me dwelling outside[32] myself, from a fleshly viewpoint, while within myself I was chewing over only such matters as my fleshly viewpoint enabled me to devour.

7. (12) I had no awareness of that other entity, the true reality, and I was being pushed, quite cleverly, to give my support to ignorant deceivers, when they posed questions to me: Where does evil comes from? Is God bounded by a physical form, and does he have hair and nails? Can those men who had many wives, and who killed people and sacrificed animals, be called righteous?[33] Ignorant of all this as I was, these questions troubled me; and while I thought I was drawing close to the truth I was actually

eam mihi videbar, quia non noveram malum non esse nisi
privationem boni usque ad quod omnino non est. (quod
unde viderem, cuius videre usque ad corpus erat oculis, et
animo usque ad phantasma?)

Et non noveram deum esse spiritum, non cui membra
essent per longum et latum nec cui esse moles esset, quia
moles in parte minor est quam in toto suo, et si infinita sit,
minor est in aliqua parte certo spatio definita quam per
infinitum, et non est tota ubique sicut spiritus, sicut deus.
et quid in nobis esset secundum quod essemus et recte in
scriptura diceremur ad imaginem dei, prorsus ignorabam.

(13) Et non noveram iustitiam veram interiorem, non
ex consuetudine iudicantem sed ex lege rectissima[11] dei
omnipotentis, qua formarentur mores regionum et dierum pro regionibus et diebus, cum ipsa ubique ac semper
esset, non alibi alia nec alias aliter, secundum quam iusti
essent Abraham et Isaac et Iacob et Moyses et David et
illi omnes laudati ore dei. sed eos ab imperitis iudicari

---

[11] rectissima *O Maur. Ver.*: lectissima *S Knöll Skut.*

---

[34] An emphatic triple anaphora of "I did not know" (*non
noveram*).   [35] I.e., his eyes could see (literally) physical things,
and his mind could see (metaphorically, i.e., "perceive") non-
physical things; but the latter were only the empty ideas of Manichaeism.   [36] A. argues for righteousness being conformity to
a divine norm.   [37] *mores* encapsulates ancient custom, pre-
cept, and habitual behavior: it is sometimes evocative of *mores
maiorum*—ancestral custom; at others it draws closer to English
"morals" or "morality," i.e., behavior inculcated by habit and ex-
pectation rather than by law.

moving away from it. For I did not know[34] that evil does not exist except as the privation of good, to the point of complete nonexistence. And how could I perceive this, when for me the act of seeing consisted simply in seeing physical things with the eye and imaginary things with the mind?[35]

And I did not know that God is a spirit and not a being   Jn 4:24 possessing parts with breadth and length, or one consisting of physical mass: after all, any physical mass is less in its parts than in its entirety; and even if it is infinite, it is less in one part of a certain defined size than it is in its infinitude. Thus it is not complete and everywhere like a spirit, like God. What it was in us that caused us to have our being, and to be defined in Scripture as "in the image of God," I had absolutely no idea.

(13) And I did not know the true righteousness[36] that dwells within and that judges not according to what is customary but according to the most equitable law of God almighty, by which the morals[37] of different places and eras were adapted to suit those countries and eras, even though meanwhile the law itself was for all times and all places—not one thing in one place and time, yet another elsewhere.[38] According to that law Abraham was righteous, and Isaac and Jacob and Moses and David and all those men who were declared to be praiseworthy by the mouth of God.[39] But they were being considered unrigh-

---

[38] An intricate play of cognate words, *alibi alia nec alias aliter.*

[39] On righteousness among the patriarchs, cf. *Doctr. Chr.* 3.12.18: "Things which appear blameworthy to the ignorant . . . are entirely figurative" (*quae autem quasi flagitiosa imperitis videntur . . . tota figurata sunt*); also ibid. 3.18.26.

CONFESSIONS

iniquos, iudicantibus ex humano die et universos mores
humani generis ex parte moris sui metientibus, tamquam
si quis nescius in armamentis quid cui membro adcommodatum sit ocrea velit caput contegi et galea calciari et mur-
muret, quod non apte conveniat; aut in uno die indicto a
promeridianis horis iustitio quisquam stomachetur non
sibi concedi quid venale proponere, quia mane concessum
est; aut in una domo videat aliquid tractari manibus a
quoquam servo quod facere non sinatur qui pocula minis-
trat, aut aliquid post praesepia fieri quod ante mensam
prohibeatur, et indignetur, cum sit unum habitaculum et
una familia, non ubique atque omnibus idem tribui. sic
sunt isti qui indignantur, cum audierint illo saeculo licuisse
iustis aliquid quod isto non licet iustis, et quia illis aliud
praecepit deus, istis aliud pro temporalibus causis, cum
eidem iustitiae utrique servierint, cum in uno homine et
in uno die et in unis aedibus videant aliud alii membro
congruere, et aliud iam dudum licuisse, post horam non
licere, quiddam in illo angulo permitti aut iuberi, quod in
isto iuxta vetetur et vindicetur. numquid iustitia varia est
et mutabilis? sed tempora, quibus praesidet, non pariter

---

[40] There is no main verb in this sentence, unless the fifth
word, *iudicari* (considered), is taken as a historic infinitive.

[41] Cf. Virg. *Aen.* 4.569–70, "woman is an inconstant and
changeable creature" (*varium et mutabile semper femina*).

teous by people judging from limited experience, basing their judgment upon human standards and sizing up the universal customs of the human race according to their own practice. They are like someone in an armory who is ignorant of what armor fits what part of the body, and wants his head covered with a greave, and a helmet put on his feet, and then grumbles because they do not fit properly; or like someone, on a day when commerce is forbidden in the afternoon, becoming dyspeptic at not being allowed to set out goods for sale, because in the morning it had been permitted; or like seeing something being handled in a house by some slave or other which even the butler is not allowed to do; or something going on behind the stable that is not allowed at dinner, and then being angry that what goes for one dwelling and one household is not equally enjoined upon each and everyone alike.[40] So it is with those who become angry when they hear of something that was permissible for righteous people in former times but that in their own time is forbidden to righteous people. This is because God has directed them to do one thing and those others to do something different, according to the requirements of particular times, although both sets of people are submitting to the same standard of righteousness, when in the case of one person, on one day, in one household, they see different things appropriate to different groups of people; or something else allowed a short time ago but after a certain time forbidden; or something being permissible or compulsory in one corner which in the corner next to it is forbidden and sanctioned. Surely righteousness is not therefore inconstant and changeable?[41] But the times over which righteousness presides do not proceed equally: they are, after all, tem-

1 Cor 4:3

115

eunt; tempora enim sunt. homines autem, quorum vita super terram brevis est, quia sensu non valent causas conexere saeculorum priorum aliarumque gentium, quas experti non sunt, cum his quas experti sunt, in uno autem corpore vel die vel domo facile possunt videre quid cui membro, quibus momentis, quibus partibus personisve congruat, in illis offenduntur, hic serviunt.

(14) Haec ergo tunc nesciebam et non advertebam, et feriebant undique ista oculos meos, et non videbam. et cantabam carmina et non mihi licebat ponere pedem quemlibet ubilibet, sed in alio atque alio metro aliter atque aliter et in uno aliquo versu non omnibus locis eundem pedem. et ars ipsa qua canebam non habebat aliud alibi, sed omnia simul. et non intuebar iustitiam, cui servirent boni et sancti homines, longe excellentius atque sublimius habere simul omnia quae praecipit et nulla ex parte variari et tamen variis temporibus non omnia simul, sed propria distribuentem ac praecipientem. et reprehendebam caecus pios patres non solum, sicut deus iuberet atque inspiraret, utentes praesentibus verum quoque, sicut deus revelaret, futura praenuntiantes.

8. (15) Numquid aliquando aut alicubi iniustum est diligere deum ex toto corde et ex tota anima et ex tota mente, et diligere proximum tamquam te ipsum? itaque

---

42 On A. and Latin poetry see Introduction, p. xxii. Cf. *Conf.* 1.13.21–22.

43 Manichaeans did not accept that the Old Testament prophesied the future.

poral. Human beings, though, whose life on earth is brief,   Ws 15:9
are incapable of understanding how to link causal factors
from earlier times and other races, of which they have no
knowledge, with factors that they do know about: whereas
when dealing with one body, or day, or household, they
find it easy to see what is proper to each member, and
moment, and part, and person. Thus while they take offense at those unfamiliar matters they do comply with
these conditions.

(14) At that time I did not understand all these matters,
and I paid them no attention. And they were bombarding
my sight on every side—and still I saw nothing. And I was
composing poems and was not allowed to put whatever
foot I liked wherever I liked, but rather in one place or
another depending on which meter it was; and even within
one particular kind of verse the same foot could not go in
every position.[42] And yet the art itself according to which
I composed did not have different rules in different places,
but all were governed alike. And still I was not perceiving
that righteousness, which all good and godly people obey,
is also governed as one, but in a much more transcendent
and exalted way; and it decrees that no part of it should be
mutable, and yet in different eras it nonetheless appor-
tions and direct all things, not in entirely the same way,
but according to what is appropriate for each. And blind
as I was, I found fault with those faithful patriarchs not
only for behaving in their own time as God directed and
inspired them but also for predicting the future, as God
disclosed it.[43]

8. (15) Surely it is never unrighteous anywhere to love
God with all your heart and with all your soul and with all
your mind, and to love your neighbor as yourself? For   Mt 22:37, 39

117

flagitia quae sunt contra naturam ubique ac semper detestanda atque punienda sunt, qualia Sodomitarum fuerunt. quae si omnes gentes facerent, eodem criminis reatu divina lege tenerentur, quae non sic fecit homines ut se illo uterentur modo. violatur quippe ipsa societas quae cum deo nobis esse debet cum eadem natura cuius ille auctor est libidinis perversitate polluitur.

Quae autem contra mores hominum sunt flagitia pro morum diversitate vitanda sunt, ut pactum inter se civitatis aut gentis consuetudine vel lege firmatum nulla civis aut peregrini libidine violetur. turpis enim omnis pars universo suo non congruens. cum autem deus aliquid contra morem aut pactum quorumlibet iubet, etsi numquam ibi factum est, faciendum est, et si omissum, instaurandum, et si institutum non erat, instituendum est. si enim regi licet in civitate cui regnat iubere aliquid quod neque ante illum quisquam nec ipse umquam iusserat, et non contra societatem civitatis eius obtemperatur, immo contra societatem non obtemperatur (generale quippe pactum est societatis humanae oboedire regibus suis), quanto magis deo regnatori[12] universae creaturae suae ad ea quae iusserit sine dubitatione serviendum est. sicut enim in potestatibus societatis humanae maior potestas minori ad oboediendum praeponitur, ita deus omnibus.

---

12 deo regnatori *codd. Skut. Ver.*: deus regnator S *Knöll*

---

44 A. distinguishes *flagitia*, which corrupt the one who commits the wrong, from *facinora* (cf. *Conf.* 3.8.16, below) by which the wrongdoer harms someone else. See also *Doctr. Chr.* 3.10.16.

45 The men of Sodom demanded that two divine messengers (in human guise) should be handed over to them to be raped.

example there are disgraceful actions[44] that are against nature in every place and always attract condemnation and punishment, such as those of the Sodomites.[45] If all nations committed this shameful act, then divine law would hold them guilty on the same charge, namely that God did not make men to exploit one another in such a way. Indeed that actual union that we ought to have with God is violated when the very nature which he created is desecrated by such a perversion of sexual desire.

Gn 19:4–5

But shameful actions that are contrary to ordinary human morality must be avoided in accordance with the multiplicity of prevailing custom, so that what is agreed within a polity, or by national custom, or supported by law, must not be violated because of one person's sexual desire, be he citizen or foreigner. Every part that is not conformed to its whole is a cause for reproach. Yet when God orders something contrary to the custom or agreement of a group of people, even if it has never been done there before, it must be done from then on; and if it has been neglected, it must be restored; and if it had not been established, then now it must be established. For if a king is allowed, in the realm which he rules over, to command something which no one before him nor he himself had ever commanded, and obeying him does not run counter to the common good of the his realm (indeed *not* to obey runs counter to the common good; for it is a universal consensus of human societies to obey their rulers), how much more should we be unhesitatingly compliant with the commands of God, the ruler over all his own creation! For just as in the authorities of human society a greater authority wins a higher obedience than a lesser, so God is obeyed above all.

(16) Item in facinoribus, ubi libido est nocendi sive per contumeliam sive per iniuriam et utrumque vel ulciscendi causa, sicut inimico inimicus, vel adipiscendi alicuius extra commodi, sicut latro viatori, vel evitandi mali, sicut ei qui timetur, vel invidendo, sicut feliciori miserior aut in aliquo prosperatus ei quem sibi aequari timet aut aequalem dolet, vel sola voluptate alieni mali, sicut spectatores gladiatorum aut inrisores aut inlusores quorumlibet.

Haec sunt capita iniquitatis quae pullulant principandi et spectandi et sentiendi libidine aut una aut duabus earum aut simul omnibus, et vivitur male adversus tria et septem, psalterium decem chordarum, decalogum tuum, deus altissime et dulcissime. sed quae flagitia in te, qui non corrumperis? aut quae adversus te facinora, cui noceri non potest? sed hoc vindicas quod in se homines perpetrant, quia etiam cum in te peccant, impie faciunt in animas suas, et mentitur iniquitas sibi sive corrumpendo ac pervertendo naturam suam, quam tu fecisti et ordinasti, vel immoderate utendo concessis rebus, vel in non concessa flagrando in eum usum qui est contra naturam. aut rei tenentur animo et verbis saevientes adversus te et adversus stimulum calcitrantes, aut cum diruptis limitibus humanae societatis laetantur audaces privatis conciliationibus aut diremptionibus, prout quidque delectaverit aut

---

46 An echo of 1 Jn 2:16: "Pride in wealth, desire of the eyes and desire of the flesh."

47 A traditional division of the Decalogue: three commandments refer to love of God, seven to love of neighbor.

48 Cf. A., *B. Coniug.* 11–12.

(16) It is the same with criminal acts, where there is a desire to do harm either by verbal abuse or by physical violence, in either case for the sake of vengeance, as one enemy does to another; or to steal another's wages, as a footpad would from a traveler; or to avoid a misfortune, as in the case of a person one fears; or because of envy, like someone in a pitiable state reacting to someone more fortunate; or someone who has prospered in some activity but is afraid that another will achieve a like success, and dreading the existence of a rival; or by pure enjoyment at another's suffering, like spectators at the gladiatorial shows or those who scoff at others and ridicule them.

These are the principal types of wrongdoing that spring from the desire to control, and observe, and experience sensually, either one of these three, or a pair, or all three together.[46] All this is to live an evil life against the Three and Seven, that psaltery of ten strings that is your Ten Commandments, O God most high and sweet.[47] But what crimes can be committed against you, who cannot be harmed? And what actions can be done against you, who cannot be injured? But you avenge whatever sins people commit against themselves, because when they sin against you, they also profane their own souls, and iniquity is self-deceiving whether in harming and perverting their nature, which you have created and set in its proper place; or by indulging in things that are permissible but doing so to excess, or in being aflame for things which are forbidden, to use them in a way that is against nature.[48] Or those people are considered guilty who rage against you in thought and speech, and who kick against the goads; or the foolhardy, who break down the limits of human society to delight in either coalitions or schisms, depending on

Ps 33:2,
144:9

Ps 27:12

Rom 1:26

Acts 9:5,
26:14

offenderit. et ea fiunt cum tu derelinqueris, fons vitae, qui es unus et verus creator et rector universitatis, et privata superbia diligitur in parte unum falsum.

Itaque pietate humili reditur in te, et purgas nos a consuetudine mala, et propitius es peccatis confitentium, et exaudis gemitus compeditorum, et solvis a vinculis quae nobis fecimus, si iam non erigamus adversus te cornua falsae libertatis, avaritia plus habendi et damno totum amittendi, amplius amando proprium nostrum quam te, omnium bonum.

9. (17) Sed inter flagitia et facinora et tam multas iniquitates sunt peccata proficientium, quae a bene iudicantibus et vituperantur ex regula perfectionis et laudantur spe frugis sicut herba segetis. et sunt quaedam similia vel flagitio vel facinori et non sunt peccata, quia nec te offendunt, dominum deum nostrum, nec sociale consortium, cum conciliantur aliqua in usum vitae, congrua et[13] tempori, et incertum est an libidine habendi, aut puniuntur corrigendi studio potestate ordinata, et incertum est an libidine nocendi. multa itaque facta quae hominibus improbanda viderentur testimonio tuo approbata sunt, et

[13] congrua et S *Knöll Skut.*: congrua G *Pell.*: congruae C D: congruentem O^1: congrue *Ver.*

---

[49] I.e., they give love to what is not the true God and therefore love only partially, rather than loving the whole.

[50] An image of arrogance; cf. Dt 33:17, with Knauer, *Psalmenzitate*, 162.   [51] Alliterative oxymoron (*peccata proficientum*).   [52] I.e., what matters, in addition to doing what is lawful, is right motives.

what delights or offends them. And this is the sort of thing which happens when you are abandoned, O wellspring of life, you who are the one true Creator and Ruler of the universe; and out of personal pride what is loved is a feigned and fractured unity.[49]

So we return to you in humble faithfulness, and you cleanse us of our faulty habits and look with mercy on the sins of those who make their confession, and you hear the groans of those who are shackled, and you free us from the chains we have made for ourselves; and all this if we no longer lift up the horns of our pretended liberty against you,[50] driven by our greed for more possessions and by the hurt of losing them completely, by loving our personal possessions more than you, who are the Good of all. Ps 102:20

Ps 75:4–5

9. (17) Amid these offenses and crimes and so many imperfections, there are the sins of those who are trying their best,[51] and those who judge rightly both criticize these, according to the standard of perfection, and also praise them in the hope that they will bear fruit, like the green blades in the cornfield. There are also certain acts that resemble offenses and crimes but are not actual sins because they do not offend against you, Lord our God, nor against our common fellowship, for example when things are procured for a particular purpose in daily life and are appropriate for the circumstances, and it is unclear whether this is from a wrongful desire for possessions; or again when punishment is meted out with lawful authority from an enthusiasm for discipline, and it is unclear whether this is done from a wrongful desire to cause harm.[52] Thus many acts that people might find reprehensible are endorsed by your validation; and many acts that Mk 4:28

multa laudata ab hominibus te teste damnantur, cum saepe se aliter habet species facti et aliter facientis animus atque articulus occulti temporis.

Cum vero aliquid tu repente inusitatum et improvisum imperas, etiamsi hoc aliquando vetuisti, quamvis causam imperii tui pro tempore occultes et quamvis contra pactum sit aliquorum hominum societatis, quis dubitet esse faciendum, quando ea iusta est societas hominum quae servit tibi? sed beati qui te imperasse sciunt. fiunt enim omnia a servientibus tibi, vel ad exhibendum quod ad praesens opus est, vel ad futura praenuntianda.

10. (18) Haec ego nesciens inridebam illos sanctos servos et prophetas tuos. et quid agebam cum inridebam eos, nisi ut inriderer abs te sensim atque paulatim perductus ad eas nugas ut crederem ficum plorare cum decerpitur et matrem eius arborem lacrimis lacteis? quam tamen ficum si comedisset aliquis sanctus, alieno sane non suo scelere decerptam, misceret visceribus et anhelaret de illa angelos, immo vero particulas dei gemendo in oratione atque ructando. quae particulae summi et veri dei ligatae fuissent in illo pomo, nisi electi sancti dente ac ventre solverentur. et credidi miser magis esse misericordiam praestandam fructibus terrae quam hominibus propter quos nasceren-

---

53 A. returns to the defense of Old Testament narratives.

54 The fig tree exudes a milk-white sap, a skin irritant, if a branch is broken.

55 I.e., a Manichaean holy person. Here A. is mocking the Manichaean belief system. The Elect are the inner circle of initiates; A. never progressed beyond the lower level of Hearer.

attract people's approval are condemned by your testimony. This is because the nature of the action is often variable, as is the intention of the perpetrator while the particular circumstances of the moment may be opaque.

Indeed when you suddenly order something unusual and unexpected, even if it is something that you previously forbade, although for the time being you conceal the reason for your command, and although it contravenes the contractual norms of some human society: who would doubt that it must be carried out, given that a human society, if it is to be just, must be obedient to you? But blessed are those who know that you have given the order! After all, everything comes about through those who serve you, either to show what is needed at the present or to foreshadow the future.

10. (18) I was ignorant of all this. I used to deride those holy servants and prophets of yours.[53] What was I doing when I laughed them to scorn? Except being laughed to scorn by you, as I was drawn gradually, little by little, to those follies, so that I came to believe a fig tree weeps when its fruits are plucked, and its mother-tree weeps milky tears![54] But if someone who was a holy person[55] ate such a fig, plucked by another, not by that person's wicked act, it would be mixed up inside his gut, and by groaning and belching while he prayed he would puff and pant out angels from eating that fig, and even crumbs of God. These crumbs of the supreme and one true God would have stayed fixed in that tree unless they were set free by the teeth and belly of a member of the holy Elect. And in my pitiable state I believed that more mercy ought to be shown to the fruits of the earth than to the human beings for whose sake those fruits came into being. For if anyone

tur. si quis enim esuriens peteret qui manichaeus non esset, quasi capitali supplicio damnanda buccella videretur si ei daretur.

11. (19) Et misisti manum tuam ex alto et de hac profunda caligine eruisti animam meam, cum pro me fleret ad te mea mater, fidelis tua, amplius quam flent matres corporea funera. videbat enim illa mortem meam ex fide et spiritu quem habebat ex te, et exaudisti eam, domine. exaudisti eam nec despexisti lacrimas eius; cum profluentes rigarent terram sub oculis eius in omni loco orationis eius, exaudisti eam. nam unde illud somnium quo eam consolatus es, ut vivere mecum cederet et habere mecum eandem mensam in domo? (quod nolle coeperat aversans et detestans blasphemias erroris mei.) vidit enim se stantem in quadam regula lignea et advenientem ad se iuvenem splendidum hilarem atque arridentem sibi, cum illa esset maerens et maerore confecta. qui cum causas ab ea quaesisset maestitiae suae cotidianarumque lacrimarum, docendi, ut adsolet, non discendi gratia, atque illa respondisset perditionem meam se plangere, iussisse illum (quo secura esset) atque admonuisse, ut attenderet et videret, ubi esset illa, ibi esse et me. quod illa ubi attendit, vidit me iuxta se in eadem regula stantem.

Unde hoc, nisi quia erant aures tuae ad cor eius, o tu bone omnipotens, qui sic curas unumquemque nostrum tamquam solum cures, et sic omnes tamquam singulos?

---

56 The first use of the term in the Latin text.

57 Cf. Introduction, p. xxvi.   58 A. thinks of her as prostrating herself to pray.   59 Perhaps with the "rule of truth" (*regula veritatis*), a way of expressing the whole content of Christian faith, in mind: cf. *Conf.* 8.12.30, with Iren. *Haer.* 2.27.1, 3.2.1, 4.35.5. *Regula* in Latin can be literal or metaphorical.

who was not a Manichaean[56] were hungry and seeking something to eat, and a morsel were given to them, that same morsel would be condemned to death.[57]

11. (19) And you sent forth your hand from on high and rescued my soul from this deep darkness when my mother, your faithful one, wept to you on my behalf more than mothers weep at physical deaths. For she was able to perceive my death through the faith and spirit that you granted her, and you heard her prayer, Lord. You heard her and you did not despise her tears. They poured out and watered the ground beneath her eyes wherever she prayed.[58] Yes, you heard her. Where did that dream come from after all, by which you consoled her so that she let me live with her and have my meals with her at home, when she had become reluctant to allow this because she loathed and detested my blasphemous heresy? She saw herself standing upon a kind of wooden ruler[59] and a glorious young man coming toward her smiling cheerfully at her, though she herself was sorrowful and overcome with grief. When the youth asked her the reasons for her sorrow and her daily weeping (to instruct her, as was fitting, rather than be instructed), she replied that she was bewailing my damnation. At this he warned her most solemnly (to reassure her) to pay attention and observe that where she was, there I was also. As soon as she heard this, she saw me standing beside her on the same ruler.

Where did this come from, unless it was the case that your ears were attentive to her deepest longing, O you who are good and all-powerful, who care for each one of us as if you care for us alone, and so care for us all like individuals?

Ps 144:7

Gal 5:5

cf. Jn 14:3

127

(20) Unde illud etiam, quod cum mihi narrasset ipsum visum, et ego ad id trahere conarer ut illa se potius non desperaret futuram esse quod eram, continuo sine aliqua haesitatione: "non," inquit, "non enim mihi dictum est, 'ubi ille, ibi et tu,' sed, 'ubi tu, ibi et ille.'" confiteor tibi, domine, recordationem meam, quantum recolo, quod saepe non tacui, amplius me isto per matrem vigilantem responso tuo, quod tam vicina interpretationis falsitate turbata non est et tam cito vidit quod videndum fuit (quod ego certe, antequam dixisset, non videram), etiam tum fuisse commotum quam ipso somnio quo feminae piae gaudium tanto post futurum ad consolationem tunc prae- sentis sollicitudinis tanto ante praedictum est.

Nam novem ferme anni secuti sunt quibus ego in illo limo profundi ac tenebris falsitatis, cum saepe surgere conarer et gravius alliderer, volutatus sum, cum tamen illa vidua casta, pia et sobria, quales amas, iam quidem spe alacrior, sed fletu et gemitu non segnior, non desineret horis omnibus orationum suarum de me plangere ad te, et intrabant in conspectum tuum preces eius, et me tamen dimittebas adhuc volvi et involvi illa caligine.

12. (21) Et dedisti alterum responsum interim quod recolo. nam et multa praetereo, propter quod propero ad ea quae me magis urguent confiteri tibi, et multa non memini. dedisti ergo alterum per sacerdotem tuum, quen-

---

60 Echoed in both Roman marriage (Quint. *Inst.* 1.7.28: "Where you are called Gaius, there I am called Gaia"—*ubi tu Gaius, ibi ego Gaia*) and Old Testament marriage (Ru 1:16–17).
    61 Cf. *Conf.* 9.8.17.

(20) From this experience came another. When she had told her vision to me and I was trying to persuade her to this conclusion, that she should not despair of one day becoming what I already was, she declared at once and without hesitation, "No, for it was not said to me, 'Where he is, there you will be,' but 'Where you are, there he will be also.'"[60] I confess to you, Lord, my recollection, as I remember it, and I have spoken of it often: I was more disturbed by that response of yours through my ever-vigilant mother, because of the fact that she was not misled by a false interpretation so close to the true one, and because she so quickly saw what was meant to be apparent in it, which I, to be sure, had not seen before she spoke. That moved me even more than did the dream itself, in which a devout woman's joy, promised for the distant future, had—to console present anxiety—been foretold so far in advance.

Almost nine years were to follow, in which I wallowed in the slime of the abyss and the shadows of falsehood. Often I tried to get myself out, but I was flung back down even deeper. From then on indeed, the hopes of that virtuous widow, devout and temperate, such as you love, grew yet more eager in her hope, while her weeping and groaning did not slacken. She persisted in lamenting over me in prayer at all hours, and her prayers entered into your presence; and still you persisted in sending me forth to be entangled and overwhelmed in that darkness.

12. (21) You gave her another answer in the meantime, which I also recall. There is much that I am omitting because I am hurrying to those events that particularly compel me to confess you; and there is much I have forgotten.[61] So you gave her another answer by means of a priest

Ps 69:2

cf. 1 Tm 5:3–16

Ps 88:2

dam episcopum nutritum in ecclesia et exercitatum in libris tuis. quem cum illa femina rogasset ut dignaretur mecum conloqui et refellere errores meos et dedocere me mala ac docere bona (faciebat enim hoc, quos forte idoneos invenisset), noluit ille, prudenter sane, quantum sensi postea. respondit enim me adhuc esse indocilem, eo quod inflatus essem novitate haeresis illius et nonnullis quaestiunculis iam multos imperitos exagitassem, sicut illa indicaverat ei. "sed" inquit "sine illum ibi. tantum roga pro eo dominum. ipse legendo reperiet quis ille sit error et quanta impietas."

Simul etiam narravit se quoque parvulum a seducta matre sua datum fuisse manichaeis, et omnes paene non legisse tantum verum etiam scriptitasse libros eorum, sibique apparuisse nullo contra disputante et convincente quam esset illa secta fugienda: itaque fugisse. quae cum ille dixisset atque illa nollet adquiescere, sed instaret magis deprecando et ubertim flendo, ut me videret et mecum dissereret, ille iam substomachans taedio, "vade" inquit "a me. ita vivas, fieri non potest, ut filius istarum lacrimarum pereat." quod illa ita se accepisse inter conloquia sua mecum saepe recordabatur, ac si de caelo sonuisset.

of yours, a certain bishop[62] who had been brought up in the Church and was learned in the Scriptures. That woman had asked him to deign to speak with me and refute my errors and disabuse me of my wrong ways and teach me good ones, as he habitually did when he found people apt for such instruction. But he refused. This was surely a wise decision, I realized later. For he replied that I was still hardened against learning, all the more because I was puffed up with the novelty of that heresy and I had already been harrying quite a few people who were unskilled in debate with some nitpicking questions—just as she had warned him. "But," he went on, "leave him be awhile. Only pray to the Lord for him. He will discover, by reading, what a mistake that heresy is, and what a gross impiety."

At the same time the bishop told her how he too had been enticed away from his mother while still quite young and delivered into the hands of the Manichaeans: there he had not only read but also copied out almost all their books. He had come to realize, without anyone arguing or persuading him, how that sect ought to be shunned. So he had shunned it. When he had told her this, she was reluctant to agree with him, but pressed him even harder with prayers and copious tears to meet me and have discussions with me. Eventually he became irritated by the monotony of this and told her, "Let me be! On your life, it is impossible that the son of your tears should perish!" As she often used to reminisce in her conversations with me, she took those words as pronouncements resounding from heaven.

[62] All bishops must first have been ordained priest—both descriptions can be applied to one man, therefore, at the same time.

LIBER IV

1. (1) Per idem tempus annorum novem, ab undevicensimo anno aetatis meae usque ad duodetricensimum, se-
ducebamur et seducebamus, falsi atque fallentes in variis
cupiditatibus, et palam per doctrinas quas liberales vocant, occulte autem falso nomine religionis, hic superbi,
ibi superstitiosi, ubique vani, hac popularis gloriae sec-
tantes inanitatem, usque ad theatricos plausus et conten-
tiosa carmina et agonem coronarum faenearum et specta-
culorum nugas et intemperantiam libidinum, illac autem
purgari nos ab istis sordibus expetentes, cum eis qui appel-
larentur electi et sancti afferremus escas de quibus nobis
in officina aqualiculi sui fabricarent angelos et deos per
quos liberaremur. et sectabar ista atque faciebam cum
amicis meis per me ac mecum deceptis.

Inrideant me arrogantes et nondum salubriter pro-
strati et elisi a te, deus meus, ego tamen confitear tibi

---

1 AD 372/3–381/2.

2 A. mingles singular and plural, switching between himself
and his fellow Manichaeans.

3 On the liberal arts, cf. Introduction, p. xxii.

4 For this opening sentence as a rhetorical tour-de-force, see
Introduction, p. xxvi.

BOOK IV

1. (1) All through this same nine-year period from my nineteenth to my twenty-eighth year,[1] we were being led astray and leading others astray,[2] we were deceived and deceiving in all kinds of desires: openly, by teaching the 2 Tm 3:13 subjects known as "liberal,"[3] but secretly under the name of that so-called religion. In the case of the one we were arrogant, in the case of the other we were superstitious, and we were vain about everything! Where education was concerned we were pursuing the vacuity of popular renown, even to the extent of applause for performances, and competitive compositions, and contests for garlands that would wither, and the triviality of stage shows, and sensual passions that were out of control. Where religion was concerned, on the other hand, we were longing for cleansing from those base impulses when we used to fetch food for those who were known as "elect" and "holy," out of which, in the "workshop of their bellies," they were to manufacture for us the angels and gods who would bring about our freedom.[4] And I followed it all, and practiced it with my friends: through me, and with me, they were deceived.

Let them laugh at me, those who are arrogant, who have not yet been laid low and struck down for their own good, O my God: and still I shall confess to you my mani-

133

dedecora mea in laude tua. sine me, obsecro, et da mihi circuire[1] praesenti memoria praeteritos circuitus erroris mei et immolare tibi hostiam iubilationis. quid enim sum ego mihi sine te nisi dux in praeceps? aut quid sum, cum mihi bene est, nisi sugens lac tuum aut fruens te, cibo qui non corrumpitur? et quis homo est quilibet homo, cum sit homo? sed inrideant nos fortes et potentes, nos autem infirmi et inopes confiteamur tibi.

2. (2) Docebam in illis annis artem rhetoricam, et victoriosam loquacitatem victus cupiditate vendebam. malebam tamen, domine, tu scis, bonos habere discipulos, sicut appellantur boni, et eos sine dolo docebam dolos, non quibus contra caput innocentis agerent sed aliquando pro capite nocentis. et deus, vidisti de longinquo lapsantem in lubrico et in multo fumo scintillantem fidem meam, quam exhibebam in illo magisterio diligentibus vanitatem et quaerentibus mendacium, socius eorum. in illis annis unam habebam non eo quod legitimum vocatur coniugio cognitam, sed quam indagaverat vagus ardor inops prudentiae, sed unam tamen, ei quoque servans tori fidem, in qua sane experirer exemplo meo quid distaret inter coniugalis placiti modum, quod foederatum esset generandi gratia, et pactum libidinosi amoris, ubi proles etiam contra votum nascitur, quamvis iam nata cogat se diligi.

---

[1] circuire *S Knöll Skut.*: circumire *codd. Maur. Ver.*

---

5 I.e., with God.

6 While he was a Manichaean.

7 Cf. Arist. *Rhet* 1.1.12 for the orator's need to be able to argue both sides.

fold disgrace, and shall do so to your praise. Permit me, in
this present memoir, allow me, I pray, to encapsulate the
whole cycle of my heretical belief, now long past, and
bring an offering to you, a sacrifice of thanksgiving. What
am I to myself, without you, if not the director of my own
downfall? Again, what am I when I am in a better state,[5]
if not a babe sucking milk from you, or tasting you, the
food which is imperishable? Again, what kind of a person
is anyone who is a human being and nothing more? Yet
though the strong and powerful laugh at us, still we who
are poor and weak will make our confession to you.

2. (2) During those years[6] I used to teach the art of
rhetoric—I who was enslaved by desire was selling all-
conquering eloquence. Yet as you know, Lord, I preferred
to have good pupils (in the ordinary sense of the term
"good") and I was teaching deceit to those who were not
then deceivers, not so that they would act against the lives
of the innocent but so that sometimes they would protect
the guilty.[7] God, you saw from afar how I stumbled in slippery places, and the glimmer of integrity in that lightless
murk that I manifested in my role as teacher to those who
loved vanity and sought after lies—and I was of their company. During those years I kept to one woman, whom
my roving desire, completely lacking in self-restraint, had
pursued. But it was not that form of union which alone is
recognized as legitimate. Still, she was the only one, and I
kept faith with her as with a spouse. With her I experienced, through my own behavior, what a gulf separates
a proper style of marriage, a covenant entered into for
the sake of procreation, and a transaction based on erotic
desire, when any offspring are born despite the couple's
prayers—though once they have been born they make
loving them inevitable.

Ps 106:47

Ps 27:5–6

Ps 50:14

Ps 8:3;
1 Cor 3:1–2

Ps 74:21

Ps 72:18

Ps 4:2

(3) Recolo etiam, cum mihi theatrici carminis certamen inire placuisset, mandasse mihi nescio quem haruspicem, quid ei dare vellem mercedis ut vincerem, me autem foeda illa sacramenta detestatum et abominatum respondisse, nec si corona illa esset immortaliter aurea muscam pro victoria mea necari sinere. necaturus enim erat ille in sacrificiis suis animantia, et illis honoribus invitaturus mihi suffragatura daemonia videbatur. sed hoc quoque malum non ex tua castitate repudiavi, deus cordis mei. non enim amare te noveram, qui nisi fulgores corporeos cogitare non noveram. talibus enim figmentis suspirans anima nonne fornicatur abs te et fidit in falsis et pascit ventos? sed videlicet sacrificari pro me nollem daemonibus, quibus me illa superstitione ipse sacrificabam. quid est enim aliud ventos pascere quam ipsos pascere, hoc est errando eis esse voluptati atque derisui?

3. (4) Ideoque illos planos quos mathematicos vocant plane consulere non desistebam, quod quasi nullum eis esset sacrificium et nullae preces ad aliquem spiritum ob divinationem dirigerentur. quod tamen christiana et vera pietas consequenter repellit et damnat. bonum est enim confiteri tibi, domine, et dicere, "miserere mei: cura animam meam, quoniam peccavi tibi," neque ad licentiam peccandi abuti indulgentia tua, sed meminisse dominicae vocis: "ecce sanus factus es; iam noli peccare, ne quid tibi

---

8 Latin *sacramenta*; the pre-Christian meaning is a legal pact or oath. A. expects his readers to recognize it also as a term for the eucharist.

9 Cf. A. *C. Faust.* 22.8.

(3) I remember too that when I had decided to enter a competition for reciting a poem in the theater, some fortune-teller sent word to me, asking what I was prepared to pay him to ensure my victory. I replied that I loathed and detested those disgusting rites[8]—not even if the victor's prize were an unfading crown of gold would I allow so much as a fly to be sacrificed to secure my victory. For he was apparently going to kill some living creatures in his sacrificial rites, and by means of those ceremonies was going to invoke the support of demons on my behalf. I did reject this evil also, but not out of pure devotion to you, O God of my heart. For I did not understand how to love you, since I did not understand how to imagine any kind of light except that which is physical.[9] Surely the soul that sighs after such fairytales is proving unfaithful to you, trusting in what is false, and supplying food for the winds? But certainly I wanted no sacrifices to demons on my behalf, even though I was sacrificing myself to them by means of my superstitious beliefs. What else does "supplying food to the winds" mean, if it is not a reference to feeding demons? In other words, causing them pleasure and laughter by going astray?

3. (4) To be sure I continued to consult those cheats known as astrologers, because it seemed to be the case that they practiced no sacrifice nor did they invoke any spirits in making their predictions. Even so, true Christian faith quite properly rejects and condemns that art. It is a good thing to confess to you, Lord, and to say, "Have mercy upon me: heal my soul for I have sinned against you," and not to abuse your forgiveness as if it were a permission to keep sinning but to remember the words of the Lord Jesus: "Look, you have been made well; now

Ps 73:27
Hos 12:1

Pss 92:1,
51:4

137

deterius contingat." quam totam illi salubritatem interfi-
cere conantur cum dicunt, "de caelo tibi est inevitabilis
causa peccandi" et "Venus hoc fecit aut Saturnus aut
Mars," scilicet ut homo sine culpa sit, caro et sanguis et
superba putredo, culpandus sit autem caeli ac siderum
creator et ordinator. et quis est hic nisi deus noster, suavi-
tas et origo iustitiae, qui reddes unicuique secundum
opera eius et cor contritum et humilatum non spernis?

(5) Erat eo tempore vir sagax, medicinae artis peritissimus atque in ea nobilissimus, qui proconsul[2] manu sua
coronam illam agonisticam imposuerat non sano capiti
meo, sed non ut medicus. nam illius morbi tu sanator, qui
resistis superbis, humilibus autem das gratiam. numquid
tamen etiam per illum senem defuisti mihi aut destitisti
mederi animae meae? quia enim factus ei eram familiarior
et eius sermonibus (erant enim sine verborum cultu viva-
citate sententiarum iucundi et graves) adsiduus et fixus
inhaerebam, ubi cognovit ex conloquio meo libris gene-
thliacorum esse me deditum, benigne ac paterne monuit
ut eos abicerem neque curam et operam rebus utilibus
necessariam illi vanitati frustra impenderem, dicens ita se
illa didicisse ut eius professionem primis annis aetatis suae
deferre voluisset qua vitam degeret et, si Hippocraten

---

[2] proconsul S *Knöll Skut*.: proconsule *codd*: pro consule *Ver.*

---

[10] Vindicianus, cf. *Conf.* 7.6.8; doctor to Valentinian II. Cf. A.
Ep. 138.13.   [11] More literally, "the books of birth-horoscope
forecasters." Cf. A. *Doctr. Chr.* 2.21.32.

[12] The name of Hippocrates of Cos (fl. mid-fifth century BC)
is associated with a number of medical and scientific writings,
known as the Hippocratic Corpus, standard medical works in A.'s
time, though mostly in Latin translations.

do not sin, lest something worse befall you!" They try to destroy that entire message of salvation when they say, "The cause of your sinning is unavoidable and is sent from heaven," and, "Venus did this—or Saturn—or Mars"! This is obviously done to absolve human beings—who are flesh and blood and proud putrefaction—from all blame; by making the Creator and Designer of the sky and stars the one at fault instead. And who is that if not you, our God, our sweet Source of righteousness, who repay each person according to their actions, and do not reject the contrite and lowly heart? Jn 5:14

Ps 51:17

(5) At that time there was a shrewd man, as skilled as he was distinguished in the art of medicine, who during his term as proconsul had with his own hand placed the victor's garland on my disordered head.[10] He did not do so in his role as a physician, for you are the Healer of that disease from which I suffered, when you resist the proud but give grace to the humble. Surely even through this old man you did not fail me, or refrain from curing my soul? For I got to know him rather well, and found that the liveliness of his opinions, though not elegantly expressed, was pleasingly serious. So I began to pay constant and careful attention to his conversation. When he found out from something I said that I was a devotee of books of horoscopes,[11] he advised me, with fatherly gentleness, to throw them away, and not to make my care and diligence over important matters depend—fruitlessly—upon such nonsense. He said that he had learned these subjects in his early years and as a result had wanted to declare it as the profession by which he would make his living: for if he had made sense of the writings of Hippocrates,[12] he could

Jas 4:6;
1 Pt 5:5

intellexisset, et illas utique litteras potuisse intellegere; et
tamen non ob aliam causam se postea illis relictis medicinam adsecutum, nisi quod[3] eas falsissimas comperisset et
nollet vir gravis decipiendis hominibus victum quaerere.
"at tu" inquit "quo te in hominibus sustentas, rhetoricam
tenes, hanc autem fallaciam libero studio, non necessitate
rei familiaris, sectaris. quo magis mihi te oportet de illa
credere, qui eam tam perfecte discere elaboravi, quam ex
ea sola vivere volui." a quo ego cum quaesissem quae causa
ergo faceret ut multa inde vera pronuntiarentur, respondit
ille ut potuit, vim sortis hoc facere in rerum natura usquequaque diffusam. si enim de paginis poetae cuiuspiam
longe aliud canentis atque intendentis, cum forte quis
consulit, mirabiliter consonus negotio saepe versus exiret,
mirandum non esse dicebat si ex anima humana superiore
aliquo instinctu nesciente quid in se fieret, non arte sed
sorte, sonaret aliquid quod interrogantis rebus factisque
concineret.

(6) Et hoc quidem ab illo vel per illum procurasti mihi,
et quid ipse postea per me ipsum quaererem, in memoria
mea deliniasti. tunc autem nec ipse nec carissimus meus
Nebridius, adulescens valde bonus et valde castus,[4] inri-
dens totum illud divinationis genus, persuadere mihi potuerunt ut haec abicerem, quoniam me amplius ipsorum
auctorum movebat auctoritas et nullum certum quale

---

3 quod *om. S*   4 castus *S Knöll Skut.*: cautus *codd. Ver.*

---

13 On the concept of "a kind of sympathy" (or "coordination
of experience") in the universe, see Introduction, p. xxiv.

14 Nebridius had an estate near Carthage, where he met A.;
he later followed him to Italy. Cf. A. *Conf.* 6.10.17, 7.2.3; *Ep.* 3–14.

surely make sense of these writings too. Nonetheless he had afterward given these subjects up and pursued medicine for precisely the reason that he had discovered them to be a complete sham, and had no desire, as a man of authority, to make his living by deceiving people. "But," he went on, "you stick to rhetoric as a means of making your living in society, yet you pursue that false trickery by free inclination and not because you need to make some income. For that reason you should believe what I say about this subject, for I once labored so thoroughly to acquire knowledge of it as to wish to make a living by it alone." When I then asked him how it therefore came about that so many predictions were made by this means which came true, he replied, as best he could, that the force of chance, all-pervasive in the universe, brought this about. For example, he said: if a person by chance consulted the pages of some poet (who wrote, and meant, something very different) and found that a line turned out to be extraordinarily appropriate to the business they had in hand, it would hardly be surprising if—by chance rather than skill—some part of the human soul (by some higher instinct that was unaware of what was taking place within itself) chimed to some extent, and was consonant with, the circumstances and actions of the questioner.[13]

(6) Whether it was by him or through him, you made provision for my needs, and you sketched in my memory something that later I would be able to inquire into for myself. At the time, though, neither he nor my dear friend Nebridius (a solidly good and modest[14] young man who ridiculed the whole subject of divination) could convince me to reject it. This was because the prestige of the writers themselves held more weight with me, though I had not

quaerebam documentum adhuc inveneram, quo mihi sine
ambiguitate appareret, quae ab eis consultis vera dicerentur, forte vel sorte non arte inspectorum siderum dici.

4. (7) In illis annis quo primum tempore in municipio
quo natus sum docere coeperam, comparaveram amicum
societate studiorum nimis carum, coaevum mihi et conflorentem flore adulescentiae. mecum puer creverat et pariter in scholam ieramus pariterque luseramus. sed nondum
erat sic amicus, quamquam ne tunc quidem sic, uti est
vera amicitia, quia non est vera nisi cum eam tu agglutinas
inter haerentes tibi caritate diffusa in cordibus nostris per
spiritum sanctum, qui datus est nobis. sed tamen dulcis
erat nimis, cocta fervore parilium studiorum. nam et a fide
vera, quam non germanitus et penitus adulescens tenebat,
deflexeram eum in superstitiosas fabellas et perniciosas,
propter quas me plangebat mater. mecum iam errabat in
animo ille homo, et non poterat anima mea sine illo. et
ecce tu imminens dorso fugitivorum tuorum, deus ultionum et fons misericordiarum simul, qui convertis nos ad
te miris modis, ecce abstulisti hominem de hac vita, cum
vix explevisset annum in amicitia mea, suavi mihi super
omnes suavitates illius vitae meae.

(8) Quis laudes tuas enumerat unus in se uno quas

---

15 I.e., Thagaste.

16 This friendship is emblematic of A.'s investment in empty
shadows of true faith, including friendships (on "true friendship"
cf. Cic. *Amic.* 6.20). This may be why the friend is not named: see
Introduction, p. xxi.

17 A. presents the friendship via the metaphor of the sweeter
taste of a fruit that is fully ripened.

18 Cf. *Conf.* 6.1.1, 16.26.

yet found any absolute proof of the kind I was looking for, to assure me beyond doubt that the things people said they had predicted accurately when consulted were only predicted by luck or blind chance, and not through their skill in astrology.

4. (7) In those years when I first began teaching in the town where I was born,[15] I had made a friend who was all too dear to me because we were united by our common interests.[16] He was the same age as I, and, like me, was maturing into the bloom of early adulthood. He had grown up with me as a boy, we had gone to school together and played together. But he was not yet such a friend to me then as he became afterward: although even then it was not that true friendship, which can only really exist when you cement it between those who hold fast to you by means of the love that is shed abroad in our hearts by the Holy Spirit, which has been given to us. But yet he was too   Rom 5:5 sweet, ripened by the warmth of our shared interests.[17] I had even wrenched him away from the true faith, to which he had no heartfelt or profound allegiance during his adolescence, and toward the superstitious and deadly fictions that my mother so lamented. Now he too, with me, was wandering from the right path as far as intellect was concerned, and my soul was helpless without him. Yet see how you were intent upon us as we turned our backs on you and fled, O God. You, both a God of vengeance and a   Ps 94:1 wellspring of pity[18] together, you convert us to you in wonderful ways; and see—you took this man, my friend, out of this life, when my friendship with him, which had barely lasted a year, was delightful to me above all other delights in my life.

(8) What individual can recount your praises that he   cf. Ps 106:2

143

expertus est? quid tunc fecisti, deus meus, et quam investigabilis abyssus iudiciorum tuorum? cum enim laboraret
ille febribus, iacuit diu sine sensu in sudore laetali et, cum
desperaretur, baptizatus est nesciens, me non curante et
praesumente id retinere potius animam eius quod a me
acceperat, non quod in nescientis corpore fiebat. longe
autem aliter erat. nam recreatus est et salvus factus, statimque, ut primo cum eo loqui potui (potui autem mox ut
ille potuit, quando non discedebam et nimis pendebamus
ex invicem), temptavi apud illum inridere, tamquam et illo
inrisuro mecum baptismum quem acceperat mente atque
sensu absentissimus, sed tamen iam se accepisse didicerat.
at ille ita me exhorruit ut inimicum admonuitque mirabili
et repentina libertate ut, si amicus esse vellem, talia sibi
dicere desinerem. ego autem stupefactus atque turbatus
distuli omnes motus meos, ut convalesceret prius essetque
idoneus viribus valetudinis, cum quo agere possem quod
vellem. sed ille abreptus dementiae meae, ut apud te ser-
varetur consolationi meae. post paucos dies me absente
repetitur febribus et defungitur.

(9) Quo dolore contenebratum est cor meum, et quidquid aspiciebam mors erat. et erat mihi patria supplicium
et paterna domus mira infelicitas, et quidquid cum illo
communicaveram, sine illo in cruciatum immanem verte-
rat. expetebant[5] eum undique oculi mei, et non dabatur.

---

[5] expetebant S *Knöll Skut.*: expectabant *codd. Ver.*

---

[19] I.e., A. doubted the power of the outward, physical sign to
effect real spiritual change.

[20] A. means his parental home in Thagaste; but the metaphor
of the prodigal (Lk 15:11–32) is also evoked.

has experienced in himself alone? What did you then do, my God? How unsearchable are the depths of your judgements? When he was struggling with fever, he lay senseless for a long time in a mortal sweat, and when all hope was lost he was baptized while unconscious. I had no objection, and assumed that his soul would rather retain what it had received from me, and not what was being done to an unconscious body.[19] But things turned out very differently. For he rallied and recovered. And at once, as soon as I was able to speak with him (for I was able as soon as he was able, since I never left him and we clung too much to one another) I tried to tease him, as if he too would join me in mocking that baptism which he had received when he was completely out of his mind, and out of his senses. But by now he had learned that he had received it: he shrank from me as if I were his adversary, and with a sudden and remarkable lack of constraint he warned me that if I wanted to be his friend I had better stop saying such things to him. I was stunned and bewildered. I postponed all of my arguments until he recovered and had sufficient strength and health for me to dispute with him as I wished. But he was snatched away from these delusions of mine, so that he could be saved and so abide with you, for my consolation. After a few days, while I was not present, he was struck by fever once more, and died.

(9) How my heart was overshadowed with grief! And whatever I looked upon, it was death. My native land was torture to me; and my father's house[20] made me extremely unhappy. Everything that I had shared in common with my friend had turned to dreadful torment without him. My eyes kept looking for him everywhere, but they were

Ps 36:6;
Rom 11:33

Lam 5:17

CONFESSIONS

et oderam omnia, quod non haberent eum, nec mihi iam dicere poterant, "ecce veniet," sicut cum viveret, quando absens erat. factus eram ipse mihi magna quaestio, et interrogabam animam meam quare tristis esset et quare conturbaret me valde, et nihil noverat respondere mihi. et si dicebam, "spera in deum," iuste non obtemperabat, quia verior erat et melior homo quem carissimum amiserat quam phantasma in quod sperare iubebatur. solus fletus erat dulcis mihi et successerat amico meo in deliciis animi mei.

5. (10) Et nunc, domine, iam illa transierunt, et tempore lenitum est vulnus meum. possumne audire abs te, qui veritas es, et admovere aurem cordis mei ori tuo, ut dicas mihi cur fletus dulcis sit miseris? an tu, quamvis ubique adsis, longe abiecisti a te miseriam nostram, et tu in te manes, nos autem in experimentis volvimur? et tamen nisi ad aures tuas ploraremus, nihil residui de spe nostra fieret. unde igitur suavis fructus de amaritudine vitae carpitur, gemere et flere et suspirare et conqueri? an hoc ibi dulce est, quod speramus exaudire te? recte istuc in precibus, quia desiderium perveniendi habent. num in dolore amissae rei et luctu, quo tunc operiebar? neque enim sperabam revivescere illum aut hoc petebam lacrimis, sed tantum dolebam et flebam. miser enim eram et

---

21 Cf. *Conf.* 3.6.10, n. 28.

22 Still evoking Ps 42, "My tears have been my food day and night" (42:3).

23 Cf. *Conf.* 3.2.2–3 on enjoying watching suffering. This type of reasoned investigation is called a *quaestio*.

disappointed. I hated everything because he was missing from everything, and there was nothing to say to me any longer: "Look—he is going to come!" as they had done when he was alive but not present. I had become the subject of my own questioning, and I challenged my soul as to why it was sad, and why it kept disquieting me so much: but it had no idea how to reply to me. And if I used to say, "Hope in God," my soul would not obey me, and rightly so, because the human being whom I had lost when he was so very dear to me was truer and better than the imaginary divinity[21] in which I kept being told to put my hope. Weeping was the only thing that held any sweetness for me, and that took the place of my friend in bringing delight to my mind.[22]

5. (10) In this present time, Lord, all that has already passed away, and time has soothed my wound. Am I able to hear from you who are Truth, and to turn the ear of my heart to your lips, so that you can tell me why weeping is sweet to those who are unhappy?[23] Or have you set our wretchedness at a distance from yourself (although you are present everywhere), while you abide in yourself, but we are embroiled in trials? Yet unless we directed our weeping for you to hear, not a particle of hope would be left to us. So where is it plucked from, this sweet fruit from the bitterness of life, this groaning and weeping and sighing and lamenting? Or is it sweet only inasmuch as we hope to hear you respond? That is right in the matter of our prayers, because their intended purpose is to reach you. But surely, when it came to grief and sorrow for what I had lost, there was no purpose in my being overwhelmed? For I was not expecting to restore him to life, nor was this the purpose of my weeping—yet still I grieved

Ps 42:5

Ps 42:5

147

amiseram gaudium meum. an et fletus res amara est et,
prae fastidio rerum quibus prius fruebamur et tunc ab eis
abhorremus, delectat?

6. (11) Quid autem ista loquor? non enim tempus quae-
rendi nunc est, sed confitendi tibi. miser eram, et miser
est omnis animus vinctus amicitia rerum mortalium, et
dilaniatur cum eas amittit, et tunc sentit miseriam qua
miser est et antequam amittat eas. sic ego eram illo tempore et flebam amarissime et requiescebam in amaritudine. ita miser eram et habebam cariorem illo amico meo
vitam ipsam miseram. nam quamvis eam mutare vellem,
nollem tamen amittere magis quam illum, et nescio an
vellem vel pro illo, sicut de Oreste et Pylade traditur, si
non fingitur, qui vellent pro invicem vel simul mori, qua
morte peius eis erat non simul vivere.

Sed in me nescio quis affectus nimis huic contrarius
ortus erat, et taedium vivendi erat in me gravissimum et
moriendi metus. credo, quo magis illum amabam, hoc magis mortem, quae mihi eum abstulerat, tamquam atrocis-
simam inimicam oderam et timebam, et eam repente
consumpturam omnes homines putabam, quia illum potuit. sic eram omnino, memini. ecce cor meum, deus
meus, ecce intus. vide, quia memini, spes mea, qui me

---

24 The paronomasia of *miser . . . eram/amiseram* is difficult to
reproduce in English.   25 A complicated thread. The inter-
linking of delight and bitterness may recall bittersweetness in the
poetry of Sappho (γλυκύπικρος [*glykopikros*] fr. 130.2), and
Horace (*inmitis Glycera, Carm.* 1.33.2).

26 Cf. Cic. *Amic.* 7.24: Pylades and Orestes both strive to be
the one to die when Orestes is sentenced to death; also *Fin.*
5.22.63.

and wept. I was miserable, and I missed my source of joy.[24]
Or is weeping a bitterness after all—one which offers us
satisfaction on account of our disdain for things which we
once enjoyed but now find repellent?[25]

6. (11) Why am I discussing these things? Now is not
the time for inquiring into this, but for making my confession to you! I was miserable, as every mind is miserable
that is fettered by its love of earthly things yet torn to
pieces when it is deprived of them and then becomes
aware of the misery that makes it miserable even before it
loses them. That was my state at that time. I was weeping
so bitterly and resting in bitterness. So I was miserable, Jb 3:20
yet I considered my own miserable life to be more precious than my friend. For although I wanted to change it,
I was more unwilling to lose it than to lose him, and I do
not know whether I might be willing to do so even for him,
as in the story of Orestes and Pylades (supposing the tale
to be true),[26] who were willing to die, either for one another or at the same time, for they considered not remaining alive together to be worse than such a death.

But in me some feeling had arisen that was completely
the opposite of this: my loathing of living and my fear of
dying were equally burdensome to me. I believe that the
more I loved that friend of mine, the more I hated and
feared death as the cruelest of enemies for stealing him
from me. I used to think it would devour all people without warning because it had such power over him. Yes, that
was the state I was in, I remember it. Regard my heart, O
my God, regard it deep within. Look—for I remember, O

mundas a talium affectionum immunditia, dirigens oculos
meos ad te et evellens de laqueo pedes meos. mirabar
enim ceteros mortales vivere, quia ille, quem quasi non
moriturum dilexeram, mortuus erat, et me magis, quia ille
alter eram, vivere illo mortuo mirabar. bene quidam dixit
de amico suo: "dimidium animae" suae. nam ego sensi
animam meam et animam illius unam fuisse animam in
duobus corporibus, et ideo mihi horrori erat vita, quia
nolebam dimidius vivere, et ideo forte mori metuebam,
ne totus ille moreretur quem multum amaveram.

7. (12) O dementiam nescientem diligere homines
humaniter! o stultum hominem immoderate humana pa-
tientem! quod ego tunc eram. itaque aestuabam, suspirabam, flebam, turbabar, nec requies erat nec consilium.
portabam enim concisam[6] et cruentam animam meam
impatientem portari a me, et ubi eam ponerem non inveniebam. non in amoenis nemoribus, non in ludis atque
cantibus, nec in suave olentibus locis, nec in conviviis
apparatis, neque in voluptate cubilis et lecti, non denique
in libris atque carminibus adquiescebat. horrebant omnia
et ipsa lux, et quidquid non erat quod ille erat improbum

---

[6] concisam S *Knöll Skut. Ver.*: conscissam *codd. Maur.*

---

[27] "Foul" because A. was indulging and enjoying his grief, just
as when he watched suffering as entertainment in *Conf.* 3.

[28] Cf. Hor. *Carm.* 1.3.8 (the poet's tribute to Virgil).

[29] Perhaps another echo of Horace, "I shall not altogether
die" (*non omnis moriar*: *Carm.* 3.30.6). When A. looks back at
Conf. years later this is the only phrase in Books 1–9 he comments
on; he dismisses it as "a frivolous piece of special pleading, not a
proper confession" (*declamatio levis quam gravis confessio*: *Retr*

my Hope, you who cleanse me from all the foulness of such affections,[27] directing my eyes toward you, and drawing my feet out of the snare. I was amazed that the rest of humanity went on living, because he whom I had loved as if he would never die had in fact died; and I was even more amazed that I remained alive when he was dead, because he was like my twin self. How rightly someone once called his friend, "half of my own self."[28] For I felt that my soul and his were one soul in two bodies, and that was why life was dreadful to me, because I did not want to live as half a person: and perhaps that was why I was afraid to die in case he whom I had loved so much would therefore die completely.[29]

Ps 25:15

7. (12) What insanity is this, not knowing how to love humanity as it really is![30] O the folly of humanity, so unable to endure its human lot with a degree of self-control! Such was my predicament at that time. How I raged, I sighed, I wept, I was distraught! I had no peace, and no purpose! I was carrying about with me my shattered, bleeding soul; it could not endure being carried by me, but I could find nowhere to set it down. Not in pleasant woodlands could it find any peace, nor in sports and music, nor in sweet-scented groves, nor in elaborate banquets, nor even in the pleasure of bed and couch, nor—finally—in books and poetry.[31] Everything was dreadful, even the light itself. Everything that was not in the same state as he was intol-

2.6.2). Though he criticizes how rhetoric trumps honesty here in *Conf.*, he does phrase the admission in a chiasmus.

[30] I.e., A. was not even capable of attaining the inadequate ideals of his classical education. [31] Each physical sense in turn fails him—sight, sound, smell, taste, and touch.

CONFESSIONS

et odiosum[7] erat praeter gemitum et lacrimas: nam in eis
solis aliquantula requies. ubi autem inde auferebatur
anima mea, onerabat me grandi sarcina miseriae.

Ad te, domine, levanda erat et curanda, sciebam, sed
nec volebam nec valebam, eo magis quia non mihi eras
aliquid solidum et firmum, cum de te cogitabam. non
enim tu eras, sed vanum phantasma et error meus erat
deus meus. si conabar eam ibi ponere ut requiesceret, per
inane labebatur et iterum ruebat super me, et ego mihi
remanseram infelix locus, ubi nec esse possem nec inde
recedere. quo enim cor meum fugeret a corde meo? quo
a me ipso fugerem? quo non me sequerer? et tamen fugi
de patria. minus enim eum quaerebant oculi mei ubi videre non solebant, atque a Thagastensi oppido veni Carthaginem.

8. (13) Non vacant tempora nec otiose volvuntur per
sensus nostros: faciunt in animo mira opera. ecce veniebant et praeteribant de die in diem, et veniendo et prae-
tereundo inserebant mihi spes alias et alias memorias, et
paulatim resarciebant me pristinis generibus delectationum, quibus cedebat dolor meus ille; sed succedebant non
quidem dolores alii, causae tamen aliorum dolorum. nam
unde me facillime et in intima dolor ille penetraverat, nisi

[7] odiosum *codd.*: taediosum S

---

[32] This technical term (*inane*) of Epicurean physics recalls
Lucretius, *DRN*.

[33] Cf. *Conf.* 2.10.18.

[34] Another echo of Horace: "Who that is exiled from his native
land also escapes himself?" (*patriae quis exul / se quoque fugit?
Carm.* 2.16.17). Cf. also A. *C. Acad.* 2.2.3.

erable and hateful; everything except for groaning and
tears. Only in these was there some small particle of peace.
But when my soul was distracted from them, it burdened
me with a heavy load of misery.

My soul should have been lifted up to you, Lord, it Ps 25:1
should have been healed, I knew it; but I neither wanted
to nor had the strength. This was mainly because to me
you were not something concrete and stable when I won-
dered about you. For you did not exist, you were just an
imaginary being; while *my* god was my own heretical belief. If I tried to set my soul down somewhere where it
could be at peace, it slid through the void[32] and came
tumbling back down upon me. I was left to be an unhappy
place where I could neither endure remaining, nor withdrawing.[33] For where could my heart flee, to escape from
my heart? Where could I flee, to escape from myself?
Where could I get to, without ending up pursuing myself?[34] Yet still I ran away from my home town, for my eyes
were not going to look so much for him in a place where
they were unused to seeing him. So I left Thagaste and
came to Carthage.

8. (13) Time does not go idly by nor flow to no purpose
through our senses. It does strange things to the mind.
Time came and went from day to day, and by that coming Ps 61:8
and going it sowed in me seeds of new hopes, and new
memories, and gradually it patched me up by means of the
kinds of pleasure I had formerly enjoyed, before my feelings of distress took precedence. Yet other things took
their place—not other distresses, but still causes of other
distresses. For how else had that pain pierced me so easily
and so deeply, if not because I had poured out my soul

quia fuderam in harenam animam meam diligendo moriturum acsi non moriturum?

Maxime quippe me reparabant atque recreabant aliorum amicorum solacia, cum quibus amabam quod pro te
amabam, et hoc erat ingens fabula et longum mendacium,
cuius adulterina confricatione corrumpebatur mens nostra pruriens in auribus. sed illa mihi fabula non moriebat-
tur, si quis amicorum meorum moreretur. alia erant quae
in eis amplius capiebant animum, conloqui et conridere et
vicissim benivole obsequi, simul legere libros dulciloquos,
simul nugari et simul honestari, dissentire interdum sine
odio tamquam ipse homo secum atque ipsa rarissima dis-
sensione condire consensiones plurimas, docere aliquid
invicem aut discere ab invicem, desiderare absentes cum
molestia, suscipere venientes cum laetitia: his atque huius
modi signis a corde amantium et redamantium proceden-
tibus per os, per linguam, per oculos et mille motus gra-
tissimos, quasi fomitibus conflare[8] animos et ex pluribus
unum facere.

9. (14) Hoc est quod diligitur in amicis, et sic diligitur
ut rea sibi sit humana conscientia si non amaverit reda-
mantem aut si amantem non redamaverit, nihil quaerens
ex eius corpore praeter indicia benivolentiae. hinc ille luc-
tus si quis moriatur, et tenebrae dolorum, et versa dulcedine in amaritudinem cor madidum, et ex amissa vita

---

[8] conflare *codd. Skut. Ver.*: flagrare *S Knöll*

---

[35] A vivid metaphor not paralleled elsewhere.

[36] Oxymoronic and chiastic. For A. and his educated readers
this artistry in arrangement would have enhanced the sentiment,
not undermined it.

upon the sand by loving someone mortal as if they were immortal?[35]

   To be sure, the consolation of other friends did much to restore and renew me. In their company I loved what I loved in place of you, but it was all a great fantasy, a massive lie, corrupting our minds with their itching ears by the stimulus of heretical ideas. Yet that fantasy of mine refused to die, no matter what friends of mine might perish. They possessed other characteristics that used to captivate my mind even more: conversation, shared laughter, doing a kindly turn for one another, reading honey-tongued books together, having fun together and being serious together, sometimes disagreeing without rancor as people might do when reflecting within themselves, and spicing up our many agreements with a sprinkling of dissent; one moment teaching a subject, the next learning from someone else; being troubled by longing for those who were absent, rejoicing to greet them on their return. By these signs and others like them, proceeding from the hearts of those who love and return the love of others, by means of the mouth, tongue, eyes and a thousand welcome gestures, we fueled the fusing of our minds and made, from many, one. 2 Tm 4:3–4

   9. (14) This is what we treasure about friends, and we treasure it in such a way that the human conscience feels guilty if it does not love what loves it in return, or does not love in return that which loves it first. It asks for nothing in return from that person except for evidence of goodwill. This is what causes grief when someone dies, and the darkness of distress, and a heart brimming over when what is sweet turns to bitterness, and, when the dying lose their hold on life, life begins to die in those who are left alive.[36]

morientium mors viventium. beatus qui amat te et amicum in te et inimicum propter te. solus enim nullum carum amittit cui omnes in illo cari sunt qui non amittitur.
et quis est iste nisi deus noster, deus, qui fecit caelum et
terram et implet ea, quia implendo ea fecit ea? te nemo
amittit nisi qui dimittit, et quia dimittit, quo it aut quo
fugit nisi a te placido ad te iratum? nam ubi non invenit
legem tuam in poena sua? et lex tua veritas et veritas tu.

10. (15) Deus virtutum, converte nos et ostende faciem
tuam, et salvi erimus. nam quoquoversum se verterit
anima hominis, ad dolores figitur alibi praeterquam in te,
tametsi figitur in pulchris extra te et extra se. quae tamen
nulla essent, nisi essent abs te. quae oriuntur et occidunt
et oriendo quasi esse incipiunt, et crescunt ut perficiantur,
et perfecta senescunt et intereunt: et non omnia senescunt, et omnia intereunt. ergo cum oriuntur et tendunt
esse, quo magis celeriter crescunt ut sint, eo magis festi-
nant ut non sint: sic est modus eorum. tantum dedisti eis,
quia partes sunt rerum, quae non sunt omnes simul, sed
decedendo ac succedendo agunt omnes universum, cuius
partes sunt. (ecce sic peragitur et sermo noster per signa
sonantia. non enim erit totus sermo, si unum verbum non
decedat, cum sonuerit partes suas, ut succedat aliud.)

---

[37] See *Conf.* 1.2.2.

[38] A. returns to his theme of alienation and return.

[39] A commonplace of classical thought; cf. Sall. *Iug.* 2.3, with
A. *Ep.* 143.6, 166.5.14.

Blessed are those who love you, and love their friend in Tb 13:14
you and their enemy because of you. Only those who hold cf. Mt 5:44;
Lk 6:27
everyone dear, in the One who can never be lost, never
lose anyone dear to them. And who is that One if not our
God, who made heaven and earth and who fills them, Jer 23:24
because by filling them he has created them? No one loses
you unless they reject you; and because they reject you
where can they go or flee except away from a kindly you Ps 139:7
to an angry you![37] Surely they find your law is everywhere
in their own punishment? And your law is truth and you Ps 119:142
are Truth.

10. (15) O God of hosts, turn us and show us your face,
and we shall be whole. For wherever a person's soul turns, Ps 80:7
everywhere it is pierced with enduring pains except in
you—even if it is stuck in things which are beautiful but
are separate from you, and separate from that soul itself.[38]
Yet those things of beauty would be nothing unless they
were from you. They arise and pass away;[39] and in arising
they begin to exist, so to speak; and they grow so that they
may reach perfection; and once they are perfected they
grow old and perish. And although not everything grows
old, still all things perish. So when things arise and strive
for existence, the faster they grow into being, they more
they hasten toward annihilation: this is their nature. This
much you have allowed them because they are parts of
things that do not all exist at the same time, but that, by
withdrawing and following on, all make up the whole universe of which they are part. In this way human speech
also is accomplished by means of sounding signs: for a
speech cannot be completed unless one word ceases to
sound once it has uttered its syllables, so that another may
take its place.

157

Laudet te ex illis anima mea, deus, creator omnium, sed non in eis figatur glutine amore per sensus corporis. eunt enim quo ibant, ut non sint, et conscindunt eam desideriis pestilentiosis, quoniam ipsa esse vult et requiescere amat in eis quae amat. in illis autem non est ubi, quia non stant: fugiunt, et quis ea sequitur sensu carnis? aut quis comprehendit, vel cum praesto sunt? tardus est enim sensus carnis, quoniam sensus carnis est: ipse est modus eius. sufficit ad aliud, ad quod factus est, ad illud autem non sufficit, ut teneat transcurrentia ab initio debito usque ad finem debitum. in verbo enim tuo, per quod creantur, ibi audiunt, "hinc" et "huc usque."

11. (16) Noli esse vana, anima mea, et obsurdescere in aure cordis tumultu vanitatis tuae. audi et tu: verbum ipsum clamat ut redeas, et ibi est locus quietis imperturbabilis, ubi non deseritur amor si ipse non deserat. ecce illa discedunt ut alia succedant, et omnibus suis partibus constet infima universitas. "numquid ego aliquo discedo?" ait verbum dei. ibi fige mansionem tuam, ibi commenda quidquid inde habes, anima mea; saltem fatigata fallaciis, veritati commenda quidquid tibi est a veritate, et non perdes aliquid, et reflorescent putria[9] tua, et sanabuntur omnes languores tui, et fluxa tua reformabuntur et reno-

9 putria *S. Maur. Knöll Skut. Ver.*: putrida *codd.*

40 Cf. *Conf.* 9.12.32; the incipit of a hymn of Ambrose.
41 For "love" and "glue" in parallel, cf. A. *Trin.* 10.5.7 (there the "glue of care").
42 Literally, "fleshly senses"; cf. *Conf.* 1.6.7, n. 17.
43 This apostrophe parallels a shorter one at *Conf.* 3.2.3.

O my God, Creator of all things,[40] let my soul praise you for all those things: but let it not be stuck fast to them with glue, with the love that comes through the bodily senses.[41] For they go where they were always going, into nonexistence, and they tear the soul apart with unhealthy desires: for the soul wishes to exist yet loves to find peace in those things that it loves. But in those things there is no place to rest, because they have no permanence: they flee away, and who can follow them with the physical senses?[42] Or who can seize them even when they are here at hand? For the physical senses are slow because, as senses, they are physical: that is their natural sphere. They are good enough for some things, for which they were made, but for that purpose they are not good enough, not for supporting transient things from their proper beginning to their proper end. There in your Word, through which they were created, they hear, "from this point," and "no further." cf. Jb 38:11

11. (16) Do not be vain, my soul, nor grow deaf in your heart's hearing with the clamor of your own vanity.[43] You too must listen: the Word himself cries out for you to return, and there is the place of peace that is always serene, where love is not forsaken, provided it does not itself opt to forsake. See how such things make way that others may succeed them and the lower universe stand fast in all its parts! The Word of God says, "Surely I shall not leave here for any other place?" O my soul, fix in that place your abiding home; entrust to that place whatever you possess. Only, when you are exhausted by deceits, entrust to the Jn 14:6 Truth whatever fraction of truth you may possess, and you will lose nothing; and all that is rotten in you will begin to flourish, and all your listless apathy will be healed, and all cf. Ps 103:3^{VL} those fleeting elements within you will be transformed and

CONFESSIONS

vabuntur et constringentur ad te, et non te deponent quo
descendunt, sed stabunt tecum et permanebunt ad semper stantem ac permanentem deum.

(17) Ut quid perversa sequeris carnem tuam? ipsa te
sequatur conversam. quidquid per illam sentis in parte est,
et ignoras totum cuius hae partes sunt, et delectant te tamen. sed si ad totum comprehendendum esset idoneus
sensus carnis tuae, ac non et ipse in parte universi acce-
pisset pro tua poena iustum modum, velles ut transiret
quidquid existit in praesentia, ut magis tibi omnia pla-
cerent. nam et quod loquimur per eundem sensum carnis
audis, et non vis utique stare syllabas sed transvolare, ut
aliae veniant et totum audias. ita semper omnia, quibus
unum aliquid constat (et non sunt omnia simul ea quibus
constat[10]): plus delectant omnia quam singula, si possint
sentiri omnia. sed longe his melior qui fecit omnia, et ipse
est deus noster, et non discedit, quia nec succeditur ei.

12. (18) Si placent corpora, deum ex illis lauda et in
artificem[11] eorum retorque amorem, ne in his quae tibi
placent tu displiceas. si placent animae, in deo amentur,

---

10 constat *codd. Maur. Knöll Skut. Ver.*: constant S
11 artificem *codd. Knöll Skut. Ver.*: artifice S

---

44 A reference to the resurrection of the body. Cf. *S.* 119.3,
"Do you wish to understand the abiding Word? Do not follow the
flowing current of the flesh. For the flesh surely is a flowing current; it does not abide."

45 Still apostrophising his soul.

46 I.e., "fleshly" (*carnis tuae*).

47 Cf. A., *Gn.c.Man.* 1.21.32, "A complete speech is beautiful
not because of any individual syllables or letters, but as a whole."

made new and bound securely about you,[44] and they will not drag you down where they themselves descend, but they will stand fast with you and abide with God, who stands fast and abides for ever.

(17) Why do you[45] go astray and follow your flesh? Let your flesh follow you, now that you have converted. Whatever you sense by means of the soul is partial, and you do not know the whole of which these are parts, and yet they delight you. If your physical[46] sense had the capacity to understand the whole, and had not, for your punishment, bowed to being properly limited to a part of the universe, you would want everything that exists in the present to pass away, so that the totality of existence could please you more. Likewise by the same physical sense you hear what people are saying, and you do not want the syllables to remain where they are but rather to fly past so that others may come, and you hear the whole speech.[47] So it always is with all the elements that make up any individual object (and not all the elements it consists of exist at the same time): as a collectivity they give more pleasure than as the individual parts, if it were possible to perceive all the elements together. But he who made all things is far better than all of these, and he is our God, and he does not leave us, because nothing can take his place.[48]

12. (18) If physical objects please you, praise God because of them, and turn your love back upon their creator, so that you do not displease him by means of what pleases you. If souls please you, let them be loved in God, because

[48] Cf. Porphyry, *Sententiae* 40 on the relations of parts to wholes; and *Sententiae* 31 on the return to the One, with *Conf.* 12.28.38.

quia et ipsae mutabiles sunt et in illo fixae stabiliuntur: alioquin irent et perirent. in illo ergo amentur, et rape ad eum tecum quas potes et dic eis: "hunc amemus: ipse fecit haec et non est longe. non enim fecit atque abiit, sed ex illo in illo sunt. ecce ubi est, ubi sapit veritas: intimus cordi est, sed cor erravit ab eo. redite, praevaricatores, ad cor et inhaerete illi qui fecit vos. state cum eo et stabitis, requiescite in eo et quieti eritis. quo itis in aspera? quo itis? bonum quod amatis ab illo est: sed quantum est ad illum, bonum est et suave; sed amarum erit iuste, quia iniuste amatur deserto illo quidquid ab illo est.

"Quo vobis adhuc et adhuc ambulare vias difficiles et laboriosas? non est requies ubi quaeratis eam. quaerite quod quaeritis, sed ibi non est ubi quaeritis. beatam vitam quaeritis in regione mortis: non est illic. quomodo enim beata vita, ubi nec vita?

(19) "Et descendit huc ipsa vita nostra, et tulit mortem nostram et occidit eam de abundantia vitae suae, et tonuit, clamans ut redeamus hinc ad eum in illud secretum unde processit ad nos, in ipsum primum virginalem uterum ubi

49 Cf. A. *Trin.* 8.5–6, "This good is not set far from each of us: for 'in him we live and move and have our being' (Acts 17:27–28). But we must stand by him in love and cleave to him, in order to enjoy to the full his presence from whom we have our being, and in whose absence we would cease to be."

50 Cf. A. *En. Ps.* 57.1, "Therefore what does that written law declare to those who have deserted the law written in their own hearts? 'Return to your heart, you transgressors!' (Rom 2:15)."

51 The nature of the blessed life exercised A. all his adult life: he wrote *Beata V.* ("On the blessed life") soon after his conversion and continued to reflect on it long after, cf. *De civ. D.* 14.26.

they too are mutable, and only when attached to God do they find a firm foundation. If they went anywhere else they would perish. Thus let them be loved in him, and take what souls you can to him with you, and say to them: "Let us love him: he made all these things, and he is not far off.[49] He has not made all this to abandon it, but all that is from him is in him. Look, there he is!—wherever truth is distinguished: he is deep within the heart, though the heart has strayed from him. Return to your heart, you transgressors,[50] and cleave to him who made you. Stand with him, and you will stand fast indeed; take your rest in him and you will find peace. Why do you make your way toward what is difficult? Why are you going there? The good that you love is from him: insofar as it refers to him, it is good and sweet; but whatever it is that comes from him, it will justly become bitter, if he has been abandoned, because then it is loved unjustly.

Is 46:8

cf. Ps 138:7

"To what purpose do you go on and on walking these difficult and wearisome ways? There is no peace where you seek it. Seek what you seek, but it is not there where you seek it. You seek a life of blessing[51] in the realm of death: it is not there. How can a life of blessing be there, where there is no life at all?

Ws 5:7

(19) "Our Life himself[52] came down to this place, and bore our death and put it to death out of the abundance of his own life; and he thundered, calling us to return from here to him, into that secret place from which he came forth to us. First, into the actual virginal womb where he

Jn 6:33
2 Tm 1:10

---

[52] I.e., Christ personified. A. continues his apostrophe to souls begun at 4.12.18, "Let us love him . . ."

ei nupsit humana creatura, caro mortalis, ne semper mortalis. et inde velut sponsus procedens de thalamo suo exultavit ut gigans ad currendam viam. non enim tardavit, sed cucurrit clamans dictis, factis, morte, vita, descensu, ascensu, clamans ut redeamus ad eum: et discessit ab oculis, ut redeamus ad eum. et discessit ab oculis, ut redeamus ad cor et inveniamus eum. abscessit enim et ecce hic est. noluit nobiscum diu esse et non reliquit nos. illuc enim abscessit unde numquam recessit, quia mundus per eum factus est, et in hoc mundo erat et venit in hunc mundum peccatores salvos facere.

"Cui confitetur anima mea et sanat eam, quoniam peccavit illi. filii hominum, quo usque graves corde? numquid et post descensum vitae non vultis ascendere et vivere? sed quo ascenditis, quando in alto estis et posuistis in caelo os vestrum? descendite, ut ascendatis, et ascendatis ad deum.[12] cecidistis enim ascendendo contra deum."

Dic eis ista, ut plorent in convalle plorationis, et sic eos rape tecum ad deum, quia de spiritu eius haec dicis eis, si dicis ardens igne caritatis.

13. (20) Haec tunc non noveram, et amabam pulchra

---

[12] ut ascendatis, et ascendatis ad deum *codd. mult. Maur. Knöll Ver.*: ut ascendatis ad deum *S Skut.*

---

[53] Cf. Eph 4:9–10, 1 Pt 3:18 for the "harrowing of hell" between the crucifixion and the resurrection, by which Christ accomplished salvation for the righteous who had died before the time of the incarnation. It is referenced in the second-century Apostles' Creed.

[54] By this series of nouns in asyndeton A. sketches a skeleton creed, which he verges on a view of the incarnation that is re-

betrothed himself to humanity's created nature, its mortal flesh, that it should not be mortal forever. Then as a bridegroom emerging from his bedchamber, he rejoiced like a giant to run his course. He did not delay, but rather ran, Ps 19:5 calling—by words, deeds, death, life, descent,[53] ascent— calling us to return to him;[54] and he departed from our sight so that we would return to him. And he departed from our sight so that we would return to our heart and Is 46:8 there find him. For he has gone, and yet look! here he is. He was unwilling to be with us for long, yet he has not abandoned us. He has gone to that place from which he never withdrew, for the world was made through him, and Jn 1:10 he was in this world and came into this world to save sinners.[55]

1 Tm 1:15

"To him does my soul make her confession, and he restores her, for she has sinned against him. O mortals, Ps 41:4 why are you so heavy-hearted? Surely now that Life has Ps 4:2 come down you are not reluctant to ascend and live? But to what purpose do you ascend, when you are on high and have turned your speech against heaven? First come Ps 73:9 down, so that you may then ascend, and that your ascent may indeed be to God. For it is by making your ascent while opposing God that you have fallen."

Tell this to them, to make those souls weep in this vale of tears, and by this means carry them off with you to God; Ps 84:6 for it is by his Spirit that you are speaking to them, if you speak as one burning with the fire of love.

13. (20) In those days I knew none of this. I used to

demptive in itself (i.e., separate from the passion and resurrection).

[55] Or "to make sinners whole."

inferiora et ibam in profundum, et dicebam amicis meis, "num amamus aliquid nisi pulchrum? quid est ergo pulchrum? et quid est pulchritudo? quid est quod nos allicit et conciliat rebus quas amamus? nisi enim esset in eis decus et species, nullo modo nos ad se moverent." et animadvertebam et videbam in ipsis corporibus aliud esse quasi totum et ideo pulchrum, aliud autem quod ideo deceret, quoniam apte adcommodaretur alicui, sicut pars corporis ad universum suum aut calciamentum ad pedem et similia. et ista consideratio scaturrivit in animo meo ex intimo corde meo, et scripsi libros "de pulchro et apto"— puto duos aut tres: tu scis, deus, nam excidit mihi. non enim habemus eos, sed aberraverunt a nobis nescio quo modo.

14. (21) Quid est autem quod me movit, domine deus meus, ut ad Hierium, Romanae urbis oratorem, scriberem illos libros? quem non noveram facie, sed amaveram hominem ex doctrinae fama, quae illi clara erat, et quaedam verba eius audieram et placuerant mihi. sed magis quia placebat aliis et eum efferebant laudibus, stupentes quod ex homine Syro, docto prius graecae facundiae, post in latina etiam dictor mirabilis extitisset et esset scientissimus rerum ad studium sapientiae pertinentium, mihi placebat. laudatur homo et amatur absens. utrumnam ab ore laudantis intrat in cor audientis amor ille? absit! sed ex amante

---

56 There is a frisson of uncleanness about this distinctive Latin verb (*scatur*[r]*io*), perhaps recalling the teeming or swarming of Lv 11:41–44, 20.25; Ps 104:25; etc.

57 Cf. *Conf.* 4.15.27; A. was about twenty-six at the time, ca. AD 380–382.

58 Either a practitioner or a teacher.

love things of lower degree that were beautiful, and to go
down into the deep and say to my friends, "Surely we must   cf. Ps 130:1
only love things that are beautiful? So what is 'a beautiful
thing'? And what is 'beauty'? What is it that attracts us and
inclines us toward the things we love? Unless they possessed qualities of grace and form they could not possibly
attract us to them." I used to observe and watch how one
object among all these things might possess a kind of com-
pleteness that made it beautiful for that reason; while another seemed graceful because it fitted so well with some
other object, like a part of the human body to the whole,
or a shoe to a foot, or something of that kind. This thought
seethed[56] in my mind, in the depth of my heart; and I   2 Mc 9:9
wrote books *On the Beautiful and the Fitting*—two books,
I think, or three: you know, O God, for I have forgotten. I
no longer possess them, they have somehow escaped me,
I am not sure how.[57]

14. (21) What is it, O Lord my God, that prompted me
to write those books for Hierius, that orator[58] in the city
of Rome? I did not know him personally but admired the
man because of his reputation as an expert, which was
widely known; and I had heard some words of his and been
impressed. But it was really because other people admired
him, and praised him to the skies: they could hardly believe that a man from Syria could learn first Greek, then
Latin, and then turn himself into a marvelous public
speaker who was so knowledgeable in all matters philosophical; that was why I favored him. Someone can be
praised and loved even when not present. Can that love
enter into the heart of a listener from the mouth of the
one who is offering praise? Of course not! But one per-

alio accenditur alius. hinc enim amatur qui laudatur, dum
non fallaci corde laudatoris praedicari creditur, id est cum
amans eum laudat.

(22) Sic enim tunc amabam homines ex hominum iudicio, non enim ex tuo, deus meus, in quo nemo fallitur. sed
tamen cur non sicut auriga nobilis, sicut venator studiis
popularibus diffamatus, sed longe aliter et graviter et ita,
quemadmodum et me laudari vellem? non autem vellem
ita laudari et amari me ut histriones, quamquam eos et
ipse laudarem et amarem, sed eligens latere quam ita
notus esse et vel haberi odio quam sic amari. ubi distri-
buuntur ista pondera variorum et diversorum amorum in
anima una? quid est quod amo in alio? quod rursus nisi
odissem, non a me detestarer et repellerem, cum sit
uterque nostrum homo? non enim sicut equus bonus amatur ab eo qui nollet hoc esse etiamsi posset. hoc et de
histrione dicendum est, qui naturae nostrae socius est.
ergone amo in homine quod odi esse, cum sim homo?
grande profundum est ipse homo, cuius etiam capillos tu,
domine, numeratos habes et non minuuntur in te: et tamen capilli eius magis numerabiles quam affectus eius et
motus cordis eius.

(23) At ille rhetor ex eo erat genere quem sic amabam
ut vellem esse me talem. et errabam typho et circumfere-

---

59 The kind of love A. is evoking here is closer to "admiration"
than "affection."

60 A *venator* was a gladiator who specialized in wild animal
hunts in the arena.

61 Cf. Prudent. *C. Symm.* 2.85–90; there the "great deep"
(*grande profundum*) is the goal of Christians (but, rejecting Symmachus' argument, not of "pagans").

son's love kindles another's. Thus someone who is praised comes to be loved, provided that the praise is reliable, a declaration coming from a sincere heart: that is, when the person who does the praising is the same one who feels the love.

(22) In those days I loved[59] people according to human standards, not according to your standards, O my God, for in you no one is deceived. But why not did I not love them in the same way I might an outstanding charioteer or a gladiator famous and acclaimed for his combats with animals,[60] but instead in a very different manner, a serious one, in the same way I myself wanted to be loved? I had no desire to be praised and loved as actors are, even though I myself used to praise and love them. Being unknown was preferable to that kind of celebrity, being detested was better than that kind of love. Where are those impulses of different and diverse loves allocated within the individual soul? Why is it that I can love in someone else something that I would only spurn and reject for myself if I really hated it, when both of us are human beings alike? It is not the same as a good horse being loved by someone who would not want to be that horse (even if such a thing were possible). We should say the same about an actor, who shares our human nature. So am I to love in another human being what I hate to be myself, though I too am human? Humanity is a great deep,[61] yet you, Lord, have counted their every hair, and none of them is lost in you. Even so, their hairs are easier to reckon with than their emotions and the impulses of their hearts.

(23) That master of oratory, though, was the kind of person which I used to love in the sense of wanting to be like him. I went astray because of my pride, and I was

bar omni vento, et nimis occulte gubernabar abs te. et
unde scio et unde certus confiteor tibi quod illum in amore
laudantium magis amaveram quam in rebus ipsis de quibus laudabatur? quia si non laudatum vituperarent eum
idem ipsi et vituperando atque spernendo ea ipsa narrarent, non accenderer in eo et non excitarer, et certe res
non aliae forent nec homo ipse alius, sed tantummodo
alius affectus narrantium.

Ecce ubi iacet anima infirma nondum haerens soliditati
veritatis: sicut aurae linguarum flaverint a pectoribus opi-
nantium, ita fertur et vertitur, torquetur ac retorquetur, et
obnubilatur ei lumen et non cernitur veritas, et ecce est
ante nos. et magnum quiddam mihi erat, si sermo meus et
studia mea illi viro innotescerent. quae si probaret, flagra-
rem magis; si autem improbaret, sauciaretur cor vanum et
inane soliditatis tuae. et tamen pulchrum illud atque aptum, unde ad eum scripseram, libenter animo versabam
ob os contemplationis meae et nullo conlaudatore mirabar.

15. (24) Sed tantae rei cardinem in arte tua nondum
videbam, omnipotens, qui facis mirabilia solus, et ibat animus per formas corporeas et pulchrum, quod per se ipsum, aptum autem, quod ad aliquid adcommodatum dece-

_____

62 As often, A. assumes knowledge of the context of his scriptural quotations: here the "winds" are winds of false doctrine.

63 A remarkable piece of self-analysis: A. pinpoints the problem of the influence of opinion.

170

carried about by every wind,[62] yet in complete secrecy you Eph 4:14
were the hand that guided me. How is it that I know, that
I can confidently confess to you, the fact that my love for
that orator had more to do with the love of those who
praised him than the actual achievements for which they
praised him? After all, if those same people had dispar-
aged him instead of praising him, and had related the same
things about him in a negative and denigratory way, I
would not have been enthusiastic about him, I would not
have been stirred. But the deeds themselves would certainly not have been different, the man himself would not
be different: only the feelings of those who spoke would
be different.[63]

Look how the soul lies stricken and helpless while it
still fails to cling to the firm reality of truth. As the breath
of tongues sounds from the chests of those who make their
views widely known, so the truth is hauled back and forth,
it is buffeted to and fro: it is overshadowed, and it goes
unnoticed—and look! that same truth is right in front of
us. It mattered a great deal to me to make my discourse
and my studies known to that man. If he approved of
them, I would be all the more thrilled; but if he disapproved, my heart, vain and lacking in your firm reality,
would be wounded. Even so, I willingly turned the subject
over in my mind's eye, that topic of "the beautiful and fit,"
of which I had written to him. Despite the lack of anyone
to join in my praise, still I was delighted with it.

15. (24) Almighty God, you alone do marvelous things: Ps 72:18
by your design I did not yet see the crux of this serious
matter. My mind was considering physical forms in turn,
and I defined as "beautiful" those that are so in themselves; but as "fitting" those that are adapted to something

171

ret, definiebam et distinguebam et exemplis corporeis
adstruebam. et converti me ad animi naturam, et non me
sinebat falsa opinio quam de spiritalibus habebam verum
cernere. et inruebat in oculos ipsa vis veri, et avertebam
palpitantem mentem ab incorporea re ad liniamenta et
colores et tumentes magnitudines et, quia non poteram ea
videre in animo, putabam me non posse videre animum.
et cum in virtute pacem amarem, in vitiositate autem odissem discordiam, in illa unitatem, in ista quandam divi-
sionem notabam, inque illa unitate mens rationalis et natura veritatis ac summi boni mihi esse videbatur, in ista
vero divisione inrationalis vitae nescioquam substantiam
et naturam summi mali, quae non solum esset substantia
sed omnino vita esset, et tamen abs te non esset, deus
meus, ex quo sunt omnia, miser opinabar. et illam "mona-
dem" appellabam tamquam sine ullo sexu[13] mentem, hanc
vero "dyadem," iram in facinoribus, libidinem in flagitiis,
nesciens quid loquerer. non enim noveram neque didiceram nec ullam substantiam malum esse nec ipsam mentem
nostram summum atque incommutabile bonum.

(25) Sicut enim facinora sunt, si vitiosus est ille animi
motus in quo est impetus et se iactat insolenter ac turbide,
et flagitia, si est immoderata illa animae affectio qua carnales hauriuntur voluptates, ita errores et falsae opiniones
vitam contaminant, si rationalis mens ipsa vitiosa est, qua-

---

[13] sexu *S Knöll Skut. Ver. GM*: sensu *codd.*

---

[64] Cf. *Conf.* 4.13.20.   [65] A. was not yet prepared to accept
the concept of immaterial existence.

[66] Violence corresponding to the masculine, and lust to the
feminine. "Monad" and "dyad" are terms from Pythagoreanism.

[67] Cf. *Conf.* 3.8.15, n. 49.

else:[64] I also classified and categorized them with concrete examples. Then I turned to the nature of the mind, and the spurious beliefs I held about spiritual entities did not let me perceive the truth.[65] Still the power of truth itself assaulted my vision, and I turned my trembling mind away from things which are incorporeal and toward shape and color and definite bulk. Because I could not see these in my mind I thought I was unable to see the mind itself. I loved the peace that is found in virtue, so likewise I hated the discord that attaches to vice. In the one I remarked its unity, in the other a kind of disunity. It seemed to me as if rational thought, and the nature of truth and of the supreme good, consisted in that unity; pitiable as I was, I imagined that some kind of concrete reality of irrational life, and the nature of ultimate evil, existed in that disunity—indeed it was not only a concrete reality but was altogether a living being. And yet apart from you it could not exist, O my God; all things come from you. I called the unity "monad" (like a mind without sexual differentiation) and the other "dyad" (as in anger in criminal acts, and lust in shameful ones).[66] I did not know what I was talking about. For I did not know, nor had I ever learned, either that evil is not a substance or that our mind is not itself the supreme unchanging good. 1 Chr 29:14; 1 Cor 8:6

(25) When the mind's impulses, which give it its force, are corrupted so that it flaunts itself with vehement arrogance, criminal acts are committed. When the soul's capacity for emotion is unrestrained, which leads to gorging on pleasures of the flesh, disgraceful acts are committed. So in the same way errors and false beliefs taint a life, if the rational mind itself is corrupt.[67] Such was the state

lis in me tunc erat nesciente alio lumine illam inlustrandam esse, ut sit particeps veritatis, quia non est ipsa natura veritatis, quoniam tu inluminabis lucernam meam, domine. deus meus, inluminabis tenebras meas, et de plenitudine tua omnes nos accepimus. es enim tu lumen verum quod inluminat omnem hominem venientem in hunc mundum, quia in te non est transmutatio nec momenti obumbratio.

(26) Sed ego conabar ad te et repellebar abs te, ut saperem mortem, quoniam superbis resistis. quid autem superbius quam ut adsererem mira dementia me id esse naturaliter quod tu es? cum enim ego essem mutabilis et eo mihi manifestum esset, quod utique ideo sapiens esse cupiebam, ut ex deteriore melior fierem, malebam tamen etiam te opinari mutabilem quam me non hoc esse quod tu es.

Itaque repellebar et resistebas ventosae cervici meae, et imaginabar formas corporeas et caro carnem accusabam, et spiritus ambulans nondum[14] revertebar ad te et ambulando ambulabam in ea quae non sunt, neque in te neque in me neque in corpore, neque mihi creabantur a veritate tua, sed a mea vanitate fingebantur ex corpore. et dicebam parvulis fidelibus tuis, civibus meis, a quibus nesciens exulabam, dicebam illis garrulus et ineptus, "cur ergo errat anima quam fecit deus?" et mihi nolebam dici, "cur ergo errat deus?" et contendebam magis incommuta-

---

14 nondum *codd. Maur. Ver.*: non S *Knöll Skut.*

---

68 Cf. *Conf.* 4.15.25, where A. thought formerly that the human mind shares God's nature as truth.

69 Cf. *Conf.* 3.6.10—his Manichaean beliefs again.

174

of my mind, while I had no idea that it needed enlightenment from some other light source in order to participate in the truth, for it is not itself the nature of truth. Instead you will light my lantern, Lord. O my God, you will lighten my darkness; we have all received of your fullness. You are the true light that lightens everyone who comes into this world, for in you is no variableness nor shadow of turning. Ps 18:28
Jn 1:16
Jn 1:9
Jas 1:17

(26) But I was trying to reach you and I kept being rebuffed by you so that I would have to taste death, for you resist the proud. What could be more arrogant than for me, in my incredible folly, to declare that I was by nature the same as you are?[68] For although I was mutable, a fact that was obvious to me because I undoubtedly longed to be wise, and thus to change from a worse state to a better, I preferred nevertheless to believe that you were subject to change, rather than that I was not what you are. Mt 16:28;
Mk 8:39;
Jn 8:52
1 Pt 5:5;
Jas 4:6

So I was rebuffed, and you thwarted my stiff-necked conceit, and I went on imagining physical forms and made accusations of fleshly substance—I who was flesh myself! I was a wandering spirit, not yet returning to you, and in my wandering I wandered into matters that have no existence, that are not in you, nor in me, nor in the body, and that were not created for me by your Truth: rather, my vanity contrived the illusion of them out of what was corporeal.[69] And I used to speak to your faithful little ones, my fellow citizens, from whom I was exiled (though I did not know it), I was voluble in my stupidity, and I said to them, "Why does the soul that God has made go astray?" But I did not want anyone to respond to me with, "So why does God go astray?" I preferred to argue that your un- Ps 78:39

175

bilem tuam substantiam coactam errare quam meam mutabilem sponte deviasse et poena errare confitebar.

(27) Et eram aetate annorum fortasse viginti sex aut
septem, cum illa volumina scripsi, volvens apud me corporalia figmenta obstrepentia cordis mei auribus, quas
intendebam, dulcis veritas, in interiorem melodiam tuam,
cogitans de pulchro et apto, et stare cupiens et audire te
et gaudio gaudere propter vocem sponsi, et non poteram,
quia vocibus erroris mei rapiebar foras et pondere superbiae meae in ima decidebam. non enim dabas auditui meo
gaudium et laetitiam, aut exultabant ossa, quae humilata
non erant.

16. (28) Et quid mihi proderat quod annos natus ferme
viginti, cum in manus meas venissent aristotelica quaedam, quas appellant decem categorias (quarum nomine,
cum eas rhetor Carthaginiensis, magister meus, buccis
typho crepantibus commemoraret et alii qui docti habe-
bantur, tamquam in nescio quid magnum et divinum sus-
pensus inhiabam), legi eas solus et intellexi? quas cum
contulissem cum eis qui se dicebant vix eas magistris eru-
ditissimis, non loquentibus tantum sed multa in pulvere
depingentibus, intellexisse, nihil inde aliud mihi dicere
potuerunt quam ego solus apud me ipsum legens cognoveram.

---

70 Cf. A. *Ep.* 138.1.5, "The beauty of the whole of time . . .
comes to completion, like a magnificent song by a singer who
defies description."

71 A. ends the book by repeating this question six times before
a climactic final address to God.   72 An exposition of what can
be argued (*katēgorein*) about, or predicated of, any thing. Cf.
Lössl and Watt, *Bible and Aristotle*, 111–20.

changeable substance was forced to go astray, rather than confessing that my own changeable substance had gone astray of its own volition, and is now going astray by way of punishment.

(27) I was perhaps twenty-six or twenty-seven years of age when I wrote those works. I was brooding over the hypothetical material images which kept clamoring to the ears of my heart, though I was concentrating my listening upon your inner music,[70] O my sweet Truth. I was reflecting on the beautiful and the fitting, and I longed to stand and hear you and to rejoice with joy at the bridegroom's voice. But I could not, because I was being carried away   Jn 3:29 by the claims of my own delusion, and the weight of my own pride tumbled me into the depths. You did not let me hear joy and gladness, nor did my bones rejoice, because they were not yet humbled.   Ps 51:8

16. (28) What good did it do me[71] that when I was scarcely twenty years old some writings of Aristotle, called the *Ten Categories*,[72] came into my hands, and I read them unaided and understood them? When my professor of rhetoric at Carthage read them aloud, his cheeks puffed out with conceit, or others who were considered learned, I would hang on the very name gaping in awe as if at some great and mighty wonder! So I brought up the subject with those who said that they had scarcely understood these books even with the most learned teachers not only explaining them but also drawing diagrams in the dust. But they could not tell me anything more than I had worked out reading them for myself.

CONFESSIONS

Et satis aperte mihi videbantur loquentes de substantiis, sicuti est homo, et quae in illis essent, sicuti est figura
hominis, qualis sit, et statura, quot pedum sit, et cognatio,
cuius frater sit, aut ubi sit constitutus aut quando natus,
aut stet an sedeat, aut calciatus vel armatus sit, aut aliquid
faciat aut patiatur aliquid, et quaecumque in his novem
generibus, quorum exempli gratia quaedam posui, vel in
ipso substantiae genere innumerabilia reperiuntur.

(29) Quid hoc mihi proderat, quando et oberat, cum
etiam te, deus meus, mirabiliter simplicem atque incommutabilem, illis decem praedicamentis putans quidquid
esset omnino comprehensum, sic intellegere conarer,
quasi et tu subiectus esses magnitudini tuae aut pulchri-
tudini, ut illa essent in te quasi in subiecto sicut in corpore,
cum tua magnitudo et tua pulchritudo tu ipse sis, corpus
autem non eo sit magnum et pulchrum quo corpus est,
quia etsi minus magnum et minus pulchrum esset, nihilo-
minus corpus esset? falsitas enim erat quam de te cogitabam, non veritas, et figmenta miseriae meae, non firma-
menta beatitudinis tuae. iusseras enim, et ita fiebat in me,
ut terra spinas et tribulos pareret mihi et cum labore pervenirem ad panem meum.

(30) Et quid mihi proderat quod omnes libros artium
quas liberales vocant tunc nequissimus malarum cupiditatum servus per me ipsum legi et intellexi, quoscumque
legere potui? et gaudebam in eis, et nesciebam unde esset
quidquid ibi verum et certum esset. dorsum enim habe-

---

73 I.e., the last of the ten categories. A. tries out philosophical
terminology of "substances" (what things are in themselves) and
"predicates" (things that can be said about a thing itself) to make
sense of God.

It was fairly obvious to me that they were discussing substances—such as humanity—and what it consists in: such as a person's shape (what form it takes); and their stature (how many feet tall they are); and their kinship, who (who is their brother); where they may be located; when they were born; whether they are standing or sitting; do they go shod or armed; what they are doing, or what is being done to them; and whatever innumerable examples are to be found either in these nine categories, of which I have described a few for illustrative purposes, or in the overall category of substance.[73]

(29) What good did it do me (in fact it stood in my way) when I tried to understand even you, O my God, extraordinarily absolute and immutable as you are, and thought that whatever existed was completely encapsulated by those ten categories? As if even you were a subject, of which greatness or beauty could be predicated, letting them exist in you as if you were their subject (as in the case of an ordinary body)! But you yourself are your own greatness and your own beauty; whereas a body is not great or beautiful by reason of its being a body, because even if it were less big and less beautiful, it would still be a body. My way of understanding you was falsehood, not truth; the creation of my own wretchedness, not the stable foundation of your bliss. For you had issued your orders, and so it came to pass in me, that the earth brought forth thorns and thistles for me, and with labor did I earn my bread. Gn 3:18–19

(30) What good did it do me either that I read and understood for myself all the books of the so-called "liberal arts," as many as I could—and I the most worthless slave of evil desires? I rejoiced in them, but as to whatever was true and sure in them, I had no idea where it

179

bam ad lumen et ad ea quae inluminantur faciem, unde ipsa facies mea, qua inluminata cernebam, non inluminabatur. quidquid de arte loquendi et disserendi, quidquid de dimensionibus figurarum et de musicis et de numeris, sine magna difficultate nullo hominum tradente intellexi.

Scis tu, domine deus meus, quia et celeritas intellegendi et dispiciendi acumen donum tuum est. (sed non inde sacrificabam tibi; itaque mihi non ad usum sed ad perniciem magis valebat, quia tam bonam partem substantiae meae sategi habere in potestate et fortitudinem meam non ad te custodiebam, sed profectus sum abs te in longinquam regionem, ut eam dissiparem in meretrices cupiditates.) nam quid mihi proderat bona res non utenti bene? non enim sentiebam illas artes etiam ab studiosis et ingeniosis difficillime intellegi, nisi cum eis eadem conabar exponere, et erat ille excellentissimus in eis qui me exponentem non tardius sequeretur.

(31) Sed quid mihi hoc proderat, putanti quod tu, domine deus veritas, corpus esses lucidum et immensum et ego frustum de illo corpore? nimia perversitas! sed sic eram nec erubesco, deus meus, confiteri tibi in me misericordias tuas et invocare te, qui non erubui tunc profiteri hominibus blasphemias meas et latrare adversum te. quid ergo tunc mihi proderat ingenium per illas doctrinas agile et nullo adminiculo humani magisterii tot nodosissimi libri enodati, cum deformiter et sacrilega turpitudine in doc-

---

74 Cf. Jer 2:27; Ez 8:16. Turning one's back was, and is, a potentially insulting action.

75 Cf. Plotinus, *Enn.* 2.2.7 on direct and indirect intellectual perception.   76 *substantia* is used here in the sense of "property" rather than as a technical philosophical term.

came from. I had my back to the light,[74] and my face to those things that are illuminated; so my face, by which I saw those things illuminated, was not itself illuminated.[75] Whatever I read on the art of public speaking and argument, on geometry and music and arithmetic I understood without difficulty and without anyone to explain it to me.

You know this, O Lord my God, for swift intelligence and keen discernment are your gift. But they did not prompt me to offer sacrifice to you; and so they were no use to me but rather contributed to my downfall. After all, I had my hands full getting control of such a large portion of my substance,[76] and I was not preserving my strength for you. Instead I was going away from you, into a far country, to fritter it away on shameless desires. What good was my ability when I made no proper use of it? For I did not feel that those arts were particularly difficult for people who are hardworking and intelligent to understand, until I started trying to explain those same ideas to them; then the person who was least slow to understand my explanation was the one who most excelled in those arts.

(31) What good did it do me, to think that you, O Lord God, O Truth, were an unfathomable, luminous body, and I a particle of that body? What extraordinary heresy! But that is how I was, and I do not blush, O my God, to confess to you your mercies toward me, and to call upon you; after all, I did not blush then to publish my blasphemies to everyone and to rant at you. What good was my intelligence to me, made so nimble by those doctrines; and all those complicated books disentangled without the help of any human tuition; when I was abandoning the teachings of the faith with my corrupt and scandalous immorality?

Lk 15:13

Ps 59:9

Jdt 11:19

181

trina pietatis errarem? aut quid tantum oberat parvulis
tuis longe tardius ingenium, cum a te longe non rece-
derent, ut in nido ecclesiae tuae tuti plumescerent et alas
caritatis alimento sanae fidei nutrirent?

O domine deus noster, in velamento alarum tuarum
speremus, et protege nos et porta nos. tu portabis et par-
vulos et usque ad canos tu portabis, quoniam firmitas nostra quando tu es, tunc est firmitas, cum autem nostra est,
infirmitas est. vivit apud te semper bonum nostrum, et
quia inde aversi sumus, perversi sumus. revertamur iam,
domine, ut non evertamur, quia vivit apud te sine ullo
defectu bonum nostrum, quod tu ipse es, et non timemus[15] ne non sit quo redeamus, quia nos inde ruimus.
nobis autem absentibus non ruit domus nostra, aeternitas
tua.

[15] timemus *S Knöll Skut. Ver.*: timebimus *codd.*

How much of an obstacle to your little ones were their far slower wits, when they did not stray far from you, so that instead, like fledglings, they could come into pin safe in the nest of your Church, and nurture their wings of love with the nourishment of a sound faith?[77]

O Lord our God, let us put our hope in the covering of your wings: protect us and carry us. You will bear us up when we are little, and you will keep on bearing us right up into old age, for when you are our firm foundation, then it is a foundation indeed; while when it is our own, it is no firm foundation at all. Our good dwells ever with you, and because we are diverted from it, we instead become perverted.[78] Let us return, Lord, so as not to be overturned,[79] for our unblemished good abides with you; for you yourself are that good, so we are not afraid that we have nowhere to return, just because we once broke away. Even while we were away our house has not fallen into decay, for it is your eternity.[80]

Ps 17:8, etc.

Is 46:4

[77] Echoing Jb 39:26, Ps 84:3, Lk 13:34; but the image is A.'s own: the feathers that the nestlings develop in order to fly suggests those who attend or attain the divine presence (Is 6:2; cf. 40.31).

[78] Paronomasia: *aversi/perversi*.

[79] Paronomasia: *revertamur/evertamur*.

[80] The house of A.'s soul was in ruins (*Conf.* 1.5.6); "our house" must refer to the Father's house (Jn 14:2).

LIBER V

1. (1) Accipe sacrificium confessionum mearum de manu
linguae meae (quam formasti et excitasti, ut confiteatur
nomini tuo), et sana omnia ossa mea, et dicant, "domine,
quis similis tibi?" neque enim docet te quid in se agatur
qui tibi confitetur, quia oculum tuum non excludit cor
clausum nec manum tuam repellit duritia hominum, sed
solvis eam cum voles, aut miserans aut vindicans, et non
est qui se abscondat a calore tuo. sed te laudet anima mea
ut amet te, et confiteatur tibi miserationes tuas ut laudet
te. non cessat nec tacet laudes tuas universa creatura tua,
nec spiritus omnis per os conversum ad te, nec animalia
nec corporalia per os considerantium ea, ut exsurgat in
te a lassitudine anima nostra, innitens eis quae fecisti et
transiens ad te, qui fecisti haec mirabiliter. et ibi refectio
et vera fortitudo.

2. (2) Eant et fugiant a te inquieti iniqui. et tu vides eos

---

¹ Cf. *Conf.* 11.11.13. In *En. Ps.* 72.30 A. explains the metaphor, "Surely a tongue does not have hands? So what does it
mean, 'in the hands of the tongue'? It means 'In the power of the
tongue.'"

² A reprise of the "confession" theme; cf Introduction, p. xix.

³ The last verse of the Psalter, 150:6, declares, "Let everything
that has breath: praise the Lord."

BOOK V

1. (1) Receive the sacrifice of my confessions from the hand of my tongue,[1] for you created it and inspired it to confess your name.[2] Heal all my bones, and let them say, "Lord, who is like you?" Anyone who makes his confession to you is not teaching you what is taking place within him, because a closed-up heart does not shut out your gaze; nor does human obduracy ward off your touch. You shatter it when you choose, whether for pity or punishment's sake, and there is no one who can hide from your fire. Let my soul praise you so that it comes to love you, and confess your mercies to you so that it comes to praise you. Your whole creation never ceases to praise you, never falls silent, nor does every living being,[3] its voice directed toward you, nor animate creatures and inanimate objects (through the voice of those who contemplate them): so our soul abandons weariness and rises up to you, making use of what you have created to find its way over to you, who made these things so wonderfully. And there is re-creation and true strength.

2. (2) Let the wicked, those who are without rest,[4] depart and flee from you. And still you see them and you

cf. Mal 1:10;
Ps 54:6

Prv 18:21

Pss 6:2,
35:10

Rom 2:5

Ps 19:6

Ps 145:2

Ps 107:8

Jb 37:5;
Ps 72:18;
Ws 19:5

---

[4] The asyndeton virtually identifies restlessness (cf. *Conf.* 1.1.1) with wickedness.

185

CONFESSIONS

et distinguis umbras, et ecce pulchra sunt cum eis omnia
et ipsi turpes sunt. et quid nocuerunt tibi? aut in quo
imperium tuum dehonestaverunt, a caelis usque in novis-
sima iustum et integrum? quo enim fugerunt, cum fu-
gerent a facie tua? aut ubi tu non invenis eos? sed fugerunt
ut non viderent te videntem se atque excaecati in te offenderent, quia non deseris aliquid eorum quae fecisti; in te
offenderent iniusti et iuste vexarentur, subtrahentes se
lenitati tuae et offendentes in rectitudinem tuam et caden-
tes in asperitatem tuam. videlicet nesciunt quod ubique
sis, quem nullus circumscribit locus, et solus es praesens
etiam his qui longe fiunt a te. convertantur ergo et quae-
rant te, quia non, sicut ipsi deseruerunt creatorem suum,
ita tu deseruisti creaturam tuam: ipsi convertantur.

Et ecce ibi es in corde eorum, in corde confitentium
tibi et proicientium se in te et plorantium in sinu tuo post
vias suas difficiles. et tu facilis terges lacrimas eorum, et
magis plorant et gaudent in fletibus, quoniam tu, domine,
non aliquis homo, caro et sanguis, sed tu, domine, qui
fecisti, reficis et consolaris eos. et ubi ego eram, quando
te quaerebam? et tu eras ante me, ego autem et a me
discesseram nec me inveniebam: quanto minus te!

3. (3) Proloquar[1] in conspectu dei mei annum illum
undetricensimum aetatis meae. iam venerat Carthaginem
quidam manichaeorum episcopus, Faustus nomine, magnus laqueus diaboli, et multi implicabantur in eo per inle-

---

[1] proloquar *codd. edd.*: proloquor S GM

---

5 For the idea of inflicting harm on God, cf. *De civ. D.* 12.3.
6 See Introduction, p. xxvi, for Faustus.

186

cleave the shadows, and look! All about them are things of beauty, yet they themselves are vile. But what wrong have they done you?[5] And how have they dishonored your sovereignty, which from the heavens to the uttermost parts of the earth is righteous and perfect? Where did they flee when they fled from your presence? What place is there where you do not encounter them? They fled to avoid seeing you see them, and in their blindness stumbled against you, for you forsake nothing that you have made. So the unrighteous stumbled against you and they were duly troubled: withdrawing from your tenderness, and stumbling at your righteousness, and falling into your severe judgment. Certainly they have no idea that you are everywhere, that you are not confined to any one place, and that you are uniquely present even with those who set themselves at a distance from you. Let them be converted, therefore, and seek you, for you have not abandoned your creation in the way that they have abandoned their creator: so let them be converted.

See—there you are, in their hearts, in the hearts of those who confess to you and cast themselves upon you, and who weep upon your bosom after all their arduous journeying. And you simply dry their tears, and they weep even more, and rejoice amid their tears, for you, Lord, are no mere human being, flesh and blood, but you, Lord, are the one who made them; and you restore them, and comfort them. So where was I, when I was searching for you? You were right in front of me, but I had even abandoned myself, and I could not find myself, never mind you!

3. (3) In the sight of my God I must describe that twenty-ninth year of my age. A certain Manichaean bishop called Faustus,[6] a powerful devil's snare, had already ar-

Rom 11:7–11

Ws 11:24–25;
Ps 145:8–9;
Ez 33:11

1 Pt 5:7

Lk 15:20

Ps 23:3

1 Tm 3:7

187

cebram suaviloquentiae. quam ego iam tametsi laudabam,
discernebam tamen a veritate rerum quarum discenda-
rum avidus eram, nec quali vasculo sermonis, sed quid
mihi scientiae comedendum apponeret nominatus apud
eos ille Faustus intuebar. fama enim de illo praelocuta
mihi erat quod esset honestarum omnium doctrinarum
peritissimus et apprime disciplinis liberalibus eruditus. et
quoniam multa philosophorum legeram memoriaeque
mandata retinebam, ex eis quaedam comparabam illis
manichaeorum longis fabulis, et mihi probabiliora ista
videbantur quae dixerunt illi qui tantum potuerunt valere
ut possent aestimare saeculum, quamquam eius dominum
minime invenerint. quoniam magnus es, domine, et humi-
lia respicis, excelsa autem a longe cognoscis, nec propin-
quas nisi obtritis corde nec inveniris a superbis, nec si illi
curiosa peritia numerent stellas et harenam et dimetiantur
sidereas plagas et vestigent vias astrorum.

(4) Mente sua enim quaerunt ista et ingenio quod tu
dedisti eis et multa invenerunt et praenuntiaverunt ante
multos annos defectus luminarium solis et lunae, quo die,
qua hora, quanta ex parte futuri essent, et non eos fefellit
numerus. et ita factum est ut praenuntiaverunt, et scrip-

---

7 A. uses the vessel metaphor to make a form/content distinction about speech; already himself a master of rhetoric, he is accordingly less impressed by Faustus' skill in that respect.

8 The psalm quotation echoes the opening sentence of *Conf.*

rived in Carthage, and many people were becoming entangled with him through the lure of his seductive eloquence. Although I extolled that eloquence, I was nonetheless beginning to distinguish it from the truth of the things that I was eager to learn. I was intent less on the vessel containing his discourse than the actual knowledge that that Faustus, so famous among the Manichaeans, gave me to devour.[7] His reputation had already been proclaimed to me, to the effect that he was an expert in all kinds of worthwhile academic subjects, and particularly accomplished in the higher forms of learning. Because I had read widely among the philosophers and committed their precepts to memory, I compared particular teachings of theirs to those protracted myths of the Manichaeans; and what the philosophers said seemed more likely to me even though they had only the capacity to measure this present world, and despite the fact that they never discovered its Lord. For you are great, Lord,[8] yet still have respect for the lowly, while you regard from afar what is lofty; and you draw near only to the broken-hearted and are beyond the perceiving of the proud, even if they had the searching intelligence to tell the number of the stars and the grains of sand, and to measure out the starry vault of heaven and to track the paths of the constellations.

(4) The philosophers seek all this in their minds, and with the intelligence which you gave them they have both discovered many things and have foretold, many years in advance, eclipses of those celestial bodies the sun and moon: on what day, what hour, to what degree they would occur, and their calculation did not let them down. So it came about that they made predictions and wrote down

Ws 13:9

Ps 138:6

serunt regulas indagatas, et leguntur hodie atque ex eis
praenuntiatur quo anno et quo mense anni et quo die
mensis et qua hora diei et quota parte luminis sui defec-
tura sit luna vel sol: et ita fiet ut praenuntiatur. et mirantur
haec homines et stupent qui nesciunt ea, et exultant atque
extolluntur qui sciunt, et per impiam superbiam rece-
dentes et deficientes a lumine tuo tanto ante solis defectum futurum praevident, et in praesentia suum non vident
(non enim religiose quaerunt unde habeant ingenium quo
ista quaerunt), et invenientes quia tu fecisti eos, non ipsi
se dant tibi, se ut serves quod fecisti, et quales se ipsi fece-
rant occidunt se tibi, et trucidant exaltationes suas sicut
volatilia, et curiositates suas sicut pisces maris quibus per-
ambulant secretas semitas abyssi, et luxurias suas sicut
pecora campi, ut tu, deus, ignis edax consumas mortuas
curas eorum, recreans eos immortaliter.

(5) Sed non noverunt viam, verbum tuum, per quod
fecisti ea quae numerant et ipsos qui numerant, et sensum
quo cernunt quae numerant et mentem de qua numerant:
et sapientiae tuae non est numerus. ipse autem unigenitus
factus est nobis sapientia et iustitia et sanctificatio, et nu-
meratus est inter nos, et solvit tributum Caesari. non no-

---

9 A. associates birds with pride, fish with curiosity, and beasts
with physical pleasures, *En. Ps.* 8.13.
10 These evocations of Scripture contrast Christ's humility
with the philosophers' pride.

rules as a result of their research; these are still being read today, and it is their prediction in what year, and on what month of the year, and on what day, and on what hour of the day, and to what degree there will be a failing of the light of moon or sun. And it will happen exactly as predicted. People who understand nothing of this field of study are amazed at this, and stunned; while those who do understand it are proud and praised to the skies, but through their ungodly pride they depart from your great light and fall away. Previously they foresee the failing of the sun, but now their own failing they do not perceive, for they do not seek in a godly way what is the source of that intelligence by which they make their investigations. When they discover that you made them, they do not surrender themselves to you, letting you save what you have created. Nor do they sacrifice themselves, such as they had made themselves, to you; or put to death their own self-glorifications like the birds of the air[9] or, like the fish of the sea, their curiosities, by which they traverse all the hidden paths of the deep, or their excess of passions like the cattle in the fields: so that you, O God, as a devouring fire can consume those dead concerns of theirs, as you re-create them to be immortal. Ps 8:8

(5) But they did not know the way—your Word, by whom you made both those things that they calculate, and themselves who do the calculating, and the capacity to reason that they employ in calculating, and the understanding by which means they make their calculations: but there is no calculating your wisdom! He, the only-begotten, was made for us wisdom and righteousness and sanctification, and he was numbered among us, and paid his dues to Caesar.[10] They did not know this way, by which they de- Jn 14:6
Ps 147:5
1 Cor 1:24, 30
Is 53:12
Mt 22:21

verunt hanc viam qua descendant ad illum a se et per eum
ascendant ad eum. non noverunt hanc viam, et putant se
excelsos esse cum sideribus et lucidos, et ecce ruerunt in
terram, et obscuratum est insipiens cor eorum. et multa
vera de creatura dicunt et veritatem, creaturae artificem,
non pie quaerunt, et ideo non inveniunt, aut si inveniunt,
cognoscentes deum non sicut deum honorant aut gratias
agunt, et evanescunt in cogitationibus suis, et dicunt se
esse sapientes sibi tribuendo quae tua sunt, ac per hoc
student perversissima caecitate etiam tibi tribuere quae
sua sunt, mendacia scilicet in te conferentes, qui veritas
es, et immutantes gloriam incorrupti dei in similitudinem
imaginis corruptibilis hominis et volucrum et quadrupe-
dum et serpentium, et convertunt veritatem tuam in mendacium, et colunt et serviunt creaturae potius quam creatori.

(6) Multa tamen ab eis ex ipsa creatura vera dicta retinebam, et occurrebat mihi ratio per numeros et ordinem
temporum et visibiles attestationes siderum, et confere-
bam cum dictis Manichaei, quae de his rebus multa scrip-
sit copiosissime delirans, et non mihi occurrebat ratio nec
solistitiorum[2] et aequinoctiorum nec defectuum luminarium nec quidquid tale in libris saecularis sapientiae didiceram. ibi autem credere iubebar, et ad illas rationes numeris et oculis meis exploratas non occurrebat, et longe
diversum erat.

2 solistitiorum S *Knöll Skut. Ver.*: solstitiorum *codd. Maur.*

11 I.e., they recognize God the Father but not his incarnate,
human, Son.

scend to him and away from themselves; and by him they ascend to him. They did not know this way, and they think themselves exalted and shining among the stars, but look how they have tumbled down to earth, and their foolish hearts are darkened! They speak many truths about the creation, but do not devoutly seek him who is Truth, the maker of creation; therefore they do not find him. Or if they do find him, even though they know God, they do not honor him as God[11] or give thanks, and they dwindle away in their own reflections, and claim to be wise by claiming for themselves what is yours. So with obstinate blindness they also attribute characteristics to you that really belong to themselves, even ascribing lies to you who are the Truth; and turning the glory of an imperishable God into the semblance of a perishable likeness of humanity, and birds, and beasts, and serpents, and they change your Truth into a lie, and they worship and serve your creation rather than the creator.

Is 14:12–15;
Rom 1:21–25

cf. Ps 106:20

(6) Still, I remembered many of their true teachings, drawn from creation itself; I found there a rational explanation by means of number and succession of times and the visible testimony of the stars. I compared these with the teachings of Manichaeus (he had written at length on these subjects, but in a totally deranged fashion), but I found there no such rational explanation, either of solstices and equinoxes, or of eclipses, or of anything on those lines that I had found out about from those books of secular wisdom. But that was where I was being instructed to put my faith: and what I was told was not consonant with the rational explanations that I had determined by calculation and personal observation, but instead was markedly different.

4. (7) Numquid, domine deus veritatis, quisquis novit ista, iam placet tibi? infelix enim homo qui scit illa omnia, te autem nescit; beatus autem qui te scit, etiamsi illa nesciat. qui vero et te et illa novit, non propter illa beatior, sed propter te solum beatus est, si cognoscens te sicut te glorificet et gratias agat, et non evanescat in cogitationibus suis. sicut enim melior est qui novit possidere arborem et de usu eius tibi gratias agit, quamvis nesciat vel quot cubitis alta sit vel quanta latitudine diffusa, quam ille qui eam metitur et omnes ramos eius numerat et neque possidet eam neque creatorem eius novit aut diligit, sic fidelis homo, cuius totus mundus divitiarum est et quasi nihil habens omnia possidet inhaerendo tibi, cui serviunt omnia, quamvis nec saltem septentrionum gyros noverit, dubitare stultum est, quin utique melior sit quam mensor caeli et numerator siderum et pensor elementorum et neglegens tui, qui omnia in mensura et numero et pondere disposuisti.

5. (8) Sed tamen quis quaerebat Manichaeum nescio quem etiam ista scribere, sine quorum peritia pietas disci poterat? dixisti enim homini, "ecce pietas est sapientia." quam ille ignorare posset, etiamsi ista perfecte nosset; ista vero quia non noverat, impudentissime audens docere,

---

12 On the symbolism (both Manichaean and Christian) of trees for A., cf. Ferrari, "Pear Theft," 234–36.

13 These words are only in the LXX, not the Latin or Hebrew text of Proverbs: "All the world of riches belongs to the one who is faithful; but not a penny goes to the unfaithful one."

14 or "Plow."

15 The pre-Vulgate Latin Bible: Hebrew, LXX and Vg all preserve a different version of this verse.

4. (7) O Lord God of truth, surely it is not people who know such things as these who are pleasing to you? How unfortunate are those who know all such things and yet do not know you! But blessed are those who know you, even if they are ignorant of such things. Anyone who knows about both them and you is not more blessed for knowing them, but they are only blessed in respect of you, if in recognizing you they glorify you for what you are, and give thanks, and do not sink into the futility of their own imaginations. In the same way someone who knows how to take care of a tree and gives thanks to you for the enjoyment of it, even though he has no idea how many cubits tall it is or how wide its spread, is better than a person who measures the tree and counts all its branches, but does not keep it properly or recognize its maker and love him.[12] So too it is pointless to wonder whether faithful people, with the whole world and all its riches[13] in their grasp, who have nothing and yet possess everything by cleaving to you whom all things serve, are surely better, even if they do not even know the orbits of the Great Bear,[14] than someone who measures heaven, and counts stars, and reflects on first principles, and forgets about you, who have arranged all things so that they have magnitude, number and weight.

Rom 1:21

Prv 17:6[LXX]
2 Cor 6:10
Ps 119:91

Ws 11:20

5. (8) But who was asking some fellow called Manichaeus to write about these subjects, given that anyone could learn reverence for God without any expertise in such matters? For you have told mortals, "Look—reverence for God is wisdom."[15] He could have been unaware of this even if he were an expert on those other subjects; but because he still had the outrageous presumption to teach them, even though he knew nothing of them, it fol-

Jb 28:28[VL]

CONFESSIONS

prorsus illam nosse non posset. vanitas est enim mundana
ista etiam nota profiteri, pietas autem tibi confiteri. unde
ille devius ad hoc ista multum locutus est, ut convictus ab
eis qui ista vere didicissent, quis esset eius sensus in ceteris quae abditiora sunt manifeste cognosceretur. non enim
parvi se aestimari voluit, sed spiritum sanctum, consola-
torem et ditatorem fidelium tuorum, auctoritate plenaria
personaliter in se esse persuadere conatus est. itaque cum
de caelo ac stellis et de solis ac lunae motibus falsa dixisse
deprehenderetur, quamvis ad doctrinam religionis ista
non pertineant, tamen ausus eius sacrilegos fuisse satis
emineret, cum ea non solum ignorata sed etiam falsa tam
vesana superbiae vanitate diceret, ut ea tamquam divinae
personae tribuere sibi niteretur.

(9) Cum enim audio christianum aliquem fratrem illum aut illum ista nescientem et aliud pro alio sentientem,
patienter intueor opinantem hominem nec illi obesse video, cum de te, domine creator omnium, non credat indigna, si forte situs et habitus creaturae corporalis ignoret.
obest autem, si hoc ad ipsam doctrinae pietatis formam
pertinere arbitretur et pertinacius affirmare audeat quod
ignorat. sed etiam talis infirmitas in fidei cunabulis a cari-

---

16 Cf. *Conf.* 4.2.2, 4.7.12 on *vanitas*.
17 Cf. *Conf.* 7.7.11 for the contrast of Christ as the Way.

lows that he could have no knowledge of such reverence. To make profession of those worldly things, even when properly understood, is vanity;[16] to make confession to you is piety. Hence he went astray[17] and spoke at length about these subjects, with the result that he was exposed as a fraud by those who really were experts in the field. This made it perfectly clear how much understanding he might possess in other, more obscure, matters. He did not want himself to be considered unimportant; so he tried to claim that the Holy Spirit, the Comforter and Enricher of your faithful ones, was personally present in him, with full authority. So when he was caught telling untruths about the heaven and the stars, and the movements of the sun and moon (even though they are not relevant to the true teaching of religion), it became quite plain that his efforts were sacrilegious. For he was making pronouncements about things that were not only beyond his comprehension but also falsehoods, and with such a deranged and vain pride that he tried to take the credit for them himself as if he were a divine being.

(9) Nowadays when I hear some one or other of my Christian brothers who is ignorant about these subjects and believes one thing rather than another, I regard him with patience while he expresses his view. Nor do I see him as having a problem if he happens to be ignorant about the situation and appearance of physical creation, provided that he has no beliefs that are unworthy of you, O Lord, creator of all. It is only a problem if he thinks his view is consistent with our foundational principles of reverence for God, and goes so far as to assert obstinately what he knows nothing about. Yet when faith is in its cradle, even a weakness like this is supported by Love,

tate matre sustinetur, donec adsurgat novus homo in virum perfectum et circumferri non possit omni vento doctrinae.

In illo autem qui doctor, qui auctor, qui dux et princeps
eorum quibus illa suaderet, ita fieri ausus est, ut qui eum
sequerentur non quemlibet hominem sed spiritum tuum
sanctum se sequi arbitrarentur, quis tantam dementiam,
sicubi falsa dixisse convinceretur, non detestandam longeque abiciendam esse iudicaret? sed tamen nondum liquido
compereram utrum etiam secundum eius verba vicissitu-
dines longiorum et breviorum dierum atque noctium et
ipsius noctis et diei et deliquia luminum et si quid eius
modi in aliis libris legeram posset exponi, ut, si forte posset, incertum quidem mihi fieret utrum ita se res haberet
an ita, sed ad fidem meam illius auctoritatem propter cre-
ditam sanctitatem praeponerem.

6. (10) Et per annos ferme ipsos novem quibus eos
animo vagabundus audivi nimis extento desiderio ventu-
rum expectabam istum Faustum. ceteri enim eorum in
quos forte incurrissem, qui talium rerum quaestionibus a
me obiectibus deficiebant, illum mihi promittebant, cuius
adventu conlatoque conloquio facillime mihi haec et si
qua forte maiora quaererem enodatissime expedirentur.
ergo ubi venit, expertus sum hominem gratum et iucun-

A. repeats the idea at *Conf.* 13.6.7; cf. *Io. Ev. Tr.* 2.4; *En. Ps.* 147.14. OD remarks that love (identified with the Holy Spirit) as the bond joining Father and Son is distinctive of A.'s theology.

Cf. Introduction, p. xxvi; "hearer" is a technical term for the lower rank of Manichaeism.

our Mother;[18] until the new person grows up into a perfect adult and can no longer be carried about by every changing wind of doctrine.

Eph 4:13

But as for that man who dared to pass himself off as the teacher, the founder, the leader and principal of those whom he tried to influence in that direction, such was his presumption that those who did follow him thought that they were following, no mere human being, but your Holy Spirit! If at any point he was convicted of having told untruths, who would not agree that such extreme delusions should be abominated and utterly rejected? But I had not yet ascertained clearly whether the changes between longer and shorter days and nights, and of night and day themselves, and the eclipses of the sun and moon, and anything of that kind which I had studied in other books, could also be construed according to his explanation. So if that remained a possibility, I was still in doubt which of the two explanations was the true one; but because I put my trust in his pure holiness, I gave preference to his authority over my own convictions.

6. (10) For almost nine years, in which my mind was aimless and destitute, and I continued a "hearer," I was all too eagerly waiting for the famous Faustus to arrive.[19] When I happened to meet other Manichaeans, and they failed to counter the objections I made on such topics, they nonetheless kept holding out to me the promise of this Faustus. His arrival, and the opportunity of discussion with him, would easily disentangle and unravel these problems for me, and any others I was investigating, including ones which were even more difficult. So when he did arrive, I found him to be agreeable and affable in his manner of speech, but he droned on with the same argu-

199

dum verbis et ea ipsa quae illi solent dicere multo suavius garrientem. sed quid ad meam sitim pretiosorum poculorum decentissimus ministrator? iam rebus talibus satiatae erant aures meae, nec ideo mihi meliora videbantur quia melius dicebantur, nec ideo vera quia diserta, nec ideo sapiens anima quia vultus congruus et decorum eloquium. illi autem qui eum mihi promittebant non boni rerum existimatores erant, et ideo illis videbatur prudens et sapiens, quia delectabat eos loquens.

Sensi autem aliud genus hominum etiam veritatem habere suspectam et ei nolle adquiescere, si compto atque uberi sermone promeretur. me autem iam docueras,[3] deus meus, miris et occultis modis (et propterea credo quod tu me docueris, quoniam verum est, nec quisquam praeter te alius doctor est veri, ubicumque et undecumque claruerit), iam ergo abs te didiceram nec eo debere videri aliquid verum dici, quia eloquenter dicitur, nec eo falsum, quia incomposite sonant signa labiorum; rursus nec ideo verum, quia impolite enuntiatur, nec ideo falsum, quia splendidus sermo est, sed perinde esse sapientiam et stultitiam sicut sunt cibi utiles et inutiles, verbis autem ornatis et inornatis sicut vasis urbanis et rusticanis utrosque cibos posse ministrari.

(11) Igitur aviditas mea, qua illum tanto tempore ex-

---

3 docueras *codd. Knöll*: docuerat *S Skut. Ver.*

20 *poculum* can mean either a cup or its contents: a fine metaphor for the form/content dichotomy.
21 Cf. Cic. *Orat.* 69; with A. *Doctr. Chr.* 4.142–44.

ments as they habitually used, albeit in a more attractive style. But what difference could it make to quenching my thirst to have a finely-dressed butler handing me a precious goblet?[20] My ears had already had their fill of such matters, nor did those subjects seem to me to be better in themselves just because they were better expressed; nor were they true because they were fluently delivered. Nor for that matter is anyone's soul wise because their face is agreeable and their eloquence congenial. The people who recommended him to me were hardly good judges of the subjects concerned. Hence he seemed to them to be knowledgeable and wise because he delighted them with his style of speaking.

I had the impression, though, that there is a type of person that holds even truth to be in doubt, and refuses to accept it if it is expressed in a elaborate and lavish style of speech. You had already taught me, O my God, by wonderful and mysterious ways (and the reason why I believe that you taught me is because it is true, and there is no other teacher of the truth but you, wherever that truth shines upon us and wherever it comes from). And so I had learned from you that nothing should appear to be spoken truthfully just because it is spoken charmingly. Also that nothing should be taken as false because the messages come from lips with an unharmonious sound. Conversely, nothing is true just because it is said in a rough and ready way, or false just because it is a glorious piece of oratory. So to conclude, wisdom and folly are like wholesome and unwholesome food; and both kinds of food can be served up through the medium of either simple or intricate speech as if from sophisticated or homely vessels.[21]

(11) I had been looking forward for so long to meeting

pectaveram hominem, delectabatur quidem motu affectuque disputantis et verbis congruentibus atque ad vestiendas sententias facile occurrentibus. delectabar autem et cum multis vel etiam prae multis laudabam ac ferebam, sed moleste habebam quod in coetu audientium non sinerer ingerere illi et partiri cum eo curas quaestionum mearum conferendo familiariter et accipiendo ac reddendo sermonem. quod ubi potui et aures eius cum familiaribus meis eoque tempore occupare coepi quo non dedeceret alternis disserere, et protuli quaedam quae me movebant, expertus sum prius hominem expertem liberalium disciplinarum nisi grammaticae atque eius ipsius usitato modo. et quia legerat aliquas tullianas orationes et paucissimos Senecae libros et nonnulla poetarum et suae sectae si qua volumina latine atque composite conscripta erant, et quia aderat cotidiana sermocinandi exercitatio, inde suppetebat eloquium, quod fiebat acceptius magisque seductorium moderamine ingenii et quodam lepore naturali. itane est, ut recolo, domine deus meus, arbiter conscientiae meae? coram te cor meum et recordatio mea, qui me tunc agebas abdito secreto providentiae tuae et inhonestos errores meos iam convertebas ante faciem meam, ut viderem et odissem.

7. (12) Nam posteaquam ille mihi imperitus earum artium quibus eum excellere putaveram satis apparuit,

---

22 A. makes scant reference to L. Annaeus Seneca (5/4 BC–ADb 65) but is steeped in Cicero.   23 Untranslatable paronomasia: "*cor*am te *cor* meum et re*cor*datio."

24 A.'s understanding of providence develops over time, from *Ord.* to *De civ. D.*: in *Gn. Litt.* 8.23.44 he refers to "the providence of God ruling and directing the entire creation."

with that man that I was hungry to relish his use of gesture and emotion in debate, and his use of harmonious diction that was well-adapted to clothing his ideas. Yes I relished it, and along with many others, perhaps even more than they, I was praising him and talking of him. But still I was annoyed because as one of the gathering of "hearers" I was not allowed to approach him and share with him the concerns raised by my inquiries in a friendly discussion and dialogue. When I did get an opportunity, I began, together with my close friends, to engage his attention (this was at a time when starting such a dialogue was not inappropriate) and brought up certain matters which were troubling me. I found him from the start to be a person ignorant of the liberal disciplines except grammar, and even in that he was nothing out of the ordinary. Just because he had read some of Cicero's speeches, one or two works of Seneca,[22] some poets, and whatever works of his own school were written in proper Latin; and just because he practiced his oratorical skills daily, he acquired a fluency that the use of his intelligence, together with a certain natural charm, made quite acceptable, and even fascinating. O Lord my God, judge of my conscience, is it really the way I remember it? My heart is open to you, and my memory,[23] for you   Nm 10:9 were leading me then through the deep mystery of your providence[24] and setting all my shameful lapses before my face, to make me see them and hate them.   Ps 50:21

7. (12) After he made it plain to me that he had no expertise in those arts in which I had expected him to excel, I began to give up hope of his unfolding and solving

desperare coepi posse mihi eum illa quae me movebant
aperire atque dissolvere; quorum quidem ignarus posset
veritatem tenere pietatis, sed si manichaeus non esset. libri quippe eorum pleni sunt longissimis fabulis de caelo
et sideribus et sole et luna; quae mihi eum, quod utique
cupiebam, conlatis numerorum rationibus quas alibi ego
legeram, utrum potius ita essent ut Manichaei libris conti-
nebantur, an certe vel par etiam inde ratio redderetur,
subtiliter explicare posse iam non arbitrabar. quae tamen
ubi consideranda et discutienda protuli, modeste sane ille
nec ausus est subire ipsam sarcinam. noverat enim se ista
non nosse nec eum puduit confiteri. non erat de talibus,
quales multos loquaces passus eram, conantes ea me docere et dicentes nihil. iste vero cor habebat, etsi non rectum ad te, nec tamen nimis incautum ad se ipsum. non
usquequaque imperitus erat imperitiae suae, et noluit se
temere disputando in ea coartare unde nec exitus ei ullus
nec facilis esset reditus: etiam hinc mihi amplius placuit.
pulchrior est enim temperantia confitentis animi quam illa
quae nosse cupiebam. et eum in omnibus difficilioribus et
subtilioribus quaestionibus talem inveniebam.

(13) Refracto itaque studio quod intenderam in Manichaei litteras, magisque desperans de ceteris eorum doc-

---

25 Cf. A. *Ep.* 190.16, "No one should be ashamed to admit that
they do not know what they do not know, in case while feigning
knowledge, they come to deserve never to know."

those matters that were disturbing me; though despite knowing nothing about them, he could still have preserved a genuine faith, but only if he had not been a Manichaean. The books of the Manichaeans are full of long mythological tales about heaven and the stars and sun and moon, but I no longer believed that he could give me what I so ardently desired, namely a persuasive account of those myths, so that I could judge them against the mathematical calculations that I had read about elsewhere, to determine whether the books of the Manichaeans gave a superior version of how the world is, or even whether they at least yield an equally cogent explanation. When I put those matters forward for inspection and scrutiny, he was at least modest enough not to risk shouldering that burden. For he knew that he did not know, and he was not ashamed to confess it. He was not one of those talkative people of the type I had often put up with, trying to teach me when they had nothing to say. He really did have a heart, and even though it was not properly directed to you, still it was not totally improvident toward himself. He was not completely ignorant of his own ignorance, and he was unwilling to debate in a rash way that would force him into corners from which he had no escape or easy retreat.[25] Even this made him more agreeable to me. For the modesty of a mind that makes a true confession holds more appeal than those matters I wanted to know about. This was how I found him in all my more challenging and detailed questions.

(13) The enthusiasm for Manichaeus' writings which I had previously maintained was now shattered. I was even less hopeful about the rest of their teachers, seeing how Faustus, who had been so renowned, had turned out in

toribus, quando in multis quae me movebant ita ille nominatus apparuit, coepi cum eo pro studio eius agere vitam,
quo ipse flagrabat in eas litteras quas tunc iam rhetor Car-
thaginis adulescentes docebam, et legere cum eo sive quae
ille audita desideraret sive quae ipse tali ingenio apta exis-
timarem.

Ceterum conatus omnis meus quo proficere in illa
secta statueram illo homine cognito prorsus intercidit, non
ut ab eis omnino separarer sed, quasi melius quicquam
non inveniens, eo quo iam quoquo modo inrueram contentus interim esse decreveram, nisi aliquid forte quod
magis eligendum esset eluceret. ita ille Faustus, qui multis
laqueus mortis extitit, meum quo captus eram relaxare iam
coeperat, nec volens nec sciens. manus enim tuae, deus
meus, in abdito providentiae tuae non deserebant animam
meam, et de sanguine cordis matris meae per lacrimas
eius diebus et noctibus pro me sacrificabatur tibi, et egisti
mecum miris modis. tu illud egisti, deus meus, nam a domino gressus hominis diriguntur, et viam eius volet. aut
quae procuratio salutis praeter manum tuam reficientem
quae fecisti?

8. (14) Egisti ergo mecum ut mihi persuaderetur Romam pergere et potius ibi docere quod docebam Carthagini. et hoc unde mihi persuasum est non praeteribo confiteri tibi, quoniam et in his altissimi tui recessus et
praesentissima in nos misericordia tua cogitanda et prae-
dicanda est. non ideo Romam pergere volui, quod maiores

---

26 Note that Faustus *hears* these works, rather than *reading*
them; cf. Introduction, p. xxxii.

the matters of the many problems that were troubling me. So I started to keep company with him, given the burning enthusiasm he displayed for those studies that at the time, as a rhetorician, I was teaching young men in Carthage. Also I read with him either works he wanted to hear[26] or that I myself thought would be suitable for an intellect like his.

But all the effort I had resolved to put into progressing in that sect collapsed completely the moment I saw him for what he was: not to the extent that I cut myself off from them completely, but rather like someone who can find nothing better. So I had decided for the time being to be content with the way I had, so to speak, stumbled upon, unless something superior happened to appear. So this man Faustus, who represented a deadly snare to many, Ps 18:5 had already begun to loosen the trap in which I was taken, without either knowing or meaning to. In that hidden place of your providence, O my God, your hands did not let go of my soul. From her own heart's blood, and by her tears day and night my mother offered her sacrifice to you, and you dealt with me in mysterious ways. That was your doing, O my God, for the steps of mortals are directed by the Lord, and he takes pleasure in their way. Ps 37:23 How can salvation be achieved except by your hand remaking what you have made?

8. (14) You guided me into a conviction that I should set out for Rome, and teach there instead what I used to teach at Carthage. I shall not neglect to confess to you why I was persuaded to do this, for in these actions both your deepest secrets and your most immanent mercy toward us demand that we reflect on them and proclaim them. I did not want to head for Rome because my friends were urg-

quaestus maiorque mihi dignitas ab amicis qui hoc suade-
bant promittebatur (quamquam et ista ducebant animum
tunc meum), sed illa erat causa maxima et paene sola,
quod audiebam quietius ibi studere adulescentes et ordi-
natiore disciplinae cohercitione sedari, ne in eius scholam
quo magistro non utuntur passim et proterve inruant, nec
eos admitti omnino nisi ille permiserit.

Contra apud Carthaginem foeda est et intemperans
licentia scholasticorum. inrumpunt impudenter et prope
furiosa fronte perturbant ordinem quem quisque discipu-
lis ad proficiendum instituerit. multa iniuriosa faciunt
mira hebetudine, et punienda legibus nisi consuetudo
patrona sit, hoc miseriores eos ostendens, quo iam quasi
liceat faciunt quod per tuam aeternam legem numquam
licebit, et impune se facere arbitrantur, cum ipsa faciendi
caecitate puniantur et incomparabiliter patiantur peiora
quam faciunt. ergo quos mores cum studerem meos esse
nolui, eos cum docerem cogebar perpeti alienos. et ideo
placebat ire ubi talia non fieri omnes qui noverant indica-
bant.

Verum autem tu, spes mea et portio mea in terra viventium, ad mutandum terrarum locum pro salute animae
meae, et Carthagini stimulos quibus inde avellerer admo-
vebas, et Romae inlecebras quibus attraherer proponebas
mihi per homines qui diligunt vitam mortuam, hinc insana

---

27 Cf. *Conf.* 3.3.6.
28 A favorite verse of A.
29 In this context, his Manichaean friends (cf. *Conf.* 5.10.18).

ing me on with the hope of greater advantages and more prestige, though both factors were influencing my thinking at that time: the principal, almost the only, reason was that I heard that there the young men went about their studies more peaceably, settled under a better-structured disciplinary regime. They would not go brazenly bursting at random into the school of a person who was not even their teacher: they would not even be allowed in unless the teacher gave permission.

It was quite the opposite at Carthage, where the students showed a disgracefully extreme lack of restraint. They blatantly invade and, in almost a frenzy of recklessness, turn to uproar the order which the teacher has imposed for the benefit of the pupils. With extraordinary stupidity they commit their manifold outrages, which would be punishable by law but for the protection of custom. This shows that they are more pitiable insofar as they behave that way as if it were authorized, but it will never be so according to your eternal law. They think that they can act with impunity, although the very blindness of their actions is their punishment, and they suffer immeasurably worse things than they inflict. So now that I was a teacher, therefore, I constantly had to endure from others that behavior in which I refused to participate when I was a student.[27] That was why it was so appealing to go where everyone in the know confirmed that such goings on did not happen.

But you, my hope and my share in the land of the living,[28] were driving me to change my domicile for the health of my soul: at Carthage you spurred me to tear myself away from the place; at Rome you provided me with allurements to tempt me by means of people who are in love with the life that is deadly,[29] some of them doing

Ps 142:5

209

facientes, inde vana pollicentes, et ad corrigendos gressus
meos utebaris occulte et illorum et mea perversitate. nam
et qui perturbabant otium meum foeda rabie caeci erant,
et qui invitabant ad aliud terram sapiebant, ego autem, qui
detestabar hic veram miseriam, illic falsam felicitatem
appetebam.

(15) Sed quare hinc abirem et illuc irem, tu sciebas,
deus, nec indicabas mihi nec matri, quae me profectum
atrociter planxit et usque ad mare secuta est. sed fefelli
eam, violenter me tenentem ut aut revocaret aut mecum
pergeret. et finxi me amicum nolle deserere donec vento
facto navigaret, et mentitus sum matri, et illi matri. et
evasi, quia et hoc[4] dimisisti mihi misericorditer servans me
ab aquis maris, plenum exsecrandis sordibus usque ad
aquam gratiae tuae, qua me abluto siccarentur flumina
maternorum oculorum, quibus pro me cotidie tibi rigabat
terram sub vultu suo. et tamen recusanti sine me redire
vix persuasi ut in loco qui proximus nostrae navi erat,
memoria beati Cypriani, maneret ea nocte.

Sed ea nocte clanculo ego profectus sum, illa autem
non; mansit orando et flendo. et quid a te petebat, deus
meus, tantis lacrimis, nisi ut navigare me non sineres? sed

---

[4] et (hoc) S *Knöll Skut.*: hoc *codd. Ver.*

---

[30] A. makes the quotations work as a metaphor for death; the
"earthly things" of the original text has become "earth," standing
more starkly for death.   [31] A cross-cultural gesture expressing
grief, cf. e.g., Hom. *Il.* 18.30–31; Lk 18:3.   [32] I.e., baptism.

[33] Cyprian was Africa's most revered martyr (d. 258); A. refers
to him as "the great sword of God" (*magna framea dei*): *Ser.* 313.5.
This chapel is not otherwise attested, unless it is to be identified

nonsensical things, others promising fruitless ones, while in secret you used their obstinacy and mine to direct my steps aright. For they were blind, those men who were troubling my peace of mind with their disgusting frenzy; but those who kept inviting me to something different were wise only in the things of this earthly existence.[30] So though I loathed real misery in one place, I was going to another in search of fake happiness.

Phil 3:19

(15) You knew, O God, the reason why I was leaving here and heading there. But you gave no sign of it to me or to my mother, who beat her breast[31] most cruelly and followed me all the way to the sea. She clung desperately to me, trying either to make me come home or to set out with me, but I tricked her. I pretended I had a friend I was unwilling to leave until there was a good wind for his sailing. I lied to my mother—and to such a mother too! So I made my escape. You have forgiven me even this sin. In your mercy you saved me, though steeped in detestable sins, from the waters of the sea, for the waters of your grace.[32] Once I was washed in that water she dried the flow of her maternal tears. Every day, right in front of me, she used to water the ground beneath her face with tears. She was still refusing to go home without me when I persuaded her to spend the night in a place close beside our ship, a chapel dedicated to blessed Cyprian.[33]

That night, however, I secretly set sail without her. She was left behind praying and weeping.[34] But what was she asking of you, O my God, with that torrent of tears? It

with one of the two chapels (*memoriae*) marking the sites of his martyrdom and burial (A. explains *memoria; Cura Mort.* 6; *De civ. D.* 22.10).   [34] See Arts, "Syntax," 119.

tu alte consulens et exaudiens cardinem desiderii eius non curasti quod tunc petebat, ut me faceres quod semper petebat. flavit ventus et implevit vela nostra et litus subtraxit aspectibus nostris, in quo mane illa insaniebat dolore, et querellis et gemitu implebat aures tuas contemnentis ista, cum et me cupiditatibus meis raperes ad finiendas ipsas cupiditates et illius carnale desiderium iusto dolorum flagello vapularet. amabat enim secum praesentiam meam more matrum, sed multis multo amplius, et nesciebat quid tu illi gaudiorum facturus esses de absentia mea. nesciebat, ideo flebat et eiulabat, atque illis cruciatibus arguebatur in ea reliquiarium Evae, cum gemitu quaerens quod cum gemitu pepererat. et tamen post accusationem fallaciarum et crudelitatis meae conversa rursus ad deprecandum te pro me abiit ad solita, et ego Romam.

9. (16) Et ecce excipior ibi flagello aegritudinis corporalis, et ibam iam ad inferos portans omnia mala quae commiseram et in te et in me et in alios, multa et gravia super originalis peccati vinculum quo omnes in Adam morimur. non enim quicquam eorum mihi donaveras in Christo, nec solverat ille in cruce sua inimicitias quas tecum contraxeram peccatis meis. quomodo enim eas solveret in cruce phantasmatis, quod de illo credideram? quam ergo falsa mihi videbatur mors carnis eius, tam vera

---

35 OD points out A.'s implicit self-justification here. Monnica's eagerness to promote a career and advantageous marriage are at odds with God's plan.   36 This is as close as A. comes to criticizing Monnica.   37 Cf. *Conf.* 1.7.11.   38 A. follows the docetic Manichaean line that Christ was neither human nor crucified: "If you are a Manichaean you do not believe he was crucified because you do not believe he was born at all" (*S.* 117.4).

could only be that you should prevent me from sailing away. In your deep counsels you heard the key point of her desire, and you did not provide what she was praying for, namely to make me what she prayed for.[35] The wind blew and filled our sails and the shore withdrew from our gaze. And on that shore, when morning came, she went mad with grief and filled your ears with lamenting and groaning. But you took no heed, for you were snatching me away from my desires in order to put an end to those very desires; and the physical element of her attachment to me was beaten into submission by the righteous scourge of sorrows. For she loved my being present with her, as mothers do, though in her case more than most; and she had no idea what joy you were going to bring about for her out of my absence. So she went on weeping and wailing, and those torments became proof in her of the legacy of Eve, in sorrow seeking what she had borne in sorrow.[36]   Gn 3:16 Still, after condemning my deceptions and cruelty, she returned to beseeching you on my behalf. She went back to her accustomed life, and I went on to Rome.

9. (16) Look! At once I fell prey there to the scourge of a physical illness and I was on my way to hell, taking with me every evil thing that I had done, whether against you or myself or others: countless, burdensome sins over and above that bond of original sin by means of which we all die in Adam.[37] For you had not forgiven me any of them   Rom 5:14; in Christ. Nor had he, by means of his cross, undone the   1 Cor 15:22 enmity I had incurred with you because of my sins. After   Eph 2:14– all, how could he undo those hostilities by the cross of (as   16; Col 2:12 I then believed about him) an imaginary being?[38] The more the death of his flesh seemed to me to be false, the more true was the death of my soul; while the more the

213

CONFESSIONS

erat animae meae, et quam vera erat mors carnis eius, tam
falsa vita animae meae, quae id non credebat.

Et ingravescentibus febribus iam ibam et peribam. quo
enim irem, si hinc tunc abirem, nisi in ignem atque tormenta digna factis meis in veritate ordinis tui? et hoc illa
nesciebat et tamen pro me orabat absens; tu autem ubique
praesens ubi erat exaudiebas eam, et ubi eram miserebaris
mei, ut recuperarem salutem corporis adhuc insanus
corde sacrilego. neque enim desiderabam in illo tanto
periculo baptismum tuum, et melior eram puer, quo illum
de materna pietate flagitavi, sicut iam recordatus atque
confessus sum. sed in dedecus meum creveram et consilia
medicinae tuae demens inridebam, qui non me sivisti talem bis mori. quo vulnere si feriretur cor matris, numquam sanaretur. non enim satis eloquor quid erga me
habebat animi, et quanto maiore sollicitudine me parturiebat spiritu quam carne pepererat.

(17) Non itaque video quomodo sanaretur, si mea talis
illa mors transverberasset viscera dilectionis eius. et ubi
essent tantae preces, et tam crebrae sine intermissione?
nusquam nisi ad te. an vero tu, deus misericordiarum,
sperneres cor contritum et humilatum viduae castae ac
sobriae, frequentantis elemosynas, obsequentis atque ser-
vientis sanctis tuis, nullum diem praetermittentis obla-
tionem ad altare tuum, bis die, mane et vespere, ad eccle-

---

39 As usual, "she" alludes to the mother A. is so cautious about
naming in *Conf.*   40 Because it worshiped that which was not
God.   41 Cf. *Conf.* 1.11.17.   42 I.e., of body and soul.

43 The Latin says "guts" (cf. Greek σπλάγχνα; Hebrew
me'iym); in each language it is the seat of emotion and feeling.

44 I.e., the Holy Communion. See A. *De civ. D.* 10.20.

214

death of his flesh was in fact true, the more false was the life of my soul, because it did not believe in it.

As my fever worsened, I was on the point of departing and dispersing. Where would I go, then, if I left this place, but into the fiery torments that my deeds deserved, according to the truth of your ordinance? She[39] did not know about it, yet kept on praying for me though I was not with her. You are present everywhere, so where she was, your heard her, and where I was, you took pity on me. So I recovered my bodily health, though my idolatrous[40] heart was still sick. Even in that time of great peril I had no wish for your baptism, so I was in a better state when, as a boy, I had pleaded with my mother's devotion for it, as I have already described and confessed.[41] But I had grown up to my own disgrace, and in this state of madness I scorned the good sense of your healing, though you did not allow me, such as I was, to endure a double death.[42] Had my mother's heart suffered such a wound, it would never have recovered. I cannot adequately express what were her feelings toward me, and how much more she struggled to give me spiritual birth than when she had given birth to me physically.

(17) So I cannot see how she could have recovered if my death in such a fashion had pierced through the visceral[43] nature of her love. And where would her urgent prayers be then, so frequent, so unceasing? Nowhere, if not with you. God of mercies, would you really have rejected the contrite, lowly heart of a modest and sober widow? someone busy with acts of charity, obedient in serving your saints, not for a single day neglecting the offering at your altar,[44] twice daily, morning and evening,

Ps 51:17
1 Tm 3:11, 5:10

215

siam tuam sine ulla intermissione venientis, non ad vanas
fabulas et aniles loquacitates, sed ut te audiret in tuis sermonibus et tu illam in suis orationibus? huiusne tu lacrimas, quibus non a te aurum et argentum petebat, nec
aliquod nutabile aut volubile bonum, sed salutem animae
filii sui, tu, cuius munere talis erat, contemneres et repel-
leres ab auxilio tuo? nequaquam, domine. immo vero aderas et exaudiebas et faciebas ordine quo praedestinaveras
esse faciendum. absit ut tu falleres eam in illis visionibus
et responsis tuis, quae iam commemoravi et quae non
commemoravi, quae illa fideli pectore tenebat et semper
orans tamquam chirographa tua ingerebat tibi. dignaris
enim, quoniam in saeculum misericordia tua, eis quibus
omnia debita dimittis, etiam promissionibus debitor fieri.

10. (18) Recreasti ergo me ab illa aegritudine et salvum
fecisti filium ancillae tuae tunc interim corpore, ut esset
cui salutem meliorem atque certiorem dares. et iungebar
etiam tunc Romae falsis illis atque fallentibus sanctis, non
enim tantum auditoribus eorum, quorum e numero erat
etiam is in cuius domo aegrotaveram et convalueram, sed
eis etiam quos electos vocant. adhuc enim mihi videbatur
non esse nos qui peccamus, sed nescio quam aliam in
nobis peccare naturam, et delectabat superbiam meam
extra culpam esse et, cum aliquid mali fecissem, non confiteri me fecisse, ut sanares animam meam, quoniam pec-
cabat tibi, sed excusare me amabam et accusare nescio
quid aliud quod mecum esset et ego non essem. verum

---

45 I.e., the Holy Scriptures.

46 Cf. *Conf.* 3.11.19.

47 This signifies both physical health and spiritual rescue. Cf.
Conf. 1.5.5, n. 12.

attending your church without fail, and not for frivolous tales and old wives' gossip, but so that she could hear you in your own words[45] and you could hear her in her own prayers! Would you have spurned this woman's tears, not shed in pleading for you to give her gold and silver, nor for some fragile or changeable good, but for the salvation of her own son's soul? Or driven her from your help though it was by your gift that she was what she was? Not under any circumstances, Lord! Indeed you were at her side, and you heard her, and you set in train what you had preordained must take place. It was impossible that you would deceive her over those visions and your responses, both those that I have already reported and those I have not reported,[46] which she kept in her faithful heart and, constant in prayer, presented before you like your own promissory note. Because your mercy is everlasting you deign to be indebted, on account of your promises, to those whose debts you have forgiven. Pss 118:1; 136:1–26

10. (18) You restored my well-being after my illness, and healed the son of your handmaid, at least in body and for the time being; so he would become someone you might grant a better and more sure salvation.[47] At Rome I associated with those false, dissembling saints, not just those who were Manichaean "hearers," one of whom was the man in whose house I had become ill and convalesced, but also those they call "elect." It still seemed to me that it is not we ourselves who commit sin, but some other nature in us which sins. My pride delighted at not being at fault, since when I did something wrong I did not have to confess that I had done so, so that you could cleanse my soul because it was sinning against you. Instead I loved to make excuses for myself and put the blame on something Ps 86:16 Ps 41:4

autem totum ego eram et adversus me impietas mea me
diviserat, et id erat peccatum insanabilius, quo me pecca-
torem non esse arbitrabar, et execrabilis iniquitas, te, deus
omnipotens, te in me ad perniciem meam, quam me a te
ad salutem malle superari. nondum ergo posueras custodiam ori meo et ostium continentiae circum labia mea, ut
non declinaret cor meum in verba mala ad excusandas
excusationes in peccatis cum hominibus operantibus iniquitatem, et ideo adhuc combinabam cum electis eorum,
sed tamen iam desperans in ea falsa doctrina me posse
proficere, eaque ipsa quibus, si nihil melius reperirem,
contentus esse decreveram iam remissius neglegentius-
que retinebam.

(19) Etenim suborta est etiam mihi cogitatio, pruden-
tiores illos ceteris fuisse philosophos quos academicos
appellant, quod de omnibus dubitandum esse censuerant
nec aliquid veri ab homine comprehendi posse decreve-
rant. ita enim et mihi liquido sensisse videbantur, ut vulgo
habentur, etiam illorum intentionem nondum intellegenti.
nec dissimulavi eundem hospitem meum reprimere a nimia fiducia quam sensi eum habere de rebus fabulosis
quibus Manichaei libri pleni sunt. amicitia tamen eorum
familiarius utebar quam ceterorum hominum qui in illa
haeresi non fuissent.

---

48 For A.'s flirtation with Carneades and the "new" (or "skeptical") Academy (partly mediated by Cicero), cf. *C. Acad.*
3.17.37–19.42. In *Ep.* 1 he doubts whether they really believed
truth to be beyond human wisdom's reach; cf. *Util. Cred.* 8.20;
Ench. 10.20.

49 Cf. *Conf.* 3.21.12, etc. In the New Testament "heresy" is a

else that was part of me but was not me myself. But the whole of it was really me, and my lack of faith had divided me against myself; and that was a sin the more incurable because I was not admitting that I was a sinner. It was also an abominable offense, almighty God, that I wanted you to be overcome in me, to bring about my own destruction, rather than letting myself be overcome by you to bring about my own salvation. Accordingly you had not set a guard on my mouth and a door of forbearance about my lips, to stop my heart inclining to evil words and so making excuses for sinning with those who commit offences. Thus I still associated with their elect but was already despairing of ever making progress in their false teaching. As a result I now kept those precepts, which I had once determined would satisfy me if I found nothing better, in a more sloppy and negligent fashion.

(19) In fact the thought even occurred to me that those philosophers known as "Academics" were wiser than the rest because they had counseled that everything must be held in doubt and had insisted that nothing of the truth could be grasped by mortals. They appeared to me, moreover, to have believed clearly what they are commonly held to believe, but I did not as yet understand their meaning.[48] I did not neglect to discourage the excessive confidence that the man who was my host seemed to maintain concerning the fantastical myths that fill the books of the Manichaeans. I kept closer ties of friendship with them than with other people who did not belong to that heresy.[49]

semi-technical word meaning a sect or party; by A.'s time it has long signified a group at doctrinal variance with the Catholic Church.

Nec eam defendebam pristina animositate, sed tamen familiaritas eorum (plures enim eos Roma occultat) pigrius me faciebat aliud quaerere, praesertim desperantem in ecclesia tua, domine caeli et terrae, creator omnium visibilium et invisibilium, posse inveniri verum, unde me illi averterant, multumque mihi turpe videbatur credere figuram te habere humanae carnis et membrorum nostrorum liniamentis corporalibus terminari, et quoniam cum de deo meo cogitare vellem, cogitare nisi moles corporum non noveram (neque enim videbatur mihi esse quicquam quod tale non esset), ea maxima et prope sola causa erat inevitabilis erroris mei.

(20) Hinc enim et mali substantiam quandam credebam esse talem et habere suam molem taetram et deformem et crassam, quam terram dicebant, sive tenuem atque subtilem, sicuti est aeris corpus, quam malignam mentem per illam terram repentem imaginantur. et quia deum bonum nullam malam naturam creasse qualiscumque me pietas credere cogebat, constituebam ex adverso sibi duas moles, utramque infinitam, sed malam angustius, bonam grandius, et ex hoc initio pestilentioso me cetera sacrilegia sequebantur. cum enim conaretur animus meus recurrere in catholicam fidem, repercutiebar, quia non erat catholica fides quam esse arbitrabar.

Et magis pius mihi videbar, si te, deus meus, cui confitentur ex me miserationes tuae, vel ex ceteris parti-

---

50 Phrases from the creed of Nicaea AD 325, appropriately as A. is questioning the credibility of its central tenet, the incarnation.   51 The same word, *moles,* is used here to mean "physical bulk" and "power/strength."

52 The adjective appears here first in *Conf.*

I was no longer defending it with my previous vehemence, but my close connections with them—for Rome ensconces quite a few of them—made me lazy about seeking something else. In particular I despaired of finding truth in your Church, Lord of heaven and earth, maker of all things visible and invisible,[50] for they had turned me away from it. It seemed to me to be very contemptible to believe that you could take the form of human flesh and confine yourself within the physical shape of a human body. Also, because when I wanted to reflect upon my God, the only way I knew how to do so was as a mass of material phenomena (for it seemed to me that these were the only things capable of existence), that was the chief, perhaps the only, cause of my unpreventable error.

Mt 11:25

(20) Because of this I used to believe that evil too was a material substance, and had physical magnitude: foul, misshapen and dense, which they called "earth," or thin and insubstantial, such as the body of air, which they picture as a malevolent mind stealing throughout that earth. My faith, such as it was, compelled me to believe that a good God had not created any evil nature; so instead I settled it for myself that there were two powers[51] opposed to one another, both infinite, but the evil one more restricted, the good more widespread. From this deadly beginning every other impiety ensued for me. For when my mind tried to hasten back to the catholic[52] faith I was knocked back, because the catholic faith was not what I believed it to be.

I felt more devout, O my God (your mercies make this confession of mine to you possible), if I believed that you

221

bus infinitum crederem, quamvis ex una, qua tibi moles
mali opponebatur, cogerer finitum fateri, quam si ex omnibus partibus in corporis humani forma te opinarer finiri.
et melius mihi videbar credere nullum malum te creasse
(quod mihi nescienti non solum aliqua substantia sed
etiam corporea videbatur, quia et mentem cogitare non
noveram nisi eam subtile corpus esse, quod tamen per loci
spatia diffunderetur) quam credere abs te esse qualem
putabam naturam mali.

Ipsumque salvatorem nostrum, unigenitum tuum,
tamquam de massa lucidissimae molis tuae porrectum ad
nostram salutem ita putabam, ut aliud de illo non crederem nisi quod possem vanitate imaginari. talem itaque
naturam eius nasci non posse de Maria virgine arbitrabar,
nisi carni concerneretur. concerni autem et non inquinari
non videbam, quod mihi tale figurabam. metuebam itaque
credere in carne natum,[5] ne credere cogerer ex carne in-
quinatum. nunc spiritales tui blande et amanter ridebunt
me, si has confessiones meas legerint, sed tamen talis
eram.

11. (21) Deinde quae illi in scripturis tuis reprehende-
rant defendi posse non existimabam, sed aliquando sane
cupiebam cum aliquo illorum librorum doctissimo conferre singula et experiri quid inde sentiret. iam enim Elpi-
dii cuiusdam adversus eosdem manichaeos coram loquen-
tis et disserentis sermones etiam apud Carthaginem

---

[5] in carne natum *codd. Maur. Skut. Ver.*: incarnatum S *Knöll*

---

[53] Otherwise unknown; his being named is an indicator that
his influence on A.'s conversion was positive. Cf. Introduction,
p. xxi.

are unbounded on every side except that one on which the power of evil stands in opposition to you. This forced me to admit that you are finite. To me this was more devout than if I held the view that you were in every respect confined within the form of a human body. It seemed to me, in my ignorance, that evil has not only some substance but in fact physical substance in particular; for I did not know how to conceptualize "mind" except as being some kind of physical mass, insubstantial yet with genuine spatial dimensions. Therefore it seemed to me better to believe that you had not created any evil than to believe that what I thought of as the nature of evil came from you.

I even imagined our Savior, your only-begotten Son, like some creature put forth for our salvation, like an extension from the mass of your most luminous substance. I would not believe anything about him except what my vain imagination could envisage. So I judged it impossible for such a nature as his to be born of the virgin Mary without being mingled with flesh. I could not see how such a thing as I had imagined for myself could be mingled without being defiled. I was afraid of believing in him as born in flesh, in case it compelled me to believe he was defiled by the flesh. Now your true Christians will laugh at me, albeit kindly and with affection, if they read these confessions of mine, but even so, that is how I was.

11. (21) Furthermore, I did not think it possible to defend what those Manichaeans had condemned in your Scriptures, but there were certainly times when I longed to discuss individual points with someone truly learned in their writings, and to put to the test what opinions he held. Even at Carthage the conversations of a man called Elpidius[53] had begun to sway me, as he spoke and held dis-

movere me coeperant, cum talia de scripturis proferret quibus resisti non facile posset. et inbecilla mihi responsio videbatur istorum, quam quidem non facile palam promebant sed nobis secretius, cum dicerent scripturas novi testamenti falsatas fuisse a nescio quibus, qui Iudaeorum legem inserere christianae fidei voluerunt, atque ipsi incorrupta exemplaria nulla proferrent. sed me maxime captum et offocatum quodam modo deprimebant corporalia cogitantem moles illae, sub quibus anhelans in auram tuae veritatis liquidam et simplicem respirare non poteram.

12. (22) Sedulo ergo agere coeperam, propter quod veneram, ut docerem Romae artem rhetoricam, et prius domi congregare aliquos quibus et per quos innotescere coeperam. et ecce cognosco alia Romae fieri, quae non patiebar in Africa. nam re vera illas eversiones a perditis adulescentibus ibi non fieri manifestatum est mihi: "sed subito," inquiunt, "ne mercedem magistro reddant, conspirant multi adulescentes et transferunt se ad alium, desertores fidei et quibus prae pecuniae caritate iustitia vilis est." oderat etiam istos cor meum, quamvis non perfecto odio. quod enim ab eis passurus eram magis oderam fortasse quam eo quod cuilibet inlicita faciebant. certe tamen turpes sunt tales et fornicantur abs te amando volatica ludibria temporum et lucrum luteum, quod cum apprehenditur manum inquinat, et amplectendo mundum fugientem, contemnendo te manentem et revocantem et

---

[54] Cf. *Conf.* 3.3.6, 5.8.14.

cussions in public against those same Manichaeans. He brought out aspects of the Scriptures that were almost irresistible. Their response seemed feeble to me, and they did not disclose it openly and straightforwardly but only in secret to us. Then they stated that the New Testament Scriptures had been falsified by persons unknown, with the aim of grafting the law of the Jews onto the Christian faith. But they themselves could not produce any uncorrupted copies. In particular, all the time I kept thinking of them as physical entities, those great masses were weighing me down, holding me prisoner, stifling me. Under their weight I gasped for the air of your truth, but pure and simple as it was I could not breathe it.

12. (22) I then became focused on what I had come there for, namely teaching the art of rhetoric at Rome. So first I gathered some people at my home; I became known to them and they made me known to others. But look: now I find that some things happen at Rome that I was not accustomed to tolerate in Africa! For it was true, what they explained to me, that the havoc[54] caused by profligate youths would not happen there. "But to avoid paying a master's fee," people told me, "a group of these young men will suddenly plot together and go off to another master, violating their good faith, holding justice cheap because of their love of money." My heart hated those youths, but not with a perfect hatred. This was because I hated what I   Ps 139:22
myself was going to suffer at their hands more, perhaps, than the fact that they were acting improperly against teachers in general. Such people are certainly disgraceful and unfaithful to you: they love the fleeting attractions of   Ps 73:27
time and filthy lucre which defiles the hand grasping it;   1 Tm 3:3, 8;
they embrace the fleeting world; they spurn you who abide   Ti 1:7, 11;
                                                                          1 Pt 5:2:

ignoscentem redeunti ad te meretrici animae humanae. et
nunc tales odi pravos et distortos, quamvis eos corrigendos diligam, ut pecuniae doctrinam ipsam quam discunt
praeferant, ei vero te deum veritatem et ubertatem certi
boni et pacem castissimam. sed tunc magis eos pati nolebam malos propter me, quam fieri propter te bonos volebam.

13. (23) Itaque posteaquam missum est a Mediolanio
Romam ad praefectum urbis, ut illi civitati rhetoricae magister provideretur, impertita etiam evectione publica, ego
ipse ambivi per eos ipsos manichaeis vanitatibus ebrios
(quibus ut carerem ibam, sed utrique nesciebamus) ut
dictione proposita me probatum praefectus tunc Symmachus mitteret. et veni Mediolanium ad Ambrosium episcopum, in optimis notum orbi terrae, pium cultorem
tuum, cuius tunc eloquia strenue ministrabant adipem
frumenti tui et laetitiam olei et sobriam vini ebrietatem
populo tuo. ad eum autem ducebar abs te nesciens, ut per
eum ad te sciens ducerer. suscepit me paterne ille homo
dei et peregrinationem meam satis episcopaliter dilexit.

Et eum amare coepi, primo quidem non tamquam doc-

---

55 Constantine gave bishops the honor of using the imperial
courier system; cf. Ammianus Marcellinus 21.16.18.

56 Q. Aurelius Symmachus, ca. AD 345–402: politician, orator,
and in AD 384 defender of the "pagan" Altar of Victory.

57 Bishop of Milan AD 374–397: cf. Introduction, p. xxi.

58 A compliment, alluding to Ambrose's morning hymn "The
Splendor of the Father's Glory" (*Splendor paternae gloriae*):
"May Christ be food for us today; may our faith be drink; let us
drink joyfully of the sober intoxication of the Holy Spirit" (*Chris-
tusque nobis sit cibus, / potusque noster sit fides; / laeti bibamus
sobriam / ebrietatem Spiritus*).

eternally and call back the unfaithful human soul as it returns to you, and grant your forgiveness. Now I hate people who are untrustworthy and crooked like that; but those who can be straightened out I love, if they come to prefer, instead of money, the true teaching that they master, and over that to prefer you, who are God, the truth and fullness of assured good and purest peace. At that time, though, I was more unwilling to put up with their wrongdoing for my own sake than wanting them to become good for your sake.

13. (23) Just then a message came from Milan to Rome for the city prefect, asking him to provide a teacher of rhetoric for that city, to be conveyed by the imperial post.[55] With the help of those same people who were steeped in the follies of Manichaeism—I was going there in order to be free of them, but neither they nor I then realized this—I applied to the then prefect, Symmachus,[56] to approve me, after prescribing a topic for a trial speech, and to send me there. So I came to Milan, to Ambrose the bishop, a man renowned among the most distinguished people in the world, but who was also your devout worshipper.[57] His powers of communication supplied your people promptly with the abundance of your wheat and the gladness of oil and the sober intoxication of wine.[58] In my state of ignorance you brought me to him, so that once I came to knowledge he could lead me to you. That man of God took me up in a fatherly fashion, and like the true bishop he was, he delighted in my coming to Milan.

I began to love him in return, not initially as a teacher

Ps 81:16

Ps 45:7

Eph 5:18;
cf. Ps 4:7

227

torem veri, quod in ecclesia tua prorsus desperabam, sed tamquam hominem benignum in me. et studiose audiebam disputantem in populo, non intentione qua debui, sed quasi explorans eius facundiam, utrum conveniret famae suae an maior minorve proflueret quam praedicabatur, et verbis eius suspendebar intentus, rerum autem incuriosus et contemptor adstabam. et delectabar suavitate sermonis, quamquam eruditioris, minus tamen hilarescentis atque mulcentis quam Fausti erat, quod attinet ad dicendi modum. ceterum rerum ipsarum nulla comparatio: nam ille per manichaeas fallacias aberrabat, ille autem[6] saluberrime docebat salutem. sed longe est a peccatoribus salus, qualis ego tunc aderam, et tamen propinquabam sensim et nesciens.

14. (24) Cum enim non satagerem discere quae dicebat, sed tantum quemadmodum dicebat audire (ea mihi quippe iam desperanti ad te viam patere homini inanis cura remanserat), veniebant in animum meum simul cum verbis quae diligebam res etiam quas neglegebam, neque enim ea dirimere poteram. et dum cor aperirem ad excipiendum quam diserte diceret, pariter intrabat et quam vere diceret, gradatim quidem. nam primo etiam ipsa defendi posse mihi iam coeperunt videri, et fidem catholicam, pro qua nihil posse dici adversus oppugnantes manichaeos putaveram, iam non impudenter adseri existimabam, maxime audito uno atque altero et saepius aenigmate

6 ille (autem) S *Knöll Skut. Ver.*: iste *Maur.*

of truth—I despaired of finding any such in your church—
but as a human being who looked kindly upon me. I listened carefully to his debates among the people, not as
attentively as I should, but as it were making trial of his
eloquence, whether it matched his reputation or whether
it was more or less fluent than I had been told. I hung upon
his words, listening carefully, but I cared little for the subject matter and stood looking on scornfully. Yet I was delighted by his attractive way of speaking, for though it was
better-informed, it was still, as far as style of delivery goes,
less crowd-pleasing and charming than that of Faustus.
Yet there was no comparison when it came to actual content: for Faustus kept wandering off into Manichaean in-
consistencies, while Ambrose was teaching wholesome
salvation. Salvation is far from sinners such as I then was,   Ps 119:155
but yet I was drawing closer, little by little, even though I
did not know it.

14. (24) I put no effort into learning what he was saying
but only into hearing how he was saying it, for that hollow
interest was all I had left, despairing as I was of a way ever
opening up for humanity to reach you. Even so, while the
words which I loved kept coming into my mind, some actual facts, to which I usually paid no attention, came with
them, for I could not keep them separate. Thus while I
was opening my heart to absorb how eloquently he was
speaking, at the same time the true subject matter of
which he spoke was entering too, though only gradually.
First I began to see that such views were defensible; and
then I began to believe that the catholic faith, which I had
thought had nothing to be said for it against the attacks of
the Manichaeans, could be proclaimed without embarrassment. Finally I heard one after another, and in fact

soluto de scriptis veteribus, ubi, cum ad litteram acciperem, occidebar.

Spiritaliter itaque plerisque illorum librorum locis expositis iam reprehendebam desperationem meam, illam dumtaxat qua credideram legem et prophetas detestantibus atque inridentibus resisti omnino non posse. nec tamen iam ideo mihi catholicam viam tenendam esse sentiebam, quia et ipsa poterat habere doctos adsertores suos, qui copiose et non absurde obiecta refellerent, nec ideo iam damnandum illud quod tenebam quia defensionis partes aequabantur. ita enim catholica non mihi victa videbatur, ut nondum etiam victrix appareret.

(25) Tum vero fortiter intendi animum, si quo modo possem certis aliquibus documentis manichaeos convincere falsitatis. quod si possem spiritalem substantiam cogitare, statim machinamenta illa omnia solverentur et abicerentur ex animo meo: sed non poteram. verum tamen de ipso mundi huius corpore omnique natura quam sensus carnis attingeret multo probabiliora plerosque sensisse philosophos magis magisque considerans atque comparans iudicabam. itaque academicorum more, sicut existimantur, dubitans de omnibus atque inter omnia fluctuans, manichaeos quidem relinquendos esse decrevi, non arbitrans eo ipso tempore dubitationis meae in illa secta mihi permanendum esse cui iam nonnullos philosophos praeponebam. quibus tamen philosophis, quod sine salutari

59 The allegorical method gave patristic exegesis a solution to many scriptural problems that modern exegetes would class as historical or literary.

60 I.e., the Christian Old Testament.

quite a lot of allegorical figures[59] from the Old Testament explained, which when I took them literally were killing me.

2 Cor 3:6

Now that many passages in those books had been interpreted in a spiritual fashion, I began to reproach myself for my despair, insofar as I had believed that there was no possible way of withstanding those who loathed and derided that law and the prophets.[60] Nevertheless I still did not feel that I ought to adopt the catholic path, on the grounds that it too could have its own learned defenders to refute objections fully and rationally; nor should that system which I used to hold be condemned simply on the grounds that the side under attack could hold its own. So it seemed to me that while the catholic side was not overthrown, it did not yet appear victorious.

(25) It was then that I turned my whole mind to whether I could somehow make use of some clear proofs to convict the Manichaeans of fraud. If only I could have grasped the concept of spiritual substance, all their stratagems would be undone in a moment and ejected from my mind. But I could not. More and more I considered and compared, and I judged that the majority of philosophers held a much more likely view about the physical form of this world and the whole of nature that bodily senses can apprehend. Therefore in the style of the Academic school, as they are generally understood, I doubted everything and wavered between different positions: then I made the decision that I had to abandon the Manichaeans. I made the judgment that at a time when I was having doubts I should not remain in that sect when I had already given my preference for certain philosophers. I absolutely refused, nonetheless, to entrust the guardianship of my

nomine Christi essent, curationem languoris animae meae committere omnino recusabam. statui ergo tamdiu esse catechumenus in catholica ecclesia mihi a parentibus commendata, donec aliquid certi eluceret quo cursum dirigerem.

soul's weakness to those philosophers, because they lacked the saving name[61] of Christ. At long last, therefore, I decided to be a catechumen[62] in the Catholic Church, which my parents had commended to me, for as long as it took until something clarified for sure in which direction I should make my way.

cf. Ps 119:9

[61] For A. as other Christians, the name was not just a title but a word of innate and effective power.

[62] I.e., receiving instruction in the faith prior to baptism; cf. *Conf.* 1.11, n. 48.

LIBER VI

1. (1) Spes mea a iuventute mea, ubi mihi eras et quo recesseras? an vero non tu feceras me et discreveras me a quadrupedibus et a volatilibus caeli sapientiorem me feceras? et ambulabam per tenebras et lubricum et quaerebam te foris a me, et non inveniebam deum cordis mei. et veneram in profundum maris, et diffidebam et desperabam de inventione veri. iam venerat ad me mater pietate fortis, terra marique me sequens et in periculis omnibus de te secura. nam et per marina discrimina ipsos nautas consolabatur, a quibus rudes abyssi viatores, cum perturbantur, consolari solent, pollicens eis perventionem cum salute, quia hoc ei tu per visum pollicitus eras.

Et invenit me, periclitantem quidem graviter desperatione indagandae veritatis, sed tamen ei cum indicassem non me quidem iam esse manichaeum, sed neque catholicum christianum, non quasi inopinatum aliquid audierit, exilivit laetitia, cum iam secura fieret ex ea parte miseriae meae in qua me tamquam mortuum sed resuscitandum

---

1 Early in AD 385.

BOOK VI

1. (1) O my hope even from my youth, where were you for me, and where had you gone?[1] Or had you not in fact made me and set me apart from the beasts and made me more intelligent than the birds of the air? Yet I was walking in darkness and slippery places, and searching for you outside myself, and I was unable to find the God of my heart. I had come to the depths of the sea, and I was in doubt and despair of ever finding your truth. By now my mother had come to me, resolute in her devotion; by land and sea she followed me, never doubting you through you in every danger. Across the perils of the seas she offered encouragement even to the sailors, who were more accustomed to offer comfort themselves to travelers inexperienced in seafaring. She assured them that they would make land safely, because you had promised her this in a vision.

She found me in dire straits indeed, in despair of ever finding my way to the truth. When I disclosed to her that I was no longer a Manichaean, though not a catholic Christian either, she did not leap for joy as if she had heard something contrary to her expectations; for she was confident about one aspect of my pitiable condition at least: that though she used to weep over me as if I were already dead, you still had the power to revive me. She was con-

Ps 71:5

Ps 10:1

Jb 35:11^{VL}

Eccl 2:14; Is
9:2; Ps 35:6

Ps 73:26

tibi flebat, et feretro cogitationis offerebat[1] ut diceres filio
viduae, "iuvenis, tibi dico, surge," et revivesceret et inci-
peret loqui et traderes illum matri suae. nulla ergo turbulenta exultatione trepidavit cor eius, cum audisset ex tanta
parte iam factum quod tibi cotidie plangebat ut fieret,
veritatem me nondum adeptum sed falsitati iam ereptum.
immo vero quia certa erat et quod restabat te daturum,
qui totum promiseras, placidissime et pectore pleno fidu-
ciae respondit mihi credere se in Christo quod priusquam
de hac vita emigraret me visura esset fidelem catholicum.
et hoc quidem mihi.

Tibi autem, fons misericordiarum, preces et lacrimas
densiores, ut accelerares adiutorium tuum et inluminares
tenebras meas, et studiosius ad ecclesiam currere et in
Ambrosii ora suspendi, ad fontem salientis aquae in vitam
aeternam. diligebat autem illum virum sicut angelum dei,
quod per illum cognoverat me interim ad illam ancipitem
fluctuationem iam esse perductum per quam transiturum
me ab aegritudine ad sanitatem, intercurrente artiore
periculo quasi per accessionem quam criticam[2] medici
vocant, certa praesumebat.

2. (2) Itaque cum ad memorias sanctorum, sicut in
Africa solebat, pultes et panem et merum attulisset atque

[1] offerebat *G O S Knöll Skut. Ver.*: efferebat *C D Maur.*
[2] criticam *codd. Maur. Knöll Skut. Ver.*: creticam *O² S*

[2] I.e., Monnica's prayers were like the bier that lifted up the
corpse of the widow's son, presenting him so that Jesus could see
and restore him.
[3] Cf. *Conf.* 2.3.5, n.18.

tinually presenting me on the bier of her anxious thoughts, for you to say to the widow's son, "Young man, I say to you, get up," and for him to arise and start speaking, and for you to hand him over to his mother.[2] So her heart did not tremble with tumultuous elation when she heard that what she implored you daily to do for her was already largely accomplished. I had not yet grasped the truth, but I was now rescued from lies and deceit. In fact because she was convinced that you would yet grant everything that was still unfulfilled of your complete promise to her, she replied to me with utter serenity, in the total faithfulness of her heart, that she believed in Christ that before she departed this life she would see me a catholic Christian.[3] She said this much to me.

Lk 7:12–14

But to you, O wellspring of mercies, her prayers and tears alike poured out more abundantly, begging you to hasten to help and to lighten my darkness. More eagerly than ever she rushed to church; she hung on Ambrose's words as if they were a spring of water welling up to eternal life. She loved that man as if he were an angel[4] of God, for she knew that during this time he had been the means of guiding me to that position of doubting hesitation. And she took it as certain that through it, after an interval of more intense danger, like the moment in the course of an illness which physicians call "critical," I would cross over from sickness to health.

Pss 70:1,
18:28

Jn 4:14
Gal 4:14

2. (2) On one occasion she brought stew and bread and wine to the chapels of the saints[5] as she used to do in Af-

---

[4] The Latinized Greek word *angelus* keeps the sense of "messenger" as well as that of "divine being."

[5] Cf. *Conf.* 5.8.15.

ab ostiario prohiberetur, ubi hoc episcopum vetuisse cognovit, tam pie atque oboedienter amplexa est ut ipse mirarer quam facile accusatrix potius consuetudinis suae quam disceptatrix illius prohibitionis effecta sit. non enim obsidebat spiritum eius vinulentia eamque stimulabat in odium veri amor vini, sicut plerosque mares et feminas qui ad canticum sobrietatis sicut ad potionem aquatam madidi nausiant, sed illa cum attulisset canistrum cum sollemnibus epulis praegustandis atque largiendis, plus etiam quam unum pocillum pro suo palato satis sobrio temperatum, unde dignationem sumeret, non ponebat, et si multae essent quae illo modo videbantur honorandae memoriae defunctorum, idem ipsum unum, quod ubique poneret, circumferebat, quo iam non solum aquatissimo sed etiam tepidissimo cum suis praesentibus per sorbitiones exiguas partiretur, quia pietatem ibi quaerebat, non voluptatem. itaque ubi comperit a praeclaro praedicatore atque antistite pietatis praeceptum esse ista non fieri nec ab eis qui sobrie facerent, ne ulla occasio se ingurgitandi daretur ebriosis, et quia illa quasi parentalia superstitioni gentilium essent simillima, abstinuit se libentissime, et pro canistro pleno terrenis fructibus plenum purgatioribus votis pectus ad memorias martyrum afferre didicerat, ut et

---

6 Cf. *Quasten*, "Vetus Superstitio et Nova Religio," 253–66.

7 Perhaps a reference to the tendency to exaggerate when drunk. Cf. *Conf.* 8.8.18 on Monnica and wine.

8 On the ancient practice of diluting wine with water, see Diggle, *Theophrastus: Characters*, 212, n. 6.

9 *Parentalia*, a festival from February 18–21, included honoring dead relatives with offerings of food and drink.

rica, and the gatekeeper stopped her; when she learned
that it was bishop Ambrose who had forbidden such offerings, she acquiesced with such obedient devotion that I
myself was astounded at how easily she became critical of
her own custom rather than disagreeing with his ban.[6] Her
spirit was not assailed by habitual drinking, nor did the
love of wine rouse her to any hatred of the truth,[7] as it does
so many husbands and wives who react to sober hymn-
singing like drunkards revolted by watered wine.[8] She, on
the other hand, used to bring her basket with its festal food
offerings to take a taste first and then share round, but she
would never set out more than a single beaker of wine,
mixed to suit her abstemious tastes, from which to sip out
of respect. If it seemed appropriate to honor a number of
chapels of the saints in this way, she would carry the self-
same beaker around to set out in each place. She would
share it in sips with her companions even though it was
now not only very watery but also far too warm. She did
this there because she was looking for devotion, not sensual enjoyment. Then she understood, therefore, that this
famous preacher and model of piety had given orders that
not even those who did so soberly were to uphold these
practices anymore, so as to give no opportunity for drink-
ers to consume alcohol to excess. So because those obser-
vances were a virtual ancestor-festival,[9] very like a non-
Christian[10] superstition, she was very glad to give them up.
In place of her basket filled with offerings of fruits of the
earth, she had learned to offer up at the martyrs' chapels

[10] The term here is a biblical one for nations outside the covenant. Cf. Introduction, p. xxxvii, on the term "pagan"; with A.
Ep. 29.9 to Alypius.

quod posset daret egentibus et sic[3] communicatio domi-
nici corporis illic celebraretur, cuius passionis imitatione
immolati et coronati sunt martyres.

Sed tamen videtur mihi, domine deus meus (et ita est
in conspectu tuo de hac re cor meum), non facile fortasse
de hac amputanda consuetudine matrem meam fuisse ces-
suram si ab alio prohiberetur quem non sicut Ambrosium
diligebat. quem propter salutem meam maxime diligebat,
eam vero ille propter eius religiosissimam conversationem,
qua in bonis operibus tam fervens spiritu frequentabat
ecclesiam, ita ut saepe erumperet, cum me videret, in eius
praedicationem gratulans mihi, quod talem matrem haberem, nesciens qualem illa me filium, qui dubitabam de
illis omnibus et inveniri posse viam vitae minime putabam.

3. (3) Nec iam ingemescebam orando ut subvenires
mihi, sed ad quaerendum intentus et ad disserendum in-
quietus erat animus meus, ipsumque Ambrosium felicem
quendam hominem secundum saeculum opinabar, quem
sic tantae potestates honorarent; caelibatus tantum eius
mihi laboriosus videbatur. quid autem ille spei gereret, et
adversus ipsius excellentiae temptamenta quid luctaminis
haberet quidve solaminis in adversis, et occultum os eius,
quod erat in corde eius, quam sapida gaudia de pane tuo
ruminaret, nec conicere noveram nec expertus eram, nec
ille sciebat aestus meos nec foveam periculi mei.

---

[3] (et) sic *P Maur. Knöll Skut.*: si *codd. Ver.*

---

[11] There was a close association between the martyr cult of
the Christians and the hero cult of the "pagan" Greeks.
[12] Perhaps A., unable to gain the close access to Ambrose that
he desired, projects onto him, with hindsight, his own interior
debate over how to integrate intellect, talent, and faith.

a heart filled with purer prayers. Then she was able to give what she could to the poor, and as a result the communion of the Lord's body was celebrated there, where the martyrs sacrificed themselves and won the crown of glory following the example of his passion.[11]

Yet regarding the curtailment of this custom, it seems to me, O Lord my God (on this subject my heart lies open to your gaze), that my mother would not have given up the practice had it been forbidden her by anyone she did not love as she loved Ambrose. She loved him most of all for his part in my salvation, while he loved her for the exceptional piety of her way of life. For she was so fervent in spirit about her good works, and she was constantly at church. So on seeing me he would often exclaim in praise of her and congratulate me on having such a mother. He did not know what kind of a son she really had: I, who had doubts about all those things and simply could not believe that the way to life was to be found!

Acts 18:25;
Rom 12:11

3. (3) I was not yet starting to groan in my prayers for you to come to my aid, but my mind was set on seeking and restless for explanations. I considered Ambrose himself to be quite the lucky man in worldly terms, for the authorities revered him. The only thing about him that seemed burdensome to me was his celibate state. What hopes he held, how he struggled against the temptations inherent in his own greatness, what comfort he had in adversities, and what was in his heart, his hidden countenance, as he chewed over the delectable joys which come from your Bread:[12] all this I did not know how to guess, and I was inexperienced, and he did not know of my fluctuating emotions nor the perilous pitfalls before me.

cf. Jn 6:35

Ps 57:6

241

Non enim quaerere ab eo poteram quod volebam, sicut
volebam, secludentibus me ab eius aure atque ore catervis
negotiosorum[4] hominum, quorum infirmitatibus serviebat. cum quibus quando non erat, quod perexiguum temporis erat, aut corpus reficiebat necessariis sustentaculis
aut lectione animum. sed cum legebat, oculi ducebantur
per paginas et cor intellectum rimabatur, vox autem et
lingua quiescebant. saepe cum adessemus (non enim veta-
batur quisquam ingredi aut ei venientem nuntiari mos
erat), sic eum legentem vidimus tacite et aliter numquam,
sedentesque in diuturno silentio (quis enim tam intento
esse oneri auderet?) discedebamus et coniectabamus eum
parvo ipso tempore quod reparandae menti suae nancis-
cebatur, feriatum ab strepitu causarum alienarum, nolle
in aliud avocari et cavere fortasse ne, auditore suspenso et
intento, si qua obscurius posuisset ille quem legeret, etiam
exponere esset necesse aut de aliquibus difficilioribus dis-
sertare quaestionibus, atque huic operi temporibus
impensis minus quam vellet voluminum evolveret, quamquam et causa servandae vocis, quae illi facillime obtun-
debatur, poterat esse iustior tacite legendi. quolibet tamen
animo id ageret, bono utique ille vir agebat.

---

[4] negotiosorum *codd. Maur. Knöll Skut.*: negotiorum S *Ver.*

---

[13] The extent to which silent reading was practiced in the
ancient world is disputed. Cf. Gillard, "More Silent Reading in
Antiquity," 689–94.

[14] Literally, "unrolled" (*evolveret*): a reminder that Ambrose's
books were papyrus rolls, not books in codex form.

I could not ask him what I wanted, as I wanted: not when flocks of busy men (for he was always tending to their frailties) were keeping me away from hearing him or speaking to him. When he was not with them, which was never for very long, he was either nourishing his body with the food it needed or nourishing his mind with reading. But when he was reading, his eyes would scan over the pages and his heart would scrutinize their meaning—yet his voice and tongue remained silent.[13] Often when we were present (no one was ever forbidden to enter, nor was it his custom to have those approaching him announced) we saw him reading like that, silently, but never aloud. We used to sit for long periods of silence—who would presume to intrude on someone so intent?—and then depart, on the assumption that in these short periods of time, carved out from the hustle and bustle of other people's problems, which he secured for refreshing his mind, he did not want to be distracted toward other things. Perhaps he was also avoiding having to explain to an engrossed and attentive listener anything that the author he was reading had put in terms unclear, or to give a commentary on some other complex subjects. Given all the time he spent on such duties, he read[14] fewer books than he wanted to, though in fact the aim of saving his voice, which all too easily became strained, could be a better justification for reading silently. Whatever his reason for doing so, a man like him was certainly doing it for the best.[15]

1 Cor 6:1

[15] A. is frustrated at not being able to get close to the man he now regards as his teacher; as the plural verbs indicate, he had to be one of the crowd instead. Ambrose may have been cautious because of A.'s Manichaean links: cf. Introduction, p. xxi.

(4) Sed certe mihi nulla dabatur copia sciscitandi quae cupiebam de tam sancto oraculo tuo, pectore illius, nisi cum aliquid breviter esset audiendum. aestus autem illi mei otiosum eum valde cui refunderentur requirebant nec umquam inveniebant. et eum quidem in populo verbum veritatis recte tractantem omni die dominico audiebam, et magis magisque mihi confirmabatur omnes versutarum calumniarum nodos quos illi deceptores nostri adversus divinos libros innectebant posse dissolvi. ubi vero etiam comperi ad imaginem tuam hominem a te factum ab spiritalibus filiis tuis, quos de matre catholica per gratiam regenerasti, non sic intellegi ut humani corporis forma te determinatum[5] crederent atque cogitarent (quamquam quomodo se haberet spiritalis substantia, ne quidem tenuiter atque in aenigmate suspicabar), tamen gaudens erubui non me tot annos adversus catholicam fidem, sed contra carnalium cogitationum figmenta latrasse. eo quippe temerarius et impius fueram, quod ea quae debebam quaerendo discere[6] accusando dixeram. tu enim, altissime et proxime, secretissime et praesentissime, cui membra non sunt alia maiora et alia minora, sed ubique totus es et nusquam locorum es, non es utique forma ista corporea, tamen fecisti hominem ad imaginem tuam, et ecce ipse a capite usque ad pedes in loco est.

[5] te determinatum *OD*: te terminatum *Maur. GM*: determinatum *codd. Knöll Skut. Ver.*

[6] discere *S Maur. Knöll Skut.*: dicere *codd. Ver.*

---

[16] In *Conf.* this verb (*regenerasti*) is always linked to baptism.

(4) It was clear that I was not going to get a chance to interrogate your holy oracle, the heart of Ambrose, as I wanted, except when some matter required a brief hearing. My storms of emotion needed his complete attention if they were to be poured out to him, but they never secured it. I used to listen to him every Sunday, preaching the word of truth in the proper fashion before the congregation. I became more and more convinced that all the tangles of false and conniving charges that those men deceived us by using to stigmatize the holy books could be undone. Then, indeed, I learned from your sons according to the spirit, whom you have made anew[16] through grace from our mother the Catholic Church, that humanity is not to be understood as made in your image in such a way that they must likewise believe and think that *you* are confined by the form of a human body. Although I had not the faintest glimmer of a notion how there could be such a thing as a "spiritual substance," I was nevertheless delighted as well as embarrassed, not because I had been opposed to the catholic faith for so many years but because I had been snarling against concepts of the physical that were entirely imaginary. I had been so impetuous and irreverent because I had made assertions and found fault concerning matters that I should have mastered through proper research. For you are both transcendent and immanent, entirely unknowable, yet close at hand; it is not that some parts of you are greater while others are smaller, but everywhere you are present in your entirety, and at the same time you are never confined to one place. You are certainly not in that physical form, yet you have made humanity in your image, and look! from head to foot humanity is physically and spatially confined.

2 Tm 2:15

Gn 1:26

245

4. (5) Cum ergo nescirem quomodo haec subsisteret imago tua, pulsans proponerem quomodo credendum esset, non insultans opponerem quasi ita creditum esset. tanto igitur acrior cura rodebat intima mea, quid certi retinerem, quanto me magis pudebat tam diu inlusum et deceptum promissione certorum puerili errore et animositate tam multa incerta quasi certa garrisse. quod enim falsa essent, postea mihi claruit; certum tamen erat quod incerta essent et a me aliquando pro certis habita fuissent, cum catholicam tuam caecis contentionibus accusarem, etsi nondum compertam vera docentem, non tamen ea docentem quae graviter accusabam. itaque confundebar et convertebar, et gaudebam, deus meus, quod ecclesia unica, corpus unici tui, in qua mihi nomen Christi infanti est inditum, non saperet infantiles nugas neque hoc haberet in doctrina sua sana, quod te creatorem omnium in spatium loci quamvis summum et amplum, tamen undique terminatum membrorum humanorum figura contruderet.

(6) Gaudebam etiam quod vetera scripta legis et prophetarum iam non illo oculo mihi legenda proponerentur quo antea videbantur absurda, cum arguebam tamquam ita sentientes sanctos tuos, verum autem non ita sentiebant. et tamquam regulam diligentissime commendaret, saepe in popularibus sermonibus suis dicentem Ambrosium laetus audiebam: "littera occidit, spiritus autem vivi-

---

17 Cf. *Conf.* 1.17.16.
18 I.e., what Christians call the Old Testament.

4. (5) Because I did not know in what way this image
of yours subsisted, I should have knocked and asked how Mt 7:7
to believe in it. I should not have been abusive and of-
fensive about the way I *thought* it was believed! The visceral anxiety gnawing at me, as to what I could consider
certain, was all the sharper the more ashamed I became
that I had been duped and deceived by the promise of
certainties; and, because of my childish error and hostility,
I had pontificated about so many uncertain matters as if
they were in fact certain. It later became clear to me that
in fact they were actually false: but at this time all that
was certain was that they were uncertain, and that I had
once considered them certain when I used to criticize your
Catholic Church with blind denunciations. Though it was
not yet apparent that she taught the truth, at least she was
not teaching what I used to denounce so fiercely. So I was
being confused and converted, and I was rejoicing, O my
God, because the one Church, the body of your only-begotten Son, in which the name of Christ had been set upon
me in my infancy,[17] had no taste for childish trivia, and had
nothing in her wholesome teaching which confined you,
who created everything, within a spatial dimension however broad or high, yet restricted you on all sides to the
configuration of human limbs.

(6) I also began to rejoice because the old Scriptures
of the law and the prophets[18] were no longer set before
me to be read with that scrutiny which had once found
them ridiculous back in the days when I used to reproach
your saints for opinions they did not actually hold. I was
delighted to hear Ambrose, when preaching to the people,
often urgently recommending this as their rule: "the letter

ficat," cum ea quae ad litteram perversitatem docere videbantur, remoto mystico velamento, spiritaliter aperiret,
non dicens quod me offenderet, quamvis ea diceret quae
utrum vera essent adhuc ignorarem. tenebam enim cor
meum ab omni adsensione timens praecipitium, et sus-
pendio magis necabar. volebam enim eorum quae non
viderem ita me certum fieri ut certus essem quod septem
et tria decem sint. neque enim tam insanus eram ut ne hoc
quidem putarem posse comprehendi, sed sicut hoc, ita
cetera cupiebam, sive corporalia, quae coram sensibus
meis non adessent, sive spiritalia, de quibus cogitare nisi
corporaliter nesciebam. et sanari credendo poteram, ut
purgatior acies mentis meae dirigeretur aliquo modo in
veritatem tuam semper manentem et ex nullo deficientem.
sed sicut evenire adsolet, ut malum medicum expertus
etiam bono timeat se committere, ita erat valetudo animae
meae, quae utique nisi credendo sanari non poterat et, ne
falsa crederet, curari recusabat, resistens manibus tuis,
qui medicamenta fidei confecisti et sparsisti super morbos
orbis terrarum et tantam illis auctoritatem tribuisti.

5. (7) Ex hoc tamen quoque iam praeponens doctrinam
catholicam, modestius ibi minimeque fallaciter sentiebam
iuberi ut crederetur quod non demonstrabatur (sive esset
quid, sed cui forte non esset, sive nec quid esset), quam

---

19 Cf. *Util. Cred.* 3.9: "Such mysteries are contained in the
precepts and commandments of the Law that every devout person understands nothing is more damaging than to take what it
contains literally (i.e., according to the word); while nothing is
more serviceable than revelation by the spirit."

20 Or "saved"; cf. *Conf.* 1.5.5, n. 12.

21 I.e., the Manichaeans.

kills, but the spirit gives life."[19] He took away the mysti- 2 Cor 3:6
cal veil and opened the spiritual sense of things which
seemed, according to the letter, to inculcate what was un-
reasonable. He did not say anything that offended me,
although I still did not know whether what he said was
true. I was restraining my feelings from giving any kind of
assent to him, fearing a headlong descent, and the sus-
pense was killing me. What I wanted was to become as
certain about what I could not see as I was that seven and
three are ten. I was not so irrational that I believed even
this to be incomprehensible. But I wanted other things to
be equally straightforward, whether physical things that
were not present to my senses or spiritual ones that I could
only conceptualize in physical terms. I could have been
saved by believing, so that my mind's eye, once it was
cleansed, could somehow have been fixed on your eternal,
never-failing truth. Instead, just as tends to happen when
someone who has endured a bad doctor is then afraid to
put any trust in a good one, so it was with the sickness of
my soul. Certainly it could not be healed[20] except by believing, and in its fear of believing untruths it refused to
be cured and resisted your hands, even though you fashioned the medicines of faith and sprinkled them upon the
world's diseases and attached such authority to them. 17:7[Vg]

5. (7) For this reason too I preferred the catholic teaching. I felt that its way of demanding my belief in what
could not be proved was expressed with greater moderation and much less uncertainty, whether that was something that could be proved (but not to just anyone) or
something not open to proof. Among them,[21] in contrast,

illic temeraria pollicitatione scientiae credulitatem inri-
deri et postea tam multa fabulosissima et absurdissima,
quia demonstrari non poterant, credenda imperari.

Deinde paulatim tu, domine, manu mitissima et misericordissima pertractans et componens cor meum, consi-
deranti quam innumerabilia crederem quae non viderem
neque cum gererentur adfuissem, sicut tam multa in his-
toria gentium, tam multa de locis atque urbibus quae non
videram, tam multa amicis, tam multa medicis, tam multa
hominibus aliis atque aliis, quae nisi crederentur, omnino
in hac vita nihil ageremus, postremo quam inconcusse
fixum fide retinerem de quibus parentibus ortus essem,
quod scire non possem nisi audiendo credidissem, persua-
sisti mihi non qui crederent libris tuis, quos tanta in omnibus fere gentibus auctoritate fundasti, sed qui non crederent esse culpandos nec audiendos esse, si qui forte
mihi dicerent, "unde scis illos libros unius veri et veracis-
simi dei spiritu esse humano generi ministratos?" idipsum
enim maxime credendum erat, quoniam nulla pugnacitas
calumniosarum quaestionum per tam multa quae legeram
inter se confligentium philosophorum extorquere mihi
potuit ut aliquando non crederem te esse quidquid esses,
quod ego nescirem, aut administrationem rerum humana-
rum ad te pertinere.

(8) Sed id credebam aliquando robustius, aliquando

---

22 From this moment on, A. writes as one under the authority
of scriptural teachings.

23 Cf. Cic. *Nat. D.* 2.1.3: "Philosophers like us divide this topic
of the immortal gods into four parts: first they teach that the gods
exist, then their nature, then how they regulate the world, and
lastly how they take thought for human affairs."

with their reckless protestations of knowledge, we were mocked for being gullible and then commanded to believe a great many fantastical and ridiculous things that could not be proved.

Then, Lord, you gradually touched my heart with your hand—so gentle and merciful!—and set it in order. I began to consider the countless things I believed in though I could not see them and had not been present when they took place, such as the many events in the history of nations, so many of them to do with places and cities that I had not seen; and so many things I learned from friends, doctors, all sorts and conditions of people. Unless we believed in them we would never take action of any kind in this life. Finally there was my unshakeable conviction about the parents who had begotten me, which I could not know except by hearing and believing it. So you persuaded me that it was not those who believed in your holy books, which you had established with such authority in almost every nation, but those who did *not* believe who were at fault: as, for example, if someone happened to say to me, "How do you know that those books have been presented to the human race by the spirit of a single true and most true god?"[22] This was the very fact that I had to trust in most completely, since no assaults by misleading questions, arising from everything that I had read of the philosophers disagreeing with one another, was enough to wrest from me an admission that at any time I did not believe either that you exist, whatever you might be (for this I did not know), or that the business of human affairs matters to you.[23]

(8) Sometimes my belief in this was relatively sturdy, sometimes rather flimsy, but I never stopped believing

exilius, semper tamen credidi et esse te et curam nostri
gerere, etiamsi ignorabam vel quid sentiendum esset de
substantia tua vel quae via duceret aut reduceret ad te.
ideoque cum essemus infirmi ad inveniendam liquida ra-
tione veritatem et ob hoc nobis opus esset auctoritate
sanctarum litterarum, iam credere coeperam nullo modo
te fuisse tributurum tam excellentem illi scripturae per
omnes iam terras auctoritatem, nisi et per ipsam tibi credi
et per ipsam te quaeri voluisses. iam enim absurditatem
quae me in illis litteris solebat offendere, cum multa ex eis
probabiliter exposita audissem, ad sacramentorum altitudinem referebam eoque mihi illa venerabilior et sacro-
sancta fide dignior apparebat auctoritas, quo et omnibus
ad legendum esset in promptu et secreti sui dignitatem in
intellectu profundiore servaret, verbis apertissimis et hu-
millimo genere loquendi se cunctis praebens et exercens
intentionem eorum qui non sunt leves corde, ut exciperet
omnes populari sinu et per angusta foramina paucos ad te
traiceret, multo tamen plures quam si nec tanto apice auctoritatis emineret nec turbas gremio sanctae humilitatis
hauriret. cogitabam haec et aderas mihi, suspirabam et
audiebas me, fluctuabam et gubernabas me, ibam per
viam saeculi latam nec deserebas. (9) Inhiabam honoribus, lucris, coniugio, et tu inridebas. patiebar in eis cupiditatibus amarissimas difficultates, te propitio tanto magis,
quanto minus sinebas mihi dulcescere quod non eras tu.

---

[24] The plural shows how A. switches between his own position
and that of humankind in general.

[25] Cf. *Conf.* 4.3.3; *sacramentum* translates the Greek *myste-
rion* (μυστήριον: as in e.g., 1 Cor 15:51; Eph 1:9; etc).

that you exist and that you have a care for us, even if I had no idea either what was the proper understanding of your substance or what path led to you or led back to you. So because we[24] were unfit to find out your truth by pure reason and therefore needed the authority of the Holy Scriptures, I began to believe that you would never have bestowed such outstanding authority across the world to that book unless you wanted belief in yourself to come through it, and the search for yourself to come through it too. For I now heard many examples of the irrationality that had always annoyed me in those writings being convincingly explained, so I started to assign them to the sublime category of holy mysteries.[25] Their authority appeared more venerable and more deserving of inviolable trust because of the way they were available for all to read while still reserving the nobility of their inner mystery for a deeper discernment. They presented themselves in the clearest of terms and the most everyday style of speaking to all kinds of people, and yet they exercised the concentration of serious thinkers. Thus Scripture gathered everyone into one inclusive embrace: it also brought a few to you by the narrow way, yet many more than if it had not possessed such a supremely preeminent authority, and drew no drew crowds within its bosom of holy humility. I was reflecting, and you were with me. I was sighing and you listened to me. I was vacillating and you directed me. I was traveling along the broad path of the world, and you did not abandon me. (9) I was gazing greedily at honors, profits, marriage, and you laughed me to scorn. By so desiring, I endured the bitterest of struggles, for the more kindly you became, the less you allowed me pleasure in anything but yourself.

Sir 19:4

Mt 7:13–14

253

Vide cor meum, domine, qui voluisti ut hoc recordarer et confiterer tibi. nunc tibi inhaereat anima mea, quam de visco tam tenaci mortis exuisti. quam misera erat! et sensum vulneris tu pungebas, ut relictis omnibus converteretur ad te, qui es super omnia et sine quo nulla essent omnia, converteretur et sanaretur. quam ergo miser eram, et quomodo egisti ut sentirem miseriam meam die illo quo, cum pararem recitare imperatori laudes, quibus plura mentirer et mentienti faveretur ab scientibus, easque curas anhelaret cor meum et cogitationum tabificarum febribus aestuaret, transiens per quendam vicum Mediolanensem animadverti pauperem mendicum, iam, credo, saturum, iocantem atque laetantem. et ingemui et locutus sum cum amicis qui mecum erant multos dolores insaniarum nostrarum, quia omnibus talibus conatibus nostris, qualibus tunc laborabam, sub stimulis cupiditatum trahens infelicitatis meae sarcinam et trahendo exaggerans, nihil vellemus aliud nisi ad securam laetitiam pervenire, quo nos mendicus ille iam praecessisset numquam illuc fortasse venturos. quod enim iam ille pauculis et emendicatis nummulis adeptus erat, ad hoc ego tam aerumnosis anfractibus et circuitibus ambiebam, ad laetitiam scilicet temporalis felicitatis. non enim verum gau-

---

26 A. uses lime or glue (used for trapping birds) repeatedly as a metaphor for death: cf. *Conf.* 6.12.22, 10.30.42; *Trin.* 8.1.3. He pictures the soul as having wings like a bird: S. 255.7, "The soul is fleshly, addicted to flesh, stuck in fleshly desires, its wings trapped by the lime of evil desires and unable to fly."

27 Valentinian II lived in Milan at this time; he had become emperor in November 375.

See my heart, Lord! It is you who wanted me to recall this and confess it to you. Now let my soul cleave to you, now that you have stripped it of the glue-trap which is death.[26] How wretched it was! You kept on pricking the soreness of its wound so that it would give everything up and be converted to you, who are above all, and without whom nothing would exist, so that it would be converted and healed. How wretched I was! So too you brought me to an awareness of my own wretchedness on that very day when I was preparing to recite my panegyric on the emperor,[27] in which I told a number of lies and won acclaim from people who knew they were lies even as I uttered them. My heart was pounding with all these anxieties, agitated by feverish and corrosive speculations. As I made my way through a certain quarter of Milan I noticed a poor beggar; at this point he was, I reckon, well fed, merry and enjoying himself.[28] Yet I groaned, and spoke to the friends who were with me about the many sorrows that accompany our follies: in all our efforts, such as those I was then grappling with—dragging the burden of my unhappiness while being goaded by desires, and making its weight heavier by the very act of dragging it—we wanted nothing else but to reach that state of happiness that is free from cares, that this beggar had reached ahead of us, and that we perhaps might never attain. What he had acquired with a few small coins obtained by begging I was still circum-navigating with difficulties and digressions—namely the joy of worldly happiness. Not that he had true joy, but I,

[28] Cf. Agamemnon in Eur. *IA* 16–18, "I envy you, old man, and everyone who lives a life free from danger in insignificant obscurity."

dium habebat, sed et ego illis ambitionibus multo falsius quaerebam. et certe ille laetabatur, ego anxius eram, securus ille, ego trepidus. et si quisquam percontaretur me utrum mallem exultare an metuere, responderem: "exultare"; rursus si interrogaret utrum me talem mallem qualis ille, an qualis ego tunc essem, me ipsum curis timoribusque confectum eligerem, sed perversitate—numquid veritate? neque enim eo me praeponere illi debebam, quo doctior eram, quoniam non inde gaudebam, sed placere inde quaerebam hominibus, non ut eos docerem, sed tantum ut placerem. propterea et tu baculo disciplinae tuae confringebas ossa mea.

(10) Recedant ergo ab anima mea qui dicunt ei, "interest unde quis gaudeat. gaudebat mendicus ille vinulentia, tu gaudere cupiebas gloria." qua gloria, domine, quae non est in te? nam sicut verum gaudium non erat, ita nec illa vera gloria et amplius vertebat mentem meam. et ille ipsa nocte digesturus erat ebrietatem suam, ego cum mea dormieram et surrexeram et dormiturus et surrecturus eram, vide quot dies! interest vero unde quis gaudeat, scio, et gaudium spei fidelis incomparabiliter distat ab illa vanitate, sed et tunc distabat inter nos. nimirum quippe ille felicior erat, non tantum quod hilaritate perfundebatur,

---

29 *Gloria* is an emotive sociopolitical term embracing fame, honor, and achievement. Christianity sought to detach it from such contexts and reapply it. Cf. Levick, "Morals, Politics, and the Fall," 53–62.

30 A vivid metaphor for the process by which his body metabolized alcohol.

with all my ambitions, was seeking a joy far less real. He was certainly happy; I was anxious. He had no worries; I was full of fears. If anyone asked me whether I would prefer to be gleeful or fearful, I would reply, "gleeful." Then again, if someone inquired whether I would like to be in the same state as the beggar, or in the state I found myself in at present, I would still choose to be myself, albeit riddled with worries and fears. But was that simply because I was obstinate? It was surely not because of truth! I ought not to put myself on a higher level than him just because I was better educated: for I got no pleasure from my education, I just used it as a way to please people, not even to teach them, no, just to please them. For this reason too you were breaking my bones with your rod of instruction.

Ps 42:10

(10) As for those, therefore, who say to my soul, "It makes a difference what is the source of a person's pleasure," let them draw back. "That beggar was happy because he was drunk," they say, "whereas you longed to take pleasure in glory."[29] In what kind of glory, Lord, if the glory is separate from you? Just as the beggar's joy was not real, so my glory was not real either, and it confused my mind even more. In the course of the same night he would digest his drunkenness[30] whereas I had gone to sleep with mine and had risen with it again: and look, I was going to keep on sleeping and arising with it for so many days ahead! I am convinced that it makes a difference what the source of a person's pleasure is, and the pleasure of a believer's hope is immeasurably different from that vanity. But even then there was a great gulf between us. Without a doubt, he was the happier, not only because he was soaked in merriment while I was being disemboweled by

1 Cor 1:31

cum ego curis eviscerarer, verum etiam quod ille bene
optando adquisiverat vinum, ego mentiendo quaerebam
typhum. dixi tunc multa in hac sententia caris meis, et
saepe advertebam in his quomodo mihi esset, et inveniebam male mihi esse et dolebam et conduplicabam ipsum
male et, si quid adrisisset prosperum, taedebat apprehen-
dere, quia paene priusquam teneretur avolabat.

7. (11) Congemescebamus in his qui simul amice vive-
bamus, et maxime ac familiarissime cum Alypio et Nebridio ista conloquebar. quorum Alypius ex eodem quo ego
eram ortus municipio, parentibus primatibus municipali-
bus, me minor natu. nam et studuerat apud me, cum in
nostro oppido docere coepi, et postea Carthagini, et diligebat multum, quod ei bonus et doctus viderer, et ego illum propter magnam virtutis indolem, quae in non magna
aetate satis eminebat. gurges tamen morum Carthaginien-
sium, quibus nugatoria fervent spectacula, absorbuerat
eum in insaniam circensium. sed cum in eo miserabiliter
volveretur, ego autem rhetoricam ibi professus publica
schola uterer, nondum me audiebat ut magistrum propter
quandam simultatem quae inter me et patrem eius erat
exorta. et compereram quod circum exitiabiliter amaret,
et graviter angebar, quod tantam spem perditurus vel
etiam perdidisse mihi videbatur. sed monendi eum et aliqua coercitione revocandi nulla erat copia vel amicitiae

---

31 A. continues to play with alimentary images.
32 Like A., Alypius was from Thagaste: he was baptized with
A. and Adeodatus at Easter 387. In 395 he became bishop of
Thagaste. Cf. *Conf.* 9.4.7. On Nebridius cf. *Conf.* 4.3.6; Introduction, pp. xx–xxi.   33 Cf. *Conf.* 4.2.2.   34 This adverb (*exitiabiliter*) is very rare and accordingly emphatic.

my anxieties,[31] but also because he had secured his supply of wine by wishing people a good day, while I was striving for self-importance by telling lies. I spoke at length to my friends about my impressions, and I often observed in them how I myself was feeling. I realized that I was in trouble and I was unhappy, and I redoubled the actual hurt; and if any good fortune smiled on me, I was reluctant to grasp it because just before I seized it, it always fluttered out of reach.

7. (11) Those of us who were living together as friends lamented all these matters. I discussed them most thoroughly and intimately with Alypius and Nebridius.[32] Of the two of them Alypius came from the same municipality as I did. His parents were in the top rank of society there, and he was younger than I. But even so, he had studied under me when I began teaching in our town, and later at Carthage. He loved me dearly because I seemed to him to be both good and learned, while I loved him for his outstanding natural virtue, which was quite apparent even in his younger days. The whirlpool of Carthage's morals, which seethes with excitement over the nonsense of the theatrical shows, had sucked him down into the frenzy of the circus entertainments. At the time when he was in a spin over them and in a pitiful state, I was using a public classroom as a teacher of rhetoric there.[33] He did not at that time, come to listen to my teaching, on account of some grudge which had arisen between his father and me. I had discovered that he had a fatal[34] fascination with the circus, and I was deeply concerned because it seemed to me that either he would squander his considerable promise or he had squandered it already. But there was no chance to warn or recall him to some sense of restraint

259

benivolentia vel iure magisterii. putabam enim eum de me
cum patre sentire, ille vero non sic erat. itaque postposita
in hac re patris voluntate salutare me coeperat veniens in
auditorium meum et audire aliquid atque abire.

(12) Sed enim de memoria mihi lapsum erat agere cum
illo, ne vanorum ludorum caeco et praecipiti studio tam
bonum interimeret ingenium, verum autem, domine, tu,
qui praesides gubernaculis omnium quae creasti, non eum
oblitus eras futurum inter filios tuos antistitem sacramenti
tui et, ut aperte tibi tribueretur eius correctio, per me
quidem illam sed nescientem operatus es. nam quodam
die cum sederem loco solito et coram me adessent discipuli, venit, salutavit, sedit atque in ea quae agebantur in-
tendit animum. et forte lectio in manibus erat, quam dum
exponerem⁷ opportune mihi adhibenda videretur simili-
tudo circensium, quo illud quod insinuabam et iucundius
et planius fieret cum irrisione mordaci eorum quos illa
captivasset insania. scis tu, deus noster, quod tunc de Alypio ab illa peste sanando non cogitaverim. at ille in se ra-
puit meque illud non nisi propter se dixisse crediddit et
quod alius acciperet ad suscensendum mihi, accepit ho-
nestus adulescens ad suscensendum sibi et ad me ardentius diligendum. dixeras enim tu iam olim et innexueras
litteris tuis, "corripe sapientem, et amabit te." at ego illum
non corripueram, sed utens tu omnibus et scientibus et

---

⁷ exponerem *codd. Vega*: exponerem et *Maur. Knöll Skut.*:
exponerem et cum *Ver.*

---

35 I.e., a bishop, presiding over the sacrament of the eucharist.
36 A. liked this proverb: cf. *Ep.* 210.2, 220.12; *Trin.* 14.1.2.

either by means of the goodwill of friendship or through a teacher's authority. For I assumed that he had the same opinion of me as did his father; but in fact he did not. And so he set aside his father's wishes in this respect and began to greet me when he came into my lecture room, and to listen for a while and then depart.

(12) It had slipped my mind to deal with him and stop him destroying a fine natural talent with his blind and headlong zeal for the vanity of the shows. But you, Lord, direct the governance of all that you have made, and you had not forgotten that he was to become an overseer of your sacrament.[35] To ensure that his amendment should be rightly attributed to you, you brought it about through me but without my being aware of it. For one day while I was sitting in my usual spot and my pupils were present before me, he arrived, greeted me, sat down, and fixed his thoughts on the subjects under discussion. By chance I had a reading in my hands, and while I was explaining it, a timely analogy with the circus games seemed to strike me that would make the point I was recommending both clearer and more appealing, because of the biting mockery of those who were in the toils of that particular frenzy. You know, our God, that I had no thoughts then of curing Alypius of that contagion. But he seized upon it and was convinced that I had directed my words at himself alone. What another person would have taken as a reason for finding fault with me, this decent young man took as a reason for finding fault with himself, and for loving me more eagerly. Long ago, you had already spoken, and put this into your Scriptures: "Reproach a wise man and he will love you."[36] It was not I who had reproached him, though, but you: you use everyone, whether we know it or   Prv 9:8

261

nescientibus ordine quo nosti (et ille ordo iustus est) de corde et lingua mea carbones ardentes operatus es, quibus mentem spei bonae adureres tabescentem ac sanares.

Taceat laudes tuas qui miserationes tuas non considerat, quae tibi de medullis meis confitentur. etenim vero ille post illa verba proripuit se ex fovea tam alta, qua libenter demergebatur et cum mira voluptate caecabatur, et excussit animum forti temperantia, et resiluerunt omnes circensium sordes ab eo ampliusque illuc non accessit. deinde patrem reluctantem evicit ut me magistro uteretur; cessit ille atque concessit. et audire me rursus incipiens illa mecum superstitione involutus est, amans in manichaeis ostentationem continentiae, quam veram et germanam putabat. erat autem illa vecors et seductoria, pretiosas animas captans nondum virtutis altitudinem scientes tangere et superficie decipi faciles, sed tamen adumbratae simulataeque virtutis.

8. (13) Non sane relinquens incantatam sibi a parentibus terrenam viam, Romam praecesserat ut ius disceret, et ibi gladiatorii spectaculi hiatu incredibili et incredibiliter abreptus est. cum enim aversaretur et detestaretur talia, quidam eius amici et condiscipuli, cum forte de prandio redeuntibus pervium[8] esset, recusantem vehementer et resistentem familiari violentia duxerunt in amphitheatrum crudelium et funestorum ludorum diebus,

---

[8] pervium *O S codd. mult. Knöll Skut. Vega Ver.*: pervius *Maur. Pell.*

---

[37] I.e., chastity.

not, in the order that you alone comprehend, and that order is just. You fashioned my heart and tongue into burning coals by which you kindled his diseased mind into a good hope, and cured it.

Let anyone who takes no thought for your mercies, which confess their thanks to you from the marrow of my bones, be silent on the subject of your praises. After those words, indeed, he snatched himself out of that pit, deep as it was, in which he was sinking of his own free will and being blinded by peculiar pleasure. With courage and self-control he gave his mind a shake and all the squalor of the circus games leaped away from him, and he went there no more. Then he prevailed upon his reluctant father to employ me as his teacher. His father gave way and gave permission for it. So he began to attend my lessons once more and became involved in that superstition with me; he admired the parade of self-restraint[37] among the Manichaeans, for he believed that it was real and true. But it was in fact senseless and false, and ensnared precious souls that as yet had no idea how to take hold of supreme virtue and were easily taken in by a surface appearance of virtue that was in fact fake and fraudulent. — Prv 6:26

8. (13) He certainly did not abandon that earthly course which his parents had dinned into him. He had made his way to Rome to learn law, and it was there that he was extraordinarily carried away by this extraordinary appetite for gladiatorial shows. For although he disliked and detested them, he happened to bump into some friends and fellow students on their way back from a dinner, and they used friendly force to drag him, still hotly protesting and resisting, into the amphitheater at a time when the deadly and cruel shows were taking place. He declared, "You may

haec dicentem: "si corpus meum in locum illum trahitis et ibi constituitis, numquid et animum et oculos meos in illa spectacula potestis intendere? adero itaque absens ac sic et vos et illa superabo." quibus auditis illi nihilo setius eum adduxerunt secum, idipsum forte explorare cupientes utrum posset efficere.

Quo ubi[9] ventum est et sedibus quibus potuerunt locati sunt, fervebant omnia immanissimis voluptatibus. ille clausis foribus oculorum interdixit animo ne in tanta mala procederet. atque utinam et aures obturavisset! nam quodam pugnae casu, cum clamor ingens totius populi vehementer eum pulsasset, curiositate victus et quasi paratus, quidquid illud esset, etiam visum contemnere et vincere, aperuit oculos.[10] et percussus est graviore vulnere in anima quam ille in corpore quem cernere concupivit, ceciditque miserabilius quam ille quo cadente factus est clamor. qui per eius aures intravit et reseravit eius lumina, ut esset qua feriretur et deiceretur audax adhuc potius quam fortis animus, et eo infirmior quo de se praesumserat, qui debuit de te. ut enim vidit illum sanguinem, immanitatem simul ebibit et non se avertit, sed fixit aspectum et hauriebat furias et nesciebat, et delectabatur scelere certaminis et cruenta voluptate inebriabatur. et non erat iam ille qui venerat sed unus de turba ad quam venerat, et verus eorum socius a quibus adductus erat. quid plura! spectavit, clamavit, exarsit, abstulit inde secum insaniam qua stimu-

---

9 quo (ubi) *P Maur. Knöll Skut. Pell.*: quod S *Vega Ver.*

10 aperuit oculos *codd. Maur. Ver. Vega*: aperuit S *Knöll Skut. Pell.*

drag my body to such a place and set it down there, but surely you cannot also fix my mind and gaze upon those performances? I shall be both present, and absent: and so I will defeat both you and them." His friends listened, then took him along with them just the same, perhaps because they were eager to test that precise point, whether he could succeed.

When they arrived there and settled into what seats they could, everything was a hotbed of monstrous gratification. He closed his eyes as a point of access, and forbade his mind to step forth into such evils. If only he had closed his ears likewise! For at one fall in a fight a loud roar from the whole crowd struck him with full force; he was overcome with curiosity and like someone prepared to condemn and subdue what he saw, whatever it might be, he opened his eyes. At once he was struck by a wound to his soul that was deeper than the wound the combatant he was now eager to watch suffered to his body. He sank down, more pitiable than the man whose fall had given rise to the shouting. That noise entered into his ears and unlocked his eyes, to make a way for the striking down and subjugation of a mind that up to this point had been confident rather than courageous, and all the weaker for relying on itself when it should have relied on you. For when he saw that blood, he drank deep of its barbarity and did not turn himself away but fixed his gaze and drank in the torments and was unaware, and found gratification in the wickedness of the contest, and became drunk on the pleasures of blood. Now he was no longer the same person as when he had come. He was one of the crowd that he had joined, a true companion of the friends who had taken him there. Why say any more? He watched, he shouted, he burned;

laretur redire non tantum cum illis a quibus prius abstrac-
tus est, sed etiam prae illis et alios trahens. et inde tamen
manu validissima et misericordissima eruisti eum tu, et
docuisti non sui habere sed tui fiduciam, sed longe postea.

9. (14) Verum tamen iam hoc ad medicinam futuram
in eius memoria reponebatur. nam et illud quod, cum adhuc studeret iam me audiens apud Carthaginem et medio
die cogitaret in foro quod recitaturus erat, sicut exerceri
scholastici solent, sivisti eum comprehendi ab aeditimis
fori tamquam furem, non arbitror aliam ob causam te per-
misisse, deus noster, nisi ut ille vir tantus futurus iam inci-
peret discere quam non facile in cognoscendis causis
homo ab homine damnandus esset temeraria credulitate.

Quippe ante tribunal deambulabat solus cum tabulis ac
stilo, cum ecce adulescens quidam ex numero scholasticorum, fur verus, securim clanculo apportans, illo non sen-
tiente ingressus est ad cancellos plumbeos qui vico argen-
tario desuper praeminent et praecidere plumbum coepit.
sono autem securis audito submurmuraverunt argentarii
qui subter erant, et miserunt qui apprehenderent quem
forte invenissent. quorum vocibus auditis relicto instru-
mento ille discessit timens, ne cum eo teneretur. Alypius
autem, qui non viderat intrantem, exeuntem sensit et celeriter vidit abeuntem et, causam scire cupiens, ingressus
est locum et inventam securim stans atque admirans con-

he took with him from that place the madness that goaded him to return, not just with those friends who had first carried him away but even before them, and taking others along. And yet you rescued him from there with a mighty and merciful hand, and you taught him to put his trust in you and not himself. But that only happened much later.

9. (14) This, however, was being stored up in his memory as a medicine for him in the future. So too was another incident. Once while he was still studying by attending my lessons in Carthage and was in the forum at noon thinking over a speech he was about to give, such as advocates often practice, you let him be arrested by the forum's temple attendants as a thief. O Lord our God, I think that you gave permission for this precise reason: to begin educating that man who would one day be so great, that when working out the reasons for things, one human being ought not to be condemned lightly by another on a basis of incautious credulity.

What happened was that he was walking up and down alone in front of the tribunal with his writing tablets and his pen. Then look: a young man, one of a group of students (this was the real thief) was secretly carrying an ax and, without Alypius noticing, went to the lead gratings that cover the top of the silversmiths' area of the market and started to cut the lead away. Once the silversmiths below heard the sound of the ax they whispered among themselves and sent people to arrest whomever they might find. The actual thief heard their voices and left in a panic, abandoning his ax so as not to be caught with it. Alypius had not heard him come in but noticed his departure and saw him make off quickly. Wanting to know why, he went into the place, found the ax, and was standing

siderabat, cum ecce illi qui missi erant reperiunt eum solum ferentem ferrum cuius sonitu exciti venerant. tenent,
attrahunt, congregatis inquilinis fori tamquam furem
manifestum se comprehendisse gloriantur, et inde offe-
rendus iudiciis ducebatur.

(15) Sed hactenus docendus fuit. statim enim, domine,
subvenisti innocentiae, cuius testis eras tu solus. cum enim
duceretur vel ad custodiam vel ad supplicium, fit eis obviam quidam architectus, cuius maxima erat cura publica-
rum fabricarum. gaudent illi eum potissimum occurrisse,
cui solebant in suspicionem venire ablatarum rerum quae
perissent de foro, ut quasi tandem iam ille cognosceret a
quibus haec fierent. verum autem viderat homo saepe Alypium in domo cuiusdam senatoris ad quem salutandum
ventitabat, statimque cognitum manu apprehensa semovit
a turbis et tanti mali causam quaerens, quid gestum esset
audivit omnesque tumultuantes qui aderant et minaciter
frementes iussit venire secum. et venerunt ad domum illius adulescentis qui rem commiserat.

Puer vero erat ante ostium, et tam parvus erat ut nihil
exinde domino suo metuens facile posset totum indicare;
cum eo quippe in foro fuit pedisequus. quem posteaquam
recoluit Alypius, architecto intimavit. at ille securim
demonstravit puero, quaerens ab eo cuius esset. qui confestim "nostra" inquit; deinde interrogatus aperuit cetera.
sic in illam domum translata causa confusisque turbis quae

---

38 On Roman social ritual centered on the morning audience
(*salutatio*), cf. Wallace-Hadrill, "Social Structure of the Roman
House," 43–97.

there considering it in puzzlement. Then all of a sudden the men who had been sent found him alone and holding the weapon that had caused the noise and prompted their coming. They grabbed him, dragged him away, and boasted to the crowd of locals that had by then gathered that they had undoubtedly apprehended a thief. Then he was led away to be committed for trial.

(15) His lesson did not go any further than this. You, Lord, went to the help of his innocence, of which you were the sole witness. For when he was being led off either to prison or to punishment, a certain architect met them, a man with principal responsibility for public buildings. They were especially pleased at running into him because he had often suspected them of pilfering items that had disappeared from the forum, since he would now at last discover who was really taking them. But this man had often seen Alypius in the house of a certain senator whose morning audience he attended regularly:[38] as soon as he recognized him he took his hand and led him away from the crowd and asked him what had caused this grave misfortune. Once he heard what happened, he ordered the whole unruly crowd, who stood there noisy and threatening, to come with him. So they arrived at the house of the young man who had committed the theft.

Beside the entrance was a boy, and he was so small that he had no reason to fear for his master and could tell the whole story: he had in fact attended that young man as his servant. Then Alypius remembered him, and told the architect, who showed the ax to the boy, and asked him whose it was. He immediately replied "Ours"; then they questioned him and he confessed the rest. So the case was transferred to that household. The crowd was con-

269

de illo triumphare iam coeperant, futurus dispensator verbi tui et multarum in ecclesia tua causarum examinator experientior instructiorque discessit.

10. (16) Hunc ergo Romae inveneram, et adhaesit mihi fortissimo vinculo mecumque Mediolanium profectus est, ut nec me desereret et de iure quod didicerat aliquid ageret secundum votum magis parentum quam suum. et ter iam adsederat mirabili continentia ceteris, cum ille magis miraretur eos qui aurum innocentiae praeponerent. temptata est quoque eius indoles non solum inlecebra cupiditatis sed etiam stimulo timoris. Romae adsidebat comiti largitionum Italicianarum. erat eo tempore quidam potentissimus senator cuius et beneficiis obstricti multi et terrori subditi erant. voluit sibi licere nescio quid ex more potentiae suae quod esset per leges inlicitum; restitit Alypius. promissum est praemium; inrisit animo. praetentae minae; calcavit, mirantibus omnibus inusitatam animam, quae hominem tantum et innumerabilibus praestandi nocendique modis ingenti fama celebratum vel amicum non optaret vel non formidaret inimicum. ipse autem iudex cui consiliarius erat, quamvis et ipse fieri nollet, non tamen aperte recusabat, sed in istum causam transferens ab eo se non permitti adserebat, quia et re vera, si ipse

---

39 Letters of A. exploring the exercise of judicial authority, and the relationship between punishment, punisher, and punished include *Ep.* 133, 134, 152–55. On bishops as judges, cf. *Op. Mon.* 29.37.   40 I.e., a legal adviser to a magistrate.

41 The Latin *comes* (whence "count" and "comte") was an imperial dignitary (originally a "companion" of the emperor); six such officials were subordinate to the official in charge of the finances of the western empire.

founded, when it had already begun to triumph over Alypius, while he—who would one day be a dispenser of your Word and a judge of many cases in your Church[39]—went away wiser and more experienced.

10. (16) I had found him at Rome. He was united with me by the strongest possible ties and had set out for Milan with me so as not to abandon me and also to practice something of the law, which he had learned to please his parents' wishes rather than his own. He had already acted as assessor[40] three times with a moderation that seemed surprising to others, although he himself was more surprised at those who put gold before guiltlessness. His nature was put to the test not only by the lure of desire but also by the spur of fear. At Rome he was assessor to the official in charge of the Italian treasuries,[41] at that time a particularly powerful senator: many were entangled in obligations to him and oppressed by terror. This man wanted permission for something that was habitually conceded, given his dominant position, but that the law forbade. Alypius stood his ground. The man tried to bribe him; from his heart he scorned it. Next came threats; he disdained them, though everyone was amazed at his remarkable courage in that although the man was so important, and of such reputation and renown, and had countless means of dispensing favors and injuries, Alypius neither chose him as a friend nor feared him as an enemy. As for the judge he was advising, he too was reluctant to give permission, yet he did not openly refuse, and instead pushed the responsibility off onto Alypius with the assertion that the latter would not let him allow it; the truth

faceret, iste discederet. hoc solo autem paene iam inlectus
erat studio litterario, ut pretiis praetorianis codices sibi
conficiendos curaret, sed consulta iustitia deliberationem
in melius vertit, utiliorem iudicans aequitatem qua prohi-
bebatur quam potestatem qua sinebatur. parvum est hoc,
sed qui in parvo fidelis est et in magno fidelis est, nec ullo
modo erit inane quod tuae veritatis ore processit: "si in
iniusto mammona fideles non fuistis, verum[11] quis dabit
vobis? et si in alieno fideles non fuistis, vestrum[12] quis
dabit vobis?" talis ille tunc inhaerebat mihi mecumque
nutabat in consilio, quisnam esset tenendus vitae modus.

(17) Nebridius etiam, qui relicta patria vicina Carthagini atque ipsa Carthagine, ubi frequentissimus erat, relicto paterno rure optimo, relicta domo et non secutura
matre, nullam ob aliam causam Mediolanium venerat, nisi
ut mecum viveret in flagrantissimo studio veritatis atque
sapientiae, pariter suspirabat pariterque fluctuabat, beatae vitae inquisitor ardens et quaestionum difficillimarum
scrutator acerrimus. et erant ora trium egentium et inopiam suam sibimet invicem anhelantium et ad te expec-

---

11 verum S *codd. Knöll Skut. Ver.*: quod verum est P *Maur.*
12 vestrum S *codd. Knöll Skut. Ver.*: quod vestrum est P *Maur.*

---

42 *codices*; the term is not used as a metonym for the book's
contents, i.e., the text.

43 A metonym for wealth, of obscure disputed origin, found
in Qumran texts in both Hebrew and Aramaic. A. thinks the word
is Punic, *Ser.* 113.2.2.

44 Hor. *Epod.* 2.1–8: the ancestral acres have a moral as well

was that if he did so, Alypius would have walked out. The only thing that nearly succeeded in tempting him was his enthusiasm for literature: for he could arrange to have books[42] copied for himself at praetorian prices. He thought about righteousness, however, and shifted his resolve for the better: he judged the sense of fairness that was restraining him to be of more real value than the power that gave him such an opportunity. It is a small matter, but the one who is faithful in a small matter is also faithful in a great one, and nothing is meaningless if it has come forth from the mouth of your truth: "If you have not been faithful in the matter of unrighteous mammon,[43] who will grant you the true riches?" This was the kind of man Alypius was in those days, when he was my close companion and, like me, was wavering about what way of life we should maintain.

Lk 16:10

Lk 16:11–12

(17) Nebridius had also left his ancestral neighborhood near Carthage, and Carthage itself, where he had lived for most of his life. He left his fine family estates.[44] He left his home and his mother, who was not going to follow him. He had come to Milan for no other reason than to live with me amid the most ardent zeal for truth and wisdom. Like me he was sighing, like me he was wavering: a passionate seeker after the blessed life, and an exceptionally keen investigator of the hardest problems.[45] And there they were, the mouths of three poor men, gasping their own neediness to one another and looking to you to give them

as a financial aspect, as a place of simple labor set apart from business, war, trade, and politics. Artistic anaphora of "left" (*relicta relicto relicta*) adds emphasis to this separation.

[45] Cf. *Ep.* 98.8 on Nebridius, and Introduction, p. xx.

tantium, ut dares eis escam in tempore opportuno. et in omni amaritudine quae nostros saeculares actus de misericordia tua sequebatur, intuentibus nobis finem cur ea pateremur, occurrebant tenebrae, et aversabamur gementes et dicebamus, "quamdiu haec?" et hoc crebro dicebamus, et dicentes non relinquebamus ea, quia non elucebat certum aliquid quod illis relictis apprehenderemus.

11. (18) Et ego maxime mirabar, satagens et recolens quam longum tempus esset ab undevicensimo anno aetatis meae, quo fervere coeperam studio sapientiae, disponens ea inventa relinquere omnes vanarum cupiditatum spes inanes et insanias mendaces. et ecce iam tricenariam aetatem gerebam, in eodem luto haesitans aviditate fruendi praesentibus fugientibus et dissipantibus me, dum dico, "cras inveniam. ecce manifestum apparebit, et tenebo. ecce Faustus veniet et exponet omnia. o magni viri academici! nihil ad agendam vitam certi comprehendi potest? immo quaeramus diligentius et non desperemus. ecce iam non sunt absurda in libris ecclesiasticis quae absurda videbantur, et possunt aliter atque honeste intellegi. figam pedes in eo gradu in quo puer a parentibus positus eram, donec inveniatur perspicua veritas. sed ubi quaeretur? quando quaeretur? non vacat Ambrosio, non vacat legere. ubi ipsos codices quaerimus? unde aut quando compara-

---

46 Ironic: A. quotes Jn 4:25 but applies it to Faustus instead of Christ. On Faustus cf. *Conf.* 5.3.3 and Introduction, p. xxvi.

47 The New Academic philosophical school held a skeptical view on reaching truth through reason. A. addresses this in the first of his Cassiciacum dialogues, *C. Acad.*, challenging their skepticism and arguing that truth is attainable (3.17–19). OD punctuates this as a statement; GM Ver. as a question.

their meat in due time. We pondered the reason why   _{Ps 104:14}
it was that we went on enduring such things, amid all
the bitterness that your mercy caused to accompany our
worldly actions; and dark shadows descended upon us.
Then we would turn away with a groan and say, "How long
must this last?" We would often talk so, but even while we
said it we did not give up our former pursuits because
there was as yet nothing clearly apparent, once we had
abandoned all that, for us to hold on to.

11. (18) I was preoccupied with my reflections and
began to marvel at how much time had passed since I was
in my nineteenth year, when I had first begun to glow with
a passion for wisdom. Once I had discovered it, I planned
to abandon all the empty expectations and deceitful delusions of my vain desires. And look, already I was in my
thirtieth year, still stuck in the same mud of hungering
after the momentary, fleeting things that were tearing me
apart. Finally I said to myself, "Tomorrow I will find it:
look, then it will be clear, and I will master it, and surely
Faustus will 'come and explain everything.'[46] O you great
Academics! is it true that nothing can be certain about how
life should be lived?[47] Well then, I must search harder and
not give up hope. After all, in the books of the Church
those things that once seemed ridiculous are no longer
ridiculous at all. They can be understood another way, and
with integrity. I shall set my feet on that step where once
my parents placed me as a child, until transparent truth is
found. But where to seek it? When to seek it? There is
no spare time for seeing Ambrose, and none for reading.
Where do I look for the actual books? Where and when

mus? a quibus sumimus? deputentur tempora, distribuan-
tur horae pro salute animae. magna spes oborta est: non
docet catholica fides quod putabamus et vani accusaba-
mus. nefas habent docti eius credere deum figura humani
corporis terminatum. et dubitamus pulsare, quo aperian-
tur cetera? antemeridianis horis discipuli occupant: ceteris quid facimus? cur non id agimus? sed quando saluta-
mus amicos maiores, quorum suffragiis opus habemus?
quando praeparamus quod emant scholastici? quando
reparamus nos ipsos relaxando animo ab intentione cura-
rum?

(19) "Pereant omnia et dimittamus haec vana et inania:
conferamus nos ad solam inquisitionem veritatis. vita misera est, mors incerta est. subito obrepat: quomodo hinc
exibimus? et ubi nobis discenda sunt quae hic negleximus?
ac non potius huius neglegentiae supplicia luenda? quid si
mors ipsa omnem curam cum sensu amputabit et finiet?
ergo et hoc quaerendum.

"Sed absit ut ita sit. non vacat, non est inane, quod tam
eminens culmen auctoritatis christianae fidei toto orbe
diffunditur. numquam tanta et talia pro nobis divinitus
agerentur, si morte corporis etiam vita animae consume-
retur. quid cunctamur igitur relicta spe saeculi conferre

---

48 Cf. *Ep.* 21.3 (AD 391): "I must scrutinize all the remedies
in his Scriptures, and by prayer and reading ensure that my soul
has adequate strength for the difficult tasks it faces. I did not do
this before because I had no time. I was ordained at the very
moment when I was planning this time of sabbatical for studying
the Holy Scriptures."

49 Cf. *Conf.* 6.3.4.

do I obtain them? Who do I borrow them from? Fixed times must be allotted, fixed periods apportioned for the good of my soul.[48] A great hope has sprung up: the catholic faith does not teach what I once used to think it did, what I falsely accused it of. The Church's teachers consider it impiety to believe that God can be encompassed by the form of a human body.[49] So why do I hesitate to knock so that the rest may be opened? All morning my pupils keep me busy: what do I do for the rest of the day? Why am I not getting on with this? Yet when am I to attend upon those influential friends on whose support I am dependent? When am I to prepare the teaching which my pupils pay for? When am I to refresh myself, giving my mind a rest from its pressing weight of anxieties? Mt 7:7

(19) "To hell with all of it! I must reject these futile follies. I must address myself solely to the pursuit of truth. Life is pitiable. Death is unaccountable: it takes us suddenly by surprise, but in what manner shall we make our departure? When are we to learn what we have neglected in this life? Must we not pay the penalty for this neglect? What if death itself cuts off all physical sensation and with it every anxious thought? This too I must investigate.

"But God forbid! It is not meaningless or for nothing that the sublime grandeur of the authority of Christian faith is spread across the entire world. Divine influence would never have provided such remarkable resources for us, if, with the death of the body, the life of the soul were also consumed![50] Now, therefore, that we have abandoned reliance on earthly things, why do we put off devoting

---

[50] A.'s use of passives and plurals here is distinctive, depersonalizing and distancing his conclusions; cf. *Conf.* 6.13.23.

nos totos ad quaerendum deum et vitam beatam? sed ex-
pecta: iucunda sunt etiam ista, habent non parvam dulce-
dinem suam; non facile ab eis praecidenda est intentio,
quia turpe est ad ea rursum redire. ecce iam quantum est
ut impetretur aliquis honor. et quid amplius in his deside-
randum? suppetit amicorum maiorum copia: ut nihil aliud
et multum festinemus, vel praesidatus dari potest. et
ducenda uxor cum aliqua pecunia, ne sumptum nostrum
gravet, et ille erit modus cupiditatis. multi magni viri et
imitatione dignissimi sapientiae studio cum coniugibus
dediti fuerunt."

(20) Cum haec dicebam et alternabant hi venti et im-
pellebant huc atque illuc cor meum, transibant tempora
et tardabam converti ad dominum, et differebam de die
in diem vivere in te et non differebam cotidie in memet
ipso mori. amans beatam vitam timebam illam in sede sua
et ab ea fugiens quaerebam eam. putabam enim me miserum fore nimis si feminae privarer amplexibus, et medicinam misericordiae tuae ad eandem infirmitatem sanandam
non cogitabam, quia expertus non eram, et propriarum
virium credebam esse continentiam, quarum mihi non
eram conscius, cum tam stultus essem ut nescirem, sicut
scriptum est, neminem posse esse continentem nisi tu
dederis. utique dares, si gemitu interno pulsarem aures
tuas et fide solida in te iactarem curam meam.

12. (21) Prohibebat me sane Alypius ab uxore ducenda,

ourselves wholly to seeking God and the blessed life? But wait: those earthly things are pleasurable, they have no small sweetness of their own. It is not easy to divert one's attention from them just because going back to them once more would be disgraceful. Just think of the distinction if political office is sought. What particular office might be especially distinguished and attractive? There are plenty of important friends to hand. If we press hard for nothing else, a modest provincial governorship can be secured. A wife would need to be taken, one with some money, to ensure that our expenditure did not cause problems. That would be the limit of my ambition. Many great men, who deserve to be emulated, have been dedicated to the pursuit of wisdom at the same time as being married."

(20) While I was arguing in this fashion, winds were blowing and driving my heart first one way and then another. Time was passing. I kept postponing the moment of conversion to the Lord. From one day to the next I was putting off a life in you, yet I was not delaying my dying in myself. I longed for the blessed life yet feared it in its proper place, and even as I fled from it I began to seek it out. I used to reckon that I would be completely wretched if deprived of intimacy with a woman, and I did not think that the medicine of your mercy could cure that precise weakness, because I had not tried it. I was convinced that chastity was the mark of a certain kind of strength of which I myself was incapable: after all I was foolish enough to be ignorant that it is written, no one can be chaste except by your gift. Undoubtedly you would have granted it if I had battered your ears with my inward groaning and, firm in my faith, had cast my care upon you.

12. (21) Very sensibly Alypius kept telling me not to

Sir 5:7

Ws 8:21

1 Pt 5:7

279

cantans nullo modo nos posse securo otio simul in amore
sapientiae vivere, sicut iam diu desideraremus, si id fecissem. erat enim ipse in ea re etiam tunc castissimus, ita ut
mirum esset, quia vel experientiam concubitus ceperat in
ingressu adulescentiae suae, sed non haeserat magisque
doluerat et spreverat et deinde iam continentissime vive-
bat. ego autem resistebam illi exemplis eorum qui coniu-
gati coluissent sapientiam et promeruissent deum et ha-
buissent fideliter ac dilexissent amicos. a quorum ego
quidem granditate animi longe aberam et deligatus morbo
carnis mortifera suavitate trahebam catenam meam, solvi
timens et quasi concusso vulnere repellens verba bene
suadentis tamquam manum[13] solventis. insuper etiam per
me ipsi quoque Alypio loquebatur serpens, et innectebat
atque spargebat per linguam meam dulces laqueos in via
eius, quibus illi honesti et expediti pedes implicarentur.

(22) Cum enim me ille miraretur, quem non parvi pen-
deret, ita haerere visco illius voluptatis ut me adfirmarem,
quotienscumque inde inter nos quaereremus, caelibem
vitam nullo modo posse degere atque ita me defenderem,
cum illum mirantem viderem, ut dicerem multum inter-
esse inter illud quod ipse raptim et furtim expertus esset,
quod paene iam ne meminisset quidem atque ideo nulla
molestia facile contemneret, et delectationes consuetudinis meae, ad quas si accessisset honestum nomen matri-

---

13 manum *codd. Maur. Knöll Skut. Vega Pell.*: manu S: manus
C^2 *Ver.*

---

51 I.e., philosophy: cf. *Conf.* 3.4.8, 8.7.17.
52 Cf. *Conf.* 6.6.9 with n. 30.
53 *caelebs* can mean "celibate," but also simply "unmarried."

take a wife. He was preaching at me that if I did so, we could never live life in peace and quiet and, at the same time, in pursuit of wisdom,[51] which was what we were always longing to do. At that time, he himself was living in perfect chastity in that respect. This was surprising, in particular because he had had sexual experience in early adolescence, but he had not persisted and instead regretted and rejected it, and from then on lived in strictest continence. I was opposing him by citing the examples of those who lived as married men yet venerated wisdom and pleased God, living faithfully and loving their friends. I was so far from their greatness of mind, so bound to that disease of the flesh with all its deadly desirability that I continued to drag my chain: I was afraid to be unfettered. It was as if I had a wound and someone had struck it: I went on rejecting the words of my wise adviser as if his hands were unbinding me. What is more, that serpent began to speak through me to Alypius too, contriving and, by my tongue, spreading sweet snares in his way. These snares were to entangle the feet of that decent man, who up till then had been free.

(22) He was surprised at me because he held me in high regard, and yet I was so stuck in the glue-trap[52] of that particular pleasure as to insist, whenever we then explored this question together, that I could not possibly life a celibate life.[53] Also, whenever I noticed his surprise, I defended myself by saying that there was a great difference between, on the one hand what he had tried only as a fleeting and clandestine experience, now barely remembered, and was therefore easily able to condemn, and on the other hand the delights of my lifestyle. If only those delights had acquired the official title of "marriage" he

281

monii, non eum mirari oportere cur ego illam vitam nequi-
rem spernere, coeperat et ipse desiderare coniugium,
nequaquam victus libidine talis voluptatis sed curiositatis.
dicebat enim scire se cupere quidnam esset illud sine quo
vita mea, quae illi sic placebat, non mihi vita sed poena
videretur. stupebat enim liber ab illo vinculo animus servitutem meam et stupendo ibat in experiendi cupidinem,
venturus in ipsam experientiam atque inde fortasse lapsu-
rus in eam quam stupebat servitutem, quoniam sponsionem
volebat facere cum morte, et qui amat periculum incidet
in illud.

Neutrum enim nostrum, si quod est coniugale decus in
officio regendi matrimonii et suscipiendorum liberorum,
ducebat nisi tenuiter. magna autem ex parte atque vehementer consuetudo satiandae insatiabilis concupiscentiae
me captum excruciabat, illum autem admiratio capien-
dum trahebat. sic eramus, donec tu, altissime, non dese-
rens humum nostram miseratus miseros subvenires miris
et occultis modis.

13. (23) Et instabatur impigre ut ducerem uxorem. iam
petebam, iam promittebatur maxime matre dante operam,
quo me iam coniugatum baptismus salutaris ablueret, quo
me in dies gaudebat aptari et vota sua ac promissa tua in
mea fide compleri animadvertebat. cum sane et rogatu

---

54 Gn 2:7.

should have had no reason for questioning why I was unable to reject that way of life. He even began to desire marriage for himself, not by any means because he was overcome by desire for such pleasure but out of curiosity. So he began to declare that he wanted to know what kind of a thing it was without which my life, which he warmly approved as it was, appeared to be not really life at all but punishment. Because his mind was free from that bondage, he was astonished at my enslavement; and he went from amazement to a desire of trying it out: he was on the brink of imitating that same experimentation and perhaps thence falling into the very enslavement which so astonished him. For he was contemplating making an engagement with death. After all, whoever loves danger is sure to fall into it.

Is 28:18; cf. Ws 1:16 Sir 3:26

Neither of us gave any serious thought to how the dignity of the married state consists in the obligations of a properly ordered marriage and the rearing of children. On the whole, it was my habit of passionately indulging my insatiable desire that held me captive and tormented me, but it was curiosity that took Alypius prisoner. And thus we remained until you, O Most Highest, took pity upon us two wretches, rather than despising us as mere earth.[54] So you rescued us by hidden yet wonderful ways.

13. (23) It became a pressing concern for me to take a wife. At once I made a proposal, and at once a bride was promised to me. My mother was assiduous in promoting this match. It was her intention that once I was pledged in marriage the saving grace of baptism would cleanse me. So she rejoiced that I was becoming daily more ready for it; and she remarked how her own prayers and your promises were being fulfilled in my faith. Certainly it was at my

283

meo et desiderio suo forti clamore cordis abs te depreca-
retur cotidie ut ei per visum ostenderes aliquid de futuro
matrimonio meo, numquam voluisiti. et videbat quaedam
vana et phantastica, quo cogebat impetus de hac re sa-
tagentis humani spiritus, et narrabat mihi non cum fiducia
qua solebat, cum tu demonstrabas ei, sed contemnens ea.
dicebat enim discernere se nescio quo sapore, quem verbis explicare non poterat, quid interesset inter revelantem
te et animam suam somniantem. instabatur tamen, et
puella petebatur, cuius aetas ferme biennio minus quam
nubilis erat, et quia ea placebat, exspectabatur.

14. (24) Et multi amici agitaveramus animo et conlo-
quentes ac detestantes turbulentas humanae vitae moles-
tias paene iam firmaveramus remoti a turbis otiose vivere,
id otium sic moliti ut, si quid habere possemus, conferre-
mus in medium unamque rem familiarem conflaremus ex
omnibus, ut per amicitiae sinceritatem non esset aliud
huius et aliud illius, sed quod ex cunctis fieret unum et
universum singulorum esset et omnia omnium, cum vide-
remur nobis esse posse decem ferme homines in eadem
societate essentque inter nos praedivites, Romanianus
maxime communiceps noster, quem tunc graves aestus
negotiorum suorum ad comitatum attraxerant, ab ineunte

---

[55] The "clamor of her heart" (*clamor cordis*) is echoed in
an anonymous twelfth-century hymn, *Jubilus Rhythmicus De Nomine Iesu, Cum Maria diluculo / Iesum quaeram in tu-
mulo / Clamore cordis querulo*.

[56] The fourth century was a time of rapid development of
monastic communities both eremitic and coenobitic: for the clas-
sic literary model, cf. Bartelink, *Vie d'Antoine*.

[57] A rich friend of A.; see Introduction, p. xxi.

request and also in accordance with her own wishes that she prayed continually every day, from the intense clamor[55] of her heart. She asked you to give her some vision about my future marriage. Yet you were never willing. She did have some visions, but always they were vain phantasms, and it was the force of a human spirit preoccupied with a particular matter that was evoking them. When she told me about them, she had none of that confidence which typified those times when you would make things plain to her. Instead she rejected them. She insisted that she could tell the difference between your granting some revelation and her own soul imagining it, by means of some kind of smell which she was unable to describe. Still the pressure continued and a girl was selected. She was almost two years below marriageable age, but since she was pleasing, there was a period of waiting.

14. (24) Many of us who were friends had animated discussions and debates, and we so disliked the tempestuous tribulations of human life that we had almost made up our minds to live a life of peace in some deserted place.[56] We would strive to build up that peace by holding in common whatever we owned, thus forging out of it all a single family unit. In this way, through the purity of our friendship it would not be a case of this thing belonging to one person and that thing to another. Instead there would be one common resource made up of everything. Our collective assets would belong to each as individuals, and each individual thing would belong to all. We took the view that we could be about ten in number in the one community. Some of us were extremely rich men, particularly Romanianus,[57] who came from my home town; some pressing business anxieties had drawn him to the court. Right from

CONFESSIONS

aetate mihi familiarissimus. qui maxime instabat huic rei
et magnam in suadendo habebat auctoritatem, quod am-
pla res eius multum ceteris anteibat. et placuerat nobis ut
bini annui tamquam magistratus omnia necessaria cu-
rarent ceteris quietis.

Sed posteaquam coepit cogitari utrum hoc mulierculae
sinerent, quas et alii nostrum iam habebant et nos habere
volebamus, totum illud placitum, quod bene formabamus,
dissiluit in manibus atque confractum et abiectum est.
inde ad suspiria et gemitus et gressus ad sequendas latas
et tritas vias saeculi, quoniam multae cogitationes erant in
corde nostro, consilium autem tuum manet in aeternum.
ex quo consilio deridebas nostra et tua praeparabas nobis,
daturus escam in opportunitate et aperturus manum atque impleturus animas nostras benedictione.

15. (25) Interea mea peccata multiplicabantur, et
avulsa a latere meo tamquam impedimento coniugii cum
qua cubare solitus eram, cor, ubi adhaerebat, concisum et
vulneratum mihi erat et trahebat sanguinem. et illa in Afri-
cam redierat, vovens tibi alium se virum nescituram, relicto apud me naturali ex illa filio meo. at ego infelix nec
feminae imitator, dilationis impatiens, tamquam post
biennium accepturus eam quam petebam, quia non ama-
tor coniugii sed libidinis servus eram, procuravi aliam, non
utique coniugem, quo tamquam sustentaretur et perduce-

58 *Mulierculae*—an unfavorable diminutive.
59 A. never names her, in accordance with his use of personal
names (always sparing in *Conf.*) to distinguish those who helped
in his conversion. They had been together for sixteen years (370–
386); their son, Adeodatus (which means "given by God"), was
born in 371/2.

286

our childhood, he and I had been the best of friends. He was particularly insistent in pressing for this plan, and his view carried great weight because he was so much richer than the rest of us. We had decided that two of us should be appointed annually, like magistrates, to take care of all practical matters and leave the rest of us free from worldly business.

But next we started to consider whether the little wives[58] would allow it: for some of us were already married, and others of us also wanted wives. So the entire plan, which we had constructed so perfectly, broke apart in our hands, shattered, and was abandoned. From that point it was all sighing and groaning and steps toward following that broad and well-worn way of the world, for there were many thoughts in my heart, while your counsel is everlasting. In accordance with your plan, you scorned mine, while making ready your own for me. You were about to give me my food at the proper time, and to open your hand, and fill my soul with blessing.

Prv 19:21; Ps 33:1

Ps 145:15–16

15. (25) In the meantime my sins were increasing in number. That woman with whom I used to share my bed[59] was torn from my side, on the grounds that she stood in the way of my marriage. My heart, which was so attached to her, was broken and pierced, leaving a trail of blood. She returned to Africa vowing to you that she would never have another man. She left behind with me my son she had borne to me. I was wretched. I could not follow even a woman's example. I was impatient with delay. As there were still two years to go before I took the wife I had chosen, and as I was not a lover of marriage but a slave of lust, I chose another woman, but not to be my wife. Thus the disease of my soul remained as great or even greater

retur vel integer vel auctior morbus animae meae satellitio
perdurantis consuetudinis in regnum uxorium. nec sanabatur vulnus illud meum quod prioris praecisione factum
erat, sed post fervorem doloremque acerrimum putresce-
bat, et quasi frigidius sed desperatius dolebat.

16. (26) Tibi laus, tibi gloria, fons misericordiarum! ego
fiebam miserior et tu propinquior. aderat iam iamque dextera tua raptura me de caeno et ablutura,[14] et ignorabam.
nec me revocabat a profundiore voluptatum carnalium
gurgite nisi metus mortis et futuri iudicii tui, qui per varias
quidem opiniones numquam tamen recessit de pectore
meo. et disputabam cum amicis meis Alypio et Nebridio
de finibus bonorum et malorum: Epicurum accepturum
fuisse palmam in animo meo, nisi ego credidissem post
mortem restare animae vitam et tractus meritorum, quod
Epicurus credere noluit. et quaerebam si essemus immor-
tales et in perpetua corporis voluptate sine ullo amissionis
terrore viveremus, cur non essemus beati aut quid aliud
quaereremus, nesciens idipsum ad magnam miseriam
pertinere quod ita demersus et caecus cogitare non possem lumen honestatis et gratis amplectendae pulchritudi-
nis quam non videt oculus carnis, et videtur ex intimo.

Nec considerabam miser ex qua vena mihi manaret
quod ista ipsa foeda tamen cum amicis dulciter confere-
bam, nec esse sine amicis poteram beatus, etiam secundum sensum quem tunc habebam in quantalibet affluentia

[14] ablutura *codd. Knöll Skut.*: ablutura me *Maur.*: ablatura
S Ver.

as this liaison sustained and prolonged it; and I was in subjection to a habit that could persist into the realm of matrimony. That wound inflicted upon me by the earlier breakup was not healed. Instead, after the passion and bitter grief of parting it began to fester. More chill and lonely than ever was its anguish.

16. (26) To you be praise, to you be glory, wellspring of mercy! I became more pitiable, and you drew closer still. At that very moment your right hand was poised to snatch me from the mire and rescue me, but I was not aware of it. All that called me back from an even deeper abyss of pleasures of the flesh was my fear of death and your impending judgment, a fear which through all my different phases of belief never left my heart. I used to argue with my friends Alypius and Nebridius about the limits of good and evil. Had I not believed that the soul, and the rewards we have deserved, persist after death, which Epicurus did not, I would have given the victory in my mind to Epicurus. Moreover I used to ask, if we were immortal and lived in perpetual pleasures of the flesh with no fear of being deprived, why were we not happy? And what else were we seeking? I did not know that this very point was the source of my wretched state, because I was so depressed and blind that I could not apprehend the light of truth and of beauty without price which was there to be embraced. For it is not the eye of flesh that sees it, rather it is beheld from within.

In my pitiable state I did not think of the source from which there flowed those conversations I used to enjoy having with friends, albeit on such unsavory subjects. Nor could I be happy without friends, even following the sensual experience that for me consisted then in the maxi-

Ps 40:2

289

carnalium voluptatum. quos utique amicos gratis diligebam vicissimque ab eis me diligi gratis sentiebam. o tor-
tuosas vias! vae animae audaci quae speravit, si a te reces-
sisset, se aliquid melius habituram! versa et reversa in
tergum et in latera et in ventrem, et dura sunt omnia, et
tu solus requies. et ecce ades et liberas a miserabilibus
erroribus et constituis nos in via tua et consolaris et dicis,
"currite, ego feram et ego perducam et ibi ego feram."

mum possible profusion of pleasures of the flesh. Certainly I loved those friends of mine unconditionally, and I knew that they loved me unconditionally in return. What tortuous paths! Alas for that presumptuous soul of mine, which had hoped that, if it withdrew from you, it would find some better place to dwell! Twist, turn, on the back or the side or the stomach: every position is uncomfortable, and you are the only rest. And look! You are at hand, you set me free from my pathetic sins and you set me on your way, and you comfort me and say, "Off you go! I will bring you, and I will guide you to the end, and even there I will bring you!"

Is 3:9^{VL}

cf. 1 Cor 9:24

Is 46:4

LIBER VII

1. (1) Iam mortua erat adulescentia mea mala et nefanda, et ibam in iuventutem, quanto aetate maior, tanto vanitate turpior, qui cogitare aliquid substantiae nisi tale non poteram, quale per hos oculos videri solet. non te cogitabam, deus, in figura corporis humani; ex quo audire aliquid de sapientia coepi, semper hoc fugi et gaudebam me hoc repperisse in fide spiritalis matris nostrae, catholicae tuae, sed quid te aliud cogitarem non occurrebat. et conabar cogitare te, homo et talis homo, summum et solum et verum deum, et te incorruptibilem et inviolabilem et incommutabilem totis medullis credebam, quia nesciens unde et quomodo, plane tamen videbam et certus eram id quod corrumpi potest deterius esse quam id quod non potest, et quod violari non potest incunctanter praeponebam violabili, et quod nullam patitur mutationem melius esse quam id quod mutari potest.

Clamabat violenter cor meum adversus omnia phantasmata mea, et hoc uno ictu conabar abigere circumvolantem turbam immunditiae ab acie mentis meae, et vix

---

¹ This book contains only A.'s thoughts, no biographical narrative.   ² Adolescence ends in the twenties, maturity lasts from then until the forties. Cf. *Conf.* 1.8.13.   ³ Cf. *Conf.* 3.6.10 with n. 23.   ⁴ An echo of Virgil's unclean Harpies (*Aen.* 3.233).

BOOK VII

1. (1)[1] My adolescence, unspeakably wicked as it was, was dead. I was entering into mature adulthood.[2] The more I increased in years, the more disgraceful was my vanity, for I could not imagine anything to be substantial unless it was of such a kind as is usually seen by these eyes of mine. Not that I was imagining you, O God, in the shape of a human body: from the time when I began to listen to philosophical teaching I always avoided this and was delighted that I had found the same principle in the faith of our spiritual mother, your Catholic Church. But I had no idea what other kind of entity you might be. I kept trying to imagine you—though I was a mere mortal, and such a mortal at that!—you who are supreme and sole and true God; and I believed with all my heart that you were imperishable and invulnerable and immutable. I did not know from where or why, yet I saw clearly and was convinced that what can be corrupted is worse than what cannot be; and what cannot be harmed I unhesitatingly preferred to what can be; and what allows of no alteration is better than what can be changed.

My heart was crying out vehemently against all my imaginary delusions[3] and with this one blow I tried to drive away the encircling swarm of immorality[4] from my mind's eye. Yet it was scarcely displaced, for—look!—in

dimota in ictu oculi, ecce conglobata rursus aderat et inruebat in aspectum meum et obnubilabat eum, ut quamvis non forma humani corporis, corporeum tamen aliquid cogitare cogerer per spatia locorum, sive infusum mundo sive etiam extra mundum per infinita diffusum, etiam ipsum incorruptibile et inviolabile et incommutabile quod corruptibili et violabili et commutabili praeponebam, quoniam quidquid privabam spatiis talibus nihil mihi esse videbatur, sed prorsus nihil, ne inane quidem, tamquam si corpus auferatur loco et maneat locus omni corpore vacuatus et terreno et humido et aerio et caelesti, sed tamen sit locus inanis tamquam spatiosum nihil.

(2) Ego itaque incrassatus corde nec mihimet ipsi vel ipse conspicuus, quidquid non per aliquanta spatia tenderetur vel diffunderetur vel conglobaretur vel tumeret vel tale aliquid caperet aut capere posset, nihil prorsus esse arbitrabar. per quales enim formas ire solent oculi mei, per tales imagines ibat cor meum, nec videbam hanc eandem intentionem qua illas ipsas imagines formabam non esse tale aliquid, quae tamen ipsas non formaret nisi esset magnum aliquid. ita etiam te, vita vitae meae, grandem per infinita spatia undique cogitabam penetrare totam mundi molem et extra eam quaquaversum per immensa sine ter-

---

5 An echo of Lucr. (*DRN* 2.154).

6 In Epicurean physics *inane* is the void in which atoms move.

7 Cf. *Conf.* 3.7.12, 5.10.19, 6.3.4–4.5.

8 A. means that the mind with which he formed those thoughts was precisely such a thing as he sought to find existent: i.e., real but not material. Cf. *Trin.* 5 proem. 2, "By what intellect can anyone grasp the concept of God, when that person does not yet grasp their own intellect by which they aim to grasp God?"

the blink of an eye the swarm was back at hand thicker than before, attacking my face and clouding my vision,[5] so that I was still compelled to imagine you, although not in the shape of a human body, as something corporeal existing in space, whether permeating the world or indeed outside the world and diffused through boundless space. Still, you were yourself something imperishable and invulnerable and immutable, which I preferred to what is perishable and vulnerable and mutable, since whatever I deprived of such existence in space seemed to me to be nothing, absolutely nothing, not even void.[6] Just as if a physical object were removed from a place, and the place remained devoid of all objects whether consisting of earth or water or air or heaven, that place would still be a void, a spatial nothing, as it were.[7]

(2) So I was becoming more and more dense in my heart, and I was not even transparent to my own self. Whatever was not extended through some degree of space, or diffused, or amassed, or enlarged, or had some kind of dimension, or was capable of so having—I judged that no such thing could exist. Just as my eyes are accustomed to range over certain physical shapes, so my heart ranged over the corresponding images, and I did not see that this actual mental effort by which I was forming those very images was not something of a physical kind. For it would not form those images unless it was something of real power.[8] So I was imagining even you, Life of my life, as a colossal being extended through infinite space in every direction, penetrating every part of the world's structure and beyond it in every direction through the bound-

Mt 13:15;
Acts 28:27

295

mine, ut haberet te terra, haberet caelum, haberent omnia et illa finirentur in te, tu autem nusquam.

Sicut autem luci solis non obsisteret aeris corpus, aeris huius qui supra terram est, quominus per eum traiceretur penetrans eum, non dirrumpendo aut concidendo sed implendo eum totum, sic tibi putabam non solum caeli et aeris et maris sed etiam terrae corpus pervium et ex omnibus maximis minimisque partibus penetrabile ad capiendam praesentiam tuam, occulta inspiratione intrinsecus et extrinsecus administrantem omnia quae creasti. ita suspicabar, quia cogitare aliud non poteram; nam falsum erat. illo enim modo maior pars terrae maiorem tui partem haberet et minorem minor, atque ita te plena essent omnia ut amplius tui caperet elephanti corpus quam passeris, quo esset isto grandius grandioremque occuparet locum, atque ita frustatim partibus mundi magnis magnas, brevibus breves partes tuas prasesentes faceres. non est autem ita, sed nondum inluminaveras tenebras meas.

2. (3) Sat erat mihi, domine, adversus illos deceptos deceptores et loquaces mutos, quoniam non ex eis sonabat verbum tuum—sat erat ergo illud quod iam diu ab usque Carthagine a Nebridio proponi solebat et omnes qui au-

---

9 Cicero's influence is detectable: *Nat. D.* 2.7.19, "These things certainly could not be so, with all the parts of the world in harmony with one another, unless a single divine and undivided spirit held them together in harmony."

10 A point paralleled in later eucharistic theology: "They receive Christ the Lord, and in each portion [of the host] he is completely present, but he is not diminished by being divided, instead offering himself whole to each person": cf. Gratian, *Decretum* 3, 2.77.

less universe. Thus the earth would contain you, and the sky would contain you, and everything would contain you: and those things would reach their limits in you—but you would have no limit.

Just as the mass of air (the air that exists above the earth) would not obstruct the light of the sun from penetrating and perforating it, not by tearing it apart or destroying it but by filling it completely, so I thought that you were able to pervade not only the physical mass of sky and air and sea, but even the physical mass of the earth as well. In all its parts, both the greatest and the least, it was accessible in such a way as to admit of your presence, by the hidden inspiration[9] which internally and externally governs everything that you have created. That was what I suspected, because I had no capacity to imagine anything else; but it was false. On that model, indeed, the greater part of the earth would contain the greater part of you; and the lesser part a lesser, and so everything would be filled with you but in such a way that the body of an elephant would hold more of you than the body of a sparrow, according to how much larger it would be than the sparrow, and how much larger a space it would occupy. So you would make parts of yourself present to the parts of the world: large parts of you to the large parts of the world, and limited elements to limited elements of the world, in a piecemeal fashion.[10] Of course this is not really how it is, but you had not yet lightened my darkness.   Ps 18:28

2. (3) It was enough for me, Lord, against those cheated cheats and speechless speakers (for the sound issuing from them was not your word), it was enough what long ago, way back in our Carthage days, Nebridius used to argue, and it struck all of us who heard it: That dubious realm of

dieramus concussi sumus: quid erat tibi factura nescio qua
gens tenebrarum, quam ex adversa mole solent opponere,
si tu cum ea pugnare noluisses? si enim responderetur
aliquid fuisse nocituram, violabilis tu et corruptibilis fores.
si autem nihil ea nocere potuisse diceretur, nulla afferre-
tur causa pugnandi, et ita pugnandi ut quaedam portio tua
et membrum tuum vel proles de ipsa substantia tua mis-
ceretur adversis potestatibus et non a te creatis naturis,
atque in tantum ab eis corrumperetur et commutaretur in
deterius ut a beatitudine in miseriam verteretur et indige-
ret auxilio quo erui purgarique posset, et hanc esse animam cui tuus sermo servienti liber et contaminatae purus
et corruptae integer subveniret, sed et ipse corruptibilis,
quia ex una eademque substantia.

Itaque si te, quidquid es, id est substantiam tuam qua
es, incorruptibilem dicerent, falsa esse illa omnia et ex-
secrabilia; si autem corruptibilem, idipsum iam falsum et
prima voce abominandum. sat erat ergo istuc adversus eos
omni modo evomendos a pressura pectoris, quia non
habebant qua exirent sine horribili sacrilegio cordis et linguae sentiendo de te ista et loquendo.

3. (4) Sed et ego adhuc, quamvis incontaminabilem et
inconvertibilem et nulla ex parte mutabilem dicerem fir-
meque sentirem deum nostrum, deum verum, qui fecisti

---

11 Manichaeism is centered on a battle between light and
darkness; particles of the light-force are trapped in all parts of the
physical world but most densely in the human soul.

12 The Manichaeans adopted the Christian schema of salvation through the Word, but without attributing to that Word all
the characteristics of true divinity which orthodox Christians did
assert, such as imperishability.

darkness, which the Manichaeans generally set up as an opposing force, what could it do to you if you were unwilling to contend against it? For if the response was, "That realm would have done you some harm," you would be vulnerable and perishable. But if it was admitted that it could not have inflicted any harm, there was no justification to be offered for clashing with it, and clashing in such a way that one part of you[11] and one limb, or offshoot from your own substance, would be mingled with enemy powers and natures not created by you; and in the end that part of you would be corrupted and mutated into something worse, and in such a way as to be transformed from felicity to wretchedness, while lacking any means of help by which it could be plucked out and purified. This was the soul that your Word[12] came to help: the free helping the enslaved, the pure helping the polluted, the whole helping the damaged; but apparently the Word was itself corruptible, because it was of one and the same substance.

And so if they said that you, whatever you are (which is to say that substance in which you consist), are imperishable, then all those assertions are abominable falsehoods; but if they said you were perishable, the argument itself would be false from the start, and no sooner spoken than unspeakable. On that subject, then, this was sufficient to counter those men whom I should have vomited out of my overburdened stomach by any possible means: for they had no way of escaping without committing dreadful sacrilege of thought and speech and mouth because of what they believed and argued about you.

3. (4) Although I said and strongly believed that our God, the true God—you who made not only our souls but also our bodies, and not only our souls and bodies but ev-

299

non solum animas nostras sed etiam corpora, nec tantum
nostras animas et corpora sed omnes et omnia, non tenebam explicatam et enodatam causam mali. quaecumque
tamen esset, sic eam quaerendam videbam, ut non per
illam constringerer deum incommutabilem mutabilem
credere, ne ipse fierem quod quaerebam. itaque securus
eam quaerebam, et certus non esse verum quod illi dicerent quos toto animo fugiebam, quia videbam quaerendo unde malum repletos malitia, qua opinarentur tuam
potius substantiam male pati quam suam male facere.

(5) Et intendebam ut cernerem quod audiebam, liberum voluntatis arbitrium causam esse ut male faceremus
et rectum iudicium tuum ut pateremur, et eam liquidam
cernere non valebam. itaque aciem mentis de profundo
educere conatus mergebar iterum, et saepe conatus mergebar iterum atque iterum. sublevabat enim me in lucem
tuam quod tam sciebam me habere voluntatem quam me
vivere. itaque cum aliquid vellem aut nollem, non alium
quam me velle ac nolle certissimus eram, et ibi esse causam peccati mei iam iamque animadvertebam.[1] quod autem invitus facerem, pati me potius quam facere videbam,
et id non culpam sed poenam esse iudicabam, qua me non
iniuste plecti te iustum cogitans cito fatebar.

---

[1] animadvertebam *codd.*: advertebam *S Knöll Skut.*

---

[13] I.e., a source of evil.
[14] Paronomasia—"evil" is *malum*, "sin" is *malitia*.
[15] In *Lib. Arb.* 3.17.14, A. asks, "What can exist before will, to
be the cause of will?" (*quae . . . esse poterit ante voluntatem causa
voluntatis*). Cf. Rist, "Augustine on Free Will and Predestination," 420–47.

eryone and everything—was imperishable and unvarying and completely immutable, I still did not consider that the cause of evil has been explained and untangled. Whatever kind of thing it was, I saw that it required investigation if I was not to be constrained to believe that the immutable God is mutable, and so become myself the very thing I was looking for.[13] So I began my search, at first without anxiety. I was sure that it was not true, what those men used to say, the ones I had begun to flee with all my heart, because I saw that by seeking where evil comes from, they came to be filled with sin,[14] in that they preferred to believe that your very being could admit of evil rather than that their own could commit it.

Rom 1:29

(5) I concentrated on evaluating what I was hearing: that the free judgment of the will was the cause of our doing evil; and that your righteous judgment was the cause of our suffering. But I had not the strength to evaluate the matter clearly. So even as I tried to draw my mind's eye up from the deep I started to sink down again. Over and over I tried, but again and again I sank. What raised me into your light was the fact that I was as convinced that I had a will[15] as I was of being alive. So when I did or did not want something, I was absolutely convinced that it was no one but myself doing the wanting or not wanting. I was on the brink of perceiving that there, in my will, was the reason for my sin. I began to realize that I was enduring rather than committing the acts which I did against my will, and I judged that this was not so much my fault as my punishment. I quickly had to admit that my punishment was not undeserved, for I considered you to be righteous.

Sed rursus dicebam, "quis fecit me? nonne deus meus, non tantum bonus sed ipsum bonum? unde igitur mihi male velle et bene nolle? ut esset cur iuste poenas luerem? quis in me hoc posuit et insevit[2] mihi plantarium amaritudinis, cum totus fierem a dulcissimo deo meo? si diabolus auctor, unde ipse diabolus? quod si et ipse perversa voluntate ex bono angelo diabolus factus est, unde et in ipso voluntas mala qua diabolus fieret, quando totus angelus a conditore optimo factus esset?" his cogitationibus deprimebar iterum et suffocabar, sed non usque ad illum infernum subducebar erroris ubi nemo tibi confitetur, dum tu potius mala pati quam homo facere putatur.

4. (6) Sic enim nitebar invenire cetera, ut iam inveneram melius esse incorruptibile quam corruptibile, et ideo te, quidquid esses, esse incorruptibilem confitebar. neque enim ulla anima umquam potuit poteritve cogitare aliquid quod sit te melius, qui summum et optimum bonum es. cum autem verissime atque certissime incorruptibile corruptibili praeponatur, sicut iam ego praeponebam, poteram iam cogitatione aliquid attingere quod esset melius deo meo, nisi tu esses incorruptibilis.

Ubi igitur videbam incorruptibile corruptibili esse praeferendum, ibi te quaerere debebam atque inde advertere ubi sit malum, id est unde sit ipsa corruptio, qua

---

[2] insevit *S. edd.*: inseruit *codd.*

---

[16] An elegant paradox with assonance requires the adverbs (*male, bene*) instead of abstract nouns.

[17] A named "character" in Scripture (cf. Satan: Jb 1–2; Mt 4:1ff.).   [18] In biographical (rather than narrative) sequence, this is A.'s first "confession."

So once more I started asking, "Who made me? Surely it was my God, who is not only good, but is Goodness itself? So how come I am capable of wanting evil and rejecting good?[16] Is it to create a reason why I deserve my punishment? Who put this into me and sowed a garden of bitterness in me, seeing that I am wholly created by my most dear God? If the Devil[17] were the instigator, where then did the Devil come from? But if he himself became a devil instead of a good angel because of his evil will, what was the origin of that malign will that made him into a devil, since he had been created as entirely an angel by the supremely good Creator?" I felt depressed and stifled by my reflections, but at least I was not completely dragged down to that hell of transgression where no one makes confession to you because they would rather believe that you endure evil than that human beings commit it.

cf. Rom 7:15

Mt 13:25;
Heb 12:15

Lk 4:2

4. (6) Now that I had verified that the imperishable is better than what is perishable, and therefore began to confess[18] that you, whatever you were, must be imperishable, I then made an effort to verify other things as well. For no soul ever has been able, or will be able, to imagine something better than you, who are the highest and greatest Good. Since the imperishable is certainly, definitely, preferable to the perishable (as indeed I did now prefer it), I now had the capacity to form a conception in my imagination which, unless you were imperishable, was more good than my God.

So where I saw that the imperishable was preferable to the perishable, it was here I had to seek you, and from there I had to consider where evil may be: which is to say, what is the origin of that quality of perishability that is

303

violari substantia tua nullo modo potest. nullo enim prorsus modo violat corruptio deum nostrum, nulla voluntate, nulla necessitate, nullo improviso casu, quoniam ipse est deus, et quod sibi vult bonum est, et ipse est idem bonum; corrumpi autem non est bonum. nec cogeris invitus ad aliquid, quia voluntas tua non est maior quam potentia tua. esset autem maior, si te ipso tu ipse maior esses: voluntas enim et potentia dei deus ipse est. et quid improvisum tibi, qui nosti omnia? et nulla natura est nisi quia nosti eam. et ut quid multa dicimus cur non sit corruptibilis substantia quae deus est, quando, si hoc esset, non esset deus?

5. (7) Et quaerebam unde malum, et male quaerebam, et in ipsa inquisitione mea non videbam malum. et constituebam in conspectu spiritus mei universam creaturam, quidquid in ea cernere possumus, sicuti est terra et mare et aer et sidera et arbores et animalia mortalia, et quidquid in ea non videmus, sicut firmamentum caeli insuper et omnes angelos et cuncta spiritalia eius, sed etiam ipsa, quasi corpora essent, locis et locis ordinavit[3] imaginatio mea. et feci unam massam grandem distinctam generibus corporum, creaturam tuam, sive re vera quae corpora erant, sive quae ipse pro spiritibus finxeram, et eam feci grandem, non quantum erat, quod scire non poteram, sed quantum libuit, undiqueversum sane finitam, te autem, domine, ex omni parte ambientem et penetrantem eam,

---

[3] ordinavit *codd.*: ordinata, ut S *edd.*

by no means able to violate your substance. For perishability is totally incapable of violating our God, neither by means of will, nor by means of necessity, nor by unforeseen chance: because he himself is God and what he wills for himself is good, and he himself is that same Good, whereas it is not good to be perishable. You are not to be constrained to act against your will, because your will is not greater than your power. It would only be greater if you yourself were greater than yourself: for God himself is synonymous with the will and power of God. And what is there which you have not foreseen, since you know everything? And no nature exists except because you know it. So why do we give many reasons why that substance which is God should not be perishable, since if it were so, it would not be God?

5. (7) So I was searching for the origin of evil, but searching in an evil way, and I did not perceive that there was evil in my very inquiry. I set out the whole of creation for my spirit to look upon: whatever we can discern in it, for example earth and sea and air and stars and trees and all living creatures, and whatever we cannot actually see in it, for example the firmament of heaven above and all the angels and all its spiritual beings. But my imagination set even these in order here and there as if they were physical bodies. I made of your creation one enormous mass, categorized according to their different types of bodies: whether they really were physical bodies or bodies that I myself had imagined for spiritual entities. Then I made that mass enormous, not its true size, which I was incapable of knowing, but a size to my liking. The mass was certainly finite in every direction, but I imagined you, Lord, as utterly without boundaries, encompassing

sed usquequaque infinitum, tamquam si mare esset
ubique et undique per immensa infinitum solum mare et
haberet intra se spongiam quamlibet magnam, sed finitam
tamen, plena esset utique spongia illa ex omni sua parte
ex immenso mari.

Sic creaturam tuam finitam te infinito plenam putabam
et dicebam, "ecce deus et ecce quae creavit deus, et bonus
deus atque his validissime longissimeque praestantior; sed
tamen bonus bona creavit, et ecce quomodo ambit atque
implet ea. ubi ergo malum et unde et qua huc inrepsit?
quae radix eius et quod semen eius? an omnino non est?
cur ergo timemus et cavemus quod non est? aut si inaniter
timemus, certe vel timor ipse malum est, quo incassum
stimulatur et excruciatur cor, et tanto gravius malum,
quanto non est, quod timeamus, et timemus. idcirco aut
est malum quod timemus, aut hoc malum est quia timemus. unde est igitur, quoniam deus fecit haec omnia bonus
bona? maius quidem et summum bonum minora fecit
bona, sed tamen et creans et creata bona sunt omnia. unde
est malum? an unde fecit ea, materies aliqua mala erat et
formavit atque ordinavit eam, sed reliquit aliquid in illa
quod in bonum non converteret? cur et hoc? an impotens
erat totam vertere et commutare, ut nihil mali remaneret,
cum sit omnipotens? postremo cur inde aliquid facere
voluit ac non potius eadem omnipotentia fecit, ut nulla

---

19 This grand metaphor echoes Plotinus, *Enn.* 4.3.9 (how
"soul" pervades the cosmos).

its every part and permeating it: as if the sea were everywhere, and everywhere through immeasurable infin-
ity sea was all there was, and that sea had within itself a
sponge, as big as you like, but still finite; that sponge would
be completely filled in all its parts from that immeasurable sea.[19]

Thus I started to think that your creation was finite and
filled with you, who are infinite; and I said, "Look, this is
God; and look, this is what God has created. God is good
and by far more excellent than these things in every way.
But even so, he who is good made things to be good; and
look how he encompasses and fills them. So where is evil?
And where is it from? And how does it worm its way in
here? What is its root and what is its seed? Or is it completely nonexistent? Why then do we fear and avoid what
is nonexistent? Or if our fears are groundless, it is at least
certain that the actual fear is an evil, because it goads and
torments the heart pointlessly. This evil that we fear, and
that does not exist, is all the more troublesome because
it is non—existent, and we certainly do fear it. For that
reason there is evil and so we are afraid of it, or it is our
fearing it which makes it evil. So where does it originate,
since God, who is good, made all these things good? The
greater and highest Good made lesser things good, but
nonetheless Creator and created things alike are all good.
So where does evil originate? Or what did he make these
things from? Was some of the material evil, but he shaped
and arranged it yet left a part of it which he did not turn
into good? If so, why? Had he no power to change or re-
place it completely so that no particle of evil remained,
given that he is omnipotent? Finally why then did he
choose to make something and did not instead use that

Gn 1:31

307

esset omnino? aut vero exsistere poterat contra eius voluntatem? aut si aeterna erat, cur tam diu per infinita retro
spatia temporum sic eam sivit esse ac tanto post placuit
aliquid ex ea facere? aut iam, si aliquid subito voluit agere,
hoc potius ageret omnipotens, ut illa non esset atque ipse
solus esset totum verum et summum et infinitum bonum?
aut si non erat bene, ut non aliquid boni etiam fabricaretur
et conderet qui bonus erat, illa sublata et ad nihilum re-
dacta materie quae mala erat, bonam ipse institueret unde
omnia crearet? non enim esset omnipotens si condere non
posset aliquid boni nisi ea quam non ipse condiderat adiu-
varetur materia."

Talia volvebam pectore misero, ingravidato curis mor-
dacissimis de timore mortis et non inventa veritate; stabi-
liter tamen haerebat in corde meo in catholica ecclesia
fides Christi tui, domini et salvatoris nostri, in multis quidem adhuc informis et praeter doctrinae normam fluitans,
sed tamen non eam relinquebat animus, immo in dies
magis magisque inbibebat.

6. (8) Iam etiam mathematicorum fallaces divinationes
et impia deliramenta reieceram. confiteantur etiam hinc
tibi de intimis visceribus animae meae miserationes tuae,
deus meus! tu enim, tu omnino (nam quis alius a morte
omnis erroris revocat nos nisi vita quae mori nescit, et
sapientia mentes indigentes inluminans, nullo indigens
lumine, qua mundus administratur usque ad arborum

very omnipotence to make it so that the evil matter would not exist at all? Or could it emerge against his will? Or if it was eternal, why did he allow it to exist for countless ages of time past, and then, so much later on, decide to make something from it? Or now, if he suddenly wanted to make something, would he rather, as the Almighty, bring it about that such matter would cease to exist, and he himself alone would be entirely the true and highest and unbounded Good? Or if it were improper that he who was good should not construct and create what is good, then, if that evil matter were removed and consigned to oblivion, might he himself provide good matter from which he could create everything? For he would not be omnipotent if he could not create something good unless with the help of some matter which he himself had not created."

I was pondering such considerations in my mind, which was afflicted and weighed down with gnawing anxieties about the fear of death and the truth I had not discovered. What remained steadfast in my heart was the faith of your Christ, our Lord and Savior, in the Catholic Church. True, on many points it was still misdirected and wavering outside the proper bounds of doctrine. But still my mind was not letting go of it, and in fact day by day it was drinking it in more and more. 2 Pt 2:20

6. (8) By now I had already rejected the false divinations and blasphemous nonsense of astrologers. O my God, let your mercies also confess that to you from the innermost depths of my soul! For it was you, only you—for who else calls us back from all our deadly error except the Life itself that does not know how to die, and the Wisdom that enlightens our needy minds while needing no light itself, and which arranges the affairs of the world Ps 107:8

volatica folia?), tu procurasti pervicaciae meae, qua obluc-
tatus sum Vindiciano acuto seni et Nebridio adulescenti
mirabilis animae, illi vehementer adfirmanti, huic cum
dubitatione quidem aliqua sed tamen crebro dicenti non
esse illam artem futura praevidendi, coniecturas autem
hominum habere saepe vim sortis et multa dicendo dici
pleraque ventura, nescientibus eis qui dicerent sed in ea
non tacendo incurrentibus—procurasti ergo tu hominem
amicum, non quidem segnem consultorem mathematicorum nec eas litteras bene callentem sed, ut dixi, consultorem curiosum et tamen scientem aliquid quod a patre
suo se audisse dicebat: quod quantum valeret ad illius
artis opinionem evertendam ignorabat.

Is ergo vir nomine Firminus, liberaliter institutus et
excultus eloquio, cum me tamquam carissimum de quibusdam suis rebus, in quas saecularis spes eius intumue-
rat, consuleret, quid mihi secundum suas quas constellationes appellant videretur, ego autem, qui iam de hac re
in Nebridii sententiam flecti coeperam, non quidem ab-
nuerem conicere ac dicere quod nutanti occurrebat, sed
tamen subicerem prope iam esse mihi persuasum ridicula
illa esse et inania, tum ille mihi narravit patrem suum
fuisse librorum talium curiosissimum et habuisse amicum
aeque illa simulque sectantem. qui pari studio et conla-
tione flatabant[4] in eas nugas ignem cordis sui, ita ut muto-

---

[4] flatabant *O edd*: flabant *G*: flagitabant *C D*: flagrabant *S*

---

[20] Not mentioned elsewhere.

even down to the changing of leaves on the trees—you who dealt with my stubbornness, with which I contended against that clever old man Vindicianus and the young Nebridius with his remarkable understanding. The former was insisting forcefully, the latter was more hesitant to be sure, but repeatedly affirmed that there was no such thing as the art of foreseeing the future and that human guess-work often had the power of luck: so because they made so many predictions some did come to pass, but those who made the predictions had no understanding, they merely stumbled upon facts because they never fell silent. So then you provided me with someone to be my friend, not some dimwitted consulter of astrologers or someone well-versed in those studies, but as I said, a curious ques-tioner with some knowledge that he said he had heard from his father, though he did not know how much influ-ence it had for overturning his opinion of that subject.

This man was called Firminus.[20] He had had a liberal education and was accomplished in rhetoric. He consulted me as one of his closest friends on the subject of certain business affairs of which he had high hopes in worldly terms, and asked what was my impression of what he called his personal horoscope. But I had already begun to incline to Nebridius' judgment on this topic. I did not ac-tually refuse to give an opinion and say what came to mind while I was undecided, but I did venture the opinion that I was now almost certain that these were ludicrous and worthless. He then told me that his father had been ex-tremely interested in books on astrology and at that time had a friend who was as keen as himself. With a like en-thusiasm and pooling of ideas they were both blowing the flames of their personal passion toward that trivia, so

rum quoque animalium, si quae domi parerent, obser-
varent momenta nascentium atque ad ea caeli positionem
notarent, unde illius quasi artis experimenta conligerent.

Itaque dicebat audisse se a patre quod, cum eundem
Firminum praegnans mater esset, etiam illius paterni
amici famula quaedam pariter utero grandescebat, quod
latere non potuit dominum, qui etiam canum suarum par-
tus examinatissima diligentia nosse curabat; atque ita factum esse, ut cum iste coniugis, ille autem ancillae dies et
horas minutioresque horarum articulos cautissima observatione numerarent, enixae essent ambae simul, ita ut
easdem constellationes usque ad easdem minutias utrique
nascenti facere cogerentur, iste filio, ille servulo. nam cum
mulieres parturire coepissent, indicaverunt sibi ambo
quid sua cuiusque domo ageretur, et paraverunt quos ad
se invicem mitterent, simul ut natum quod parturiebatur
esset cuique nuntiatum: quod tamen ut continuo nuntia-
retur, tamquam in regno suo facile effecerant.

Atque ita qui ab alterutro missi sunt tam ex paribus
domorum intervallis sibi obviam factos esse dicebat, ut
aliam positionem siderum aliasque particulas momento-
rum neuter eorum notare sineretur. et tamen Firminus
amplo apud suos loco natus dealbatiores vias saeculi cur-

much so that even if some dumb animals were giving birth in their household they used to observe the moment of the births and make a note of the disposition of the heaven at that moment, so that they could gather together the results of their so-called art.

So he used to tell how he had heard from his father that when his mother was pregnant with him, Firminus, a certain female slave belonging to his father's friend was at the same stage of pregnancy. Of course this could not escape the notice of a master who was scrupulously careful to ensure he was informed even when his own dogs were producing litters. So it transpired that when the two men calculated the days, the hours and the smallest fractions of time with most particular care, Firminus' father for his wife, and the friend for his slave, the two women went into labor at the same time, so that they were obliged to make the same horoscope for both babies, right down to the slightest space of time, the one man for his son, and the other for his new little slave. For as soon as the women went into labor the two men both sent word to each other of what was happening in their two houses. And they both had messengers ready to send to each other giving news of the birth immediately after it took place. As each man was in his own domain they had easily arranged for this, so as to ensure that the news came at once.

As it happened, he said, the messengers, who were sent from each place at precisely the same moment, met up exactly halfway between their homes. This meant that neither of them could record a different arrangement of stars or a different fraction of a moment. Yet Firminus was born to a high rank in his parents' house and trod the brighter paths of the world, comparatively speaking; his

sitabat, augebatur divitiis, sublimabatur honoribus, servus
autem ille conditionis iugo nullatenus relaxato dominis
serviebat, ipso indicante qui noverat eum.

(9) His itaque auditis et creditis (talis quippe narraverat) omnis illa reluctatio mea resoluta concidit, et primo
Firminum ipsum conatus sum ab illa curiositate revocare,
cum dicerem, constellationibus eius inspectis ut vera pro-
nuntiarem, debuisse me utique videre ibi parentes inter
suos esse primarios, nobilem familiam propriae civitatis,
natales ingenuos, honestam educationem liberalesque
doctrinas; at si me ille servus ex eisdem constellationibus
(quia et illius ipsae essent) consuluisset, ut eidem quoque
vera proferrem, debuisse me rursus ibi videre abiectissi-
mam familiam, conditionem servilem et cetera longe a
prioribus aliena longeque distantia. unde autem fieret ut
eadem inspiciens diversa dicerem, si vera dicerem, si autem eadem dicerem, falsa dicerem, inde certissime conlegi
ea quae vera consideratis constellationibus dicerentur non
arte dici sed sorte, quae autem falsa, non artis imperitia
sed sortis mendacio.

(10) Hinc autem accepto aditu, ipse mecum talia rumi-
nando, ne quis eorundem delirorum qui talem quaestum
sequerentur, quos iam iamque invadere atque inrisos refellere cupiebam, mihi ita resisteret, quasi aut Firminus
mihi aut illi pater falsa narraverit, intendi considerationem
in eos qui gemini nascuntur, quorum plerique ita post

wealth grew and his prestige increased. The slave, on the other hand, went on serving his masters with no loosening of that yoke of his servile status. Firminus himself confirmed this, for he knew the slave concerned.

(9) When I heard all this and believed it, given the reliability of the narrator, all my resistance gave way and collapsed. I first tried to draw Firminus back from his curiosity on that subject by saying that if I scrutinized his horoscope in order to give a true report, I must certainly have seen there parents of high rank among their own social group, a family of distinction in its own city, free-born status, an honorable upbringing and a liberal education; but if that slave asked my opinion of the same horoscope, for these were his stars too, and if I told the truth to him as well, I should have seen there the humblest of homes, the status of a slave, and everything else completely different and utterly removed from that of Firminus. Thus it was that while I investigated this same matter, if I spoke the truth I would say they were different, whereas if I said they were the same I would be telling a lie. From this I established conclusively that what was predicted accurately based on horoscopes was a matter of chance, not skill. Whereas whatever was incorrectly predicted was the result of luck letting us down, not some lack of technical expertise.

(10) Approaching the subject from this angle, I kept mulling over the subject to myself, to prevent any of the fools intent on that pursuit from putting up any defense against me, for I was already eager to attack, ridicule and refute them. For example, had Firminus or his father been telling me lies? I focused my reflection on those who are born twins, for they are mostly expelled from the womb

invicem funduntur ex utero ut parvum ipsum temporis intervallum, quantamlibet vim in rerum natura habere contendant, conligi tamen humana observatione non possit litterisque signari omnino non valeat quas mathematicus inspecturus est ut vera pronuntiet. et non erunt vera, quia easdem litteras inspiciens eadem debuit dicere de Esau et de Iacob, sed non eadem utrique acciderunt. falsa ergo diceret aut, si vera diceret, non eadem diceret: at eadem inspiceret. non ergo arte sed sorte vera diceret.

Tu enim, domine, iustissime moderator universitatis, consulentibus consultisque nescientibus occulto instinctu agis ut, dum quisque consulit, hoc audiat quod eum oportet audire occultis meritis animarum ex abysso iusti iudicii tui. cui non dicat homo, "quid est hoc?" "ut quid hoc?" non dicat, non dicat; homo est enim.

7. (11) Iam itaque me, adiutor meus, illis vinculis solveras, et quaerebam unde malum, et non erat exitus. sed me non sinebas ullis fluctibus cogitationis auferri ab ea fide qua credebam et esse te et esse incommutabilem substantiam tuam et esse de hominibus curam et iudicium tuum et in Christo, filio tuo, domino nostro, atque scripturis sanctis quas ecclesiae tuae catholicae commendaret auctoritas, viam te posuisse salutis humanae ad eam vitam quae post hanc mortem futura est.

---

21 I.e., celestial phenomena.

22 Cf. *Conf.* 4.3.5.

23 See A. *De civ. D.* 5.2; Hegedus, *Early Christianity*, 43–61. The anaphora is unusual and marks heightened emotion.

in such quick succession that the space of time between, however much impact people may insist that this has in the nature of things, is too small to be reckoned by human observation. It certainly cannot be set out in formulae with the precision that the astrologer looks for in order to make accurate predictions. In any case they will not be true, because an inspection of the same formulae should have led to the same predictions about Esau and Jacob, Gn 25–36 but what befell them was not the same. So the astrologer would predict what did not happen, or if he predicted what did, he would not predict the same for both: and yet what he observed[21] would be the same. So his predictions would prove accurate not by skill but by chance.

Lord, you are the most righteous Ruler of the universe. Although they do not realize it, you act by a hidden inspiration upon those who consult about astrology and those who are consulted,[22] so when someone does go for a consultation, that person hears what it is right for them to hear according to each soul's secret deserving out of the bottomless depths of your righteous judgment. Let no one say Ps 36:6 to you, "What is this?" or "why is this?"; let no one say this, Sir 39:21 let no one say that, for all are mere mortals.[23]

7. (11) So, my Helper, you had already freed me from Ps 18:2 those chains and I was now searching for the origin of evil, but there was no way through. But you did not allow any fluctuations of thought to carry me away from that faith I believed: that you exist, that your substance is unchanging, that your care for humanity is real and your judgment, and that you have established a way for humanity to be saved into the life that is to be after this death, in Christ your Son, our Lord, and in the holy Scriptures that the authority of your Catholic Church enjoins.

His itaque salvis atque inconcusse roboratis in animo meo, quaerebam aestuans unde sit malum. quae illa tormenta parturientis cordis mei, qui gemitus, deus meus! et ibi erant aures tuae nesciente me. et cum in silentio fortiter quaererem, magnae voces erant ad misericordiam tuam tacitae contritiones animi mei. tu sciebas quid patiebar, et nullus hominum. quantum enim erat quod inde digerebatur per linguam meam in aures familiarissimorum meorum! numquid totus tumultus animae meae, cui nec tempora nec os meum sufficiebat, sonabat eis? totum tamen ibat in auditum tuum quod rugiebam a gemitu cordis mei, et ante te erat desiderium meum, et lumen oculorum meorum non erat mecum. intus enim erat, ego autem foris, nec in loco illud.

At ego intendebam in ea quae locis continentur, et non ibi inveniebam locum ad requiescendum, nec recipiebant me ista ut dicerem, "sat est et bene est," nec dimittebant redire ubi mihi satis esset bene. superior enim eram istis, te vero inferior, et tu gaudium verum mihi subdito tibi et tu mihi subieceras quae infra me creasti. et hoc erat rectum temperamentum et media regio salutis meae, ut manerem ad imaginem tuam et tibi serviens dominarer corpori.

Sed cum superbe contra te surgerem et currerem adversus dominum in cervice crassa scuti mei, etiam ista infima supra me facta sunt et premebant, et nusquam erat laxamentum et respiramentum. ipsa occurrebant undique

---

24 Cf. *Conf.* 10.27.38.

25 I.e., in the middle, between God and the rest of creation.

26 A. refers to a pre-Vg Latin version of Jb 15:26: at *Adn. Iob* 15.25 he interprets this as an assumption of not being vulnerable.

Once all these matters were safe and confirmed unshakeably in my mind, I began to seek feverishly for the origin of evil. How great were the torments of my heart as it went into labor, O my God, and the cries of pain! And your ears were there to hear, though I did not know it. Though I searched valiantly in silence, the silent sufferings of my soul were loud cries for your mercy. You knew what I suffered, though no mortal did. How little of it did my tongue impart to the ears of my dearest friends! Certainly it was not the whole tumult of my soul that sounded for them: there was neither time nor words enough for that! Yet what I roared from the disquietude of my heart entered into your hearing, and my desire was before you, and the light of my eyes was not at hand: instead it was within me, and I was outside myself,[24] and it was not located in space.

cf. Jer 48:41, 49:22

Ps 38:8–10

Meanwhile I was scrutinizing those things that are contained in space, and there I found no place to rest, and those things did not welcome me in such a way that I could say, "This is enough, this is good"; nor did they release me to return to what I would find good enough. I was a higher creature than those things were, but certainly inferior to you: you are true joy to me when I am in subjection under you, and you had placed in subjection under me those things that you created as inferior to me. This was the proper median and central zone of my salvation,[25] to remain in your image and serve you by governing my body.

But when I rose up in pride against you and ran headlong against the Lord with the thick boss of my shield,[26] even those lower things were placed above me and pressed upon me, and there was no respite or breathing space. These things stood in my way on every side in heaps and

Jb 15:26^VL

319

acervatim et conglobatim cernenti, cogitanti autem imagines corporum ipsae opponebantur redeunti, quasi diceretur, "quo is, indigne et sordide?" et haec de vulnere meo
creverant, quia humilasti tamquam vulneratum super-
bum, et tumore meo separabar abs te et nimis inflata facies
claudebat oculos meos.

8. (12) Tu vero, domine, in aeternum manes et non in
aeternum irasceris nobis, quoniam miseratus es terram et
cinerem. et placuit in conspectuo tuo reformare deformia
mea, et stimulis internis agitabas me ut impatiens essem
donec mihi per interiorem aspectum certus esses. et resi-
debat tumor meus ex occulta manu medicinae tuae
aciesque conturbata et contenebrata mentis meae acri
collyrio salubrium dolorum de die in diem sanabatur.

9. (13) Et primo volens ostendere mihi quam resistas
superbis, humilibus autem des gratiam, et quanta misericordia tua demonstrata sit hominibus via humilitatis, quod
verbum tuum caro factum est et habitavit inter homines,
procurasti mihi per quendam hominem immanissimo typho turgidum quosdam platonicorum libros ex graeca lingua in latinam versos, et ibi legi, non quidem his verbis
sed hoc idem omnino multis et multiplicibus suaderi rationibus, quod in principio erat verbum et verbum erat apud
deum et deus erat verbum. hoc erat in principio apud
deum. omnia per ipsum facta sunt, et sine ipso factum est
nihil. quod factum est in eo vita est, et vita erat lux homi-

27 A vivid turn of phrase: perhaps A. had once observed an
allergic reaction causing swelling.
28 Cf. A.'s self-descriptions at *Conf.* 3.3.6, 3.5.9.

piles when I looked; while when I reflected, the visual impressions of these physical objects stood before me as I went to turn back, as if to say, "Where are you going, worthless and defiled as you are?" These things had burgeoned from my wound because you have brought down the proud like one who is wounded; and because of my pride I was separated from you, and my face was so puffed-up that it forced my eyes shut.[27] Ps 89:10

8. (12) O Lord, you endure forever but not forever are you angry with us; you take pity on earth and ash. It was pleasing in your sight to reform my deformities. You began to vex me with inner torments that made me impatient until you became clear to me in terms of my inner vision. Thanks to the unseen touch of your hand doing its healing work, my swelling began to go down, while my mental perception, formerly agitated and obscured, was getting better day by day thanks to the effective ointment of wholesome afflictions. Ps 102:12
Ps 85:5
Jb 42:6; Sir 17:31

Rv 3:18

9. (13) At first you wanted to show me how you resist the proud but give grace to the humble, and how by your immense mercy the way of humility was made apparent to mortals, because your Word was made flesh and dwelt among mortals. So by means of a certain person who was puffed up with monumental conceit[28] you acquired for me some books of the Neoplatonists translated from Greek into Latin. There I read the very same idea, with many and varied arguments to persuade me, albeit not in precisely the same words, that in the beginning was the Word and the Word was with God and the Word was God. He was in the beginning with God. All things were made by him and without him nothing was made. What was made in him is life, and the life was the light of humanity, and the Prv 3:34;
James 4:6;
1 Pt 5:5

321

num; et lux in tenebris lucet, et tenebrae eam non comprehenderunt. et quia hominis anima, quamvis testimonium perhibeat de lumine, non est tamen ipsa lumen, sed verbum deus est[5] lumen verum, quod inluminat omnem hominem venientem in hunc mundum. et quia in hoc mundo erat, et mundus per eum factus est, et mundus eum non cognovit. quia vero in sua propria venit et sui eum non receperunt, quotquot autem receperunt eum, dedit eis potestatem filios dei fieri credentibus in nomine eius, non ibi legi.

(14) Item legi ibi quia verbum, deus, non ex carne, non ex sanguine non ex voluntate viri neque ex voluntate carnis, sed ex deo natus est; sed quia verbum caro factum est et habitavit in nobis, non ibi legi. indagavi quippe in illis litteris varie dictum et multis modis quod sit filius in forma patris, non rapinam arbitratus esse aequalis deo, quia naturaliter idipsum est, sed quia semet ipsum exinanivit formam servi accipiens, in similitudinem hominum factus et habitu inventus ut homo, humilavit se factus oboediens usque ad mortem, mortem autem crucis: propter quod deus eum exaltavit a mortuis et donavit ei nomen quod est super omne nomen, ut in nomine Iesu omne genu flectatur caelestium terrestrium et infernorum, et omnis lingua

5 deus (est) *codd. Ver. Pell.*: deus ipse *S edd.*: dei deus *codd. Maur.*

29 A. begins with neuter pronouns for the "Word" (which is grammatically neuter but imagined as masculine with reference to the incarnate Word) but shifts here to the masculine.

light shines in the darkness, and the darkness has not appropriated it. I also read there that the human soul is not itself the light, although it bears witness concerning the light, but rather the Word is God, the true Light that enlightens every person coming into this world. Also that he[29] was in this world, and the world was made by him, and the world did not recognize him. But that he came to what belonged to him, and that his own people did not recognize him, though as many as did receive him, he gave to those who believed in his name the power to become sons of God: that I did not read there. Jn 1:1–5

Jn 1:8–12

(14) Again[30] I read there that the Word, which is God, was born not of flesh, nor of blood nor of human will nor of the will of the flesh, but of God. But that the Word was made flesh and dwelt among us: that I did not read there. Indeed I investigated what was said in those writings, in many different ways, that the Son in is the form of the Father but did not consider it robbery to be equal to God because he is naturally identical; and that he emptied himself, accepting the form of a slave, was made in human likeness and, being found human in appearance, he humbled himself and was made obedient to the point of death, even the death of the cross; that God has therefore raised him from the dead and given him a name that is above every name, that at the name of Jesus every knee should bend in heaven, on earth and in the world below; and that Jn 1:13–14

Phil 2:6

[30] The Scripture saturation in this section reaches a peak of intensity, as A. sets out side by side where the two belief systems coincide, and where Christianity contains what classical wisdom lacks.

confiteatur quia dominus Iesus in gloria est dei patris, non
habent illi libri. quod enim ante omnia tempora et supra
omnia tempora incommutabiliter manet unigenitus filius
tuus coaeternus tibi, et quia de plenitudine eius accipiunt
animae ut beatae sint, et quia participatione manentis in
se sapientiae renovantur ut sapientes sint, est ibi; quod
autem secundum tempus pro impiis mortuus est, et filio
tuo unico non pepercisti, sed pro nobis omnibus tradidisti
eum, non est ibi. abscondisti enim haec a sapientibus et
revelasti ea parvulis, ut venirent ad eum laborantes et one-
rati et reficeret eos, quoniam mitis est et humilis corde, et
diriget mites in iudicio et docet mansuetos vias suas, vi-
dens humilitatem nostram et laborem nostrum et dimit-
tens omnia peccata nostra. qui autem cothurno tamquam
doctrinae sublimioris elati non audiunt dicentem, "discite
a me quoniam mitis sum et humilis corde, et invenietis
requiem animabus vestris," etsi cognoscunt deum, non
sicut deum glorificant aut gratias agunt, sed evanescunt in
cogitationibus suis et obscuratur insipiens cor eorum; dicentes se esse sapientes stulti facti sunt.

(15) Et ideo legebam ibi etiam immutatam gloriam
incorruptionis tuae in idola et varia simulacra, in similitudinem imaginis corruptibilis hominis et volucrum et qua-
drupedum et serpentium, videlicet Aegyptium cibum quo
Esau perdidit primogenita sua, quoniam caput quadrupe-
dis pro te honoravit populus primogenitus, conversus

---

31 A. thinks of lentils (from which was made Esau's "mess of
pottage"; cf. *En. Ps.* 46.6), which were commonly grown in Egypt.
For A., Esau selling his birthright represents God's people abandoning their true inheritance. His thoughts here are compressed.

every tongue should confess that Jesus the Lord is in the glory of God the Father: those books do not contain this. As for the fact that your only-begotten Son, who is co-eternal with you, continues unchangeably before all times and beyond all times, and that out of his fullness souls accept that they are in bliss, and that by participation of the wisdom that abides in them they are renewed so as to become wise: that is found there; but that in due time he died for the ungodly, and that you did not spare your only Son but handed him over in place of us all: that is not found there. For you hid these things from the wise and have revealed them to little ones, so that those who labor and are heavy-laden might come to him, and that he might restore them: for he is gentle and humble in heart, and he shall direct those who are gentle in judgment, and shall teach the self-effacing his ways, as he looks upon our low-liness and trouble and forgives us all our sins. Those who are exalted as if by the sublimity of a grander teaching do not hear him saying, "Learn from me, for I am gentle and humble in heart, and you will find rest for your souls." Even if they recognize God, they do not glorify him as God, or give thanks; but they have come to nothing with their powers of reason, and their foolish hearts are blinded. By claiming that they are wise, they have made themselves foolish.

(15) And so I was reading there also that the glory of your imperishability was changed into idols and various representations, into the likeness of a perishable image of a human and of birds and beasts and reptiles. These in-deed are food in Egypt for which Esau abandoned his own birthright,[31] since your firstborn people venerated the

Phil 2:7–11

Jn 1:16

Ws 7:27

Rom 5:6

Rom 8:32

Mt 11:25

Mt 11:28

Ps 25:9

Ps 25:18

Mt 11:29

Rom 1:21–22

Rom 1:23

Nm 11:5

Gn 25:34

corde in Aegyptum et curvans imaginem tuam, animam
suam, ante imaginem vituli manducantis faenum. inveni
haec ibi et non manducavi. placuit enim tibi, domine,
auferre opprobrium diminutionis ab Iacob, ut maior ser-
viret minori, et vocasti gentes in hereditatem tuam. et ego
ad te veneram ex gentibus et intendi in aurum quod ab
Aegypto voluisti ut auferret populus tuus, quoniam tuum
erat, ubicumque erat. et dixisti Atheniensibus per apostolum tuum quod in te vivimus et movemur et sumus, sicut
et quidam secundum eos dixerunt, et utique inde erant illi
libri. et non attendi in idola Aegyptiorum, quibus de auro
tuo ministrabant qui transmutaverunt veritatem dei in
mendacium, et coluerunt et servierunt creaturae potius
quam creatori.

10. (16) Et inde admonitus redire ad memet ipsum,
intravi in intima mea duce te, et potui, quoniam factus es
adiutor meus. intravi et vidi qualicumque oculo animae
meae supra eundem oculum animae meae, supra mentem
meam, lucem incommutabilem, non hanc vulgarem et
conspicuam omni carni, nec quasi ex eodem genere gran-
dior erat, tamquam si ista multo multoque clarius clares-
ceret totumque occuparet magnitudine. non hoc illa erat

---

32 *Diminutio/deminutio* can refer to legal forfeiture or alienation of land.   33 Greek word for a Hebrew term referring
to nations other than Israel. The younger son Jacob represents
the younger faith, Christianity, taking the place of the elder people (as Esau, the elder son), the Jews. Cf. A. *En. Ps.* 137.10.

34 The riches taken from Egypt at the exodus become a trope
for Christian appropriation of non-Christian wisdom: cf. Justin
Apol. 2.13.4, "Whatever has been said well by any persons belongs
to us Christians."

head of a beast in place of you, and they bowed your image (their own souls) before the image of a calf feeding on hay. These things I found there, but I did not feed on them. It pleased you, Lord, to take away Jacob's shame in being the lesser son[32] so that the elder served the younger, and you called the gentiles[33] into your inheritance. And I had come to you from the gentiles and fixed my attention on the gold[34] that you desired your people to bring out of Egypt, for wherever it was, it belonged to you. What is more, you told the Athenians by your apostle that in you we live and move and have our being, just as some among them also said: and certainly those books came from a similar source.[35] I paid no heed to the idols of the Egyptians, for they served them with the use of your gold, and changed the truth of God into a lie, and worshipped and served the creation rather than the Creator.

Ps 106:20

Ps 119:22;
Gn 27:1–40

Ex 3:22

Acts 17:28

Rom 1:25

10. (16) All this warned me to come back to myself.[36] I entered deep within myself under your guidance, for you became my helper. I entered and saw, as it were with the eye of my soul, above that same eye of my soul, above my mind, the unchangeable light. It was not this ordinary light, which all flesh can behold, nor was it a grander version, as it were, of the same kind, as if it had the power to light everything up much, much more brightly, and to fill the whole with its abundance. That light was not like this;

Ps 30:10

1 Tm 6:16;
Jn 1:9

---

[35] Athens is the home of early Greek philosophy, Egypt of Neoplatonism. A. believes Ambrose's argument that Plato had met Jeremiah in Egypt and learned from him: cf. *Doctr. Chr.* 2.28.43, 2.40.60.

[36] Cf. the prodigal son (Lk 15:17) and the Plotinian progress into the self (*Enn.* 1.6.9).

sed aliud, aliud valde ab istis omnibus. nec ita erat supra
mentem meam, sicut oleum super aquam nec sicut caelum
super terram, sed superior, quia ipsa fecit me, et ego inferior, quia factus ab ea. qui novit veritatem, novit eam, et
qui novit eam, novit aeternitatem; caritas novit eam. o
aeterna veritas et vera caritas et cara aeternitas, tu es deus
meus, tibi suspiro die ac nocte! et cum te primum cognovi,
tu adsumpsisti me ut viderem esse quod viderem, et nondum me esse qui viderem. et reverberasti infirmitatem
aspectus mei, radians in me vehementer, et contremui
amore et horrore. et inveni longe me esse a te in regione
dissimilitudinis, tamquam audirem vocem tuam de ex-
celso: "cibus sum grandium: cresce et manducabis me. nec
tu me in te mutabis sicut cibum carnis tuae, sed tu muta-
beris in me." et cognovi quoniam pro iniquitate erudisti
hominem, et tabescere fecisti sicut araneam animam
meam, et dixi, "numquid nihil est veritas, quoniam neque
per finita neque per infinita locorum spatia diffusa est?"
et clamasti de longinquo, "immo vero ego sum qui sum."
et audivi, sicut auditur in corde, et non erat prorsus unde
dubitarem, faciliusque dubitarem vivere me quam non
esse veritatem, quae per ea quae facta sunt intellecta con-
spicitur.

---

37 A.'s first mystical experience; but not his last. Cf. *Conf.*
9.24–26.　　　38 *Reverberasti*: A. thinks of his eye projecting a
beam of light, which the superior light repels back.

39 Cf. Plotinus, *Enn.* 6.9.8: "They do not differ from one another in location but in unlikeness and differentness" (ἑτερότητι
δὲ καὶ διαφορᾷ).

40 In *En. Ps.* 38.18^{Vg} he notes that a soul punished for sin is as
fragile as a spider's web.

it was something else, something utterly different from all these things. It was not above my mind in the way that oil floats above water or sky above land; it was greater than that, because it made me, and I was lesser because I was its creation.[37] One who knows the Truth knows this light, and one who knows it knows eternity too. Love knows it. O everlasting Truth, and true Love, and beloved Eternity, you are my God: day and night I sigh for you! When I first recognized you, you lifted me up, to let me see that there was something I must see, but I was not yet capable of seeing it. Your beams of light reflected back[38] the weakness of my sight, so brightly did they shine upon me, and I trembled with love and awe. Then I discovered that I was far away from you, in a place of unlikeness[39] as if I heard your voice from on high: "I am the food of those who have come of age: grow up and you shall taste of me. You will not transform me into you as you do your fleshly food, but you will be transformed into me." And I realized that you have rebuked humanity because of our sin, and have made my soul dwindle away like the threads of a cobweb,[40] and I said, "Can nothing then be the truth, for it is not spread abroad either in the finite or infinite regions of space?" and you called from far off, "Truly I am who I am." And I heard you as one hears in one's heart, and from that moment there was no room for doubt, and I would sooner doubt that I was alive than that that truth was existent, for it is visible and understood through the things that have been made.[41]

cf. Jer 9:1;
Ps 42:3
Ps 27:10

Ps 39:11

Ex 3:14

[41] Polysyndeton (repetition of "and") marks heightened emotion.

11. (17) Et inspexi cetera infra te et vidi nec omnino esse nec omnino non esse: esse quidem, quoniam abs te sunt, non esse autem, quoniam id quod es non sunt. id enim vere est quod incommutabiliter manet. mihi autem inhaerere deo bonum est, quia, si non manebo in illo, nec in me potero. ille autem in se manens innovat omnia, et dominus meus es, quoniam bonorum meorum non eges.

12. (18) Et manifestatum est mihi quoniam bona sunt quae corrumpuntur, quae neque si summa bona essent neque nisi bona essent corrumpi possent; quia si summa bona essent, incorruptibilia essent, si autem nulla bona essent, quid in eis corrumperetur non esset. nocet enim corruptio et, nisi bonum minueret, non noceret. aut igitur nihil nocet corruptio, quod fieri non potest, aut, quod certissimum est, omnia quae corrumpuntur privantur bono. si autem omni bono privabuntur, omnino non erunt. si enim erunt et corrumpi iam non poterunt, meliora erunt, quia incorruptibiliter permanebunt. et quid monstrosius quam ea dicere omni bono amisso facta meliora? ergo omni bono privabuntur, omnino nulla erunt: ergo quamdiu sunt, bona sunt. ergo quaecumque sunt, bona sunt, malumque illud quod quaerebam unde esset non est substantia, quia si substantia esset, bonum esset. aut enim

---

42 In Latin this verb is cognate with the nouns and adjectives translated "im/perishable" above.

43 *substantia*: real physical existence or being; used in Trinitarian theology to define what unites the Father, Son, and Holy Spirit.

11. (17) And I contemplated the other, lower, things, and perceived that they are neither completely existent nor completely nonexistent: they do exist because they are from you, but they do not exist because they are not what you are: that is, what really abides unchangingly. Yet it is good for me to cleave to God, because if I do not abide in him I cannot abide in myself. Abiding in himself, however, he makes all things new; and you are my God, for you need no goods of mine.

Ps 73:28

Ws 7:27;
Rv 21:5
Ps 16:2

12. (18) It was also made apparent to me that the things that are perishable[42] are still good because it would be impossible for them to become perishable if they were either a supreme good or were not good at all. For if they were a supreme good, they would be imperishable, but if they were not a good at all there would be nothing in them with the capacity to be perishable. For perishability entails change to a worse state, and such change could not be inflicted without diminishing what was once good. So either perishability entails no change for the worse, which is impossible, or (which is beyond dispute) all things that are perishable are deprived of some good. But if things are deprived of good completely, they will altogether cease to exist. For if they go on existing but are no longer perishable they will be in a better state because they will abide enduringly and imperishably. And what could be more unnatural than to declare that the loss of all good has made those things better? Therefore, if they are to be deprived of all good they will cease to exist altogether; therefore, for as long as they do exist, they are good. Therefore, whatever they are, they are good: and evil itself, whose source I kept trying to discover, has no physical existence[43] because if it did have physical existence it would have to

esset incorruptibilis substantia, magnum utique bonum,
aut substantia corruptibilis esset, quae nisi bona esset, corrumpi non posset. itaque vidi et manifestatum est mihi
quia omnia bona tu fecisti et prorsus nullae substantiae
sunt quas tu non fecisti. et quoniam non aequalia omnia
fecisti, ideo sunt omnia, quia singula bona sunt, et simul
omnia valde bona, quoniam fecit deus noster omnia bona
valde.

13. (19) Et tibi omnino non est malum, non solum tibi
sed nec universae creaturae tuae, quia extra non est aliquid quod inrumpat et corrumpat ordinem quem impo-
suisti ei. in partibus autem eius quaedam quibusdam quia
non conveniunt, mala putantur; et eadem ipsa conveniunt
aliis et bona sunt et in semet ipsis bona sunt. et omnia
haec, quae sibimet invicem non conveniunt, conveniunt
inferiori parti rerum, quam terram dicimus, habentem
caelum suum nubilosum atque ventosum congruum sibi.
et absit iam ut dicerem, "non essent ista," quia etsi sola ista
cernerem, desiderarem quidem meliora, sed iam etiam de
solis istis laudare te deberem, quoniam laudandum te
ostendunt de terra dracones et omnes abyssi, ignis, grando,
nix, glacies, spiritus tempestatis, quae faciunt verbum
tuum, montes et omnes colles, ligna fructifera et omnes
cedri, bestiae et omnia pecora, reptilia et volatilia pinnata.
reges terrae et omnes populi, principes et omnes iudices

be good. For it would either be an imperishable substance, which is certainly a definite good, or a perishable one, which unless it were good would have no capacity for becoming perishable. So I saw, and it was made clear to me, that you have made all things good and certainly there are no substances that you did not make. And because you did not make all things alike, they are therefore manifold, because as individual things they are good, while collectively they are all *very* good, since our God made all things very good.

13. (19) Accordingly, for you absolutely nothing is evil, and not just for you but for your entire creation: because there is nothing outside of it that could burst into it and cause the order that you have placed upon it to become perishable. Yet among all its parts there are some that, because they are inconsistent with others, are considered to be evil, while those same parts, being consistent with other, different, elements, now appear to be good in themselves, and good in their consistency with those other parts. All these things that are inconsistent with one another in themselves are still consistent with the lower part of creation, which we call "earth," with its own cloudy and windy sky to suit it. Far be it from me, then, to say, "Those things would not exist," because even if they were the only things I could perceive, I should still long for better ones. Yet I ought to praise you even for these things taken on their own, because the creatures of earth demonstrate that you deserve praise: dragons and all deeps, fire, hail, snow, ice, stormy wind: all these fulfill your word; mountains and all hills, fruitful trees and all cedars, beasts and all cattle, every creeping thing and feathered fowl; earthly kings and all nations, princes and all earthly judges, young men

Gn 1:4, 10, 12, 18, 21, 25, 31

333

terrae, iuvenes et virgines, seniores cum iunioribus laudent nomen tuum. cum vero etiam de caelis te laudent, laudent te, deus noster: in excelsis omnes angeli tui, omnes virtutes tuae, sol et luna, omnes stellae et lumen, caeli caelorum et aquae quae super caelos sunt laudent nomen tuum. non iam desiderabam meliora, quia omnia cogitabam, et meliora quidem superiora quam inferiora, sed meliora omnia quam sola superiora iudicio saniore pendebam.

14. (20) Non est sanitas eis quibus displicet aliquid creaturae tuae, sicut mihi non erat cum displicerent multa quae fecisti. et quia non audebat anima mea ut ei displiceret deus meus, nolebat esse tuum quidquid ei displicebat. et inde ierat in opinionem duarum substantiarum, et non requiescebat, et aliena loquebatur. et inde rediens fecerat sibi deum per infinita spatia locorum omnium et eum putaverat esse te et eum conlocaverat in corde suo, et facta erat rursus templum idoli sui abominandum tibi, sed posteaquam fovisti caput nescientis et clausisti oculos meos, ne viderent vanitatem. cessavi de me paululum, et consopita est insania mea, et evigilavi in te et vidi te infinitum aliter, et visus iste non a carne trahebatur.

15. (21) Et respexi alia, et vidi tibi debere quia sunt et in te cuncta finita, sed aliter, non quasi in loco, sed quia tu

---

44 The Latin *virtutes* renders LXX "powers" and Hebrew "hosts" (i.e., armies of divine beings) rather than good qualities or theological virtues.

45 I.e., to Manichaeism; cf. Introduction, p. xxv.

and maidens, older and younger people together: let them praise your name. To be sure, when they praise you from heaven, let all your angels on high praise you, our God, and all your hosts,[44] sun and moon, all stars and light, the heaven of heavens and the waters above the heavens, let them praise your name. I no longer yearned for individual things to be better, because I was thinking about things as a whole. With clearer insight I considered higher things as better than the lower ones, but now I was regarding everything taken together as better, rather than individual higher things by themselves. Ps 148:7–12

14. (20) There is no health in those people who disapprove of some part of your creation, as in myself for example, when I disapproved of many things that you made. And because my soul felt it was presumptuous to find my God displeasing, it did not want anything of which it disapproved to be from you. Because of this it had inclined to a dualistic theory of substances,[45] and it found no rest, and simply recited other people's ideas. And then it had come back and formed a god for itself, which would be throughout the boundless regions of all space, and had thought that this god was you, and had established it in its heart. Then for a second time my soul had become a temple containing its very own idol, an abomination to you. But afterward you cherished me in my foolishness, and you closed my eyes to stop me looking upon vanity. I had a brief respite from myself, and my madness was lulled to sleep; then I awoke in you and saw that you were immeasurably different, and that vision of mine was not drawn from the realm of the flesh. Ps 38:3 Ez 14:7 Ps 119:37

15. (21) Then I looked back at other things, and I saw that they owe their existence to you, and they are all con-

es omnitenens manu veritate, et omnia vera sunt in quantum sunt, nec quicquam est falsitas, nisi cum putatur esse
quod non est. et vidi quia non solum locis sua quaeque suis
conveniunt sed etiam temporibus et quia tu, qui solus
aeternus es, non post innumerabilia spatia temporum coe-
pisti operari, quia omnia spatia temporum, et quae prae-
terierunt et quae praeteribunt, nec abirent nec venirent
nisi te operante et manente.

16. (22) Et sensi expertus non esse mirum quod palato
non sano poena est et panis qui sano suavis est, et oculis
aegris odiosa lux quae puris amabilis. et iustitia tua displicet iniquis, nedum vipera et vermiculus, quae bona creasti,
apta inferioribus creaturae tuae partibus, quibus et ipsi
iniqui apti sunt, quanto dissimiliores sunt tibi, apti autem
superioribus, quanto similiores fiunt tibi. et quaesivi quid
esset iniquitas et non inveni substantiam, sed a summa
substantia, te deo, detortae in infima voluntatis perversitatem, proicientis intima sua et tumescentis foras.

17. (23) Et mirabar quod iam te amabam, non pro te
phantasma, et non stabam frui deo meo, sed rapiebar ad
te decore tuo moxque diripiebar abs te pondere meo, et

---

46 Countering the sponge metaphor, *Conf.* 7.5.7.

47 LXX is more concrete, "It casts its entrails away": a reminder of human mortality. For A. the bowels here are figurative,
referring to the indwelling of God (cf. *Mus.* 6.13.40).

tained in you, but in a specific way: not as if in physical space[46] but because you hold all things in your hand by means of truth; and all things are true insofar as they exist, nor is anything a falsehood except when it is believed to exist but does not. Next I saw that everything is contained not only within its proper space but also within its own time, and that you who alone are everlasting did not begin your work after countless periods of time, because all periods of time, both past and yet to come, would neither pass nor arrive unless you brought them about, while yourself abiding eternally.

16. (22) I also realized from experience that it was not surprising that the bread that is pleasing to a healthy palate is a trial to a disordered appetite, and that unhealthy eyes find loathsome the light that is lovely to those who are undefiled. So too the unjust find your righteousness disagreeable, and even more so the viper and the worm, which you created good and which belong to the lower regions of your creation. Likewise those who are unjust belong to those same regions, in proportion to how little they resemble you; but they belong to the higher regions in proportion to how much they resemble you. And I asked what injustice was, and I did not find it to be a physical entity but rather a deviation of the will that is misdirected away from the highest essence, which is you who are God, and toward the lowest form of being, a will that casts out what lies deep within it[47] and puffs itself up in public. Sir 10:9

17. (23) Now I was amazed at my beginning to love you instead of some illusory image of you. I was unable to stand firm in my enjoyment of my God; rather I was transported to you by your beauty and all too soon was severed from you by my own weight, and with a groan I tumbled

ruebam in ista cum gemitu; et pondus hoc consuetudo
carnalis. sed mecum erat memoria tui, neque ullo modo
dubitabam esse cui cohaererem, sed nondum me esse qui
cohaererem, quoniam corpus quod corrumpitur adgravat
animam et deprimit terrena inhabitatio sensum multa
cogitantem, eramque certissimus quod invisibilia tua a
constitutione mundi per ea quae facta sunt intellecta
conspiciuntur, sempiterna quoque virtus et divinitas tua.
quaerens enim unde approbarem pulchritudinem corporum, sive caelestium sive terrestrium, et quid mihi praesto
esset integre de mutabilibus iudicanti et dicenti, "hoc ita
esset debet, illud non ita"—hoc ergo quaerens, unde iudicarem cum ita iudicarem, inveneram incommutabilem et
veram veritatis aeternitatem supra mentem meam com-
mutabilem.

Atque ita gradatim a corporibus ad sentientem per corpus animam atque inde ad eius interiorem vim, cui sensus
corporis exteriora nuntiaret, et quousque possunt bestiae,
atque inde rursus ad ratiocinantem potentiam ad quam
refertur iudicandum quod sumitur a sensibus corporis.
quae se quoque in me comperiens mutabilem erexit se ad
intellegentiam suam et abduxit cogitationem a consuetudine, subtrahens se contradicentibus turbis phantasma-
tum, ut inveniret quo lumine aspergeretur, cum sine ulla

---

48 Cf. Cic. *Tusc.* 1.6.38: "It is the mark of a great intelligence
(*ingenii*) to withdraw the mind from the physical senses and direct thought (*mentem*) away from its habitual path."

49 Cf. *Conf.* 3.6.10, n. 23.

downward into those base things, and this weight was my sexual behavior. Yet the memory of you stayed with me, and I had no doubt at all that there was One I could cleave to, even though I was not yet in a fit state to do so. This was because a body that is being corrupted weighs the mind down, and its earthly habitation presses down upon the mind while it is meditating upon many things. I was utterly convinced that right from the foundation of the world your invisible nature is discernible and can be understood by means of what has been created, including your eternal power and divinity. For I was looking for a reason for affirming beauty in physical things, whether heavenly or earthly, and what resources I might have at hand for making a sound judgment and pronouncement about changeable entities, "This ought to be this way, and that should be otherwise." This was what I was asking: when I made judgments in such a way, what were the grounds for my judgment? I had found that the eternity of truth is true unchangeably, beyond my mutable mind.

Ws 9:15

Rom 1:20

So in stages I progressed from physical entities to the soul, which experiences sensation by means of the body, and thence to the soul's inner power, to which physical sensation would communicate the world around it. This is as far as the capacities of animals can go. From there I went on to the power of reason: to this everything gathered from bodily sensation is referred for assessment. This reasoning power in me also ascertained that it was changeable, so it raised itself up to face its own understanding and directed my thoughts away from their habitual path.[48] At the same time it withdrew itself from conflicting crowds of illusory images[49] in order to find what light had been scattered upon it: when it cried out, without any hesita-

dubitatione clamaret incommutabile praeferendum esse
mutabili unde nosset ipsum incommutabile (quod nisi aliquo modo nosset, nullo modo illud mutabili certa praepo-
neret), et pervenit ad id quod est in ictu trepidantis aspectus. tunc vero invisibilia tua per ea quae facta sunt intellecta
conspexi, sed aciem figere non evalui, et repercussa infir-
mitate redditus solitis non mecum ferebam nisi amantem
memoriam et quasi olefacta desiderantem quae comedere
nondum possem.

18. (24) Et quaerebam viam comparandi roboris quod
esset idoneum ad fruendum te, nec inveniebam donec
amplecterer mediatorem dei et hominum, hominem
Christum Iesum, qui est super omnia deus benedictus in
saecula, vocantem et dicentem, "ego sum via et veritas et
vita," et cibum, cui capiendo invalidus eram, miscentem
carni, quoniam verbum caro factum est ut infantiae nostrae lactesceret sapientia tua, per quam creasti omnia. non
enim tenebam deum meum Iesum, humilis humilem, nec
cuius rei magistra esset eius infirmitas noveram. verbum
enim tuum, aeterna veritas, superioribus creaturae tuae
partibus supereminens subditos erigit ad se ipsam, in inferioribus autem aedificavit sibi humilem domum de limo
nostro, per quam subdendos deprimeret a seipsis et ad se

---

50 Cf. *Conf.* 7.10.16 with Ex 3:14 (the true identity of God: for
A. this meant his name "I Am That I Am" (*ego sum qui sum/qui
est*), not the fullness of the Hebrew, which is, perhaps, closer to
"I will become to you the one who comes alongside" (cf. Ps 124:1
and ctr. Hos 1:9). Language and thought here draw on Scripture
and Plotinus; cf. *Conf.* 9.10.25.   51 As if his eye emits a beam
of light, which strikes the object he beholds. Cf. *Conf.* 7.10.16.

52 Central in *Conf.* as a whole both spatially and conceptually.

tion, that the unchangeable is preferable to the change-able, what was the source of its knowing the concept of unchangingness? For if it did not know it by some means, it could not by any means be sure in preferring it to what is changeable. And with the stroke of one trembling glance it arrived at that which truly is.[50] Then in truth I perceived that your invisible nature is understood by means of your creation, but I had not the strength to fix my gaze; instead my weakness rebounded[51] and I was returned to my old habits, carrying with me no more than a loving memory and, as it were, longing to smell the sweet savor of food that I could not as yet consume.

18. (24) I began to look for a way to gain enough strength to enjoy you, but I did not find one until I em-braced the mediator between God and humanity. This was the man Christ Jesus, who is over all things, God blessed for ever, who calls and says, "I am the Way, the Truth and the Life,"[52] and who mingles with flesh the food that I was too weak to take. For the Word was made flesh so that your Wisdom, through whom you created all things, could start to produce the spiritual milk for our infancy. I was not holding fast to Jesus as my God; I was not humble enough to cleave to him who is humble, and I did not realize what lesson his weakness was going to teach me. Your Word, the eternal Truth, towers over the higher regions of your cre-ation, and raises up those who submit themselves to him; but in creation's lower regions he has built for himself a humble dwelling from the clay of our humanity through which he can constrain those who need to be changed from themselves, and can bring them across to himself.

1 Cor 15:52

Rom 1:20

1 Tm 2:5

Rom 9:5
cf. Jn 14:6

1 Cor 3:2;
Heb 5:12, etc.

Mt 11:29

Gn 2:7, 3:19;
Prv 9:1

traiceret, sanans tumorem et nutriens amorem, ne fiducia
sui progrederentur longius, sed potius infirmarentur, videntes ante pedes suos infirmam divinitatem ex participatione tunicae pelliciae nostrae, et lassi prosternerentur in
eam, illa autem surgens levaret eos.

19. (25) Ego vero aliud putabam tantumque sentiebam
de domino Christo meo, quantum de excellentis sapientiae viro cui nullus posset aequari, praesertim quia mirabiliter natus ex virgine, ad exemplum contemnendorum
temporalium prae adipiscenda immortalitate, divina pro
nobis cura tantam auctoritatem magisterii meruisse videbatur. quid autem sacramenti haberet verbum caro factum, ne suspicari quidem poteram. tantum cognoveram ex
his quae de illo scripta traderentur quia manducavit et
bibit, dormivit, ambulavit, exhilaratus est, contristatus est,
sermocinatus est, non haesisse carnem illam verbo tuo nisi
cum anima et mente humana. novit hoc omnis qui novit
incommutabilitatem verbi tui, quam ego iam noveram,
quantum poteram, nec omnino quicquam inde dubitabam. etenim nunc movere membra corporis per voluntatem, nunc non movere, nunc aliquo affectu affici, nunc
non affici, nunc proferre per signa sapientes sententias,
nunc esse in silentio, propria sunt mutabilitatis animae et
mentis. quae si falsa de illo scripta essent, etiam omnia

---

53 Gn 3:21 refers to literal clothing. Here "garments of skins"
represents humanity's mortality in its corrupted condition (cf. A.
En. Ps. 103.1.8; with Rv 6:11, etc.; Mt 22:12; 2 Cor 5:2–3; the
second century AD pseudepigraphical Ascension of Isaiah 9.68–9
comes closest: "And he took me up into the seventh heaven . . .
and there I saw all the righteous from the time of Adam onward
. . . stripped of (their) robes of the flesh; and I saw them in their

Then he can heal their swollen pride and feed their love,
to stop them going on any longer in self-reliance, and so
that instead they can let themselves be weak. For they see
before their own feet a divinity that is fragile because of
its participation in our garments of skins,[53] and in their
exhaustion they prostrate themselves upon that divinity,
but it rises up and sets them on their feet.

cf. 1 Cor
1:25
Gn 3:21

19. (25) But I thought differently. I was imagining
Christ my Lord only as a man who excelled in wisdom, a
man beyond compare, especially because it appeared that
he was miraculously born of a virgin to give us an example
of the rejection of worldly things in comparison with the
prize of immortality; and because of God's concern on our
behalf he deserved the highest authority as a teacher. But
as for the mystery encapsulated in the Word made flesh, I
could not even begin to imagine it. I had only learned,
from the writings handed down about him, that he ate and
drank, slept, walked, felt joy and sorrow, and conversed,
that his flesh was not joined to your Word in such a way as
to lack a soul and a human mind. Everyone who knows the
unchangeableness of your Word knows this, and now I
knew it too, as far as I could; and from that point on, I had
no doubt whatever. For these things are characteristic of
the changeability of soul and mind: one moment to move
the body's limbs at will, and the next not to move them;
one moment to be affected by some emotion and the next
to be unaffected, one moment to proffer wise opinions by
means of signs and the next to remain silent. But if what
had been written about him were untrue, the falsehood

Jn 1:14

robes of above, and they were like the angels": see Hunt, *Clothed
in the Body*, ch. 10.

periclitarentur mendacio neque in illis litteris ulla fidei salus generi humano remaneret. quia itaque vera scripta sunt, totum hominem in Christo agnoscebam, non corpus tantum hominis aut cum corpore sine mente animum, sed ipsum hominem, non persona veritatis, sed magna quadam naturae humanae excellentia et perfectiore participatione sapientiae praeferri ceteris arbitrabar.

Alypius autem deum carne indutum ita putabat credi a catholicis ut praeter deum et carnem non esset in Christo, animam mentemque hominis non existimabat in eo praedicari. et quoniam bene persuasum tenebat ea quae de illo memoriae mandata sunt sine vitali et rationali creatura non fieri, ad ipsam christianam fidem pigrius movebatur. sed postea haereticorum apollinaristarum hunc errorem esse cognoscens catholicae fidei conlaetatus et contemperatus est.

Ego autem aliquanto posterius didicisse me fateor, in eo quod verbum caro factum est, quomodo catholica veritas a Photini falsitate dirimatur. improbatio quippe haere-

---

54 I.e., A. still recognizes only the humanity, not the divinity, of Christ.

55 *catholici*: the term is derived from the Greek for "universal, comprehensive"; in this period it denotes Christians identified by the writer using the term as holding right beliefs ("orthodox").

56 I.e., that the incarnate Christ had no human soul. The belief that the Logos or Word (*Verbum*) took the place of the human soul in Christ was judged to be heretical: see n. 67.

57 "living" corresponds to the "soul," and "rational" to the "mind" of the previous sentence, factors which Alypius could not (yet) bring himself to acknowledge in Christ.

would endanger everything, and no surety of faith would remain for the human race in those writings. And so because the Scriptures were true, I acknowledged the complete humanity in Christ: not just the body of a man, or a spirit with a body but no mind, but truly a human being; and I judged that he was to be preferred to others not because he took on the role of Truth[54] but because of the supreme quality of that human nature that he possessed, and because of his more perfect participation in wisdom.

Alypius, on the other hand, thought that catholic[55] Christians believed God was clothed in human flesh to such an extent that apart from what was God and what was flesh there was nothing in Christ:[56] he did not accept that Christ could be said to possess a human soul and mind. Because he remained convinced that those things that he had committed to memory concerning Christ could not be done except by a living and rational being,[57] he progressed more slowly toward true Christian faith. Later on, though, he recognized that this was the misconception of the Apollinarian heretics,[58] and he found joy in the catholic faith and watered down his views.[59]

I admit that I learned somewhat later how, concerning the one who is the Word made flesh, catholic truth is divergent from the falsehood of Photinius.[60] Rejection of

[58] Apollinaris was a bishop of Laodicea (condemned by the Council of Constantinople in 381, d. 390); he denied that Christ had a human soul.

[59] Cf. A. *En. Ps.* 29, 2.2.

[60] Fourth-century bishop of Sirmium, who denied the pre-existence of Christ.

ticorum facit eminere quid ecclesia tua sentiat et quid
habeat sana doctrina. oportuit enim et haereses esse, ut
probati manifesti fierent inter infirmos.

20. (26) Sed tunc, lectis platonicorum illis libris,
posteaquam inde admonitus quaerere incorpoream veritatem, invisibilia tua per ea quae facta sunt intellecta
conspexi et repulsus sensi quid per tenebras animae meae
contemplari non sinerer, certus esse te et infinitum esse
nec tamen per locos finitos infinitosve diffundi et vere te
esse, qui semper idem ipse esses, ex nulla parte nulloque
motu alter aut aliter, cetera vero ex te esse omnia, hoc solo
firmissimo documento quia sunt, certus quidem in istis
eram, nimis tamen infirmus ad fruendum te. garriebam
plane quasi peritus et, nisi in Christo, salvatore nostro,
viam tuam quaererem, non peritus sed periturus essem.
iam enim coeperam velle videri sapiens plenus poena mea
et non flebam, insuper et inflabar scientia. ubi enim erat
illa aedificans caritas a fundamento humilitatis, quod est
Christus Iesus? aut quando illi libri me docerent eam? in
quos me propterea, priusquam scripturas tuas considera-
rem, credo voluisti incurrere, ut imprimeretur memoriae
meae quomodo ex eis affectus essem et, cum postea in
libris tuis mansuefactus essem et curantibus digitis tuis

---

61 A word rooted in the New Testament concept of factions or
parties within the Church. By A.'s time it stood for those whose
teachings excluded them from the Church; cf. Acts 24:14; Gal
5:20; Ti 3:10; 2 Pt 2:1.   62 A. echoes the words of *Conf.* 7.17.23.

63 Paronomasia on *peritus* (skilled) and *periturus* (about to
perish); sometimes rendered "not so much skilled as killed."

64 He first weeps truly in the garden at his conversion: *Conf.*
8.12.28; cf. 9.12.29.

heretics[61] certainly makes it clear what your church approves and what sound doctrine holds. For there had to be heresies so that those who are in the right may become apparent among the weak.

1 Cor 11:19

20. (26) Back in those days, though, I had read those books of the Neoplatonists, and following on from them I had been taught to seek truth which is incorporeal. I perceived that your invisible realities can be understood by means of the physical creation.[62] Although I was thwarted,

Rom 1:20

I still glimpsed what the shadows of my soul were preventing me from contemplating: I was sure that you exist and are infinite and yet are not dispersed through finite or infinite space; and that you truly exist in that you yourself are always the same, being in no aspect and by no movement one way or another; and that all other things truly derive from you on the grounds of this most convincing

Rom 11:36

proof: that they exist. I was sure about all this but too weak to enjoy you. I was pontificating like an expert, and unless I was seeking your way in Christ our Savior I was not so much expert as destined to expire.[63] I had already begun to want to appear wise: I was filled with a torment of my own making, and instead of shedding tears I grew bloated with learning.[64] Where was that love which builds up from

1 Cor 8:1

a foundation of humility, namely Christ Jesus? After all,

1 Cor 3:11

when were all those books of mine going to teach me that? Because of this, I believe it was your will that I should come across those books before I gave my attention to your Scriptures, so that it would be imprinted on my memory how I was affected by them. Then afterward, when I grew to be gentle by means of your books, and my wounds felt the touch of your healing fingers, I discerned and re-

contrectarentur vulnera mea, discernerem atque distin-
guerem quid interesset inter praesumptionem et confes-
sionem, inter videntes quo eundum sit nec videntes qua,
et viam ducentem ad beatificam patriam non tantum
cernendam sed et habitandam. nam si primo sanctis tuis
litteris informatus essem et in earum familiaritate obdul-
cuisses mihi, et post in illa volumina incidissem, fortasse
aut abripuissent me a solidamento pietatis, aut si in affectu
quem salubrem inbiberam perstitissem, putarem etiam ex
illis libris eum posse concipi, si eos solos quisque didicis-
set.

21. (27) Itaque avidissime arripui venerabilem stilum
spiritus tui, et prae ceteris apostolum Paulum, et perie-
runt illae quaestiones in quibus mihi aliquando visus est
adversari sibi et non congruere testimoniis legis et prophetarum textus sermonis eius, et apparuit mihi una facies
eloquiorum castorum, et exultare cum tremore didici. et
coepi et inveni, quidquid illac verum legeram, hac cum
commendatione gratiae tuae dici, ut qui videt non sic glo-
rietur, quasi non acceperit non solum id quod videt, sed
etiam ut videat (quid enim habet quod non accepit?) et ut
te, qui es semper idem, non solum admoneatur ut videat,
sed etiam sanetur ut teneat, et qui de longinquo videre
non potest, viam tamen ambulet qua veniat et videat et
teneat, quia, etsi condelectetur homo legi dei secundum

---

65 The density of scriptural allusion in this final part of Book
7 is a marker of high emotion. Cf. *Conf.* 7.9.14, n. 30.

66 I.e., the Scriptures consist of a unity forged from different
authors.

marked what a difference there was between presumption and confession, between those who see what direction they should go but do not see how [to go there], and the Way who leads to the land of bliss that is not just for looking at but also for living in. For if I had been molded from the beginning by your holy writings, and through my knowledge of them you had grown sweet to me, and I had later chanced upon those books, they might perhaps have torn me away from the framework of my dutiful observance. Or if I had persisted in the devotion that I had imbibed as health-giving, I might still think that such devotion could be absorbed from those books even if everyone had studied nothing but them.

Jn 14:6

21. (27) So I clutched that sacred writing of your Spirit eagerly, and principally the apostle Paul.[65] Then all those problems disappeared, in which I previously found that the account of his preaching contradicted itself and disagreed with the testimonies of the law and the prophets. I now discerned a single face with different pure voices[66] and I learned to rejoice with trembling. And I made a start and found that whatever truth I had read in those other books was proclaimed in this book, with the additional recommendation of your grace: and to such an extent that none who see can boast as if not only what they see but also the actual capacity for seeing have not been bestowed upon them, for who possess what they have not received? Moreover they are not only warned that they will see you who are the same forever, but also that they will be healed so they can hold fast to you. Those who are too far off to see you, meanwhile, must walk the way that leads them to come and see and hold fast, because even if they delight in God's law in their inner being, what are they to do con-

Ps 11:6

Ps 2:11

1 Cor 4:7

349

interiorem hominem, quid faciet de alia lege in membris suis repugnante legi mentis suae et se captivum ducente in lege peccati, quae est in membris eius?

Quoniam iustus es, domine, nos autem peccavimus, inique fecimus, impie gessimus, et gravata est super nos manus tua, et iuste traditi sumus antiquo peccatori, praeposito mortis, quia persuasit voluntati nostrae similitudinem voluntatis suae, qua in veritate tua non stetit. quid faciet miser homo? quis eum liberabit de corpore mortis huius, nisi gratia tua per Iesum Christum dominum nostrum, quem genuisti coaeternum et creasti in principio viarum tuarum, in quo princeps huius mundi non invenit quicquam morte dignum, et occidit eum? et evacuatum est chirographum quod erat contrarium nobis.

hoc illae litterae non habent: non habent illae paginae vultum pietatis huius, lacrimas confessionis, sacrificium tuum, spiritum contribulatum, cor contritum et humilatum, populi salutem, sponsam civitatem, arram spiritus sancti, poculum pretii nostri. nemo ibi cantat, "nonne deo subdita erit anima mea? ab ipso enim salutare meum: etenim ipse deus meus et salutaris meus, susceptor meus: non movebor amplius." nemo ibi audit vocantem: "venite ad me, qui laboratis." dedignantur ab eo discere quoniam mitis est et humilis corde. abscondisti enim haec a sapientibus et prudentibus et revelasti ea parvulis. et aliud est de silvestri cacumine videre patriam pacis et iter ad eam non invenire et frustra conari per invia circum obsidentibus et

---

67 The orthodox position was that Christ was begotten and not created; so A. takes the Proverbs text (which is a Christological crux) as a reference to Christ's human nature only, not his whole self.

cerning the other law, that of their physical bodies, that fights against the law of their minds and leads them captive in the law of sin that is in their physical bodies? Rom 7:22–23

For you are righteous, Lord, but we have sinned, we have acted unjustly, we have behaved wickedly and your hand has grown heavy upon us, and we are justly handed over to that ancient sinner, to the captain of death, because he has persuaded our will into becoming like his will, which does not abide in your truth. What is humanity to do in its wretchedness? Who will rescue it from this body of death if not your grace through Jesus Christ our Lord, whom you have begotten as one coeternal with yourself, and created[67] in the beginning of your ways, in whom the prince of this world found nothing to deserve death yet still he killed him? Thus the written record of the debt we owed was annulled. Ps 119:137;
cf. Tb 3:2
Ps 106:6
Ps 32:4
Heb 2:14;
1 Jn 3:8
Jn 8:44; cf.
Is 14:12–14;
Lk 10:18
Prv 8:22
Lk 23:14–15;
Jn 14:30
Col 2:14

Those other books contain nothing of this: their pages do not contain the devoted countenance, the tears of confession, your sacrifice, the troubled spirit, the heart repentant and humbled, the salvation of your people, the city that is your bride, the pledge of the Holy Spirit, or the cup that is the price of our ransom! No one there is singing, "Surely my soul will be subject to God, for from him comes my salvation: truly he is my God and my salvation, he is my helper, I shall be troubled no more." No one there hears him calling, "Come to me, you who are struggling": they are not worthy to learn from him, for he is gentle and humble in heart. You have hidden these matters from the wise and cautious and have revealed them to little ones. It is one thing to see the homeland of peace from a wooded mountain top, then fail to find the way to it and try in vain to get through impenetrable terrain while all around fugi- Ps 51:17; Rv
21:2; 2 Cor
1:22, 5:5;
Mt 20:28;
cf. Lk 22:42
Ps 61:2–3
Mt 11:28–29
Mt 11:25

351

insidiantibus fugitivis desertoribus cum principe suo
leone et dracone, et aliud tenere viam illuc ducentem cura
caelestis imperatoris munitam, ubi non latrocinantur qui
caelestem militiam deseruerunt; vitant enim eam sicut
supplicium. haec mihi inviscerabantur miris modis, cum
minimum apostolorum tuorum legerem, et considerave-
ram opera tua et expaveram.

tives and deserters, under the command of the lion and
dragon, lie in wait to attack; and quite another to stick to   Ps 91:13
the way that leads there, a way under the protection of the
ruler of heaven, where there are no deserters from the
heavenly host to commit highway robbery, for they avoid
that way as if it were a torment to them. In a way beyond
comprehension, all this was implanted deep within me
when I read the least of your apostles and had contem-   1 Cor 15:9
plated your works: and I was utterly terrified.

LIBER VIII

1. (1) Deus meus, recorder in gratiarum actione tibi et confitear misericordias tuas super me. perfundantur ossa mea dilectione tua et dicant: "domine, quis similis tibi?" dirupisti vincula mea: sacrificem tibi sacrificium laudis. quomodo dirupisti ea narrabo, et dicent omnes qui adorant te, cum audiunt haec, "benedictus dominus in caelo et in terra; magnum et mirabile nomen eius."

Inhaeserant praecordiis meis verba tua, et undique circumvallabar abs te. de vita tua aeterna certus eram, quamvis eam in aenigmate et quasi per speculum videram; dubitatio tamen omnis de incorruptibili substantia, quod ab illa esset omnis substantia, ablata mihi erat, nec certior de te sed stabilior in te esse cupiebam. de mea vero temporali vita nutabant omnia et mundandum erat cor a fermento veteri. et placebat via ipse salvator, et ire per eius angustias adhuc pigebat.

Et immisisti in mentem meam visumque est bonum in conspectu meo pergere ad Simplicianum, qui mihi bonus apparebat servus tuus et lucebat in eo gratia tua. audieram

BOOK VIII

1. (1) O my God, let me, by giving thanks to you, call to mind and confess your mercies toward me. Let my very bones be flooded with love for you and cry out: "Lord, who is like you?" You have torn away my bonds: let me offer to you a sacrifice of thanksgiving. How you tore them away, I shall now recount, and let everyone who worships you say, when they hear these things, "Blessed is the Lord in heaven and on earth: great and wonderful is his name." Ps 86:13; cf. Is 63:7

Ps 35:10

Ps 116:16

Ps 72:18

Ps 8:2, 76:1

Your words were firmly implanted in my heart, and you encompassed me on every side. I was now convinced of your eternal life, although I had seen it only as a mystery and like a reflected image. As for every doubt about imperishable substance, because every kind of substance is derived from it, it was taken from me. Now I longed to be more firmly established in you rather than more convinced about you. But concerning my earthly life everything was in a state of flux: my heart was yet to be cleansed of its old leaven. The Way himself, my Savior, won favor with me, and yet I was still hesitating to pass through his narrow gate.

Is 29:2^{Vg}

1 Cor 13:12

1 Cor 5:7–8

Jn 14:6

Mt 7:14

Then you put an idea in my mind, and it seemed good in my sight: to make my way to Simplicianus, who seemed to me to be your good servant, for your grace shone in

etiam quod a iuventute sua devotissime tibi viveret; iam vero tunc senuerat et longa aetate in tam bono studio sectandae vitae[1] tuae multa expertus, multa edoctus mihi videbatur: et vere sic erat. unde mihi ut proferret volebam conferenti secum aestus meos quis esset aptus modus sic affecto ut ego eram ad ambulandum in via tua.

(2) Videbam enim plenam ecclesiam, et alius sic ibat, alius autem sic, mihi autem displicebat quod agebam in saeculo et oneri mihi erat valde, non iam inflammantibus cupiditatibus, ut solebant, spe honoris et pecuniae ad tolerandam illam servitutem tam gravem. iam enim me illa non delectabant prae dulcedine tua et decore domus tuae, quam dilexi, sed adhuc tenaciter conligabar ex femina, nec me prohibebat apostolus coniugari, quamvis exhortaretur ad melius, maxime volens omnes homines sic esse ut ipse erat.

Sed ego infirmior eligebam molliorem locum et propter hoc unum volvebar, in ceteris languidus et tabescens curis marcidis, quod et in aliis rebus quas nolebam pati congruere cogebar vitae coniugali, cui deditus obstringebar. audieram ex ore veritatis esse spadones qui se ipsos absciderunt propter regnum caelorum, sed "qui potest," inquit, "capere, capiat." vani sunt certe omnes homines

---

[1] vitae *O S Ver.*: viae *mss, edd.*

---

[1] Successor to Ambrose as bishop of Milan, influential on him as well as on A; d. 400/1.

[2] Or (with the MSS) "a way."

[3] This moment of crisis resolved itself into acceptance of continence as the prerequisite for baptism.

him.[1] I had heard that his life had been completely devoted to you even from his youth. By now he was grown old, and I thought he would be well-versed and widely experienced because of the long years he had spent in the worthy task of pursuing a life[2] you would approve: and so it proved. I wanted him, when I laid my perplexities before him, to bring forth for me what would be the appropriate way forward for someone in my condition, so that I could become fit to walk in your way.

(2) I saw your Church full, one person going one way, someone else going another way. But I was unhappy with the fact that I was still living a secular life, and one that put me under great strain, now that I no longer had any burning desires, as previously, hoping for distinction and wealth to make such a burdensome enslavement bearable.[3] No longer did those factors attract me in preference to your sweetness and the beauty of your house, which I now loved; but I was still very much entangled on account of a woman—not that the apostle forbade me to marry, though he did urge me toward the better choice, for he was especially hopeful that everyone would live as he himself did.

But I was weaker than he. I chose the softer option, and only because of this I was in turmoil, apathetic about the worries that were wearing me down, listless about everything else, because in other aspects that I was far from eager to put up with I was being forced to adapt myself to the married state, and if I committed myself to that I was going to be completely trapped. I had heard from the mouth of Truth that there are eunuchs who have castrated themselves for the sake of the kingdom of heaven, but let those who can accept this, he said, accept it. Surely every-

Mt 13:52

Ps 128:1

cf. 1 Cor 7:7

Ps 26:8

Jn 14:6

Mt 19:12

357

CONFESSIONS

quibus non inest dei scientia, nec de his quae videntur
bona potuerunt invenire eum qui est. at ego iam non eram
in illa vanitate. transcenderam eam et contestante universa creatura inveneram te creatorem nostrum et verbum
tuum apud te deum tecumque unum deum, per quod
creasti omnia. et est aliud genus impiorum, qui cognoscentes deum non sicut deum glorificaverunt aut gratias
egerunt. in hoc quoque incideram, et dextera tua suscepit
me et inde ablatum posuisti ubi convalescerem, quia
dixisti homini, "ecce pietas est sapientia," et, "noli velle
videri sapiens, quoniam dicentes se esse sapientes stulti
facti sunt." et inveneram iam bonam margaritam, et ven-
ditis omnibus quae haberem emenda erat, et dubitabam.

2. (3) Perrexi ergo ad Simplicianum, patrem in acci-
pienda gratia tunc episcopi Ambrosii et quem vere ut patrem diligebat. narravi ei circuitus erroris mei. ubi autem
commemoravi legisse me quosdam libros platonicorum,
quos Victorinus, quondam rhetor urbis Romae, quem
christianum defunctum esse audieram, in latinam linguam
transtulisset, gratulatus est mihi quod non in aliorum philosophorum scripta incidissem plena fallaciarum et de-
ceptionum secundum elementa huius mundi, in istis autem omnibus modis insinuari deum et eius verbum.

Deinde, ut me exhortaretur ad humilitatem Christi
sapientibus absconditam et revelatam parvulis, Victori-

---

4 Gaius Marius Victorinus: like A., for whom he was in part a
model, he began as a student of philosophy and teacher of rhetoric, and ended as a Christian. Cf. Ammianus Marcellinus 14.6.8
on honorific statues.

one who lacks the knowledge of God is vain and they have been unable to find him, who is Goodness itself, among those things that seem good. I was no longer in that state of vanity. I had surmounted it and the whole creation bore witness, and I had discovered you, our Creator, and your Word, who abides with you and is God, and with you is one God, through whom you created all things. Yet there is a race of wicked people who know God but do not glorify him as God or give him thanks. In the past I too had fallen into that error, but your right hand took me up and carried me away from all that and laid me in a place where I could recover my strength, for you have said to humanity, "Look, devotion to God is a form of wisdom" and, "Do not desire to appear wise, for those who claim to be wise have made themselves fools." And I had found the fine pearl, and I was supposed to sell everything I possessed to buy it. And still I hesitated.

Ws 13:1

Jn 1:1–3

cf. Jb 28:28

Prv 26:5;
Rom 1:22

2. (3) So I made my way to Simplicianus, who became father to the then bishop, Ambrose, who really did love him like a father, at the time when the latter received the grace of baptism. I told him how I had been going around in circles of sinfulness. But when I recounted how I had read certain Neoplatonist books that Victorinus,[4] the former professor of rhetoric at Rome, who, so I hear, had died a Christian, had translated into the Latin language, he congratulated me for not having happened upon the writings of other philosophers, for they were full of falsehoods and deceits in accordance with the principles of this world, whereas God and his Word were intimately enmeshed in the Neoplatonist works in every way.

Next, when he urged me to accept the humility of Christ, which is hidden from the wise and revealed to

num ipsum recordatus est, quem Romae cum esset familiarissime noverat, deque illo mihi narravit quod non si-
lebo. habet enim magnam laudem gratiae tuae confitendam
tibi, quemadmodum ille doctissimus senex et omnium liberalium doctrinarum peritissimus quique philosophorum tam multa legerat et diiudicaverat, doctor tot nobi-
lium senatorum, qui etiam ob insigne praeclari magisterii,
quod cives huius mundi eximium putant, statuam Romano
foro meruerat et acceperat, usque ad illam aetatem vene-
rator idolorum sacrorumque sacrilegorum particeps, quibus tunc tota fere Romana nobilitas inflata spirabat, †popi-
liosiam†[2] et omnigenum deum monstra et Anubem
latratorem, quae aliquando contra Neptunum et Venerem
contraque Minervam tela tenuerant et a se victis iam
Roma supplicabat, quae iste senex Victorinus tot annos ore
terricrepo defensitaverat, non erubuerit esse puer Christi
tui et infans fontis tui, subiecto collo ad humilitatis iugum
et edomita fronte ad crucis opprobrium.

(4) O domine, domine, qui inclinasti caelos et descen-
disti, tetigisti montes et fumigaverunt, quibus modis te
insinuasti illi pectori? legebat, sicut ait Simplicianus, sanc-

2 Pompilii deos iam *cj. OD*: popilios iam *S*: popilius iam *D*:
populiosiam *P*: populique iam *G*

5 The text is hopelessly corrupt: OD's conjecture is translated
here: *Pompilii deos iam.* Cf. *Ep.* 102.2.13; *De Civ. D.* 7.35; 3.9–12
for Numa Pompilius ("that most inquisitive of Rome's kings")
introducing gods into Rome.
6 Virg. *Aen.* 8.698–700; cf. Propertius 3.11.41. Anubis is the
dog-headed god in Egyptian mythology.
7 An elaborate way of marking Victorinus' baptism; the peri-

babes, he recalled Victorinus himself, with whom he had   Mt 11:25
been closely acquainted when he was at Rome, and he told
me something of him that I will not fail to mention. Indeed
it expresses great praise of your grace that I must confess
to you. That most learned old man, an expert in all the
liberal disciplines, who had read so much of the philosophers and had judged them against each other, a teacher,
too, of so many high-ranking senators, because of his distinguished teaching record had earned the distinction of
a statue in the forum at Rome, which the citizens of this
world regard as a signal honor, and had agreed to it. Up to
this moment in his life he had been a worshipper of idols
and a participant in the blasphemous rituals that almost
all the Roman aristocracy, in their arrogance, lived and
breathed at that time: the gods of Numa Pompilius[5] and
the "the gods of every kind and Anubis the Barker; they
all bore arms at one time against Neptune, Venus and Mi-
nerva,"[6] and now Rome was on her knees before the gods
she once had conquered. Over many years the old man
Victorinus had often defended those monstrous creatures
in thundering tones. Now he was not ashamed to be a child
of your Christ and a baby baptized by you, bending his
neck to the yoke of humility, his head submitting to the
shame of the cross.[7]   Gal 5:11

(4) O Lord, Lord, you have bowed the heavens and
come down, you have touched the mountains and made
them smoke: by what means did you infiltrate his heart?   Ps 144:5
As Simplicianus told the story, Victorinus was reading the

odic sentence climaxes in the antithesis of *senex* and *puer*; the old
man becomes a child. The cross marked on the forehead is part
of the baptismal rite.

tam scripturam omnesque christianas litteras investigabat
studiosissime et perscrutabatur, et dicebat Simpliciano,
non palam sed secretius et familiarius, "noveris me iam
esse christianum." et respondebat ille, "non credam nec
deputabo te inter christianos, nisi in ecclesia Christi vi-
dero." ille autem inridebat dicens, "ergo parietes faciunt
christianos?" et hoc saepe dicebat, iam se esse christianum, et Simplicianus illud saepe respondebat, et saepe ab
illo parietum inrisio repetebatur. amicos enim suos reve-
rebatur offendere, superbos daemonicolas, quorum ex
culmine Babylonicae dignitatis quasi ex cedris Libani,
quas nondum contriverat dominus, graviter ruituras in se
inimicitias arbitrabatur.

Sed posteaquam legendo et inhiando hausit firmitatem
timuitque negari a Christo coram angelis sanctis, si eum
timeret coram hominibus confiteri, reusque sibi magni
criminis apparuit erubescendo de sacramentis humilitatis
verbi tui et non erubescendo de sacris sacrilegis super-
borum daemoniorum, quae imitator superbus acceperat,
depuduit vanitati et erubuit veritati subitoque et inopina-
tus ait Simpliciano, ut ipse narrabat, "eamus in ecclesiam:
christianus volo fieri." at ille non se capiens laetitia per-
rexit cum eo. ubi autem imbutus est primis instructionis
sacramentis, non multo post etiam nomen dedit ut per
baptismum regeneraretur, mirante Roma, gaudente ecclesia. superbi videbant et irascebantur, dentibus suis stride-

---

8 Cf. Thuc. 7.77.7 for a polity defined by its people not its
surrounding wall.

9 Babylon in the Old Testament is emblematic of pride.

Holy Scriptures and thoroughly examining all the Christian texts and searching through them; and he used to say to Simplicianus, not openly but somewhat privately, between the two of them, "You know that I am already a Christian." And Simplicianus used to reply, "I shall not believe or count you a Christian unless I see you in the Church of Christ." But then he would laugh and say, "So do walls define Christians then?"[8] And he would often declare that he was already a Christian, and Simplicianus would regularly reply in those terms, and he would often repeat his joke about the walls. He was afraid of offending his friends, those proud demon-worshippers, for he thought that their enmities against himself were going to come crashing down from the pinnacle of their Babylonian arrogance,[9] as if from cedars of Lebanon that the Lord had not yet brought down.

Afterward, though, he drew strength from reading and listening and was afraid of being disowned by Christ in the presence of his holy angels if he remained afraid to confess him openly before other people. In his own eyes he stood guilty of a serious charge: being ashamed of the sacrament of humility that is your Word's, and not being ashamed of the blasphemous rites of the proud demons. He had copied their pride in participating in these, brass-faced in his vanity, shame-faced at the truth, and suddenly, unexpectedly, he said to Simplicianus, as he himself used to tell the tale, "Let us go to church: I want to become a Christian." The latter could hardly contain his joy, and off he went with him. So when he was initiated in the primary sacrament as a catechumen, he soon afterward signed up for the rebirth of baptism. Rome was stunned, the Church was delighted. The proud watched and were furious; they

Ps 29:5

Lk 12:9

bant et tabescebant. servo autem tuo dominus deus erat
spes eius, et non respiciebat in vanitates et insanias mendaces.

(5) Denique ut ventum est ad horam profitendae fidei,
quae verbis certis conceptis retentisque memoriter de
loco eminentiore in conspectu populi fidelis Romae reddi
solet ab eis qui accessuri sunt ad gratiam tuam, oblatum
esse dicebat Victorino a presbyteris ut secretius redderet,
sicut nonnullis qui verecundia trepidaturi videbantur of-
ferri mos erat; illum autem maluisse salutem suam in conspectu sanctae multitudinis profiteri. non enim erat salus
quam docebat in rhetorica, et tamen eam publice professus erat. quanto minus ergo vereri debuit mansuetum gre-
gem tuum pronuntians verbum tuum, qui non verebatur
in verbis suis turbas insanorum? itaque ubi ascendit ut
redderet, omnes sibimet invicem, quisque ut eum noverat,
instrepuerunt nomen eius strepitu gratulationis (quis autem ibi non eum noverat?) et sonuit presso sonitu per ora
cunctorum conlaetantium, "Victorinus, Victorinus." cito
sonuerunt exultatione, quia videbant eum, et cito silue-
runt intentione, ut audirent eum. pronuntiavit ille fidem
veracem praeclara fiducia, et volebant eum omnes rapere
intro in cor suum. et rapiebant amando et gaudendo: hae
rapientium manus erant.

3. (6) Deus bone, quid agitur in homine, ut plus gau-

---

10 This "profession of faith" is that now known as the Apostles'
Creed; it was spoken aloud rather than written down (a normal
practice in ancient mystery cults to reserve words of power to the
initiated).

ground their teeth and were consumed with anger. As for   Ps 112:10
your servant, the Lord God was his hope, and he had no
regard any longer for vanities and deceiving madness.   Ps 40:4

(5) At last the time came for making the profession of
faith. Those persons who are about to attain to your grace
usually repeat it[10] from memory according to a set form of
words, in a prominent place and in the sight of the Christian community at Rome. Simplicianus claimed that the
priests had offered Victorinus the chance to repeat the
profession more privately; they had a custom of offering
this to certain individuals who seemed to be rather too shy
and nervous. But he preferred to declare that he was saved
in the sight of the whole company of saints. After all, he
had not usually taught salvation in rhetoric, and he had
still professed that subject before the people. How much
less, then, should he fear the reactions of your peaceable
people when declaring your word, after he had no fear of
raging crowds when relying only on words of his own! So
when he went up to make the profession, one after another all the people, each of those who knew him, shouted
his name in an outburst of rejoicing, and who was there
who did not know him! And there sounded a distinct cry
on the lips of all those who were celebrating with him,
"Victorinus, Victorinus!" Their joy resounded swiftly because they saw him; and their silence followed swiftly because they were concentrating on hearing him. He declared the true faith with conspicuous confidence; and
everyone was longing to gather him into the depths of
their heart. By their love and rejoicing, indeed, they were
reaching out to grasp him: such were the groups of wor-
shippers who took him for their own.

3. (6) Good God, what is it about mortals that makes

deat de salute desperatae animae et de maiore periculo liberatae quam si spes ei semper adfuisset aut periculum minus fuisset? etenim tu quoque, misericors pater, plus gaudes de uno paenitente quam de nonaginta novem iustis quibus non opus est paenitentia. et nos cum magna iucunditate audimus, cum audimus quam exultantibus pastoris umeris reportetur ovis quae erraverat, et drachma referatur in thesauros tuos conlaetantibus vicinis mulieri quae invenit, et lacrimas excutit gaudium sollemnitatis domus tuae, cum legitur in domo tua de minore filio tuo quoniam "mortuus erat et revixit, perierat et inventus est." gaudes quippe in nobis et in angelis tuis sancta caritate sanctis. nam tu semper idem, qui[3] ea quae non semper nec eodem modo sunt eodem modo semper nosti omnia.

(7) Quid ergo agitur in anima, cum amplius delectatur inventis aut redditis rebus quas diligit quam si eas semper habuisset? contestantur enim et cetera et plena sunt omnia testimoniis clamantibus, "ita est." triumphat victor imperator, et non vicisset nisi pugnavisset, et quanto maius periculum fuit in proelio, tanto est gaudium maius in triumpho. iactat tempestas navigantes minaturque naufragium: omnes futura morte pallescunt: tranquillatur caelum et mare, et exultant nimis, quoniam timuerunt nimis. aeger est carus et vena eius malum renuntiat: omnes qui eum salvum cupiunt aegrotant simul animo: fit ei

---

3 qui *codd. Maur.*: quia S *Knöll Skut.*

---

11 Hypallage—the participle "rejoicing" agrees with the "shoulders," not the "shepherd."

12 Literal not metaphorical: a Roman general's honorific military procession following exceptional military success.

366

us rejoice over the salvation of a lost soul set free from serious danger more than if that soul had always dwelt in hope or been in less danger? Even you, merciful Father, rejoice more over one penitent than over ninety-nine righteous persons who do not need to repent. And we listen with great joy when we hear that a sheep which had gone astray is being carried home on the shepherd's shoulders, with rejoicing;[11] and that a coin is returned to your treasure chests amid the rejoicing of the neighbors of the woman who found it; while the joy of the celebration in your house produces weeping, when in your house we read of that younger son who had been dead and is alive again, who had been lost but now was found. Surely you rejoice in us and in your angels who are sanctified by their holy love. For you are always the same: as for what is not eternal and what is not always the same, in one and the same way you know it all, and forever. `Lk 15:4–7`

`Lk 15:5;`
`Ps 119:176`

`Lk 15:8–9`

`Lk 15:24–32`

(7) So what is at work in the soul when it takes more pleasure in whatever it finds or recovers and then loves than it would if it had always possessed them? Other things bear witness to the same, and all kinds of things provide abundant evidence as they call out, "It is true!" A victorious general has his triumph,[12] but if he had never fought he would never have conquered either: the greater the danger in battle, the greater the joy in his triumph. A storm buffets sailors and threatens shipwreck: everyone blanches with fear as death looms. The sky and sea grow calm, and they are overjoyed because just now they were over-fearful. A dear one falls ill and his pulse warns of danger: everyone who longs for him to be well again is sick

recte et nondum ambulat pristinis viribus, et fit iam tale gaudium quale non fuit cum antea salvus et fortis ambularet.

Easque ipsas voluptates humanae vitae etiam non inopinatis et praeter voluntatem inruentibus, sed institutis et voluntariis molestiis homines adquirunt. edendi et bibendi voluptas nulla est, nisi praecedat esuriendi et sitiendi molestia. et ebriosi quaedam salsiuscula comedunt, quo fiat molestus ardor, quem dum exstinguit potatio, fit delectatio. et institutum est ut iam pactae sponsae non tradantur statim, ne vile habeat maritus datam quam non suspiraverit sponsus dilatam.

(8) Hoc in turpi et exsecranda laetitia, hoc in ea quae concessa et licita est, hoc in ipsa sincerissima honestate amicitiae, hoc in eo qui mortuus erat et revixit, perierat et inventus est: ubique maius gaudium molestia maiore praeceditur. quid est hoc, domine deus meus, cum tu aeternum tibi, tu ipse, sis gaudium, et quaedam de te circa te semper gaudeant? quid est quod haec rerum pars alternat defectu et profectu, offensionibus et conciliationibus? an is est modus earum et tantum dedisti eis, cum a summis caelorum usque ad ima terrarum, ab initio usque in finem saeculorum, ab angelo usque ad vermiculum, a motu primo usque ad extremum, omnia genera bonorum et omnia iusta opera tua suis quaeque sedibus locares et suis

at heart. He then recovers, though his walking is no longer as fit as formerly, but still such joy ensues as was never the case before he was ill, when his stride was confident.

These are the actual human pleasures of life that people strive for, not only derived from difficulties that are unexpected and unlooked for but also from those that have been anticipated and willingly accepted. There is no pleasure in eating and drinking unless they are preceded by the discomfort of hunger and thirst. Those who are drunk tend to eat salty snacks to create an uncomfortable longing, and when drinking slakes the thirst it causes pleasure. Likewise it is established custom that young women are not given to their fiancés immediately after the betrothal, so that the husband does not hold her in contempt once he has his bride in his possession, just because he has not languished after her during the interval of their betrothal.

(8) This holds true concerning gratification that is vile and detestable, it holds true concerning what is permissible and lawful, it holds true concerning the purest integrity of friendship, it holds true concerning him who died and came to life again, who was lost and then found: in every case, great joy is preceded by commensurate hardship. Why is this, my Lord and God, when you, your own yourself, are your own eternal joy; and those who dwell about you always rejoice in you? Why is it that one part of things alternates between advance and decline, conflict and reconciliation? Or is this their proper sphere, and this only have you allotted them, although from the heights of heaven down to the depths of the earth, from the beginning to the end of the ages, from the angels to the smallest worm, from the first action to the last, you set all kinds of good things, and all your just works, each in its proper

Lk 15:24, 32

369

quaeque temporibus ageres? ei mihi, quam excelsus es in excelsis et quam profundus in profundis! et nusquam recedis, et vix redimus ad te.

4. (9) Age, domine, fac, excita et revoca nos, accende et rape, flagra,[4] dulcesce: amemus, curramus. nonne multi ex profundiore tartaro caecitatis quam Victorinus redeunt ad te et accedunt et inluminantur recipientes lumen? quod si qui recipiunt, accipiunt a te potestatem ut filii tui fiant. sed si minus noti sunt populis, minus de illis gaudent etiam qui noverunt eos. quando enim cum multis gaudetur, et in singulis uberius est gaudium, quia fervefaciunt se et inflammantur ex alterutro. deinde quod multis noti, multis sunt auctoritati ad salutem et multis praeeunt secuturis, ideoque multum de illis et qui eos praecesserunt laetantur, quia non de solis laetantur.

Absit enim ut in tabernaculo tuo prae pauperibus accipiantur personae divitum aut prae ignobilibus nobiles, quando potius infirma mundi elegisti ut confunderes fortia, et ignobilia huius mundi elegisti et contemptibilia, et ea quae non sunt tamquam sint, ut ea quae sunt evacuares. et tamen idem ipse minimus apostolorum tuorum, per cuius linguam tua ista verba sonuisti, cum Paulus proconsul[5] per eius militiam debellata superbia sub lene iugum Christi tui missus esset, regis magni provincialis effectus,

4 flagra *codd. edd.*: fragla S: fragra *Knöll*
5 proconsul *codd. pauc. Maur.*: pro consule S. *codd. Knöll Skut. Ver.*

13 A. means that they expect others to follow the example of those who convert.

place and activate each one at its proper time? Alas for me! How high you are in the heights, and how unfathomable in the depths! You are nowhere absent, yet we struggle to return to you. `Ps 113:4`

4. (9) Rouse yourself to action, O Lord, summon and call us, kindle and capture us, set us on fire, make yourself desirable to us: let us fall in love, let us run to you! Surely many people return to you from a deeper hell of blindness than Victorinus, and draw near, and are illumined when they are given the light? And if they are given it, they accept from you the power to become your children. But if they are less well-known to the congregations, even those who know them are less delighted for them. This is because when joy arises among many people, even as individuals their joy is more copious, because they fire themselves up, and are also inflamed by one another. Furthermore, because they are known to many, they can influence many toward salvation and they lead the way for many to follow: so also those who have gone before them rejoice greatly over them, because they are rejoicing over more than just individuals.[13] `Ps 34:5` `Jn 1:9, 12`

Heaven forbid that in your tabernacle rich people should be more welcome than poor, or the wellborn than those of baser origin! For you have preferred what is weak in the world, to throw what is strong into confusion, and you have preferred things that are base and scorned, and treated nonentities as if they did exist, so that you could bring to nothing the things which do exist. And still that man who was the least of your apostles, by whose mouth those words of yours resounded, instead of his former name Saul now loved to be called Paul: this was the mark of a great victory when the proconsul Paulus had his `1 Cor 1:27–28; Rom 4:17` `1 Cor 15:9` `Acts 13:7`

ipse quoque ex priore Saulo Paulus vocari amavit ob tam magnae insigne victoriae.

Plus enim hostis vincitur in eo quem plus tenet et de quo plures tenet. plus autem superbos tenet nomine nobilitatis et de his plures nomine auctoritatis. quanto igitur gratius cogitabatur Victorini pectus, quod tamquam inexpugnabile receptaculum diabolus obtinuerat, Victorini lingua, quo telo grandi et acuto multos peremerat, abundantius exultare oportuit filios tuos, quia rex noster alligavit fortem, et videbant vasa eius erepta mundari et aptari in honorem tuum et fieri utilia domino ad omne opus bonum.

5. (10) Sed ubi mihi homo tuus Simplicianus de Victorino ista narravit, exarsi ad imitandum: ad hoc enim et ille narraverat. posteaquam vero et illud addidit, quod imperatoris Iuliani temporibus lege data prohibiti sunt christiani docere litteraturam et oratoriam. quam legem ille amplexus, loquacem scholam deserere maluit quam verbum tuum, quo linguas infantium facis disertas. non mihi fortior quam felicior visus est, quia invenit occasionem vacandi tibi, cui rei ego suspirabam, ligatus non ferro alieno sed mea ferrea voluntate. velle meum tenebat inimicus et inde mihi catenam fecerat et constrinxerat me.

---

14 A reapplication of classical prophecy: Virg. *Aen.* 6.853.

15 Double military metaphor: *provincialis* (inhabitant of a province) to denote lay persons, and *milites* (soldiers) to denote clergy. 16 The enemy is Satan: Mt 13:39, Lk 10:19, Acts 13:10, etc. A.'s expression is congested to construct a paradox that does not stand up to scrutiny. 17 Julian "the Apostate" (AD 331–363); rescript "On Christian Teachers" in *Ep.* 61 (Bidez, *L'empereur Julien*). Cf. Socrates, *Hist. Eccl.* 3.16.

pride conquered[14] by that apostle's campaign, submitted to Christ's easy yoke, and was made a mere ordinary citizen[15] of the High King.

Mt 11:29–30

When the Enemy has great control over a person and through that person controls still more people, his overthrow is proportionately greater too: he has more control over those who are proud because they have noble titles, and through them he controls yet more people who hold the power of political office.[16] So the heart of Victorinus was regarded with all the more gladness, because the devil had considered it as an invincible stronghold; and the tongue of Victorinus, a terrible sharp sword for annihilating multitudes: it was right that your children should exult more plenteously, because our King has bound the strong man, and they saw his capacities taken away to be cleansed and made fit for your honor, and becoming useful to the Lord for every good work.

Mt 12:29

2 Tm 2:21

5. (10) But when your servant Simplicianus recounted all this to me about Victorinus, I was on fire with enthusiasm to follow his example. Indeed that was why he had told the story. Later he added the fact that during the reign of the emperor Julian Christians were prohibited by law from teaching literature and oratory.[17] Victorinus had accepted this law: he preferred to abandon a school of wordiness rather than your Word by whom you make eloquent the tongues of infants. He seemed to me to be as courageous as he was fortunate, because he found an opportunity of becoming open to you. I myself was longing for this very thing, yet I was bound: not by someone else's iron chains but by my own iron will. The enemy still held sway over the exercise of my will, and from that had fashioned a chain for me and bound me in fetters. In fact, my feelings

Ws 10:21;
Ps 8:2

quippe ex voluntate perversa facta est libido, et dum servitur libidini, facta est consuetudo, et dum consuetudini non resistitur, facta est necessitas. quibus quasi ansulis sibimet innexis (unde catenam appellavi) tenebat me obstrictum dura servitus.

Voluntas autem nova quae mihi esse coeperat, ut te gratis colerem fruique te vellem, deus, sola certa iucunditas, nondum erat idonea ad superandam priorem vetustate roboratam. ita duae voluntates meae, una vetus, alia nova, illa carnalis, illa spiritalis, confligebant inter se atque discordando dissipabant animam meam.

(11) Sic intellegebam me ipso experimento id quod legeram, quomodo caro concupisceret adversus spiritum et spiritus adversus carnem, ego quidem in utroque, sed magis ego in eo quod in me approbabam quam in eo quod in me improbabam. ibi enim magis iam non ego, quia ex magna parte id patiebar invitus quam faciebam volens, sed tamen consuetudo adversus me pugnacior ex me facta erat, quoniam volens quo nollem perveneram. et quis iure contradiceret, cum peccantem iusta poena sequeretur? et non erat iam illa excusatio qua videri mihi solebam propterea me nondum contempto saeculo servire tibi, quia incerta mihi esset perceptio veritatis: iam enim et ipsa certa erat. ego autem adhuc terra obligatus militare tibi

---

18 Literally, "fleshly." Cf. *Conf.* 1.6.7, n. 17.

of sexual desire were formed out of the perversion of my will. While my will was in thrall to sexual desire, it grew into a habitual behavior: while I was capitulating to that habitual behavior, it grew into something I could not live without. These quite small links joined themselves together into the bond I called my chain: it was a cruel slavery that had me in shackles.

Yet I had begun to own a new will, a wish to worship you voluntarily and to enjoy you, O God, the only sure pleasure; but it was not yet ready to overcome my former will, strengthened as it was by its long duration. And so my two wills, one old, the other new, one physical,[18] the other spiritual, were in conflict with one another and by their strife were shattering my soul.

(11) Thus I was my own test case: and I began to understand what I had read, how the flesh has desires in opposition to the spirit and the spirit has desires in opposition to the flesh. I was enmeshed in both but more in Gal 5:17 the form of desire that I approved of in myself than in the one I disapproved of. No more did I venture in that direction, because I was to a great extent already enduring it against my will rather than engaging in it willingly. Even so, force of habit had become stronger to subvert me, for of my own free will I had come to a place I was unwilling to be. Who could reasonably speak in my defense, since the punishment that pursues a sinner is just? No longer cf. Prv 13:21 did I have that excuse with which I habitually contented myself, namely that I had not yet spurned the world and begun to serve you because my comprehension of truth was still unconfirmed: for now it was indeed confirmed. But I was still in bondage to the earth, and persisted in

recusabam et impedimentis omnibus sic timebam expediri, quemadmodum impediri timendum est.

(12) Ita sarcina saeculi, velut somno adsolet, dulciter premebar, et cogitationes quibus meditabar in te similes erant conatibus expergisci volentium, qui tamen superati soporis altitudine remerguntur. et sicut nemo est qui dormire semper velit omniumque sano iudicio vigilare praestat, differt tamen plerumque homo somnum excutere cum gravis torpor in membris est, eumque iam displicentem carpit libentius quamvis surgendi tempus advenerit: ita certum habebam esse melius tuae caritati me dedere quam meae cupiditati cedere, sed illud placebat et vincebat, hoc libebat et vinciebat.

Non enim erat quod tibi responderem dicenti mihi, "surge qui dormis et exsurge a mortuis, et inluminabit te Christus," et undique ostendenti vera te dicere, non erat omnino quid responderem veritate convictus, nisi tantum verba lenta et somnolenta: "modo," "ecce modo," "sine paululum." sed "modo et modo" non habebat modum et "sine paululum" in longum ibat. frustra condelectabar legi tuae secundum interiorem hominem, cum alia lex in membris meis repugnaret legi mentis meae et captivum me duceret in lege peccati quae in membris meis erat. lex enim peccati est violentia consuetudinis, qua trahitur et

---

19 A. continues the military metaphor—*sarcina* is a soldier's pack.

refusing to serve in your army; I was as afraid of being relieved of all my burdens as I should have been at shouldering them! 2 Tm 2:3–4

(12) So I was being pleasantly laden with worldly baggage[19] as sometimes happens during sleep, and the reflections by which I was meditating on you were like the efforts of people who try to awaken but are overwhelmed and plunged back into a deep slumber. And just as no one wants to sleep all the time, and the sensible consensus gives preference to being awake, still a lot of people delay shaking off sleep because they feel a heavy lethargy in their limbs, which agreeably weakens their resolve despite their intention, and although the time to get up is at hand. Likewise I was convinced that it was better for me to give myself up to your love than to give myself up to my desire; but although the former course of action was both attractive and convincing, the former was more tempting and had me in its coils. Ps 63:7

So there was nothing for me to say in reply to your words to me, "Get up, you who are asleep, and arise from the dead, and Christ will give you light." In every direction you made it clear that you were speaking the truth, and I was convinced by your truth, and there was absolutely nothing I could say in reply excepting only slothful, sleepy words: "In a moment," "Look, just wait a moment," "Give me just a second." As for "in a moment, yes a moment," the moment never came, and as for "give me a second," that second just went on and on. It was in vain that I delighted in your law in my innermost self, when another law, the one at work in my physical body, was rebelling against the law of my mind and leading me captive in the law of sin which was in my physical body. For the law of sin is Eph 5:14

Rom 7:22–2

377

tenetur etiam invitus animus eo merito quo in eam volens inlabitur. miserum ergo me quis liberaret de corpore mortis huius nisi gratia tua per Iesum Christum, dominum nostrum?

6. (13) Et de vinculo quidem desiderii concubitus, quo artissimo tenebar, et saecularium negotiorum servitute quemadmodum me exemeris, narrabo et confitebor nomini tuo, domine, adiutor meus et redemptor meus. agebam solita, crescente anxitudine, et cotidie suspirabam tibi. frequentabam ecclesiam tuam, quantum vacabat ab eis negotiis sub quorum pondere gemebam. mecum erat Alypius otiosus ab opere iuris peritorum post adsessionem tertiam, expectans quibus iterum consilia venderet, sicut ego vendebam dicendi facultatem, si qua docendo praestari potest. Nebridius autem amicitiae nostrae cesserat, ut omnium nostrum familiarissimo Verecundo, Mediolanensi et civi et grammatico, subdoceret, vehementer desideranti et familiaritatis iure flagitanti de numero nostro fidele adiutorium, quo indigebat nimis. non itaque Nebridium cupiditas commodorum eo traxit (maiora enim posset, si vellet, de litteris agere) sed officio benivolentiae petitionem nostram contemnere noluit, amicus dulcissimus et mitissimus. agebat autem illud prudentissime cavens innotescere personis secundum hoc saeculum

---

20 Cf. *Conf.* 6.10.16.

21 Owner of the estate at Cassiciacum (near Milan), where A. gathered a small community after his conversion: cf. *Conf.* 9.7.4.

22 Cf. *Conf.* 1.13.20, and Introduction, p. xxii.

the brutality of habitual behavior: it drags and masters the mind even against its will, and it deserves this, because it sinks into such habits of its own free will. Wretch that I am, who will rescue me from this body of death, if not your grace through Jesus Christ, our Lord?

6. (13) So now I shall now relate how you delivered me from the chains of sexual desire, by which I was so tightly constrained, and from my enslavement to worldly affairs; and I shall confess your name, O Lord, my helper and my redeemer. I carried on with my usual activities, but my anguish mounted, and every day I was longing for you. I attended your church constantly, as often as I had time off from the duties of my employment, for I was groaning under the burden of them. Alypius was with me. He was having a break from his work as a legal expert after his third term as an assessor[20] and looking around him for clients to whom he could sell his legal services next, in the same way as I was selling my talent for public speaking, if indeed teaching can impart such excellence. But Nebridius had made a concession to our friendship by agreeing to do a little teaching under that very dear friend of us all, Verecundus,[21] who was both a citizen and a grammarian[22] of Milan and who was most eager for, and by right of friendship even demanded the reliable assistance from one of us that he urgently needed. It was not desire for advantage that attracted Nebridius, for if he so wished he could do better in this respect from his scholarship, but being the dearest and kindest of friends, he was unwilling to reject our request in regard for our friendship. So Nebridius accomplished the task with the utmost discretion, taking care not to attract the attention of persons of importance in the eyes of the world. In such matters, there-

Ps 19:14, 54:6

379

maioribus, devitans in eis omnem inquietudinem animi,
quem volebat habere liberum et quam multis posset horis
feriatum ad quaerendum aliquid vel legendum vel audiendum de sapientia.

(14) Quodam igitur die (non recolo causam qua erat
absens Nebridius) cum ecce ad nos domum venit ad me
et Alypium Ponticianus quidam, civis noster in quantum
Afer, praeclare in palatio militans: nescio quid a nobis
volebat. et consedimus ut conloqueremur. et forte supra
mensam lusoriam quae ante nos erat attendit codicem.
tulit, aperuit, invenit apostolum Paulum, inopinate sane:
putaverat enim aliquid de libris quorum professio me
conterebat. tum vero arridens meque intuens gratulatorie
miratus est, quod eas et solas prae oculis meis litteras repente comperisset. christianus quippe et fidelis erat, et
saepe tibi, deo nostro, prosternebatur in ecclesia crebris
et diuturnis orationibus.

Cui ego cum indicassem illis me scripturis curam maxi-
mam impendere, ortus est sermo ipso narrante de Antonio
Aegyptio monacho, cuius nomen excellenter clarebat
apud servos tuos, nos autem usque in illam horam latebat.
quod ille ubi comperit, immoratus est in eo sermone, insi-
nuans tantum virum ignorantibus et admirans eandem
nostram ignorantiam. stupebamus autem audientes tam
recenti memoria et prope nostris temporibus testatissima
mirabilia tua in fide recta et catholica ecclesia. omnes

---

23 Otherwise unknown.   24 As the book is a *codex* not
a *volumen* it is "opened," not "unrolled."   25 The monastic
life of Antony of Egypt (AD ca. 251–ca. 356) was recorded in a
work attributed to Athanasius of Alexandria (AD ca. 298–373).
Cf. A. *Conf.* 8.12.29; *Doctr. Chr.* preface §4. Evagrius of Antioch
(AD 349–399) translated the *Vita Antoni* into Latin.

fore, he avoided any disturbance of mind, for he wanted his mind to be kept free and unengaged for as much time as possible, to allow for doing a piece of research, or reading, or listening to something about wisdom.

(14) One day, then, when Nebridius was away (I do not remember why), look! someone came to the house to see us, namely me, Alypius and Ponticianus.[23] He was a fellow citizen of ours in that he was African, and he held a position of distinction at court. I do not know what he wanted from us. Anyway we sat down and talked with one another. Then he happened to notice a book on the side-table, which was in front of us. He picked it up, opened it,[24] found the apostle Paul: this was certainly unforeseen, because he had expected it to be something from the books which I was wearing myself down teaching. At that point he smiled as he looked at me, expressing his congratulations and surprise alike that he had unexpectedly found these works and these alone before my eyes. He was himself a Christian, certainly, and had been baptized; in church he often prostrated himself before you, our God, with continual daily prayers.

When I explained to him that I attached the highest importance to those Scriptures, it prompted him to tell the story of the monk Antony of Egypt,[25] whose reputation was outstandingly distinguished among your servants, though up until that moment it was unknown to us. Once he realized this, he lingered over that story, recommending the great man to us, though we knew nothing of him, and expressing his surprise at our ignorance. We were staggered to hear that in recent memory, almost in our own times, your wonderful works were so completely manifested in proper faith and in the Catholic Church. All

mirabamur, et nos, quia tam magna erant, et ille, quia inaudita nobis erant.

(15) Inde sermo eius devolutus est ad monasteriorum greges et mores suaveolentiae tuae et ubera deserta heremi, quorum nos nihil sciebamus. et erat monasterium Mediolanii plenum bonis fratribus extra urbis moenia sub Ambrosio nutritore, et non noveramus. pertendebat ille et loquebatur adhuc, et nos intenti tacebamus. unde incidit ut diceret nescio quando se et tres alios contubernales suos, nimirum apud Treveros, cum imperator promeridiano circensium spectaculo teneretur, exisse deambulatum in hortos muris contiguos atque illic, ut forte combinati spatiabantur, unum secum seorsum et alios duos itidem seorsum pariterque digressos; sed illos vagabundos inruisse in quandam casam ubi habitabant quidam servi tui spiritu pauperes, qualium est regnum caelorum, et invenisse ibi codicem in quo scripta erat vita Antonii. quam legere coepit unus eorum et mirari et accendi, et inter legendum meditari arripere talem vitam et relicta militia saeculari servire tibi. erant autem ex eis quos dicunt agentes in rebus. tum subito repletus amore sancto et sobrio pudore, iratus sibi, coniecit oculos in amicum et ait illi, "dic, quaeso te, omnibus istis laboribus nostris quo ambimus pervenire? quid quaerimus? cuius rei causa militamus? maiorne esse poterit spes nostra in palatio

---

26 An allusion to the smell of a burned sacrifice: e.g., Gn 8:21.

27 Former capital of the western empire. Athanasius may have brought the eremitic life there during his exile of 335–337.

28 This garden location parallels A.'s looming garden encounter at *Conf.* 8.8.19.   29 A privileged group of officials employed by the later emperors on confidential matters.

of us were amazed, we because they were so momentous, and he because we had never heard of them.

(15) Then his story got around to the flocks in the monasteries and their customs (which were a pleasing savor[26] to you) and the fruitful barrenness of the desert, of which we were altogether ignorant. There was a monastery in Milan, full of faithful brothers; it was outside the city walls, but under the care of Ambrose, and we did not know! He went on with his story and spoke at length, and we listened in rapt silence. So it happened that he began to tell us of a time when he and three other people who were friends of his, at Trier as a matter of fact,[27] left to stroll into the gardens[28] alongside the walls, while the emperor was detained by the morning show at the circus. They paired off to go walking about, one separately with him and the other two likewise wandering off by themselves. During their stroll this other pair happened to chance upon a dwelling where some of your servants were living, men poor in spirit, and the kingdom of heaven consists of such people. There the two of them discovered a book containing the life of Antony. One of them began to read it and to be amazed, and to be kindled; and while the reading was going on he was thinking how to adopt such a way of life, to abandon his imperial service and serve you. They were from the company of men known as special agents.[29] The one suddenly felt himself full of a holy love and clearheaded sense of remorse: angry with himself, he turned his gaze upon his friend and said to him, "Tell me, please; in all these works of ours, what is it that we are aiming to achieve? What are we seeking? For whose cause are we campaigning? Can we find some higher hope than achiev-

cf. Acts 20:28–29; 1 Pt 5:2–3

Mt 5:3

quam ut amici imperatoris simus? et ibi quid non fragile plenumque periculis? et per quot pericula pervenitur ad grandius periculum? et quando istuc erit? amicus autem dei, si voluero, ecce nunc fio."

Dixit hoc et turbidus parturitione novae vitae reddidit oculos paginis. et legebat et mutabatur intus, ubi tu videbas, et exuebatur mundo mens eius, ut mox apparuit. namque dum legit et volvit fluctus cordis sui, infremuit aliquando et discrevit decrevitque meliora, iamque tuus ait amico suo, "ego iam abrupi me ab illa spe nostra et deo servire statui, et hoc ex hac hora, in hoc loco aggredior. te si piget imitari, noli adversari." respondit ille adhaerere se socium tantae mercedis tantaeque militiae. et ambo iam tui aedificabant turrem sumptu idoneo relinquendi omnia sua et sequendi te.

Tunc Ponticianus et qui cum eo per alias horti partes deambulabat, quaerentes eos, devenerunt in eundem locum et invenientes admonuerunt ut redirent, quod iam declinasset dies. at illi, narrato placito et proposito suo quoque modo in eis talis voluntas orta esset atque firmata, petiverunt ne sibi molesti essent si adiungi recusarent. isti

---

30 A select group instituted by the emperor Augustus.

ing the status of 'friends of the emperor' at court?[30] And is anything in that environment lasting or free from dangers? How many such dangers must we pass through, just to encounter still greater danger? When will this be achieved? But if I want to be a friend of God, look: I can become one immediately!"

So he spoke, and, struggling to give birth to this new life, he turned his eyes back to the pages. And he went on reading and was inwardly changed, where you looked on, Mt 6:18 and his mind shook off the world, as quickly became apparent. For while he was reading and reflecting on his heart's fluctuations, he stormed at himself sporadically and determined and decided upon a better course. And now he belongs to you, and says to his friend, "I have rescued myself from that former ambition of ours and have decided to serve God: and this, from this moment, in this place, is to be my goal. If you are too embarrassed to follow my example, at least do not oppose it." His friend replied that he would stick by his companion in pursuit of such a prize and such a contest. And now they both belonged to you and were building a strong tower with sufficient funds, Lk 14:28 by giving up everything and following you. Mt 4:20

Then Ponticianus and the companion who was strolling with him in another part of the garden went to look for them and found them in the same place; and when they found them they reminded them to go back, because the day was already coming to an end. But those two explained their resolution and proposal, and how their choice had originated and become settled. They requested that if Ponticianus and his companion decided against joining in, they would nonetheless not try to oppose them. Although Ponticianus and his companion were not at all changed

385

autem nihilo[6] mutati a pristinis fleverunt se tamen, ut dicebat, atque illis pie congratulati sunt, et commendaverunt se orationibus eorum et trahentes cor in terra abierunt in palatium, illi autem affigentes cor caelo manserunt in casa. et habebant ambo sponsas quae, posteaquam hoc audierunt, dicaverunt etiam ipsae virginitatem tibi.

7. (16) Narrabat haec Ponticianus. tu autem, domine, inter verba eius retorquebas me ad me ipsum, auferens me a dorso meo, ubi me posueram dum nollem me attendere, et constituebas me ante faciem meam, ut viderem quam turpis essem, quam distortus et sordidus, maculosus et ulcerosus. et videbam et horrebam, et quo a me fugerem non erat. sed si conabar avertere a me aspectum, narrabat ille quod narrabat, et tu me rursus opponebas mihi et impingebas me in oculos meos, ut invenirem iniquitatem meam et odissem. noveram eam, sed dissimulabam et cohibebam et obliviscebar.

(17) Tunc vero quanto ardentius amabam illos de quibus audiebam salubres affectus, quod se totos tibi sanandos dederunt, tanto exsecrabilius me comparatum eis oderam, quoniam multi mei anni mecum effluxerant (forte duodecim anni) ex quo ab undevicensimo anno aetatis meae, lecto Ciceronis Hortensio, excitatus eram studio sapientiae et differebam contempta felicitate terrena

---

6 nihilo *codd. Maur. Ver.*: nihil S *Knöll Skut.*

---

31 Vivid metaphor; unparalleled in Scripture or classical literature (but cf. Virg. *Aen.* 5.468): A. means that they were still attached to earthly things.

32 A. echoes Sen. *Dial.* 3 (*de ira*), 2.36.1, as well as Lk 16:20[VL]; cf. A. *En. Ps.* 33.2.25 (on verses 22–23).

from their former ways they still wept, so Ponticianus told us, and offered the other two their sincere congratulations, and asked that they would remember them in their prayers. Then they departed for the imperial residence, dragging their hearts in the dust,[31] while the other two fixed their hearts on heaven and remained in the poor dwelling. Both of them had been engaged to be married, and after their future wives heard about this, they too consecrated their virginity to you.

7. (16) Such was Ponticianus' story. But while he spoke, Lord, you were wrenching me back toward myself, taking me away from the place behind my back where I had set myself while I was refusing to look properly at myself. And you placed me before my very eyes so that I could see how vile I was, how deformed and filthy, how besmirched and full of sores.[32] And I did see, and was horrified, and I had nowhere to run to away from myself. But if I tried to turn my gaze away from myself he kept on telling his tale, and once again you set me against myself and impressed me upon my own eyes, so that I would find out my own sin and hate it. I knew it all right, but I was pretending I did not, and was suppressing and forgetting it.

(17) From that time, indeed, the more intensely I loved those salutary intentions that I heard of, because they gave themselves up completely to you for healing, the more I came to detest and loathe myself in comparison with them. After all, many years of my life, twelve years, perhaps, had by now trickled away, as I myself had likewise, since that nineteenth year of my life when I had read Cicero's *Hortensius* and had been roused by a thirst for wisdom: and even though I had already despised earthly pros-

Ps 50:21

cf. Ps 139:7

387

ad eam investigandam vacare, cuius non inventio sed vel sola inquisitio iam praeponenda erat etiam inventis thesauris regnisque gentium et ad nutum circumfluentibus corporis voluptatibus. at ego adulescens miser valde, miser in exordio ipsius adulescentiae, etiam petieram a te castitatem et dixeram, "da mihi castitatem et continentiam, sed noli modo." timebam enim ne me cito exaudires et cito sanares a morbo concupiscentiae, quem malebam expleri quam exstingui. et ieram per vias pravas superstitione sacrilega, non quidem certus in ea sed quasi praeponens eam ceteris, quae non pie quaerebam sed inimice oppugnabam.

(18) Et putaveram me propterea differre de die in diem contempta spe saeculi te solum sequi, quia non mihi apparebat certum aliquid quo dirigerem cursum meum. et venerat dies quo nudarer mihi et increparet in me conscientia mea: "ubi est lingua? nempe tu dicebas propter incertum verum nolle te abicere sarcinam vanitatis. ecce iam certum est, et illa te adhuc premit, umerisque liberioribus pinnas recipiunt qui neque ita in quaerendo attriti sunt nec decennio et amplius ista meditati." ita rodebar intus et confundebar pudore horribili vehementer, cum Ponticianus talia loqueretur. terminato autem sermone et

---

33 In Scripture, wings are a divine attribute; cf. Ps 17:8, etc. A. is also thinking of the philosopher's reward of wings in Pl. *Phaedr.* 249.

perity I was putting off making time to seek that wisdom out, even though not only finding it but even the simple act of seeking it ought to be preferable to discovering hoards of treasure and kingdoms of the world, or to copious physical pleasures on demand. But in my youth I was utterly wretched, wretched in the beginning of adolescence; I had even asked you for chastity and had said, "Grant me chastity and celibacy, but not just yet!" For I was afraid that you would hear me straightaway and would cleanse me of the disease of desiring, which I would much rather have explored than expunged! So I had continued through wicked ways in my unholy superstition, certainly not because I was sure about it but rather as if I preferred it to the alternatives, which I struggled against as if they were the enemy, rather than dutifully seeking them out.

Sir 2:16

(18) I had thought that I was postponing from one day to the next a decision to spurn worldly ambition and follow you alone only because I could see no clear target at which to direct my course. The day had come when I was to be laid bare to myself, and my conscience was crying out against me, "Where is that fluent tongue now? You definitely used to say that you were unwilling—because truth is uncertain—to cast aside your burden of vanity. But look! Now it *is* certain, and still the burden is weighing you down. In contrast, those who have not been so ground down with searching and who have not been pondering all that for a decade and more, their shoulders are eased and they are given wings instead."[33] Thus was I being gnawed from within and completely overwhelmed by a dreadful sense of shame, while Ponticianus was recounting his story. When his story, and the reason for his coming, were concluded, he went his way, and I turned to

Ps 55:6; cf.
Rv 12:14

causa qua venerat, abiit ille, et ego ad me. quae non in me dixi? quibus sententiarum verberibus non flagellavi animam meam, ut sequeretur me conantem post te ire? et renitebatur, recusabat, et non se excusabat. consumpta erant et convicta argumenta omnia. remanserat muta trepidatio et quasi mortem reformidabat restringi a fluxu consuetudinis, quo tabescebat in mortem.

8. (19) Tum in illa grandi rixa interioris domus meae, quam fortiter excitaveram cum anima mea in cubiculo nostro, corde meo, tam vultu quam mente turbatus invado Alypium: exclamo, "quid patimur? quid est hoc? quid audisti? surgunt indocti et caelum rapiunt, et nos cum doctrinis nostris sine corde, ecce ubi volutamur in carne et sanguine! an quia praecesserunt, pudet sequi et non pudet nec saltem sequi?" dixi nescio qua talia, et abripuit me ab illo aestus meus, cum taceret attonitus me intuens. neque enim solita sonabam. plus loquebantur animum meum frons, genae, oculi, color, modus vocis quam verba quae promebam.

Hortulus quidam erat hospitii nostri, quo nos utebamur sicut tota domo: nam hospes ibi non habitabat, dominus domus. illuc me abstulerat tumultus pectoris, ubi nemo impediret ardentem litem quam mecum aggressus eram, donec exiret—qua tu sciebas, ego autem non: sed tantum insaniebam salubriter et moriebar vitaliter, gnarus quid mali essem et ignarus quid boni post paululum futu-

---

34 A decisive shift from words into silence.

35 As elsewhere in A., *cubiculum* (chamber) is used metaphorically of the heart: cf. *S. Dom. M.* 2.3.11; *En. Ps.* 35.5; *Io. Ev. Tr.* 10.1.   36 These verbs are in the historic present tense: the switch is markedly vivid.

myself. What did I not accuse myself of? With what rods of condemnation did I not lash my soul, to make it follow me as I tried to go after you? And it resisted, recoiled, but did not excuse itself. Every argument was exhausted and refuted. All that was left was a wordless agitation,[34] and my soul shuddered as if it were death to be restrained from its lax habits, though in fact they were making it disintegrate into death.

8. (19) The fierce quarrel, which I had provoked against my soul in the chamber of my heart,[35] went on in my interior dwelling, and my expression was as troubled as my mind. Then I seize upon Alypius, I cry out,[36] "What is wrong with us? What is it that you have heard? People with no education are rising up and seizing heaven, and we, with all our learning, look on! We are entangled in flesh and blood! Or is it just because they have gone first that we are ashamed to follow, or at any rate we are not ashamed *not* to follow?" I said something along these lines, but when he looked at me in silent amazement, my torment carried me away from him. I did not sound like I usually did. My forehead, cheeks, eyes, complexion, tone of voice, all spoke my mind more clearly than the words I was uttering.

There was a little garden at our lodgings, which we made use of along with the rest of the house, for our host, the master of the house, did not live there. The turmoil in my breast had taken me there, where no one would get in the way of the passionate disputation that I had undertaken within myself, until it resulted—in what? You knew, but I did not, but I was out of my mind for my own good, and I was dying in such a way as to live. I knew that I was 2 Cor 6:9 an evil creature and I had no idea how good a creature I

391

rus essem. abscessi ergo in hortum, et Alypius pedem post pedem. neque enim secretum meum non erat, ubi ille aderat. aut quando me sic affectum desereret? sedimus quantum potuimus remoti ab aedibus. ego fremebam spiritu, indignans indignatione turbulentissima quod non irem in placitum et pactum tecum, deus meus, in quod eundum esse omnia ossa mea clamabant et in caelum tollebant laudibus. et non illuc ibatur navibus aut quadrigis aut pedibus, quantum saltem de domo in eum locum ieram ubi sedebamus. nam non solum ire verum etiam pervenire illuc nihil erat aliud quam velle ire, sed velle fortiter et integre, non semisauciam hac atque hac versare et iactare voluntatem parte adsurgente cum alia parte cadente luctantem.

(20) Denique tam multa faciebam corpore in ipsis cunctationis aestibus, quae aliquando volunt homines et non valent, si aut ipsa membra non habeant aut ea vel conligata vinculis vel resoluta languore vel quoquo modo impedita sint. si vulsi capillum, si percussi frontem, si consertis digitis amplexatus sum genu, quia volui, feci. potui autem velle et non facere, si mobilitas membrorum non obsequeretur. tam multa ergo feci, ubi non hoc erat velle quod posse: et non faciebam quod et incomparabili affectu amplius mihi placebat, et mox ut vellem possem, quia mox ut vellem, utique vellem. ibi enim facultas ea,

---

37 As often, the context of the Scriptural quotation is significant—A. is following the example of Christ.

38 Cf. *Conf.* 1.6.8: a regression to infant helplessness.

39 A. thinks of both good intentions unfulfilled (e.g., Mt 26:41) and male sexual arousal in terms of movement of a limb (*membrum*) outside the control of the will: cf. e.g., *De civ. D.* 14.23.

might become a short while later. So I withdrew into the garden, and Alypius followed in my footsteps. It was not the case that when he came with me I had no privacy; after all, how could he abandon me in such distress? We sat down as far away from the house as possible. I was groaning in spirit,[37] I was furiously indignant that I could not enter into a covenant and agreement with you, my God, when all my bones were crying out that I should do so, and were praising it to the skies. There is no going there by boat or chariot, or on foot; it is not even as far as my movement from the house to this place where we were sitting. For not only heading there but also arriving there was simply a matter of having the will to go there; but it must be a constant and complete willingness, with no tossing and turning a half-wounded will this way and that, hesitating while one part seeks to ascend and the other to sink.

Jn 11:33, 38

Ps 35:10

(20) At last, amid these very torments of indecision, the bodily gestures I made were like the ones people sometimes make when they have the will but not the strength,[38] for example if they do not have the necessary limbs, or those limbs are bound in chains or enfeebled by weakness, or hampered in some other way. If I pulled out my hair, if I beat my breast, if I linked my fingers and hugged my knees, I did so because I wanted to. But I could have had the will and still not acted, if my limbs' capacity for movement had been unable to obey me.[39] I did so many things, then, where being willing was not the same as being able; but I was not doing what I was infinitely more eagerly resolved on, which as soon as I willed it I could attain, because as soon as I willed it I would be willing! For in that circumstance, the ability was identical with the will,

393

quae voluntas, et ipsum velle iam facere erat; et tamen non
fiebat, faciliusque obtemperabat corpus tenuissimae voluntati animae, ut ad nutum membra moverentur, quam
ipsa sibi anima ad voluntatem suam magnam in sola voluntate perficiendam.

9. (21) Unde hoc monstrum? et quare istuc? luceat
misericordia tua, et interrogem, si forte mihi respondere
possint latebrae poenarum hominum et tenebrosissimae
contritiones filiorum Adam. unde hoc monstrum? et quare
istuc? imperat animus corpori, et paretur statim; imperat
animus sibi, et resistitur. imperat animus ut moveatur
manus, et tanta est facilitas ut vix a servitio discernatur
imperium: et animus animus est, manus autem corpus est.
imperat animus ut velit animus, nec alter est nec facit tamen.

Unde hoc monstrum? et quare istuc, inquam, ut velit
qui non imperaret nisi vellet, et non facit quod imperat?
sed non ex toto vult: non ergo ex toto imperat. nam in
tantum imperat, in quantum vult, et in tantum non fit
quod imperat, in quantum non vult, quoniam voluntas
imperat ut sit voluntas, nec alia, sed ipsa. non itaque plena
imperat; ideo non est quod imperat. nam si plena esset,
nec imperaret ut esset, quia iam esset. non igitur mon-

---

40 Double perspective: A.'s apostrophe at the time, and his
later reflection when writing *Conf.*

41 Cf. *Conf.* 1.8.14.

42 A. uses "will" (*voluntas*) in two senses: the capacity for volition, and the thing that is willed.

and to be willing was the same as already doing. But still it was not coming to pass; instead my body was all too easily controlling the feeble will of my soul to move its limbs on demand, instead of the soul obeying itself to accomplish, in its will alone, its own robust will.

9. (21) Where does this perversion come from?[40] And what is its purpose? Let the light of your mercy illuminate this question, and let me ask whether perhaps the enigma of human sufferings, and the darkened griefs of Adam's offspring, can reply.[41] Where does this perversion come from? And what is its purpose? The mind rules over the body and is instantly obeyed, but when the mind rules over itself it is resisted. The mind commands a hand to move, and so prompt is the response that the command is virtually indistinguishable from the obedient response. Yet mind is mind, but the hand is part of the body. It is the mind, and not something else, that commands what the mind is to will, and yet it does not accomplish what it wills.

Where does this perversion come from? And what is its purpose, I say, that it should will something, and it would not so command unless it willed it, and still does not do what it tells itself to? In fact it does not exercise its will completely. For this reason it does not have complete command. Insofar as it commands, to that extent does it exercise its will; and insofar as it does not accomplish what it commands, to that extent does it really will it: for the will commands into being that will, which is none other than itself.[42] So it does not have complete command, and therefore it cannot be identical with the things which it commands. For if its command were complete, it would not command itself to exist, because it would exist already. It is not, therefore, a perversion to be partly willing, and

cf. Jas 4:1

395

strum partim velle, partim nolle, sed aegritudo animi est,
quia non totus adsurgit veritate consuetudine praegrava-
tus. et ideo sunt duae voluntates, quia una earum tota non
est et hoc adest alteri quod deest alteri.

10. (22) Pereant a facie tua, deus, sicuti pereunt, vani-
loqui et mentis seductores qui, cum duas voluntates in
deliberando animadverterint, duas naturas duarum men-
tium esse adseverant, unam bonam, alteram malam. ipsi
vere mali sunt, cum ista mala sentiunt, et idem ipsi boni
erunt, si vera senserint verisque consenserint, ut dicat eis
apostolus tuus, "fuistis aliquando tenebrae, nunc autem
lux in domino." illi enim dum volunt esse lux, non in domino sed in se ipsis, putando animae naturam hoc esse
quod deus est, ita facti sunt densiores tenebrae, quoniam
longius a te recesserunt horrenda arrogantia, a te vero
lumine inluminante omnem hominem venientem in hunc
mundum. attendite quid dicatis, et erubescite et accedite
ad eum et inluminamini, et vultus vestri non erubescent.

Ego cum deliberabam ut iam servirem domino deo
meo, sicut diu disposueram, ego eram qui volebam, ego
qui nolebam: ego eram. nec plene volebam nec plene
nolebam. ideo mecum contendebam et dissipabar a me
ipso, et ipsa dissipatio me invito quidem fiebat, nec tamen
ostendebat naturam mentis alienae sed poenam meae. et

---

[43] Cf. *Conf.* 8.5.10.

partly unwilling; but it is a sickness of the mind. This is because the mind cannot rise up completely by means of the truth, for it is already weighed down with habit. So there are two wills, because each of them is incomplete, and each has what the other lacks.

10. (22) Let them perish from your sight, O God, just as those people perish whose talk is vanity and who seduce the minds of others, who, once they have noticed that in our decision-making there are two wills present, proceed to claim that there are two natures that exist in two minds, one good, the other evil. Certainly they themselves are evil when they hold those evil beliefs, and in the same way anyone is good who holds to truths and agrees with truths. As your apostle says to them, "Once you were darkness, but now you are light in the Lord." Although those people want to be light, they are not in the Lord but instead immersed in themselves, because they think that the nature of the soul can be identical with God. So they have become deeper darkness, because their dreadful arrogance has drawn them away from you, and you are the true light that enlightens every human being who comes into the world. Just listen to what you are saying, and blush with shame, and draw near to him and become enlightened, and then your faces will blush with shame no longer.

Ps 68:1;
Ti 1:10

Eph 5:8

Jn 1:9

cf. Ps 34:6

While I was weighing up how to serve the Lord my God, which I had intended to do for a long time, I was the one who was willing, but I was also the one who was unwilling: it all came down to me. I was not wholly willing, nor wholly unwilling. So I was in conflict with myself, and my very identity was disintegrating,[43] and the actual disintegration was in fact taking place quite against my will. Even so, it was not revealing the nature of a different

397

CONFESSIONS

ideo non iam ego operabar illam, sed quod habitabat in me peccatum de supplicio liberioris peccati, quia eram filius Adam.

(23) Nam si tot sunt contrariae naturae quot voluntates sibi resistunt, non iam duae sed plures erunt. si deliberet quisquam utrum ad conventiculum eorum pergat an ad theatrum, clamant isti, "ecce duae naturae, una bona hac ducit, altera mala illac reducit, nam unde ista cunctatio sibimet adversantium voluntatum?" ego autem dico ambas malas, et quae ad illos ducit et quae ad theatrum reducit. sed non credunt nisi bonam esse qua itur ad eos.

Quid si ergo quisquam noster deliberet et secum altercantibus duabus voluntatibus fluctuet, utrum ad theatrum pergat an ad ecclesiam nostram, nonne et isti quid respondeant fluctuabunt? aut enim fatebuntur quod nolunt, bona voluntate pergi in ecclesiam nostram, sicut in eam pergunt qui sacramentis eius imbuti sunt atque detinentur, aut duas malas naturas et duas malas mentes in uno homine configere putabunt, et non erit verum quod solent dicere, unam bonam, alteram malam, aut convertentur ad verum et non negabunt, cum quisque deliberat, animam unam diversis voluntatibus aestuare.

---

44 A. is driven to challenge Manichaean dualism: cf. A. *C. Adim.* 26: "Evil has a double definition: the sort that human beings do, the other that they have done to them. What they do is sin; what they endure is punishment."

45 A. held that Adam had greater freedom than his descendants in that he had the capacity *not* to sin; this still fell short of the actual inability to sin, which A. ascribed to those in heaven: cf. *Corrept.* 12.33: "There is being able not to sin; and there is not being able to sin" (*posse non peccare, et non posse peccare*).

46 Because the person exhibits two negative wills in conflict with respect to two differing apparent evils.

398

person's mind but rather the penalty being paid by my own mind.[44] So it was no longer I who was effecting that, but the sin which dwelt within me, arising from the punishment of a sin committed despite greater freedom: for I was a son of Adam.[45]

Rom 7:17, 20

(23) For if there are as many contrary natures as there are wills to resist you, there will no longer be two kinds, but instead they will be a multiplicity. If someone were to make a decision whether to go to the theater or to the Manichaean assembly, those Manichaeans cry out, "Look, that's the two natures! The good one leads in this direction, the other, which is evil, leads back in that direction: where else does that hesitation between conflicting wills in a person come from?" But I declare that both of them are evil: both the one which takes them one way, to the assembly, and the other which takes them another way, to the theater. They, however, will only believe that the way which leads to their assembly is good.

So what if some catholic Christian were to be hesitating and vacillating internally, as the two wills came into conflict, whether he should go to the theater or instead to our church? Surely those Manichaeans will be vacillating as to what they should reply? Either they will admit what they do not want to, that it is a good will which makes people go to our church (as, for example, those who have been steeped in her sacraments and remained involved there); or they must think that there are *two* evil natures and *two* evil minds in conflict in a single human being,[46] so what they usually say (that there is one good and one evil nature) will not be true; or they will be converted to the truth and will stop denying that when a person is hesitating between two courses of action, one soul can be wavering between conflicting wills.

CONFESSIONS

(24) Iam ergo non dicant, cum duas voluntates in homine uno adversari sibi sentiunt, duas contrarias mentes de duabus contrariis substantiis et de duobus contrariis principiis contendere, unam bonam, alteram malam. nam tu, deus verax, improbas eos et redarguis atque convincis eos, sicut in utraque mala voluntate, cum quisque deliberat utrum hominem veneno interimat an ferro, utrum fundum alienum illum an illum invadat, quando utrumque non potest, utrum emat voluptatem luxuria an pecuniam servet avaritia, utrum ad circum pergat an ad theatrum, si uno die utrumque exhibeatur; addo etiam tertium, an ad furtum de domo aliena, si subest occasio; addo et quartum, an ad committendum adulterium, si et inde simul facultas aperitur; si omnia concurrant in unum articulum temporis pariterque cupiantur omnia quae simul agi nequeunt, discerpunt enim animum sibimet adversantibus quattuor voluntatibus vel etiam pluribus in tanta copia rerum quae appetuntur, nec tamen tantam multitudinem diversarum substantiarum solent dicere.

Ita et in bonis voluntatibus. nam quaero ab eis utrum bonum sit delectari lectione apostoli et utrum bonum sit delectari psalmo sobrio et utrum bonum sit evangelium disserere. respondebunt ad singula: "bonum." quid si ergo pariter delectent omnia simulque uno tempore, nonne diversae voluntates distendunt cor hominis, dum deliberatur quid potissimum arripiamus? et omnes bonae sunt

47 Burglary and adultery are much more convenient when the householder is out at a show.
48 Paul.

(24) Therefore when they perceive two opposing wills in a single person, they should no longer say that two contrary minds from two contrary substances and from two contrary origins are in conflict, and that one is good, the other evil. For you, God of truth, condemn those people, and confound and conquer them. For instance, in a case when both wills are evil: when someone chooses whether to kill another person with poison or a weapon; whether to usurp one portion or another of someone's estate (assuming that usurping both is impossible); or whether to buy pleasure through extravagance or hoard money out of greed; whether to go to the circus or to the theater if there are shows on at both on the same day. And I add a third possibility to this: whether to burgle someone else's house should the opportunity arise; and a fourth: whether to commit adultery, if a favorable opportunity opens up.[47] If everything comes together to a single moment of time, and each thing is desired to the same degree but cannot be achieved at the same time (for they tear the mind apart between themselves by the effect of four conflicting wills, or even more, given the wealth of objects ripe for our desiring), nonetheless they do not usually declare that this is a plethora of different substances.

It is just the same when the will is for something good. I might ask those Manichaeans whether it is a good thing to enjoy reading the Apostle,[48] and whether it is good to enjoy the austerity of a psalm, and whether it is good to converse about the gospel. They would reply to each individual instance, "It is good." What then if we enjoy all those things equally, and at one and the same time? Surely divergent inclinations make the heart swell, while we consider which one it is best to opt for? And they are all good,

Jn 3:33

401

et certant secum, donec eligatur unum quo feratur tota
voluntas una, quae in plures dividebatur. ita etiam cum
aeternitas delectat superius et temporalis boni voluptas
retentat inferius, eadem anima est non tota voluntate illud
aut hoc volens et ideo discerpitur gravi molestia, dum illud
veritate praeponit, hoc familiaritate non ponit.

11. (25) Sic aegrotabam et excruciabar, accusans memet ipsum solito acerbius nimis ac volvens et versans me
in vinculo meo, donec abrumperetur totum, quo iam ex-
iguo tenebar, sed tenebar tamen. et instabas tu in occultis
meis, domine, severa misericordia, flagella ingeminans
timoris et pudoris, ne rursus cessarem et non abrumperetur idipsum exiguum et tenue quod remanserat, et reva-
lesceret iterum et me robustius alligaret. dicebam enim
apud me intus, "ecce modo fiat, modo fiat," et cum verbo
iam ibam in placitum. iam paene faciebam et non faciebam, nec relabebar tamen in pristina sed de proximo stabam et respirabam. et item conabar, et paulo minus ibi
eram et paulo minus, iam iamque attingebam et tenebam:
et non ibi eram nec attingebam nec tenebam, haesitans
mori morti et vitae vivere, plusque in me valebat deterius
inolitum quam melius insolitum, punctumque ipsum temporis quo aliud futurus eram, quanto propius admoveba-

---

[49] Paronomasia: *inolitum/insolitum.*

but they conflict with one another until one thing is chosen. Then the will is united and drawn toward that one
thing, even though it was previously fragmented into a
number of inclinations. So when eternity above delights
us, and when pleasure in earthly prosperity keeps us down
below, the soul is the same soul. It does not wish for one
thing or the other with a complete will, and so ends up
torn apart by its severe difficulties, as it prefers one thing
for the sake of the truth, and yet because of ingrained
habit fails to set the other thing aside.

11. (25) So I was sick and tormented. I blamed myself
much more vehemently than I usually would have done. I
was twisting and turning in my chains, until they were utterly broken; until then they were restraining me, but only
just. And you, Lord, pressed on in my innermost being   Ps 51:6
with your relentless mercy. You redoubled the lashes of
fear and shame to stop me from giving up again, from
keeping that thin remaining link of chain unbroken, and
allowing it to become strong again and bind me more securely. In my heart I was saying, "Look, let it happen now,
let it happen now!" and as I was saying it, I was coming to
the point of decision. One moment I was about to do it,
and then I was failing to do it. Yet I was not slipping back
into my former state but stopping very close and catching
my breath. Then I was trying again, and I was a little
closer, and closer, and at that very moment I was about to
touch it, about to grasp it: but I did not make it, I missed
touching it, I failed to grasp it—I was hesitating about
dying to death and living to life, for habitual wrongdoing   cf. Rom 6:2
had more power over me than goodness, which was unfa-
miliar.[49] The closer that moment came, that point of time
when I was to become different, the more it made me

403

tur, tanto ampliorem incutiebat horrorem. sed non recutiebat retro nec avertebat, sed suspendebat.

(26) Retinebant nugae nugarum et vanitates vanitantium,[7] antiquae amicae meae, et succutiebant vestem meam carneam et submurmurabant, "dimittisne nos?" et "a momento isto non erimus tecum ultra in aeternum" et "a momento isto non tibi licebit hoc et illud ultra in aeternum." et quae suggerebant in eo quod dixi "hoc et illud," quae suggerebant, deus meus, avertat ab anima servi tui misericordia tua! quas sordes suggerebant, quae dedecora! et audiebam eas iam longe minus quam dimidius, non tamquam libere contradicentes eundo in obviam, sed velut a dorso mussitantes et discedentem quasi furtim vellicantes, ut respicerem. tardabant tamen cunctantem me abripere atque excutere ab eis et transilire quo vocabar, cum diceret mihi consuetudo violenta, "putasne sine istis poteris?"

(27) Sed iam tepidissime hoc dicebat. aperiebatur enim ab ea parte qua intenderam faciem et quo transire trepidabam casta dignitas continentiae, serena et non dissolute hilaris, honeste blandiens ut venirem neque dubitarem, et extendens ad me suscipiendum et amplecten-

---

[7] vanitantium *codd. Knöll Skut.*: vanitatium S *Ver.*: vanitatum *codd. Maur.*

---

[50] Ironic. A. borrows a classical metaphor for a "trifling matter" (*nuga*: "nut") and adapts it as a parallel with the scriptural idea of Sir 1:2; cf. Ws 2:16, 4:12; Zep 3:18.

[51] Cf. *Conf.* 7.18.24, n. 53.

[52] *mussitantes . . . vellicantes*: "a touch of colloquialism," OD 2:53.

shiver with dread. And yet it did not knock me back, nor
did it divert me. It merely left me hanging in the balance.

(26) My old friends, utter frivolity and complete vanity,[50] were restraining me. Beneath my garment of flesh[51]
they were pinching me gently and whispering softly, "Are
you going to send us away?" and, "from that moment we
shall no longer be with you forever" and, "from that moment you will not be allowed to do such and such ever
again." As for the things they were reminding me of, in
that "such and such" I just referred to, what they were
reminding me of, O my God, let your mercy turn it aside
from the soul of your servant! What filth, what shame they
were reminding me of! I was not even half-listening to
them, and they no longer argued with me in an open attack. Instead they were grumbling behind my back and, as
it were, furtively nagging me,[52] even as I was abandoning
them, to look back.[53] They slowed me down as I hesitated   Gn 19:26
to snatch myself away from them and shake them off, and
to make the leap to where I was being called; for my impetuous habits kept calling to me, "Do you think you can
cope without those things?"

(27) But that call of habit was now barely lukewarm,
for from the direction where I had turned my face, and   cf. Lk 9:51
where I trembled to move across, there appeared the pure
excellence of Chastity.[54] She was tranquil rather than care-
lessly merry, she was frankly coaxing me to come on and
not hesitate, she held out holy hands to support me and

---

[53] The dangerous-retrospection motif has classical as well as
biblical resonance; Virg. G. 4.490–91.

[54] A. personifies chastity as the antonym of the human/physi-
cal in her desirability.

dum pias manus plenas gregibus bonorum exemplorum.
ibi tot pueri et puellae, ibi iuventus multa et omnis aetas,
et graves viduae et virgines anus, et in omnibus ipsa continentia nequaquam sterilis, sed fecunda mater filiorum
gaudiorum de marito te, domine.

Et inridebat me inrisione hortatoria, quasi diceret, "tu
non poteris quod isti, quod istae? an vero isti et istae in se
ipsis possunt ac non in domino deo suo? dominus deus
eorum me dedit eis. quid in te stas et non stas? proice te
in eum! noli metuere. non se subtrahet ut cadas: proice te
securus! excipiet et sanabit te." et erubescebam nimis,
quia illarum nugarum murmura adhuc audiebam, et cunc-
tabundus pendebam. et rursus illa, quasi diceret, "ob-
surdesce adversus immunda illa membra tua super terram, ut mortificentur. narrant tibi delectationes, sed non
sicut lex domini dei tui." ista controversia in corde meo
non nisi de me ipso adversus me ipsum. at Alypius affixus
lateri meo inusitati motus mei exitum tacitus opperieba-
tur.

12. (28) Ubi vero a fundo arcano alta consideratio traxit
et congessit totam miseriam meam in conspectu cordis
mei, oborta est procella ingens ferens ingentem imbrem
lacrimarum. et ut totum effunderem cum vocibus suis,
surrexi ab Alypio (solitudo mihi ad negotium flendi aptior

---

55 *controversia* is a rhetorical term for an argument usually in
a forensic context.

embrace me. Those hands were overflowing with flocks of encouraging examples: there were so many boys and girls, a host of young people and people of every age, venerable widows and elderly virgins. Among all of them Chastity herself was by no means barren: rather she was a fruitful mother of children born of her joys in you, O Lord, her husband.

cf. Ps 113:9

She began to tease me with laughter meant to encourage me, as if she were saying, "Are you not able to do what these men, even these women do? Surely these men and women would have no such power in themselves, instead of in the Lord their God? It was the Lord their God who granted me to them. Why stand by yourself, and so fail to stand? Cast yourself upon him! Do not be afraid! He will not step away and let you fall, so cast yourself upon him without fear! He will pick you up, and heal you." My cheeks burned, because I could still hear the whispering of those frivolities. Full of hesitation, I was hanging in the balance. And there she was again, as if to say: "Make yourself deaf to those parts of you which are unclean in your earthly existence, so as to put them to death. They do tell you of pleasures; but nothing like the law of the Lord your God." This debate[55] took place within my heart; it was myself arguing against myself. And all the while Alypius stayed by my side, waiting in silence for the outcome of my abnormal agitation.

Col 3:5

12. (28) When this profound reflection dragged up my complete wretchedness from the uttermost depths and piled it up in the sight of my heart, a mighty tempest arose, bringing with it a mighty storm of tears. I needed to let it all pour out, in words as well, so I got up from Alypius, for I felt that the business of weeping was better suited to

suggerebatur) et secessi remotius quam ut posset mihi onerosa esse etiam eius praesentia. sic tunc eram, et ille sensit: nescio quid enim, puto, dixeram in quo apparebat sonus vocis meae iam fletu gravidus, et sic surrexeram. mansit ergo ille ubi sedebamus nimie stupens.

Ego sub quadam fici arbore stravi me nescio quomodo, et dimisi habenas lacrimis, et proruperunt flumina oculorum meorum, acceptabile sacrificium tuum, et non quidem his verbis, sed in hac sententia multa dixi tibi: "et tu, domine, usquequo? usquequo, domine, irasceris in finem? ne memor fueris iniquitatum nostrarum antiquarum." sentiebam enim eis me teneri. iactabam voces miserabiles: "quamdiu, quamdiu, 'cras' et 'cras'? quare non 'modo'? quare non hac hora finis turpitudinis meae?"

(29) Dicebam haec et flebam amarissima contritione cordis mei. et ecce audio vocem de vicina[8] domo cum cantu dicentis et crebro repetentis, quasi pueri an puellae, nescio: "tolle lege, tolle lege." statimque mutato vultu intentissimus cogitare coepi utrumnam solerent pueri in aliquo genere ludendi cantitare tale aliquid. nec occurrebat omnino audisse me uspiam, repressoque impetu lacrimarum surrexi, nihil aliud interpretans divinitus mihi iuberi nisi ut aperirem codicem et legerem quod primum caput invenissem. audieram enim de Antonio quod ex

---

[8] vicina *codd Maur. Skut. Ver.*: divina *S Knöll*

---

56 A. wants to be sure that it is a genuine message for himself, not random chance.

57 A parallel use of "sacred" text is divination by random consultation of the *Aeneid*, called *sortes Virgilianae*; cf. Introduction, p. xxxiv, with *Scriptores Historiae Augustae Hadr.* 2.8.

solitude. I withdrew to a place so secluded that even his presence could not be a burden to me. That was the state I was in, and he knew it: I suppose I had said something which gave it away that the sound of my voice was laden with weeping, and that was why I had got up. So he stayed where we had sat down, in complete consternation.

Somehow or other I cast myself upon the ground beneath a fig tree, and I gave free rein to my tears and they flowed in torrents from my eyes, an acceptable sacrifice to you. I spoke to you at length, not in these actual words, but along these lines, "As for you, how long, Lord? Lord, how long will you be angry, for ever? Do not remember our former sins any more." For I felt that I was in their grip. I sobbed out my pitiful cries, "How long? How long must it be 'tomorrow' and 'tomorrow'? Why not 'now'? Why not an end to my degradation from this very moment?"

(29) These were my words, and in grief of heart I wept bitterly. And look!—from the house next door I hear a voice—I don't know whether it is a boy or a girl—singing some words over and over: "Pick it up and read it, pick it up and read it!" Immediately my expression transformed. I started to ask myself eagerly whether it was common for children to chant such words when they were playing a game of some kind.[56] I could not recall ever having heard anything quite like it. I checked the flow of my tears and got up. I understood it as nothing short of divine providence that I was being ordered to open the book and read the first passage I came across.[57] I had heard of Antony, how he had been challenged by a reading from the gospel

cf. Ps 51:17, 19

Ps 79:5, 8

409

evangelica lectione cui forte supervenerat admonitus fuerit, tamquam sibi diceretur quod legebatur: "vade, vende
omnia quae habes, et da pauperibus et habebis thesaurum
in caelis; et veni, sequere me," et tali oraculo confestim ad
te esse conversum.

Itaque concitus redii in eum locum ubi sedebat Alypius: ibi enim posueram codicem apostoli cum inde surrexeram. arripui, aperui, et legi in silentio capitulum quo
primum coniecti sunt oculi mei: "non in comessationibus
et ebrietatibus, non in cubilibus et impudicitiis, non in
contentione et aemulatione, sed induite dominum Iesum
Christum et carnis providentiam ne feceritis in concupis-
centiis." nec ultra volui legere nec opus erat. statim quippe
cum fine huiusce sententiae quasi luce securitatis infusa
cordi meo omnes dubitationis tenebrae diffugerunt.

(30) Tum interiecto aut digito aut nescio quo alio signo
codicem clausi et tranquillo iam vultu indicavi Alypio. at
ille quid in se ageretur (quod ego nesciebam) sic indicavit.
petit videre quid legissem. ostendi, et attendit etiam ultra
quam ego legeram. et ignorabam quid sequeretur. sequebatur vero: "infirmum autem in fide recipite." quod ille ad
se rettulit mihique aperuit. sed tali admonitione firmatus
est placitoque ac proposito bono et congruentissimo suis
moribus, quibus a me in melius iam olim valde longeque
distabat, sine ulla turbulenta cunctatione coniunctus est.
inde ad matrem ingredimur, indicamus: gaudet. narramus
quemadmodum gestum sit: exultat et triumphat et bene-

58 Cf. Athanasius, *Vita Antoni* 2.
59 I.e., a book (*codex*) containing letters of the apostle Paul.

which he happened to encounter,[58] as if what he was reading was being spoken for himself: "Go, sell everything you possess and give to the poor, and you will have treasure in the heavens: and come, follow me!" Straightaway that oracle had converted him to you. Mt 19:21

In great excitement I returned to the place where Alypius was sitting, for when I stood up I had put down a volume of the apostle[59] down there. I snatched it up, opened it, and read silently the first chapter that my eyes lit upon: "Not in partying and drunkenness, not in promiscuity and shamelessness, not in fighting and jealousy, but clothe yourself in the Lord Jesus Christ and make no provision for the flesh concerning its physical desires." I neither wanted nor needed to read further. Immediately, the end of the sentence was like a light of sanctuary poured into my heart; every shadow of doubt melted away. Rom 13:13–14

cf. Jn 1:9

(30) Then I put my finger, or some other marker, into the book and closed it. My expression now calm, I showed it to Alypius. But this prompted him to show what his inner feelings had been, which I was unaware of. He asked to see what I had read. I showed him, and he looked even further on than I had read. I did not know what came next. But this was what did come next: Receive the one who is weak in faith. He referred this text to himself, and showed it to me. But he took strength from this suggestion, and from the decision and the good resolution that he had made. It was in keeping with his own character; in that respect he had already been markedly different from me for a long time, and for the better. Without any commotion or delay he joined me. Next we go to my mother. We tell her the news. She is delighted. We tell her how it happened. She is jubilant, and celebrates, and she began to Rom 14:1

411

dicebat tibi, qui potens es ultra quam petimus et intelle-
gimus facere, quia tanto amplius sibi a te concessum de
me videbat quam petere solebat miserabilibus flebilibus-
que gemitibus. convertisti enim me ad te, ut nec uxorem
quaererem nec aliquam spem saeculi huius, stans in ea
regula fidei in qua me ante tot annos ei revelaveras, et
convertisti luctum eius in gaudium multo uberius quam
voluerat, et multo carius atque castius quam de nepotibus
carnis meae requirebat.

bless you, who have power to act beyond what we ask and conceive, because she could see that you had granted her _{Eph 3:10} so much more for me than she regularly asked for with her pitiful crying and groaning. For you converted me to you, not to seek either a wife nor any worldly hope, but to take my stand on that rule of faith[60] on which you had revealed me to her so many years ago. And you converted her grief into joy in a way much more fruitful than she had desired, _{Ps 30:11} and much more precious and pure than she used to look for from having grandchildren physically begotten by me.

[60] Cf. *Conf.* 3.11.19, and Iren. *Haer.* 2.27.1, 3.2.1